Study Guide

for use with

Macroeconomics:
Updated Edition

J. Bradford DeLong
University of California, Berkeley

Prepared by
Martha Olney
University of California, Berkeley

McGraw-Hill
Irwin

Boston   Burr Ridge, IL   Dubuque, IA   Madison, WI   New York   San Francisco   St. Louis
Bangkok   Bogotá   Caracas   Kuala Lumpur   Lisbon   London   Madrid   Mexico City
Milan   Montreal   New Delhi   Santiago   Seoul   Singapore   Sydney   Taipei   Toronto

McGraw-Hill
Irwin

Study Guide for use with
Macroeconomics: Updated Edition
J. Bradford DeLong

Published by McGraw-Hill/Irwin, an imprint of the McGraw-Hill Companies, Inc., 1221 Avenue of the
Americas, New York, NY 10020. Copyright © 2002 by the McGraw-Hill Companies, Inc.
All rights reserved.

1 2 3 4 5 6 7 8 9 0 CUS/CUS 0 9 8 7 6 5 4 3 2 1

ISBN 0-07-283627-X

www.mhhe.com

Contents

ABOUT THE AUTHOR

Martha L. Olney is a nationally-recognized award-winning teacher. She currently teaches economics at the University of California, Berkeley. She received her Ph.D. from Berkeley in 1985. Her research focuses on consumer spending and indebtedness in the early twentieth century. She is the author of *Buy Now, Pay Later: Advertising, Credit, and Consumer Durables in the 1920s* (University of North Carolina Press, 1991), and several articles. In 1991, Professor Olney received the Distinguished Teaching Award from the University of Massachusetts, Amherst. In 1997, she was awarded the Jonathan Hughes Prize for Excellence in Teaching by the Economic History Association. Over 5,000 students have learned intermediate macroeconomics directly from Professor Olney.

Preface

WELCOME!

I think macroeconomics is an exciting and important subject. When I can help you, the student understand the material, or when I can help nurture your enthusiasm about macroeconomics, I have succeeded as a teacher. I hope that this study guide helps you learn macroeconomics. And I hope it helps make you excited about the subject.

I have designed a study guide that emphasizes active learning. Passive learning – reading with a highlighter in hand is one example – is a much less effective way to learn material than is active learning. If you want to just *read* a summary of the textbook, you probably don't want to buy this study guide. Active learning – working through problems and thinking about concepts – is a way to *really* learn material so that it makes sense, can be applied to new situations, and sticks with you after the final exam. If you are ready to learn, grab your pencil and come along.

Properly used, this study guide should have no resale value. Designing the study guide in such a way is not an attempt to undermine the used book market, I promise! But if the study guide is used as intended, it will be filled from one end to the other with your answers, derivations, data, and graphs.

HOW THE STUDY GUIDE IS ORGANIZED

Each chapter begins with two bulleted paragraphs in which I have condensed the main points of the chapter to just two statements.

A "Learning Guide" follows the summary. The Learning Guide tells you what is covered in the chapter, how many new models are in the chapter, and how the material in the chapter fits in with the other chapters in the textbook. Some of you come to the study guide the night before the exam (bad strategy) hoping to get some last-minute help; "Short on Time?" offers suggestions for what to study if you don't have enough time to study the entire chapter.

Each chapter of the study guide is then divided into five sections.
- **A. Basic Definitions.** You have to be able to run through the definitions. Three types of questions are provided in Section A: fill in the blank, circle the correct word, and multiple-choice questions. There are very few multiple-choice questions in the study guide because I think the best way to learn material for a multiple-

choice exam is not to practice multiple-choice questions but to simply *learn* the material.

- **B. Manipulation of Concepts and Models.** Section B is the longest part of most study guide chapters. Here, you are asked to work with the concepts and models introduced in the chapter. I think of the Section B questions as typical problem set questions. With a few exceptions, the Section B questions would not make good exam questions. But with few exceptions, the Section B questions will improve your understanding so you can answer exam questions that ask you to apply the concepts and models to real-world situations.

- **C. Applying Concepts and Models.** Section C contains the sorts of questions I like to put on exams: See if you can apply this particular concept to this real-world situation. You are given the real-world situation. You are told what concept to use. You have to figure out how to use the concept to explain the real-world situation.

- **D. Explaining the Real World.** Section D questions are more challenging. In Section D, you are given a real-world situation, but you have to figure out which concept to apply. It is a little easier than an exam situation because your choice of concepts or models is limited to that particular chapter. If you want to study for an exam that covers several chapters, you might try photocopying the Section D questions from each of the chapters on the exam, cut the photocopied questions into individual strips with one question on each strip, and then randomly pick a question. Can you figure out which concept to apply even when you don't know which chapter the question is from?

- **E. Possibilities to Ponder.** Section E contains questions that do not lend themselves to quick answers. I would not worry about these questions if you are simply trying to study for an exam. But if you want to think about macroeconomics more generally, take a look at some of these questions and ponder them.

- **Solutions.** The solutions to every question in Sections A, B, C, and D are given at the end of each chapter. The solution pages have a dark bar along the side of the page to make it a bit easier to locate the solutions as you thumb through the book.

There are two chapters in the Study Guide that do not directly correspond to textbook chapters. **Chapter A** runs through concepts you should know from your Principles course. If there is material in Chapter A that is unfamiliar, you will want to review your principles textbook. **Chapter B** presents the math tools that you need throughout the Study Guide. If you get stuck on a math tool at any point in the study guide, try reviewing that tool in Chapter B.

FEEDBACK

I am grateful to my students at U.C. Berkeley who sent me suggestions for this study guide. I think a fair summary of their comments is: "Include problems, problems, and more problems (and please explain confusing graphs)." I have tried to be true to their suggestions.

Now it is your turn. I welcome your comments and feedback. Great questions, bad questions, helpful questions, misleading questions, wrong answers, great answers – all of your feedback will help make the next edition of this guide even better than the first. Please send your comments to me via email: molney@econ.berkeley.edu.

THE UPDATED EDITION

The first edition of the study guide proved very successful with students who used it. The updated edition of the study guide is therefore very similar to the first edition. Errors have been corrected; some formatting has been improved; and changes have been made to reflect corresponding changes in the textbook.

ACKNOWLEDGMENTS

My colleague Brad DeLong wrote an innovative and exciting new textbook; I am grateful for the opportunity to join him in this joint effort to help students learn modern macroeconomics. Paul Shensa and Tom Thompson of McGraw-Hill Higher Education deserve the lion's share of thanks; they have my gratitude. My partner and our son sacrificed more than anyone else as I worked away; they have my never-ending love.

Peace be with you.

Martha L. Olney
El Cerrito, California

Chapter A
Things You Should Remember From Principles

There are several concepts that you should have learned in your principles class that you need to remember before you begin studying intermediate macroeconomics. The concepts are listed in this preliminary chapter.

If you do not remember the concept at all, dig out your principles textbook and review it. If you remember a concept but would be hard-pressed to explain it to someone, that is ok. You will wind up reviewing every concept listed below as you work through this study guide.

- Gross domestic product (GDP) is simultaneously a measure of aggregate output and aggregate income.

  *Aggregate output refers to **what** is produced: a shirt, a book, your pen, advice from a therapist, a computer, a concrete mixer, a dump truck, police protection, justice – final goods and services. Aggregate income refers to **what we earn** for producing that output. The dollar values of aggregate output and aggregate income are the same and equal "gross domestic product."*

- The unemployment rate is not a perfect indicator of the "unemployment problem."

  The unemployment rate, the number of people unemployed expressed as a percentage of the labor force, includes only those people who fit the government's definition of what it means to be "unemployed." People who want work but have not looked for work in the last four weeks are not "unemployed"; they are "discouraged workers" who are counted as "out of the labor force." People who are working but are overqualified for their current positions or are working fewer hours than they wish to work are not "unemployed"; they are counted as "employed" and thus "in the labor force" even though they are underemployed. But the economy is producing below its potential whenever there are discouraged or underemployed workers. The economy's unemployment problem therefore includes discouraged workers and underemployment even though they are not included in the unemployment rate.

- In the Keynesian model, Aggregate Demand (AD) equals C + I + G + NX.

  John Maynard Keynes taught us that we could best simplify total spending in the economy by dividing it into four components: consumption spending (C) by households, investment spending (I) by businesses, government purchases (G) by government agencies, and net export spending (NX) by the rest of the world.

- Macroeconomic equilibrium in the short-run Keynesian model occurs when aggregate output equals aggregate demand. That is, equilibrium is the level of output and income (GDP) such that $Y = C + I + G + NX$.

The simplest definition of short-run macroeconomic equilibrium is that output equals aggregate demand. When GDP equals that level of output, everyone is able to purchase the final goods and services they wish to purchase, and no final goods and services are produced that are not purchased or deliberately added to inventory holdings.

- In the short run, the economy's adjustment to macroeconomic equilibrium is an *output* adjustment process.

If the amount of output does not equal aggregate demand, then in the short run the economic variable that changes in order to bring the macroeconomy into equilibrium is the amount of output. If real GDP is initially greater than aggregate demand, businesses will reduce their production of output. If real GDP is initially smaller than aggregate demand, businesses will increase their production of output.

- Disposable income (Y^d) equals Income (Y) + Transfer Payments (TR) - Tax Payments (TA). That is, $Y^d = Y + TR - TA$.

Disposable income is what households have available to spend on final goods and services. Disposable income begins with the income we earn for producing goods and services (Y). It also includes transfer payments (TR) – funds we receive from the government for which we produce no goods and services in exchange. Social Security payments, welfare payments, and military pension payments are all examples of transfer payments. From income, we subtract our tax payments (TA) – funds we pay the government for the services they provide us. Income taxes, sales taxes, excise taxes, and user fees are all examples of tax payments.

- Consumption increases with disposable income. The change in consumption (C) is generally less than the corresponding change in disposable income (Y^d). That is, $C = C_0 + C_y \cdot Y^d$, where C_y is the marginal propensity to consume, and $0 < C_y < 1$.

Consumption spending by households is purchases of final goods and services by households. In general, the greater is disposable income, the greater is consumption spending. The marginal propensity to consume (mpc) tells us how much consumption spending changes when disposable income changes. The mpc is greater than 0 because households do increase consumption when disposable income increases; they do not save all of an increase in disposable income. The mpc is less than 1 because households tend to use part but not all of the additional disposable income to buy goods and services.

- Investment and interest rates tend to be inversely related. Interest rates are not the *only* determinant of investment, however.

  Investment spending by businesses is purchases of durable goods, construction of new buildings, and changes in the value of business inventory holdings. An increase in interest rates tends to cause a decrease in investment spending. A decrease in interest rates tends to cause an increase in investment spending. But investment spending is volatile and can change for many reasons in addition to changes in interest rates.

- Only government purchases of goods and services are included in aggregate demand. Other government spending (transfer payments) is part of Y^d.

  Aggregate demand, $C + I + G + NX$, is demand for the final goods and services that are counted as part of real GDP. G includes spending by government agencies for items such as pencils and computers and electricity, and salaries of government workers. But government agencies also spend funds supporting the population through various transfer payment programs: Social Security, TANF, unemployment compensation, veterans' pensions, and so on. These transfer payments are not part of aggregate demand because there is no good or service produced and given to the government in exchange for the transfer payment.

- Adjusting G, TR (transfer payments), or TA (tax payments) to achieve macroeconomic goals is *fiscal* policy.

  Fiscal policy is undertaken by the government. In the United States, Congress with the approval of the President conducts fiscal policy.

- Adjusting the money stock or interest rates to achieve macroeconomic goals is *monetary* policy.

  Monetary policy is undertaken by the central bank. In the United States, the Federal Reserve (the Fed) conducts monetary policy.

- Capital (K) includes structures (buildings), equipment (machines), and items in inventory. Money, stocks, bonds, or other financial assets are *not* included in capital.

  Physical capital is all that is included in K. Financial capital is not included. Because many people – especially people in the business world – use the word "capital" to mean money, it is easy to forget that to an economist and in an economics class, capital is nothing more and nothing less than buildings, machines, and inventory holdings.

- The aggregate production function tells us the relationship between output and inputs. It is often expressed as $Y = F(K, L)$.

The aggregate production function simply says that output is produced with inputs. If we assume that the inputs to production are simply capital (K) and labor (L), then the aggregate production function says output, Y, is produced with inputs, K and L. That is, $Y = F(K, L)$.

Chapter B
Math Skills You Will Need

There are several math skills you will need in order to work through the material in this course. A brief review of the math skills is provided below. If further review is needed, dig out a math textbook.

GRAPHING

Economists always graph in just two dimensions. Unlike in a math class, economists do not always put the independent or exogenous variable on the horizontal axis and the dependent or endogenous variable on the vertical axis. We may have it reversed, or it may be that some factors not depicted on the horizontal or vertical axis are jointly determining the variables on the axes.

Many students get confused when trying to figure out whether there is a movement along a curve or a shift of a curve. Here is the key: If there is a change in a variable that is **not** on one of the two axes, the curve shifts. If there is a change in a variable that **is** on one of the axes, we move along the curve.

WEIGHTED AVERAGES

A weighted average is an average which uses weights. Your grade point average is an example of a weighted average. In computing your g.p.a., each course grade is weighted by the number of units. For example, suppose you have earned an A in a 2-unit course, a B in a 5-unit course, and an A– in a 1-unit course. Your g.p.a. would then be

$$\frac{4.0 \cdot 2 + 3.0 \cdot 5 + 3.7 \cdot 1}{2 + 5 + 1} = \frac{26.7}{8} = 3.34$$

ALGEBRA

You need to be able to solve one equation with one unknown, and two equations with two unknowns. The rules to remember are:

- You can add the same thing to both sides of the equation.
- You can subtract the same thing from both sides of the equation.
- You can multiply both sides of the equation by the same thing.
- You can divide both sides of the equation by the same thing, so long as you are not dividing by 0.
- You can raise both sides of the equation to the same power.
- $1 \cdot x = x$, for any variable x.
- You can factor out common terms.

With those rules, you should be able to solve any algebraic equation. For example, what value of Y makes this equation true: $Y = 100 + 0.6Y$?

$$Y = 100 + 0.6Y$$
$$Y - 0.6Y = 100 \qquad \textit{subtracting } 0.6Y \textit{ from both sides}$$
$$(1 - 0.6)Y = 100 \qquad \textit{factoring out } Y$$
$$0.4Y = 100 \qquad \textit{simplifying}$$
$$Y = \frac{100}{0.4} \qquad \textit{dividing both sides by } 0.4$$
$$Y = 250 \qquad \textit{simplifying}$$

There are several methods for solving two equations with two unknowns. In economics, most systems of two equations and two unknowns lend themselves to the easiest solution method. Set both equations equal to the same value, then use the transitivity rule: if A = B and B = C, then A = C. For example, what values of Y and r make both of these equations true: $Y = 400 - 20r$ and $Y = 250 + 30r$?

$$Y = 400 - 20r \textit{ and } Y = 250 + 30r$$
$$400 - 20r = 250 + 30r \qquad \textit{applying transitivity rule}$$
$$150 = 50r \qquad \textit{subtracting } 250 - 20r \textit{ from both sides}$$
$$3 = r \qquad \textit{dividing both sides by } 50$$

Now you substitute this value of r back into either equation for Y. You should obtain the same value of Y regardless of which equation you use.

$$Y = 400 - 20(3) = 340 \qquad \textit{substituting } r = 3$$
$$\textit{or, } Y = 250 + 30(3) = 340 \qquad \textit{substituting } r = 3$$

In your high school algebra class, you no doubt learned more complicated methods for solving two equations with two unknowns. For this class, you are unlikely to need those methods.

RATES OF CHANGE

Economists often consider the rate of change of a variable. The rate of change is simply the change in the variable's value divided by its initial value. For example,

$$\%\Delta X = \frac{X_{new} - X_{old}}{X_{old}}$$

PROPORTIONAL GROWTH RULES

Proportional growth – percentage change – is often of interest in economics. A handful of proportional growth rules are used in the textbook and study guide. The textbook uses the shorthand 'g' to stand for percentage change: g(x) = %Δ(x).

- The growth rate of a product equals the sum of the growth rates of the two terms. $\%\Delta(a \cdot b) = \%\Delta a + \%\Delta b$, or $g(a \cdot b) = g(a) + g(b)$
- The growth rate of a quotient equals the difference between the growth rates o the two terms. $\%\Delta\left(\dfrac{a}{b}\right) = \%\Delta a - \%\Delta b$, or $g\left(\dfrac{a}{b}\right) = g(a) - g(b)$
- The growth rate of one variable raised to a power equals the power times the growth rate of the variable. $\%\Delta(a^b) = b \cdot \%\Delta a$, or $g(a^b) = b \cdot g(a)$

EXPONENT RULES

Particularly in the material that covers long-run growth, you need to be able to manipulate exponents. Again, a handful of rules is all you need.

- Any variable raised to the power 0 equals 1. $x^0 = 1$
- Any variable raised to the power 1 equals the variable. $x^1 = x$
- The product of a variable raised to some power and the same variable raised to some other power is the variable raised to the sum of the powers. $x^a \cdot x^b = x^{a+b}$
- The quotient of a variable raised to some power and the same variable raised to some other power is the variable raised to the difference between the powers. $\dfrac{x^a}{x^b} = x^{a-b}$
- The reciprocal of a variable raised to a power equals the variable raised to the negative of that power. $\dfrac{1}{x^b} = x^{-b}$
- A variable raised to a power and then raised to another power equals the variable raised to the product of the powers. $\left(x^a\right)^b = x^{a \cdot b}$

CALCULUS

At some institutions, calculus is a prerequisite to this course. At other institutions, it is not. Professor DeLong wrote the textbook so that it can be used in institutions where intermediate macroeconomics students do not know calculus. But there are many equations in the textbook that can only be derived with calculus. In the study guide, calculus is therefore used on occasion.

You need only a few rules from calculus to follow what is used in the study guide.

- The derivative of a constant, k, is zero. $\dfrac{dk}{dx} = 0$

- The derivative of a constant times a variable, with regard to that variable, is the constant. $\dfrac{d(kx)}{dx} = k$

- The derivative of a variable raised to the power n is n times the variable raised to the power n-1. $\dfrac{dx^n}{dx} = nx^{n-1}$

- A partial derivative is just a derivative where lots of stuff is assumed to be a constant. For example, the partial derivative of f(x, y, z) with regard to x, $\dfrac{\partial f(x,\, y,\, z)}{\partial x}$, assumes that y and z are constants.

- A total differential shows how changes in a function depend upon changes in the determining variables. For example, if Y = F(K, L) is a function that combines the variables K and L to determine Y, then the change in Y (dY) depends upon the changes in K (dK) and in L (dL).

$$dY = \frac{\partial F(K,\, L)}{\partial K} dK + \frac{\partial F(K,\, L)}{\partial L} dL$$

Chapter 1
Introduction to Macroeconomics

- Macroeconomics deals with questions about the economy as a whole. The most important questions consider the long-run determinants of economic growth and the short-run determinants of unemployment and inflation.

- Economic statistics are used to track the behavior of the macroeconomy. The six most important indicators for macroeconomics are real GDP, unemployment rate, inflation rate, interest rate, stock market value, and exchange rate.

LEARNING GUIDE

Introductory chapters are necessary because they set the stage for what is to come. But introductory chapters are not a very useful place to begin studying. The material presented in Chapter 1 is a combination of overview of the Big Questions of macroeconomics and definitions of some basic variables. There are no models presented in this chapter.

Most of the terms in this chapter should be familiar to you from your study of Economics Principles. You should not really need to *study* this chapter. All of the questions in the Study Guide for Chapter 1 are Section A questions.

Short on time?

 If you are familiar with all the terms introduced in the Chapter and listed at the end of the chapter, you can probably dive right in to Chapter 2.

If you do not know what macroeconomics is all about, be sure to read the first and last sections of Chapter 1. Otherwise, just be sure you know the definitions of each of the chapter's key terms and then move on to Chapter 2.

A. BASIC DEFINITIONS

Before you apply knowledge, you need a basic grasp of the fundamentals. In other words, there are some things you just have to know. Knowing the material in this section won't guarantee a good grade in the course, but not knowing it will guarantee a poor or failing grade.

USE THE WORDS OR PHRASES FROM THE LIST BELOW TO COMPLETE THE SENTENCES. SOME ARE USED MORE THAN ONCE; SOME ARE NOT USED AT ALL.

business cycle
cyclical unemployment
exchange rate
fiscal
frictional unemployment
growth
inflation rate
macroeconomics

microeconomics
monetary
nominal GDP
real GDP
stock market
unemployment
unemployment rate

1. A period of fluctuation in production and employment is a(n) _____.

2. _____ is the part of unemployment that rises and falls with the business cycle.

3. The amount of final goods and services produced in an economy in a year is _____.

4. _____ is the branch of economics that deals with the economy "in the small."

5. The nominal _____ is the rate at which the currencies of different countries can be exchanged for one another.

6. _____ includes people who are out of work and actively looking for work.

7. The _____ measures how fast the overall price level is rising.

8. _____ is the branch of economics related to the economy as a whole.

9. The level of the _____ is an indicator of expectations about the future.

10. The _____ reports the share of the labor force that is unemployed.

11. The government's _____ policy is designed to affect the long-run rate of economic growth.

12. _____ is the part of unemployment that allows qualified workers to match up with firms that can use their skills.

> **NOTE:** The six key variables – real GDP, unemployment rate, inflation rate, interest rate, stock market level, and exchange rate – are explored in further detail in Chapter 2.

CIRCLE THE CORRECT WORD OR PHRASE IN EACH OF THE FOLLOWING SENTENCES.

13. When production and employment are growing, the economy is experiencing a(n) expansion / recession.

14. Macroeconomists assume that both prices and output / only output adjust(s) as we move to an equilibrium of supply and demand.

15. Macroeconomists try to understand what determines the level and rate of change of individual / overall prices.

16. The nominal / real exchange rate is expressed in terms of goods and services.

17. The real interest rate is expressed in terms of money / goods and services.

18. The nominal / real interest rate is expressed in terms of money.

19. Microeconomists assume that prices / output adjusts as we move to an equilibrium of supply and demand.

20. When production is falling and unemployment is rising, the economy is experiencing a(n) expansion / recession.

SELECT THE ONE BEST ANSWER FOR EACH MULTIPLE-CHOICE QUESTION.

21. Which of the following activities is **not** an economic activity that is counted in the NIPA?
    - A. You buy a tank of gas for your car.
    - B. The clerk at the gas station is paid her weekly wages.
    - C. The gas station owner pays taxes to the federal government.
    - D. The gas station owner transfers funds from his checking account to a stock mutual fund.

22. A recession is said to occur when
    A. real GDP growth slows.
    B. real GDP declines for two or more quarters.
    C. real GDP is smaller in one year than it was in the previous year.
    D. real GDP grows more slowly than the labor force.

23. Because real GDP includes purchases of machines and buildings that replace worn out and obsolete machines and buildings, it is
    A. *real*, not nominal, GDP.
    B. real *gross*, not net, domestic product.
    C. real gross *domestic*, not national, product.
    D. none of the above.

24. Because real GDP includes output produced in the United States but excludes output produced in U.S.-owned factories in other countries, it is
    A. *real*, not nominal, GDP.
    B. real *gross*, not net, domestic product.
    C. real gross *domestic*, not national, product.
    D. none of the above.

25. Economists refer to "the" interest rate because
    A. all interest rates tend to rise and fall together.
    B. there is only one interest rate in the economy.
    C. there is only one interest rate that matters to macroeconomics.
    D. it simplifies their models, but it is an unrealistic and misleading assumption.

> **NOTE:** There are no Section B, Section C, or Section D questions in this Chapter.

E. POSSIBILITIES TO PONDER

The more you learn, the more you realize you have more to learn. These questions go beyond the textbook material. They are the sort of questions that distinguish A+ or A work from A-work. Some of them may even serve as starting points for junior or senior year research papers.

1. Which topic should be studied first: microeconomics or macroeconomics? Why?

2. Were there business cycles in planned economies such as the former Soviet Union?

3. Are the lessons of macroeconomics applicable to agriculturally-based economies? Are they applicable to poverty-stricken countries in Africa?

SOLUTIONS SOLUTIONS SOLUTIONS SOLUTIONS

A. BASIC DEFINITIONS

1. business cycle
2. cyclical unemployment
3. real GDP
4. microeconomics

5. exchange rate
6. unemployment
7. inflation rate
8. macroeconomics

9. stock market
10. unemployment rate
11. growth
12. frictional unemployment

---

13. expansion
14. both prices and output
15. overall

16. real
17. goods and services
18. nominal

19. prices
20. recession

---

21. D. When wealth is transferred between any two forms (here, between money and stock), no output is created, no employment is generated, and thus no economic activity has occurred.

22 B. In most cases, answer "C" will also be correct, but it need not be. A recession can be only six months long and thus it may not be reflected in annual data. Answer "D" produces what is sometimes called a "growth recession"; real GDP is growing, so it is not technically a recession, but because real GDP growth is outstripped by labor force growth, the unemployment rate is rising.

23. B.   24. C.   25. A.

E.   POSSIBILITIES TO PONDER

No solutions are given to these questions. The questions are designed to be somewhat open ended. Each question draws on your understanding of the concepts covered in this chapter.

Have you checked out the Online Learning Center for this textbook? You should! Go to

www.mhhe.com/economics/delong

The "Student Center" includes self-grading multiple choice exams with twenty questions per chapter, graphing exercises, applying the theory exercises, and working with data exercises. A full set of PowerPoint© slides are also available for each chapter.

So when you're surfing, hop on over to

www.mhhe.com/economics/delong

and check it out. We think you'll want to come back again and again!

Chapter 2
Measuring the Macroeconomy

- Six variables are used to measure the macroeconomy: exchange rates, stock market, interest rates, prices, unemployment rate, and gross domestic product.

- For these variables, their current values, trends over time, future projected values, methods of calculation, and meanings are all important to know.

LEARNING GUIDE

There is a lot of material in this chapter, some of which must be memorized and some of which can be learned through application. There is only one model, Okun's law. There are many conceptual points.

You will need some math skills in this chapter. Math skills that are covered in Chapter B are indicated with

Be sure you can define each of the six variables in a sentence; identify which variable is relevant in an applied setting; calculate the value of each variable; give a reasonable estimate of the current value of the variable; and explain the strengths and shortcomings of each variable.

Short on time?

Some professors expect students to know how to manipulate each of the variables. Others are less concerned with manipulation of the variables and instead want you to know the conceptual aspects of each variable. Be sure you know what you are expected to learn before you begin.

Everyone will need to be very clear on the definitions of the six variables. You cannot understand the rest of the course if you are not clear on the definitions of real GDP, unemployment, inflation, interest rates, and exchange rates. It is worth spending a lot of time on this chapter.

A. BASIC DEFINITIONS

Before you apply knowledge, you need a basic grasp of the fundamentals. In other words, there are some things you just have to know. Knowing the material in this section won't guarantee a good grade in the course, but not knowing it will guarantee a poor or failing grade.

USE THE WORDS OR PHRASES FROM THE LIST BELOW TO COMPLETE THE SENTENCES. SOME ARE USED MORE THAN ONCE; SOME ARE NOT USED AT ALL.

an index number	I.O.U.
bilateral trade	imports
businesses	labor force
Consumer Price Index	Laspeyres
exports	nominal exchange rate
GDP deflator	nominal interest rate
gross national product (GNP)	Paasche
gross domestic product (GDP)	real interest rate
households	stock market

1. The dollar price of foreign exchange is another phrase for the _____.

> **HINT**: Exchange rates are no different than the dollar price of any other good or service. For example, we can talk about the market for 8-ounce cups of chocolate-flavored frozen yogurt. The price of frozen yogurt, P_{yogurt}, is the number of dollars (perhaps a fraction of a dollar, such as 0.75 or 75¢) for one cup of yogurt. Similarly, the nominal dollar-peso exchange rate, e_{peso}, is the number of dollars (perhaps a fraction of a dollar, such as 0.11 or 11¢) for one Mexican peso.

2. A(n) _____ index uses fixed quantity weights from a base year.

3. I of the equation GDP = C + I + G + NX measures spending by _____ on machinery, construction of new buildings, and changes in the value of inventory holdings.

4. _____ measures final goods and services produced in one year in a nation's economy.

5. The _____ indicates relative pessimism or optimism of investors.

6. _____ is/are the value of goods and services sold to residents and businesses of other countries.

7. The real exchange rate is the _____ adjusted for differences in prices between two countries.

8. The _____ includes people with jobs (the employed) and people looking for jobs (the unemployed).

9. The _____ measures average prices of consumer goods, using a fixed market basket of goods and services.

10. The _____ equals $\frac{nominal\ GDP}{real\ GDP} \cdot 100$.

11. The _____ measures how much we pay in goods and services to borrow money.

12. C of the equation GDP = C + I + G + NX measures spending by _____ on foreign and domestically produced goods and services.

13. _____ is/are the value of goods and services sold to residents of the U.S. by residents and businesses of other countries.

14. "The" exchange rate is _____ constructed with a weighted average of "bilateral" exchange rates. The weights are the levels of _____ in a base year.

15. The unemployment rate is the number of unemployed people expressed as a percentage of the _____.

16. A bond is a(n) _____ from a corporation or government agency to the bond owner.

17. A(n) _____ index adjusts weights each year.

> **HINT**: The only way to keep straight Paasche and Laspeyres is to memorize the difference. This trick works for me: Paasche and Present both begin with "P"; a Paasche index uses "present year" (current year) weights. Laspeyres and Last both begin with "L"; a Laspeyres index uses "last year" (base year, not actually *last* year but it's just a memorization trick not a definition) weights.

CIRCLE THE CORRECT WORD OR PHRASE IN EACH OF THE FOLLOWING SENTENCES.

18. The <u>demand for / supply of</u> foreign exchange depends upon the domestic demand for foreign goods and services and upon the domestic demand for foreign assets.

19. The <u>real / nominal</u> exchange rate compares the cost of living in two countries.

20. In the 1990s, the real exchange rate index rose until 1995 and then fell. Between 1995 and 1998, on average, U.S. consumers therefore paid <u>more / less</u> for foreign goods and services than they did before 1995.

21. The higher the risk, the <u>higher / lower</u> the interest rate.

22. Discouraged workers <u>are / are not</u> counted as unemployed; they <u>are / are not</u> part of the economy's unemployment problem.

23. Real GDP for 2001, using a 1996 base year, is calculated with <u>1996 / 2001</u> quantities and <u>1996 / 2001</u> prices.

24. Intermediate goods are items that are "used up" when they are used to produce something else. Investment goods are items that continue to exist when they are used to produce something else. <u>Intermediate / investment</u> goods are excluded from GDP; <u>intermediate / investment</u> goods are included in GDP.

SELECT THE ONE BEST ANSWER FOR EACH MULTIPLE CHOICE QUESTION.

25. When the dollar depreciates relative to the Japanese yen,
    A. one dollar buys fewer yen.
    B. one dollar buys more yen.
    C. one dollar buys one yen.
    D. one yen buys one dollar.

26. Real exchange rates increase in the U.S. when
    A. nominal exchange rates fall.
    B. U.S. prices rise more rapidly than prices abroad.
    C. U.S. prices rise less rapidly than prices abroad.
    D. the dollar appreciates.

CAREFUL! "Investors" as used in the next question refers to people and firms and institutions who buy and sell stock and other financial assets. Buying stock is *NOT* <u>investment</u> to an economist. Investment means buying machines, constructing buildings, or changing inventory holdings. Buying stock is a decision about an asset portfolio.

27. If the expected return on a stock is 6 percent and the return on a bond is 6 percent,
    A. most investors will be indifferent between buying the stock and buying the bond.
    B. most investors will purchase the stock.
    C. most investors will purchase the bond.
    D. most investors will want more information before deciding what to purchase.

28. Changes in the CPI can overstate the "true" change in the cost of living because
    A. the CPI only includes consumer prices.
    B. the prices of all consumer goods and services are not included in the CPI.
    C. the value of household services is excluded from the CPI.
    D. the changes in what consumers purchase are not reflected right away in the weights used for calculating the CPI.

29. Which one of the following is considered unemployed?
    A. A full-time student who has no job during the school year.
    B. A college senior who is interviewing for post-graduation jobs.
    C. A stay-at-home mom who is home-schooling her children.
    D. A man who last worked eight months ago but who hasn't looked for work for the last two months.

30. Okun's law states a relationship between the
    A. growth of real GDP and changes in the unemployment rate.
    B. level of real GDP and changes in the unemployment rate.
    C. growth of real GDP and the level of the unemployment rate.
    D. level of real GDP and the level of the unemployment rate.

31. G of the equation GDP = C + I + G + NX measures spending by local, state, and federal government agencies on
    A. all goods and services.
    B. final goods and services.
    C. transfer payments.
    D. goods and services and transfer payments.

B. MANIPULATION OF CONCEPTS AND MODELS

Most instructors expect you to be able to do basic manipulation of the concepts. Being able to do so often means you can earn a C in a course. But if you want a better grade, you'll need to be able to complete this next section easily and move on to Sections C and D.

1. Graph the market for foreign exchange (fx) at the right. The demand and supply curves are already drawn but need to be labeled. Draw in an additional curve showing an increase in demand for foreign exchange. What effect does an increase in demand for foreign exchange have on the price of foreign exchange, e?

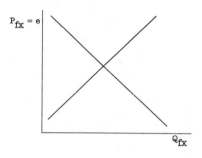

2. Suppose the nominal exchange rate is $1.00 for €0.83.
   A. What are €100 worth in dollars?

   B. Michelle, a tourist from France, is visiting Chicago. She wants to buy a $25 sweatshirt. How many euros (€) does she need?

   Suppose the nominal exchange rate changes to $1.00 for €0.70.
   C. How many euros does Michelle now need to buy a $25 sweatshirt?

   D. Has the dollar appreciated or depreciated relative to the euro?

   E. Are U.S. goods now more or less expensive relative to French goods?

HINT: Whenever you read "real exchange rate," say to yourself instead "relative price of foreign goods and services." You already know how price effects work: when the relative price of something increases, quantity demanded falls. It's no different with foreign trade. When the relative price of foreign goods and services increases, our demand for foreign goods and services falls. In the language of economics: When the real exchange rate (the relative price of foreign goods and services) increases, U.S. imports (demand for foreign goods and services) falls.

3. Suppose prices in Mexico rise more rapidly than prices in the United States. Suppose the nominal exchange rate is initially unchanged.

A. All else constant, is the initial effect of the difference in inflation rates an increase or decrease in the real exchange rate for pesos?

Now, trace through the subsequent effects on the nominal and real exchange rate:

B. Does the difference in inflation rates increase or decrease the U.S. demand for the Mexican peso?

C. Does the difference in inflation rates increase or decrease the Mexican demand for the U.S. dollar?

D. Does the difference in inflation rates increase or decrease the nominal exchange rate for the Mexican peso?

E. Does the difference in inflation rates ultimately increase or decrease the real exchange rate for the Mexican peso?

 MATH: To complete the next problem, you must understand rates of change. This math skill is covered in Chapter B.

4. Consider the following table.

	e_{peso}	CPI_{Mexico}	$CPI_{U.S.}$	ε_{peso}
year 1	0.25	600	140	
year 2				
year 3				

A. Suppose the annual inflation rate is 10 percent in Mexico and 5 percent in the United States. Complete the columns for CPI_{Mexico} and $CPI_{U.S.}$.

B. Suppose the nominal exchange rate is unchanged between year 1 and year 2, but appreciates 10 percent between year 2 and year 3. Complete the column for e_{peso}.

C. Complete the last column. Does the real exchange rate rise or fall between year 1 and year 2? Does it rise or fall between year 2 and year 3?

D. Relative to U.S. goods and services, are Mexican goods and services more or less expensive in year 2 than they were in year 1? In year 3 than in year 2?

NOTE: The *Economic Report of the President (ERP)* is an annual document produced by the Council of Economic Advisers, economists chosen by the President and appointed by Congress to advise the Office of the President on economic matters. The *ERP* can be purchased through the U.S. Government Printing Office. Many professors order it for economics courses, so it may be available in your campus bookstore. Every library will have a copy in the Reference section. And it is available online at http://w3.access.gpo.gov/usbudget/index.html. For example, the 2002 *Economic Report of the President* is available in pdf format at http://w3.access.gpo.gov/usbudget/fy2003/pdf/2002_erp.pdf. There are over one hundred tables in the *Economic Report*. They can be downloaded at http://w3.access.gpo.gov/usbudget/fy2003/erp.html in spreadsheet format.

5. Using the *Economic Report of the President (ERP)*, look up the nominal exchange rate between the U.S. dollar and any two countries' currencies for 1995, 1996, 1997, and 1998. (In *ERP 2002*, the data were in Table B110.) Write the data in the table below. Find the consumer price index values for the U.S. and each of the other two countries for the same years. (In *ERP 2002*, the data were in Table B108.) Write the data in the table below. Calculate the real exchange rate between the U.S. dollar and each of the two other countries' currency for 1995, 1996, 1997, and 1998. (The countries are labelled "A" and "B" in the table.) Write the answers in the table below. Is the pattern you found consistent with the graph in textbook Figure 2.2?

CAREFUL! The exchange rates reported in the *Economic Report of the President* are sometimes expressed as number of dollars per one unit of foreign currency and sometimes as number of units of foreign currency per one dollar. Be sure to read the table headings and the footnotes to be sure you know whether you have e or 1/e.

	e_A	CPI_A	$CPI_{U.S.}$	ε_A	e_B	CPI_B	$CPI_{U.S.}$	ε_B
1995								
1996								
1997								
1998								

6. Suppose there are five countries: U.S., Americas, Africa, Europe, and Asia. The nominal exchange rates, consumer price indexes, and total trade (T) are given below. The major trading partners are Americas and Asia. Africa is experiencing extremely high rates of inflation.

	$P_{U.S.}$	$e_{Americas}$	$P_{Americas}$	$T_{Americas}$	$\varepsilon_{Americas}$	e_{Africa}	P_{Africa}	T_{Africa}	ε_{Africa}
year 1	140	1.06	40	800		12	50	100	
year 2	147	1.03	43	900		11	100	100	
year 3	154	1.05	44	1000		10	200	100	

	e_{Europe}	P_{Europe}	T_{Europe}	ε_{Europe}	e_{Asia}	P_{Asia}	T_{Asia}	ε_{Asia}
year 1	0.30	100	400		64	20	700	
year 2	0.33	110	450		56	25	800	
year 3	0.31	140	500		50	30	900	

 To complete this problem, you must understand weighted averages. This math skill is covered in Chapter B.

A. Calculate the value of the real exchange rate for each country in each year. Write your answers in the table above and also in the table below part D.

B. Calculate the annual rates of change in the real exchange rates. Then, calculate the average of the annual rates of change. Write your answers in the table below part D where "%Δ" stands for "percent change from previous year."

C. Let year 1 be the base year. Calculate the value of the exchange rate index (XR index) in each year. Write your answers in the table below part D.

 HINT: To calculate the exchange rate index, you will need to calculate a weighted average of the real exchange rates, using each countries' share of total trade in the base year as its weight in the index. So the first thing you need to do is calculate total trade (T) by summing the four trade amounts across rows for year 1. Then you need to calculate each country's share of trade. For example, the Americas' share of trade with the U.S. in year 1 is 800 / (800 + 100 + 400 + 700) = 0.4.

D. Calculate the rate of change of the exchange rate index. Write your answers in the table below.

	$\varepsilon_{Americas}$	$\%\Delta$	ε_{Africa}	$\%\Delta$	ε_{Europe}	$\%\Delta$	ε_{Asia}	$\%\Delta$	Avg $\%\Delta$	XR index	$\%\Delta$
year 1											
year 2											
year 3											

E. Why does the exchange rate index grow at a slower rate than the annual average of exchange rates you calculated in part B?

7. A. Suppose you buy stock at $10 per share. The stock pays 60¢ dividends per share annually. What is the nominal return on the stock?

    B. Suppose you buy stock at $10 per share. The stock pays 50¢ dividends per share annually. What is the nominal return on the stock?

    C. Suppose you buy stock at $12 per share. The stock pays 60¢ dividends per share annually. What is the nominal return on the stock?

    D. The calculations in parts A-C assumed that you anticipate no increase in the price of a share of the stock. Suppose instead you anticipated an increase in its price and you planned to sell the stock after holding it for a few years. Would this new assumption increase, decrease, or not affect the nominal return of the stock? Why?

8. Suppose for the economy as a whole, on average

    $r = 6$ percent
    $P^S = \$8.00$
    $E^a = 0.50$

    What is the value of the risk premium?

9. If you buy a $1,000 bond for three years that pays 5 percent simple interest (that is, the interest is calculated once a year), and you receive interest payments once a year, how much interest will you receive in total?

HINT: Each and every bond has a face value, maturity date, and interest rate. The face value is printed on the bond; it is the amount the bondholder receives "at maturity." The maturity date is the date on which the face value will be paid. The interest rate determines the amount of interest the borrower pays the bondholder each year. Suppose you bought a bond with face value of $10,000, maturity date of 12/31/2015, and interest rate of 6 percent. You would receive 6 percent interest per year ($600) and you would also receive the face value of $10,000 on 12/31/2015. If you paid face value for the bond ($10,000), then buying the bond is equivalent to putting $10,000 into a savings account that pays 6 percent annually, withdrawing the $600 interest you've earned on the savings account once a year, and then withdrawing the full $10,000 in 2015. Your nominal rate of return on the bond is 6 percent.

10. Assume a credit card charges 21 percent annual interest on outstanding balances. Interest is calculated monthly on outstanding balances. Suppose you carry a balance of $500 on your credit card. Each month you pay interest only. How much interest will you pay per month? How much will you pay per year?

11. Suppose nominal interest rates are 21 percent and inflation is 3 percent. What is the real interest rate?

12. Assume the Federal Reserve (Fed) decreases nominal interest rates on federal funds from 7 to 6 percent. If there is no change in prices, what is the effect on real interest rates? If the expected inflation rate simultaneously decreases from 3 to 2 percent, what is the effect on real interest rates?

13. Consider the following actual annual values for the consumer price index for the United States. CPI-U is the CPI for all urban consumers; food, medical, and housing are CPIs for those subsets of items.

	CPI-U	inflation rate	food	inflation rate	medical	inflation rate	housing	inflation rate
1982	96.5		97.3		92.5		96.9	
1983	99.6		99.5		100.6		99.5	
1984	103.9		103.2		106.8		103.6	
1990	130.7		132.4		162.8		128.5	
1991	136.2		136.3		177.0		133.6	
1992	140.3		137.9		190.1		137.5	
1993	144.5		140.9		201.4		141.2	
1994	148.2		144.3		211.0		144.8	

A. The base year for the CPI is said to be "1982-84=100." That means the average value for 1982, 1983, and 1984 should equal 100 for each index. Confirm this is the case.

B. For 1991-1994, calculate the inflation rate for each spending category. Write your answers in the table above.

C. Social Security benefits, which are received primarily by those age 65 and over, increase when the CPI-U increases. But the primary expenses for senior citizens are food, medical care, and housing. For 1991-94, did changes in the CPI-U reflect changes in the cost of living for seniors? Explain.

14. Use data from the *Economic Report of the President* to answer the following questions. For the most recent data, you can start with the Economics Statistics Briefing Room of the White House at http://www.whitehouse.gov/fsbr/esbr.html.

A. What was the average inflation rate, as calculated with the CPI, in the 1960s? The 1970s? The 1980s? The 1990s? What is it today? Did the inflation rate increase or decrease in the past year?

B. What was the average unemployment rate in the 1960s? The 1970s? The 1980s? The 1990s? What is it today? Has the unemployment rate been increasing or decreasing in the past twelve months?

C. What demographic group has the highest unemployment rate? The lowest? In recessions, does the gap between the unemployment rates of Black and White workers increase or decrease? Why?

D. What was the average 3-month treasury bill rate in the 1960s? The 1970s? The 1980s? The 1990s? What is it today? Has this interest rate been increasing or decreasing in the past twelve months?

E. What was the average Aaa corporate bond rate in the 1960s? The 1970s? The 1980s? The 1990s? What is it today? Has this interest rate been increasing or decreasing in the past twelve months? Why is the Aaa corporate bond rate generally greater than the 3-month Treasury bill rate?

F. What are recent values of consumption (C), investment (I), government spending (G), and net exports (NX)? What share of GDP is C? I? G? NX? Are the shares today approximately the same as they were in the 1960s?

 MATH: To complete the next two problems, you must understand algebra. This math skill is covered in Chapter B.

15. Suppose employment is 125 million and the unemployment rate is 5.3 percent. How large is the labor force?

16. Suppose the unemployment rate is 4.9 percent and 8 million people are unemployed. How many people are employed?

17. Are each of the following people employed, unemployed, or out of the labor force?
A. A student who works for pay part-time during the school year

B. A student who is interviewing for post-graduation jobs

C. A stay-at-home mom

D. A man who volunteers with American Foundation for AIDS Research 40 hours per week

E. A professor

F. A man who wants to find a job but who got so discouraged by the lack of employment opportunities that he has not actively looked for work for the past six weeks

18. For each activity listed below, indicate where the activity would be recorded on the expenditure side of GDP accounting. Your choices are C, I, G, EX (exports), IM (Imports), and NR (not recorded). Give a brief explanation for each answer.

A. You buy a new CD, manufactured in California, at Tower Records.

B. You buy a used CD at a local music shop.

C. You buy a used bookcase at a garage sale.

D. Tower Records buys new permanent CD display racks that were manufactured in North Carolina.

E. Tower Records buys paint with which to paint sale signs on the windows.

F. The City of Ann Arbor, Michigan, buys new parking meters that were manufactured in Russellville, Arkansas.

G. Workers for the City of Ann Arbor remove broken parking meters.

H. A student from South Africa visiting Indiana University for the summer buys lunch at a local Bloomington hamburger joint.

I. A resident of Las Cruces, New Mexico, visits Russia and buys trinkets to bring home.

J. You buy a new Toyota that was manufactured in Kentucky.

K. McDonald's purchases a new frying machine that was manufactured in Italy.

L. McDonald's purchases paper napkins that were produced in Washington state.

M. A student at the University of Massachusetts Amherst (a public school) pays her fees.

N. The parents of a student at Amherst College (a private school) pay his tuition and fees.

O. You take three weeks of dirty laundry to the neighborhood laundromat.

P. You take three weeks of dirty laundry home and sweet talk Mom into doing it.

Q. MARTA (Metropolitan Atlanta Rapid Transit Authority, a government agency) purchases new transit cars from a Japanese manufacturer.

19. Suppose the following describes the economy (all figures in billions):

GDP	$9,000
Investment	1,500
Consumption	5,000
Government purchases of goods and services	1,000

What is the value of net exports?

20. Assume inventory holdings are 0 at the beginning of year 1. Assume changes in inventory holdings are the only form of investment spending. Assume government spending and net exports are 0. Fill in the table.

	year 1	year 2	year 3
sell to consumers	2700	2700	2700
end-of-year inventory	300	100	100
C			
I			
production (GDP)			

21. Consider the following data for a college student, Natalya. "P" is the price of each good. "Q" is the quantity Natalya purchased during a year. "Share" will be the share of total spending accounted for by each of the five products.

	books			coffee			lattes			phone cards			CDs		
year	P	Q	share	P	Q	share	P	Q	share	P	Q	share	P	Q	share
1	80.00	8		1.00	250		2.50	500		20.00	12		16.00	10	
2	84.00	8		1.05	275		2.85	475		19.20	12		16.16	10	
3	88.20	8		1.10	450		3.30	300		18.40	13		16.32	10	
4	92.60	8		1.15	550		3.80	200		17.70	13		16.48	10	

A. For each year, calculate Natalya's total spending and the share of her spending accounted for by each of the five products. Write your answers in the table above.

B. Assume year 1 is the base year. What is the value of the price index in each year, if the expenditure shares from year 1 are used in every year? What is the inflation rate? Write your answers in the table at the right.

Year	Price Index	Rate
1		███
2		
3		
4		

C. As the price of lattes increased, what happened to the quantity of lattes consumed per year by Natalya? Does her behavior make economic sense?

D. Would the inflation rate be higher or lower if we used year 4 expenditure shares instead of year 1 shares? (Can you answer this question without recomputing the values of the price index for each year?)

E. Recalculate the price index assuming it is a Paasche index and year 1 is the base year. What is the inflation rate in each year? Write your answers in the table at the right.

Year	Price Index	Rate
1		███
2		
3		
4		

$\mathcal{C}$. Applying Concepts and Models

Now we're getting to the good stuff. Being able to apply a specific concept or model to a real world situation — where you are told which model to apply but you have to figure out how to apply it — is often what you need to earn a B in a course. This is where macroeconomics starts to become interesting and the world starts to make more sense.

1. Hoof and mouth disease became an epidemic in Europe in 2001. To prevent further spread of the disease, hundreds of thousands of animals were destroyed. Worldwide warnings and misinformation led many Americans to cancel vacation trips to Britain. All else constant, what effect should this event have had on the dollar-pound exchange rate?

2. Electricity outages were expected to be rampant in California in Summer 2001. Fears of tourists being trapped in high-rise hotel elevators resulted in a large drop in international tourism. All else constant, what effect should this event have had on the dollar-yen exchange rate?

3. Electricity outages in California were expected to disrupt production in the Silicon Valley, home of the high-tech industry. As a result, foreign demand for ownership of California-based high tech companies decreased. All else constant, what effect should this event have had on the nominal exchange rate?

4. Kavita is very risk averse (she dislikes risk a lot). She estimates that her risk premium, σ^S, is 10 percent. The rate of return on bonds is 6 percent. What rate of return does Kavita want on a stock to make her indifferent between buying stocks and buying bonds?

5. Use the concept of risk premium to explain why some investors would prefer to hold bonds while, at the same time, facing the same rates of return, other investors prefer to hold stocks.

6. In the late 1990s, price-earnings ratios increased dramatically. If the market had been in equilibrium (it wasn't), what did the rise in price-earnings ratios tell you about what was happening to the risk premium?

7. Interest rates on bonds fall. Assuming there is no change in the risk premium, what is the effect on stock prices? Why?

8. Hector borrows $1,000 at 10 percent to buy DVDs, which cost $25 each. One year later when he repays the loan, DVDs cost $20 each. Is Hector's real interest rate greater than, less than, or equal to 10 percent? Explain.

TO THE CHALKBOARD:
Explaining Figure 2.8

The Okun's law graph in textbook Figure 2.8 may be a bit confusing. For now, ignore the diagonal lines in the graph. Each dot in the graph represents one year's values of "percent change in real GDP" and "percentage-point change in unemployment rate." For instance, real GDP fell by 0.5 percent in 1991, so the "percent change in real GDP" was -0.5 in 1991. The unemployment rate was 5.6 in 1990 and 6.8 in 1991, meaning the "percentage-point change in unemployment rate" for 1991 was +1.2. The dot for 1991 is therefore in the lower right of the graph, where -0.5 on the vertical axis and +1.2 on the horizontal axis come together.

Now look at the lines. Professor DeLong performed *regression analysis* on the annual data (the points in the graph). Regression analysis comes up with a linear equation that is a "best fit" for the points on the graph. Professor DeLong estimated two equations: one using the data from before 1974 only, and a second equation that used all of the years of data. The equations were both of the form %ΔGDP = <intercept> + <slope>*ΔUnemployment-rate. In both cases, the slope is -2.5. That is why both lines — the one for pre-1974 and the one for all years — slope down at a rate of -2.5. The intercept with the pre-1974 data was about 4; that is why the top line crosses the vertical axis at about 4. The intercept with all years was about 2.3; that is why the bottom line crosses the vertical axis at about 2.3. Professor DeLong also estimated that same equation using just the data for 1974-1995. The slope was again -2.5 but the intercept was 2.8. The intercept gives the "percent change in real GDP" when the "percentage-point change in unemployment rate" is zero; that is, it tells us what real GDP growth rate will, on average, keep the unemployment rate constant. That is why Professor DeLong states, "Between 1974 and 1995, the unemployment rate was constant when real GDP growth was about 2.8 % per year."

---

9. Use Okun's law to answer these questions.

   A. If real GDP grows by 6 percent annually, potential GDP grows at 2 percent annually, and the initial unemployment rate is 6 percent, what is the unemployment rate at the end of the year?

   B. If the unemployment rate is initially 4 percent but rises to 5 percent by the end of the year, and potential GDP grows at 2.5 percent annually, what is the rate of growth of real GDP?

   C. If real GDP grows by 2 percent annually and unemployment rises by 0.5 percentage points, what is the rate of growth of potential GDP?

D. EXPLAINING THE REAL WORLD

Most instructors are delighted when you are able to figure out which concept or model to apply to a real world situation. Being able to do so means you thoroughly understand the material and is often what you need to do to earn an A in a course. This is where you experience the power of macroeconomic theory.

1. Ruby, who is 85 years old, prefers to hold her wealth in bonds. Jerome, who is 30 years old, prefers to hold his wealth in stocks. Why?

2. The economy appears to be heading into a recession. What is the effect on the stock market? Why?

3. Don's Concrete Mixing Company is considering purchasing a new concrete mixer, and he can borrow $50,000. What price is relevant to his decision to borrow the money: the price of his inputs (gravel, sand, water, electricity, gas, and so on); the price he can charge for a yard of mixed concrete; the GDP price deflator; or the consumer price index? Why?

4. Prices have been rising for all goods and services. A new commissioner for the Bureau of Labor Statistics proposes updating the weights used to calculate the consumer price index. Which weights are likely to be lowered when the weights are updated: the weights of goods with high price elasticity of demand or those with low price elasticity of demand? Why? What is the likely effect of the change in weights on the inflation rate?

5. Why does the GDP deflator generally record lower inflation rates than the CPI? Which is the better index: the CPI or the GDP deflator?

6. Suppose unemployment is mostly low-skill, low-productivity workers whose contribution to output is relatively small. Would a decrease in the unemployment rate of 1 percentage point require faster or slower growth of real GDP than when unemployment is mostly high-productivity workers? Why?

7. In the 1840s and 1850s, the U.S. labor force swelled as unskilled immigrants from Western Europe migrated to America. In the 1990s, the U.S. labor force grew rapidly due in part to immigration of high-skilled workers from Asia. Would the Okun's law tradeoff have been the same in the 1990s as it was in the 1840s and 1850s? Why?

8. Economists are forecasting weak annual growth of real GDP in the range of 2 percent. Assuming the rate of growth of potential GDP is 2.5 percent, is the unemployment rate expected to increase or decrease? Why?

9. Real GDP increased at an annual rate of 4.1 percent between 1960 and 1970. Married women's labor force participation rate increased from 31.9 to 40.5 percent over the same period. Explain any connections between these increases in output and in labor force participation.

10. What price index should be used to determine annual increases in Social Security benefits? Why?

11. An oil tanker runs aground in San Francisco Bay, spilling thousands of gallons of fuel into the bay. Hundreds of volunteers spend thousands of hours rescuing shore birds. The oil refining company hires workers to clean the beaches of fuel. Could someone possibly say this is "good for the economy"? Explain.

12. Linda studied in Japan on an exchange program during her sophomore year. She is returning to Japan for the summer following graduation. The exchange rate was 131 yen (¥) to the dollar during her exchange year and is 108 ¥ to the dollar now. Does that mean her post-graduation trip will be more expensive than her earlier trip?

13. The GDP of the United States is about twice as large as the GDP of Japan. Are Americans therefore better off than the Japanese? Explain.

E. POSSIBILITIES TO PONDER

The more you learn, the more you realize you have more to learn. These questions go beyond the textbook material. They are the sort of questions that distinguish A+ or A work from A- work. Some of them may even serve as starting points for junior or senior year research papers.

1. Suppose there are no government-imposed limits on nominal exchange rates. Can differences in inflation rates between the United States and Mexico continue unabated year after year? Is it economically possible? Is it politically possible?

2. If you ask economists, "What is the effect on stock prices of some event (such as an oncoming recession)?," they can answer the question. But if you say, "Suppose stock prices fell; explain why," economists cannot provide an answer. Why can they answer the first question but not the second?

3. When economists discuss real interest rates, they typically distinguish between *ex ante* and *ex post* real interest rates. *Ex ante* real interest rates are calculated using future expected price inflation. *Ex post* real interest rates are calculated using past actual price inflation. If you were calculating *ex ante* real interest rates, how would you measure expected inflation?

4. Many politicians and economists believe the nation's goal should be an unemployment rate of 4 or 4.5 percent. But a national unemployment rate of 4 percent typically means an unemployment rate of about 2 percent for married men with spouse present, 7 percent for women who maintain families (single moms), 3 percent for white women over age 20, and 35 percent for black teens. If 4 percent is considered a "good" level of unemployment and 7 percent is a "bad" level, then why are we content when some groups have an unemployment rate in excess of 7 percent?

5. Okun's law states that a one-percentage-point change in the unemployment rate corresponds to a certain rate of growth in real GDP. Currently it takes 2.5 percent growth in real GDP to lower the unemployment rate by one percentage point. But a decade ago, it took only 2 percent real GDP growth to lower the unemployment rate by one percentage point. Why would the ratio between change in the unemployment rate and real GDP growth change over time?

SOLUTIONS	SOLUTIONS	SOLUTIONS	SOLUTIONS

A. BASIC DEFINITIONS

* indicates there are notes below related to this question.

1. Nominal exchange rate
2. Laspeyres index
3. businesses
4. Gross Domestic Product*

5. stock market
6. Exports

7. nominal exchange rate
8. labor force
9. Consumer Price Index
10. GDP deflator
11. real interest rate*
12. households*

13. Imports
14. an index number; bilateral trade
15. labor force
16. I.O.U.
17. Paasche index

*4.   The difference between GDP and GNP is whether the resources producing output are located within or owned by a nation and its citizens. Gross **National** Product measures final goods and services produced **with a nation's resources**, regardless of where those resources are located.

*11.   The key phrase in the question is "in goods and services."

*12.   Note that consumption measures spending for both domestically produced **and foreign produced** products. The same is true of investment spending and government spending. It is the inclusion of spending for foreign produced products in C, I, and G that makes it necessary to subtract these imports (IM) when calculating total spending for domestically produced goods and services, GDP.

18. demand for
19. real
20. more

21. higher
22. are not; are

23. 2001 quantities; 1996 prices
24. Intermediate; investment

25. A. The dollar depreciating means that one dollar is worth fewer units of foreign currency. It is equivalent to the nominal exchange rate, e, rising.

26. C. An increase in real exchange rates is equivalent to an increase in the relative price of foreign goods and services. Foreign goods and services become more expensive if prices abroad rise more rapidly than prices in the U.S. The other answers are all consistent with a decrease in real exchange rates.

27. C. Most investors, though not all, are at least slightly risk averse. They want to be compensated for taking on risk. That means that most investors want a higher return on stock than on bonds. Stocks are always riskier than bonds because, according to the law, bondholders must be repaid before stockholders when a company declares bankruptcy.

28. D. All four statements are true statements but only "D" is an explanation for the tendency of the CPI to overstate the "true" cost of living.

29. B. The student, mom, and out-of-work man are all out of the labor force. The college senior is actively looking for work.

30. A. Just have to remember this one.

31. A. This is an important quirk to remember. Consumption spending measures spending for *final* goods and services. Investment spending includes businesses' spending for investment goods but not for *intermediate* goods and services. But government spending includes spending for all goods and services by government agencies. The final good or service provided by the government is justice, or police protection, or education, or paved roads — things that do not have a price determined in a market.

Rather than try to figure out how to price justice, the national income accounting system implicitly assumes that the "price" of justice is the cost of the inputs — the salaries, pencils, computer disks, law books, electricity, and so on. In effect, national income accounting assumes that government passes justice and other goods and services on to us at cost and therefore we can use the value of the intermediate goods (inputs) to measure the market price of justice. Businesses generally charge more than cost, so if we counted just the inputs we would not measure the full market price of the product.

B. MANIPULATION OF CONCEPTS AND MODELS

1. An increase in demand for foreign exchange is shown as a shift to the right of the demand curve. The increase in demand **increases** the price of foreign exchange, e.

2. A. $\$120.50 = 100€ \cdot \dfrac{\$1}{0.83€}$

   B. $20.75€ = \$25 \cdot \dfrac{0.83€}{\$1}$

   C. $17.5€ = \$25 \cdot \dfrac{0.70€}{\$1}$

   D. Dollar depreciated. The initial exchange rate, e_1, was
   $\dfrac{1}{0.83} = 1.205$. The second exchange rate, e_2, was $\dfrac{1}{0.70} = 1.429$.

   E. Assuming no changes in prices, U.S. goods are now less expensive relative to French goods.

3. Use the real exchange rate equation, $\varepsilon = \dfrac{e \cdot P_{Mexico}}{P_{U.S.}}$.

   A. Increase in real exchange rate, as prices in Mexico rise more rapidly than prices in the U.S.

   B. Decrease in U.S. demand for Mexican pesos, due to increase in real exchange rate (increase in relative price of Mexican goods and services). This would be shown in the graph above as a shift to the left in the demand curve.

   C. Increase in Mexican demand for U.S. dollars, due to increase in relative price of Mexican goods and services which is equivalent to decrease in relative price of U.S. goods and services. Increase in Mexican demand for U.S. dollars is equivalent to increase in Mexican supply of pesos, and would be shown as a shift to the right in the Supply curve.

   D. Decrease in nominal exchange rate for Mexican pesos, due to decrease in demand for pesos and increase in supply of pesos.

   E. The first effect (part A) was an increase in the real exchange rate; the subsequent effect (part D) was a decrease in the real exchange rate. Without more information, we do not know which effect is larger so we don't know if there is an overall increase, decrease, or no change in the real exchange rate.

4.

	e_{peso}	CPI_{Mexico}	$CPI_{U.S.}$	ε_{peso}
year 1	0.25	600	140	1.07
year 2	0.25	660	147	1.12
year 3	0.225	726	154	1.06

   A. $660 = 600 + 600 \cdot 0.10 = 600 \cdot (1.10)$ $147 = 140 + 140 \cdot 0.05 = 140 \cdot (1.05)$
   $726 = 660 + 660 \cdot 0.10 = 660 \cdot (1.10)$ $154 = 147 + 147 \cdot 0.05 = 147 \cdot (1.05)$

   B. $0.225 = 0.25 - 0.25 \cdot 0.10 = 0.25 \cdot (0.90)$

C. $1.07 = 0.25 \cdot 600/140$

$1.12 = 0.25 \cdot 660/147$

$1.06 = 0.225 \cdot 726/154$

D. Mexican goods and services are more expensive in year 2 than in year 1; 1.12 > 1.07. Because inflation is greater in Mexico than in the U.S. and nominal exchange rates have not adjusted, the real exchange rate (relative price of Mexican goods and services) has increased.

Mexican goods and services are less expensive in year 3 than in year 2; 1.06 < 1.12. Inflation continues to be greater in Mexico than in the U.S. but now nominal exchange rates have adjusted. The real exchange rate (relative price of Mexican goods and services) has decreased between year 2 and year 3 and is almost back to its year 1 level.

5. Answers will vary. You should have used the equation $\varepsilon_A = \dfrac{e \cdot P_A}{P_{u.s.}}$. Be sure the nominal exchange rate you took from the *Economic Report* was expressed as dollars per unit of foreign currency. In the 2001 *ERP*, only the euro and the British pound are expressed that way.

6.

	$\varepsilon_{Americas}$	% Δ	ε_{Africa}	% Δ	ε_{Europe}	% Δ	ε_{Asia}	% Δ	Avg % Δ	XR index	% Δ
year 1	0.303		4.286		0.214		9.143			100	
year 2	0.301	-0.52	7.483	74.6	0.247	15.2	9.524	4.17	22.3	108.0	8.0
year 3	0.300	-0.43	12.99	73.6	0.282	14.1	9.740	2.27	22.8	118.4	9.6

A. $0.303 = 1.06 \cdot 40/140$ $0.214 = 0.30 \cdot 100/140$

$0.301 = 1.03 \cdot 43/147$ $0.247 = 0.33 \cdot 110/147$

$0.300 = 1.05 \cdot 44/154$ $0.282 = 0.31 \cdot 140/154$

$4.286 = 12 \cdot 50/140$ $9.143 = 64 \cdot 20/140$

$7.483 = 11 \cdot 100/147$ $9.524 = 56 \cdot 25/147$

$12.99 = 10 \cdot 200/154$ $9.740 = 50 \cdot 30/154$

B. Note that the answers given in the table above and detailed below were calculated before rounding. If you round and then calculate the rate of change, you will get slightly different results. For instance, after rounding a drop from 0.303 to 0.301 is a drop of 0.0066 or 0.66 percent.

$-0.0052 = -0.52\% = (0.303/0.301) - 1$ $0.152 = 15.2\% = (0.247/0.214) - 1$

$-0.0043 = -0.43\% = (0.300/0.301) - 1$ $0.141 = 14.1\% = (0.282/0.247) - 1$

$0.746 = 74.6\% = (7.483/4.286) - 1$

$0.736 = 73.6\% = (12.99/7.483) - 1$ $0.0417 = 4.17\% = (9.524/9.143) - 1$

                                                $0.0227 = 2.27\% = (9.740/9.524) - 1$

$0.2233 = 22.33\% = (-0.52 + 74.6 + 15.2 + 4.17) / 4$

$0.2285 = 22.85\% = (-0.43 + 73.6 + 14.1 + 2.27) / 4$

C. $100 = 100 \times \left[\left(\dfrac{0.303}{0.303} \cdot 0.4 \right) + \left(\dfrac{4.286}{4.286} \cdot 0.05 \right) + \left(\dfrac{0.214}{0.214} \cdot 0.2 \right) + \left(\dfrac{9.143}{9.143} \cdot 0.35 \right) \right]$

$$108.0 = 100 \times \left[\left(\frac{0.301}{0.303} \cdot 0.4 \right) + \left(\frac{7.483}{4.286} \cdot 0.05 \right) + \left(\frac{0.247}{0.214} \cdot 0.2 \right) + \left(\frac{9.740}{9.143} \cdot 0.35 \right) \right]$$

$$118.4 = 100 \times \left[\left(\frac{0.300}{0.303} \cdot 0.4 \right) + \left(\frac{12.99}{4.286} \cdot 0.05 \right) + \left(\frac{0.282}{0.214} \cdot 0.2 \right) + \left(\frac{9.740}{9.143} \cdot 0.35 \right) \right]$$

D. $8.0 = (108.0/100) - 1$ \hspace{3cm} $9.6 = (118.4/108.0) - 1$

E. The real exchange rate between the U.S. and Africa is rising very rapidly due to rampant inflation in Africa and an absence of nominal exchange rate adjustment. When the annual rates of change of the real exchange rates are simply averaged, as in Part B, the rapid increase in the U.S.-Africa real exchange rate has the same influence on the average as does that for every other country. But only 5 percent of trade is between the U.S. and Africa. By contrast, the exchange rate index is a weighted average of the real exchange rates, with weights equal to each country's share of trade with the U.S. The rapid rise in the U.S.-Africa real exchange rate affects the exchange rate index but its influence on the index is relatively small. The exchange rate index gives a better indication of average changes in the cost of the foreign goods and services those in the U.S. actually buy.

7. A. $6.0\% = \dfrac{0.60}{10}$ \hspace{2cm} B. $5.0\% = \dfrac{0.50}{10}$ \hspace{2cm} C. $5.0\% = \dfrac{0.60}{12}$

D. Expected returns would increase if I anticipated an increase in the price of the stock. My total return would then equal not only the dividends received, but also the increase in the stock's price. To determine the annual rate of return for a stock held more than one year, I would need to take a finance course.

8. Use $P^S = \dfrac{E^S}{r + \sigma^S}$. Thus $\sigma^S = \dfrac{E^S}{P^S} - r = \dfrac{0.50}{8} - 0.06 = 0.0625 - 0.06 = 0.0025 = 0.25\%$

9. $150 total. $0.05 \cdot 1000 = 50$. Three years at $50 per year is $150 total.

10. $8.75 per month in interest charges. $21\% = 0.21$ is the annual rate. If interest is calculated monthly, then the monthly interest rate is $0.21 / 12 = 0.0175 = 1.75\%$ monthly. An outstanding balance of $500 incurs $500 \cdot 0.0175 = \$8.75$ in interest each month. Annual interest payments will be $105 = 12 \cdot 8.75$.

11. 18% is the real interest rate. Use real interest rate = nominal interest rate - inflation rate. $18 = 21 - 3$.

12. Real interest rates fall by 1 percentage point when the Fed lowers the federal funds rate from 7 to 6 percent, if there is no change in the expected inflation rate. Real interest rates are unchanged if the inflation rate declines from 3 to 2 percent at the same time.

13.

	CPI-U	inflation rate	food	inflation rate	medical	inflation rate	housing	inflation rate
1990	130.7		132.4		162.8		128.5	
1991	136.2	4.2	136.3	2.9	177.0	8.7	133.6	4.0
1992	140.3	3.0	137.9	1.2	190.1	7.4	137.5	2.9
1993	144.5	3.0	140.9	2.2	201.4	5.9	141.2	2.7
1994	148.2	2.6	144.3	2.4	211.0	4.8	144.8	2.5

A. Confirmed. For example, $100 = (96.5 + 99.6 + 103.9)/3$.

B. Example: $4.2 = 100 \cdot [(136.2/130.7)-1]$

C. It depends. Food prices rose at a slower pace than CPI-U, but medical expenses rose much more rapidly than CPI-U. Whether CPI-U reflected changes in the cost of living for seniors depends upon the shares of their total spending that are allocated to food, medical care, and housing. The more that seniors spend on medical care, the less useful is the CPI-U index as a measure of seniors' cost of living.

14. The point of this question is to get you to actually look up the data, play with it, and get a feel for how the economy compares today with the economy of the late twentieth century. You can't get that feel for data from just reading the answers; you actually have to play with the figures. So go for it!

15. 132 million. Use $unemployment\ rate\ (u) = \dfrac{number\ unemployed\ (U)}{number\ unemployed\ (U)\ +\ number\ employed\ (E)}$ and

labor force (LF) = number employed (E) + number unemployed (U).

$$u = \frac{U}{U + E}$$
$$0.053 = \frac{U}{U + 125}$$
$$0.053U + 0.053 \cdot 125 = U$$
$$6.625 = U - 0.053U$$
$$6.625 = (1 - 0.053) \cdot U$$
$$6.625 = 0.947U$$
$$\frac{6.625}{0.947} = U$$
$$7.0 = U$$
$$LF = E + U$$
$$LF = 125 + 7 = 132$$

16. 155.3 million.

$$0.049 = \frac{8}{8 + E}$$
$$0.049 \cdot E + 0.049 \cdot 8 = 8$$
$$0.049 \cdot E = 8 \cdot 0.951$$
$$0.049 \cdot E = 7.608$$
$$E = \frac{7.608}{0.049} = 155.3$$

17. A. Employed. A paycheck is received. It doesn't matter how much time is spent in school versus at work.

   B. Unemployed. Once you begin looking for work, you are counted as unemployed.

   C. Out of the labor force. She is not paid.

   D. Out of the labor force. He is not paid. If he did exactly the same work for AmFAR and received a paycheck for his efforts, then he would be counted as employed.

   E. Employed. Presumably she or he is paid.

   F. Out of the labor force. He has to have looked for work at some point in the last four weeks. "Looking for work" can include anything from reading the "help wanted" advertisements to interviewing for a potential job.

18. A. C. You are (part of) a household, buying a final good.

   B. Mostly not recorded, but there is an entry in Consumption. The markup of the used CD is in C. The rest is not recorded. If the shop bought the CD for $5 for Rashanda and sold it for $8 to Imani, then $3 ($8-$5) is in Consumption and $5 is not recorded.

   C. Not recorded. This is just a transfer of assets between two households; nothing was produced.

   D. I. The racks are permanent; they are not used up in the process of producing the final product, CDs for sale to consumers.

   E. Not recorded. The paint is an intermediate good; it is an input that is used up in the process of producing the final product, CDs for sale to consumers. Look inside the paint can at the end of the day and the paint can will be empty. It was used up.

   F. G. The city is a local government agency buying a product.

G. G. The city is a local government agency. Payment of wages to city employees is part of government spending.

H. EX. The student has purchased a U.S.-produced service, a restaurant meal.

I. C and IM. Buying trinkets is Consumption spending by a household. But the trinkets were produced in Russia, so it is an import as well. "Not recorded" would be the wrong answer because the purchase of trinkets *is* recorded – twice! The net effect on U.S. GDP is zero, because the consumption spending is exactly offset by the imports. That makes sense: no product was produced in the U.S. and no employment was generated in the U.S. from the act of buying trinkets in Russia.

J. C. You are (part of) a household, buying a final good. If you were a business, this would be investment spending because the car is not used up when it is driven. But assuming you're a person (And it's hard to imagine a business doing all these questions, now isn't it?), this is Consumption. The fact the Toyota Motor Corporation is a Japanese-owned corporation is irrelevant to the determination of GDP; what matters is the location of the factory not its ownership. The Toyota factory in Georgetown, Kentucky, generates employment in the U.S. and so its product is counted as part of U.S. GDP. If we were discussing GNP (gross national product), then the ownership of the factory would matter.

K. I and IM. It is investment because the fry machine is not used up in the process of producing fries. It is also counted in imports because the machine itself was produced in Italy, generating employment in machine factories in Italy. See also part "I" above.

L. Not recorded. Napkins are an intermediate good; they are an input that is used up in the process of producing the final product, burgers and sodas. Napkins are not an item on the menu. They are definitely used up; look inside the napkin dispenser at the end of the lunch hour and it will be empty. (By the way, the napkin dispenser is so well made it lasts for a few years; it is therefore investment spending.)

M. Not recorded. Payment of tuition and fees to public schools (government agencies) are not consumption spending; they are counted as "taxes," which reduce disposable income relative to income. The expenses of a public school (a government agency) are in G. So if you are at UMass, the salary of the person teaching this course is counted as a final product in Government spending.

N. C. Payment of tuition and fees to a private school is part of consumption spending. The payroll expenses of the private school are inputs to the production of their final product, education. So if you are at Amherst College, the salary of the person teaching this course is an intermediate good.

O. C. You are paying for a service, the use of the washers and dryers.

P. Not recorded, because Mom's efforts to make your life joyful (or at least less smelly) are not part of GDP. But the flowers you buy to thank her will be in Consumption spending.

Q. G and IM. MARTA is a government agency, so its purchase of anything is part of G. But the cars were produced abroad, so their value is also included in IM. See also part "I" above.

19. 1500.

$$GDP = C + I + G + NX$$
$$GDP - C - I - G = NX$$
$$9000 - 5000 - 1500 - 1000 = NX$$
$$1500 = NX$$

20.

	year 1	year 2	year 3
C	2700	2700	2700
I	+300	-200	0
production (GDP)	3000	2500	2700

Remember that investment spending includes the *changes* to inventory holdings, not the actual inventory holdings. Inventories was 0 at the beginning of year 1 and 300 at the end of year 1, so the change in inventory (investment) is 300 in year 1. At the end of year 2, inventory holdings are 100, so inventories fell by 200 during year 2; the change in inventory (investment) is -200. Total production (GDP) is the sum of Consumption and Investment.

21.

	books			coffee			lattes			phone cards			CDs			Total
year	P	Q	share	P	Q	share	P	Q	share	P	Q	share	P	Q	share	Spending
1	80.00	8	0.252	1.00	250	0.098	2.50	500	0.492	20.00	12	0.094	16.00	10	0.063	2540.00
2	84.00	8	0.248	1.05	275	0.107	2.85	475	0.500	19.20	12	0.085	16.16	10	0.060	2706.50
3	88.20	8	0.272	1.10	450	0.191	3.30	300	0.382	18.40	13	0.092	16.32	10	0.063	2593.00
4	92.60	8	0.293	1.15	550	0.250	3.80	200	0.301	17.70	13	0.091	16.48	10	0.065	2528.20

A. See table. For example, total spending in year 1 is $2540 = 80 \cdot 8 + 1 \cdot 250 + 2.5 \cdot 500 + 20 \cdot 12 + 16 \cdot 10$. The share spent on books is $80 \cdot 8 / 2540 = 0.252$.

B.

Year	Price Index	Rate
1	100	
2	108.33	8.33
3	118.69	9.56
4	130.14	9.65

E.

Year	Price Index	Rate
1	100	
2	108.50	8.50
3	116.30	7.20
4	123.15	5.89

B. See above table. In each year, the weights used in the weighted average will be the expenditure shares from the base year, year 1. For example, the year 2 price index is 108.33.

$$108.33 = 100 \cdot \left(\frac{84.00}{80.00} \cdot 0.252 + \frac{1.05}{1.00} \cdot 0.098 + \frac{2.85}{2.50} \cdot 0.492 + \frac{19.20}{20.00} \cdot 0.094 + \frac{16.16}{16.00} \cdot 0.063 \right)$$

C. Natalya decreased her demand for lattes as their relative price increased. This makes sense. Unless her demand for lattes is perfectly price inelastic, an increase in the relative price of lattes will cause Natalya to decrease the quantity of lattes demanded. Notice that what is relevant here is the *relative* price of lattes. The price of coffee increased, but her quantity of coffee demand also increased. That makes sense because the *price of coffee relative to the price of related goods (lattes)* fell; lattes increased in price more rapidly than cups of coffee.

D. Lower. The inflation rate would be lower if we used year 4 expenditure shares because by year 4, Natalya is devoting only 30 percent of her total spending to lattes, whose price is increasing rapidly. In year 1, she was devoting over 49 percent of her spending to lattes. When the price index is calculated, the weight applied to any product is its share in total expenditure. Applying a weight of 0.301 to the most rapidly increasing price, rather than a weight of 0.492, will result in a lower weighted average.

E. See above table. In each year, the weights used in the weighted average will be the expenditure shares from that year. For example, the year 2 price index is 108.50.

$$108.50 = 100 \cdot \left(\frac{84.00}{80.00} \cdot 0.248 + \frac{1.05}{1.00} \cdot 0.107 + \frac{2.85}{2.50} \cdot 0.500 + \frac{19.20}{20.00} \cdot 0.085 + \frac{16.16}{16.00} \cdot 0.060 \right)$$

C. APPLYING CONCEPTS AND MODELS

1. The question is about determinants of nominal exchange rates, so you should use a model of supply and demand for foreign currency. The dollar-pound exchange rate will fall; that is, the dollar will appreciate relative to the pound. Decreased tourism from the U.S. lowers U.S. demand for British pounds, which decreases the price in dollars of one British pound. Or, symbolically: $\downarrow$Tourism $\Rightarrow$ $\downarrow$U.S. $D_£ \Rightarrow \downarrow P_£ = \downarrow e_£$.

2. The question is about determinants of nominal exchange rates, so you should use a model of supply and demand for foreign currency. The dollar-yen exchange rate will rise; that is, the dollar will depreciate relative to the yen. Decreased tourism from Japan lowers Japanese demand for the U.S. dollar, which is equivalent to a decline in Japanese supply of Japanese yen being exchanged for dollars, which increases the price in dollars of one Japanese yen. Or, symbolically: $\downarrow$Tourism $\Rightarrow$ $\downarrow$Japanese $D_\$ =$ $\downarrow$Japanese $S_¥ \Rightarrow \uparrow P_¥ = \uparrow e_¥$

3. The question is about determinants of nominal exchange rates, so you should use a model of supply and demand for foreign currency. The nominal exchange rate will rise; that is, the dollar will depreciate relative to foreign currencies. Decreased foreign investment in the United States lowers foreign demand for U.S. dollars, which lowers the supply of foreign exchange (fx), which increases the price in dollars of foreign exchange. Or, symbolically: $\downarrow$foreign investment $\Rightarrow$ $\downarrow$foreign $D_\$ \Rightarrow \downarrow S_{fx} \Rightarrow \uparrow P_{fx} = \uparrow e_{fx}$.

4. The question is about stock and bond rates of return, so you should use the equation in Figure 2.3. Kavita wants a rate of return of at least 16 percent.

$$P^S \le \frac{E^S}{r + \sigma^S}$$

$$r + \sigma^S \le \frac{E^S}{P^S}$$

$$6 + 10 \le \frac{E^S}{P^S}$$

$$\frac{E^S}{P^S} \ge 16$$

5. The question is about stock and bond rates of return, so you should use the equation in Figure 2.3. Risk premiums vary. One person may have a high risk premium because he is very risk averse, while someone else has a low risk premium because he is not very risk averse (is more risk loving). Suppose the rate of return on bonds is 7 percent and the expected rate of return on stocks is 10 percent. Someone with a risk premium that is less than 3 percent will buy the stock; someone with a risk premium that is more than 3 percent will buy the bond.

6. The question is about stock returns and risk premiums, so you should use the equation in Figure 2.3. The equation is usually stated in terms of rates of return (E^S/P^S), but the question refers to price-earnings ratios. Price-earnings ratios (P^S/E^S) are just the inverse of the stock's rate of return when we assume no anticipated changes in the stock's price. Use the equation $r + \sigma = E/P$.

Mathematically, $\uparrow P/E \Leftrightarrow \uparrow \frac{1}{E/P} \Leftrightarrow \downarrow (E/P) \Leftrightarrow \downarrow (r + \sigma)$. For the market to be in equilibrium, a higher price-earnings ratio means a lower bond return or a lower risk premium. One interpretation of the dramatic increase in price-earnings ratios in the 1990s, then, is that the public's risk premium had decreased just as dramatically. This interpretation invokes two implicit assumptions: one, that no capital gains were anticipated; and two, that the stock markets were in equilibrium and not in a "bubble."

7. The question is about stock and bond returns, so you should use the equation in Figure 2.3. Lower interest rates on bonds mean higher stock prices.

Mathematically, $\downarrow r \Rightarrow \downarrow (r + \sigma) \Rightarrow \downarrow (E/P) \Rightarrow \uparrow P$. Economically, lower rates of return on bonds leads some investors to substitute stocks for bonds in their portfolios, increasing demand for stock and thus increasing the price of stock.

8. The question is about real interest rates, so you should use the equation for real interest rates: real interest rates = nominal interest rates - inflation rates.

Greater than 10 percent. Mathematically, since DVD prices have decreased, the inflation rate is negative (a deflation rate). Therefore, the real interest rate is greater than the nominal rate. Conceptually, when Hector borrowed $1,000, he was able to buy 40 DVDs at $25 each. At that price, Hector would have repaid $1,100 ($1,000 principal plus $100 interest), or the equivalent of 44 DVDs. But DVD prices fell to $20 each, so the $1,100 he repays is equivalent to 55 DVDs. The real cost, 15 DVDs, is much greater than the nominal cost, 4 DVDs, of borrowing $1,000.

9. The question is about Okun's law, so you should use the equation: $\%\Delta$ real GDP = $\%\Delta$ potential real GDP $- 2.5\cdot(U_t - U_{t-1})$.

A. 4.4 percent.
$$\%\Delta\ GDP = \%\Delta\ Potential\ GDP - 2.5\cdot(U_2 - U_1)$$
$$6 = 2 - 2.5\cdot(U_2 - 6)$$
$$4 = -2.5\cdot(U_2 - 6)$$
$$-1.6 = U_2 - 6$$
$$6 - 1.6 = U_2 = 4.4$$

B. 0 percent.
$$\%\Delta\ GDP = \%\Delta\ Potential\ GDP - 2.5\cdot(U_2 - U_1)$$
$$\%\Delta\ GDP = 2.5 - 2.5\cdot(5 - 4)$$
$$\%\Delta\ GDP = 2.5 - 2.5 = 0$$

C. 3.25 percent. Note that this situation would not constitute a recession, even though the unemployment rate is rising, because real GDP is not decreasing.
$$\%\Delta\ GDP = \%\Delta\ Potential\ GDP - 2.5\cdot(U_2 - U_1)$$
$$2 = \%\Delta\ Potential\ GDP - 2.5\cdot(0.5)$$
$$2 = \%\Delta\ Potential\ GDP - 1.25$$
$$3.25 = \%\Delta\ Potential\ GDP$$

D. EXPLAINING THE REAL WORLD

1. The question is asking about stocks and bonds, so use the equation in Figure 2.3.

An 85 year old and a 30 year old probably have different degrees of risk aversion. The 85 year old is very risk averse; she cannot afford to risk losing very much of her principal if the market fluctuates because she frankly doesn't have that many years to recoup her losses. The 30 year old is much less risk averse; he can afford to risk losing some of his principal if his goal is saving for retirement because he has another thirty or forty years to recoup his losses. Because their risk premiums differ, there is a range of rates of return where Ruby will prefer bonds while Jerome prefers stocks.

2. The question asks about the stock market, so use the equation in Figure 2.3.

Stock prices will probably fall. For most companies, a recession means lower sales and thus lower expected earnings. Mathematically, if there is no change in $(r+\sigma)$, then in equilibrium E/P must not change. A lowering of earnings would therefore be offset by a fall in stock prices. Behaviorally, lower expected earnings decreases the expected rate of return on stocks, leading some investors to decrease their demand for stocks, which in turn lowers the price of stock.

3. The question is asking about the real interest rate.

   The answer is not obvious without more information. The real interest rate is the nominal interest rate minus the inflation rate, and he wants to consider the real – not nominal – interest rate in making his decision. But the relevant inflation rate depends upon his opportunity costs. What is Don giving up when he repays the loan? The answer determines which price is relevant to his decision.

4. The question is asking about the consumer price index, and it draws on both your understanding of some microeconomic theory (price elasticity) and how weighted averages work.

   The weights that will be lowered are those for goods with high price elasticity of demand, because those are products whose quantity demanded changes a lot even when relative price changes only a little, and therefore whose total revenue (p·q) declines when relative prices rise. The share of these products in total spending will therefore decline as their relative prices increase. The effect of changing the weights will be to lower the measured inflation rate.

5. The question is asking you to compare the GDP deflator and the consumer price index, so you need to draw on your understanding of the difference between Paasche (GDP deflator) and Laspeyres (CPI) indexes.

   The GDP deflator generally records lower inflation rates than the CPI because, as some products become relatively more expensive, quantity demanded for those products declines. Only the GDP deflator takes into account the changes in demand patterns; the weights used to calculate the GDP deflator are changed each year to reflect actual spending patterns. The weights used to calculate the CPI are from some base year and do not change as our spending patterns change.

   Which index is better depends upon the purpose. There is no one definition of "better" or "best"; there is just "best for this purpose." The question is unanswerable without knowing the purpose to which the index will be put. But if you *were* asked just this question on an exam, the strategic answer would not be to point out that the question is unanswerable as written. The better answer would be to give the conditions under which the CPI is best, and then give the conditions under which the GDP deflator is best. That sort of answer would better demonstrate your knowledge of the differences between the two indexes, which is what the question is trying to assess.

6. The question is asking about the relationship between unemployment and real GDP growth, so it is drawing on the concepts in Okun's law.

   Slower growth in real GDP is needed to decrease the unemployment rate by 1 percentage point when unemployment is mostly of low-skill, low-productivity workers. Low-productivity workers by definition do not produce very much output (GDP) per hour. Employing a certain number of low-productivity workers therefore results in relatively low growth in GDP. Turning it around, when unemployment is mostly of low-productivity workers, relatively slow growth in real GDP is needed to reduce the unemployment rate by 1 percentage point.

7. The question is asking about the relationship between employment and real GDP growth, so it is drawing upon the concepts in Okun's law.

   Different tradeoffs probably applied in the 1840s than in the 1990s. The answer depends upon which type of workers were more likely to experience unemployment in each period. Assuming that low-productivity workers were more likely to experience unemployment in the 1840s than in the 1990s, then the tradeoff was probably greater than it was in the 1840s and 1850s. When workers have high productivity, then a large increase in output (real GDP) is required to provide enough jobs to decrease unemployment by one percentage point. But when workers have low productivity, a smaller increase in GDP is needed to provide enough jobs to decrease unemployment by one percentage point.

The question doesn't ask, but the more obvious effect of the difference between the 1840s and the 1990s would be on the intercept of the equation; that is, on the rate of growth of potential GDP. When labor force growth is primarily of low-productivity workers, then real GDP doesn't need to grow very rapidly to absorb the additional workers; the rate of growth of potential GDP is relatively low. On the other hand, when labor force growth is primarily of high-productivity workers, then real GDP needs to grow relatively quickly to absorb the additional workers; the rate of growth of potential GDP is relatively high. In the Okun's law equation, the rate of growth of potential GDP is the intercept of the equation. See also the next question.

8. The question is asking about the relationship between employment and real GDP growth, so it is drawing on the concepts in Okun's law.

Increase in the unemployment rate is expected. The rate of growth of potential GDP tells us how much output needs to grow just to keep the labor force fully employed. That rate of growth is more than 0 because the labor force is growing. If output grows by only 2 percent and the rate of growth of potential GDP is 2.5 percent, then unemployment will increase. The increase in output produced will not be sufficient to provide jobs for everyone who has entered the labor force.

9. The question is asking about the connection between labor force growth and real GDP. But it is not asking about Okun's law. It is drawing on your understanding of the limitations of real GDP.

There are two obvious connections between the change in married women's labor force participation and real GDP growth. First, the increase in the labor force is associated with an increase in real GDP. For the purposes of this question you don't need to know what led to the increase in women's labor force participation; a larger labor force of any sort, assuming no matching increase in unemployment, is associated with production of more output (GDP). (By the way, you should know that 4.1 percent growth of real GDP is high by historical standards. What were the average rates of growth in the subsequent decades?)

Second, the increase in married women's labor force participation also increased real GDP because of the substitution of market for home production of goods and services used in the home. Consumption of restaurant meals (including "fast food") increases rapidly starting in the 1960s; Mom is too tired to cook after a full day at work so the family grabs dinner at McDonald's. Had Mom cooked burgers, her efforts would not have been counted in real GDP; but because a for-profit company charged a price for their efforts at cooking burgers, those efforts count in real GDP. Similarly, hiring help to clean the house, watch the kids, do the laundry, and so on also leads to measured increases in real GDP. The house is just as clean, the kids are just as watched, the laundry is just as folded, the burgers are just as bad, but because these activities now take place in the market rather than in the home, they are recorded in real GDP.

10. The question is asking about price indexes, so it draws on your understanding of the differences between the CPI and the GDP deflator.

There is no good answer to the question as stated! We need to know the goal of policy in order to determine the best index to use to determine changes in Social Security benefits. (A strategic answer would not end there; it would go on to state possible policy goals and related price index choices.) If the goal is to let seniors buy the same goods and services over time, maintaining their material standard of living, then an index that measures what they buy should be used. The Bureau of Labor Statistics regularly conducts surveys of spending patterns. They could survey senior citizens, then design a price index based on their spending patterns.

11. The question is asking about what is counted in GDP and employment.

   Job creation is considered "good for the economy" even when it is bad for the environment. The volunteers who rescue shore birds do not contribute to the local economy. (Indeed, if they take unpaid leave from their jobs, the time they spend rescuing shore birds is a drain on the economy.) But when the oil refinery hires workers to clean the beaches, they have created additional jobs. Some would say the oil spill, in an ironic way, is therefore "good for the economy."

   Note that cleaning up oil off the beaches is not the production of a final good or service. The workers are an input to the production of oil; cleaning the beach is an intermediate product in the production of oil. Therefore while there is a contribution to employment from hiring workers, there is no direct contribution to GDP.

12. The question is asking about nominal versus real exchange rates.

   Linda's post-graduation trip may not be more expensive than her exchange year even though the nominal exchange rate has increased. She needs to compare not just the nominal exchange rates, but also what has happened to prices in the U.S. and in Japan. If the real exchange rate has also increased, then the post-graduation trip will be more expensive than her exchange year.

13. The question is asking about the definition of real GDP and what it means to be "better off," so it is drawing on your conceptual understanding of GDP and also on your ability to criticize an argument.

   Americans are not necessarily better off than the Japanese even though the GDP of the United States is about twice as large as the GDP of Japan. There are several criticisms. One, the comparison should be of per capita (per person) GDP, not of levels of GDP. Two, a comparison of GDP per capita does not take into account distributional issues; perhaps the distribution of income or wealth is much more skewed in one country than the other, which would enter into a consideration of who is "better off." Third, most people would say that more than just material standards of living are important in determining how "well off" they are; political freedoms, educational opportunities, and so on also matter. A fourth criticism is valid but relatively minor: we need to be sure the statement is comparing real, not nominal, levels of GDP.

E. POSSIBILITIES TO PONDER

No solutions are given to these questions. The questions are designed to be somewhat open ended. Each question draws on your understanding of the concepts covered in this chapter.

NOTE: Economists typically graph things in two dimensions, with a horizontal axis and a vertical axis. So what do you do when you have a relationship that involves three variables? You choose the most important two variables and graph the relationship between those two, holding the values of the other variables constant.

One of the most important variables will *always* be the dependent (endogenous) variable. The other most important variable depends upon the question that is being addressed. Usually — but not always — economists put the dependent variable on the vertical axis and the independent variable on the horizontal axis.

Chapter 3
Thinking Like an Economist

- Economics is a *social* science: it uses models, analytical thought, and mathematics, but is based on human behavior so does not lend itself to the experimentation that is common in the natural or physical sciences.

- Economists use metaphors: circular flow, markets, and equilibrium. Economists also use graphs and diagrams to express economic relationships.

LEARNING GUIDE

The material in this chapter is all conceptual. Some of it is applied to economic growth models that will be covered in depth in Chapter 4. You can do the mathematical applications to those models now, before you have learned the models. Or you can wait and return to the questions about the production function and the balanced growth equation after you have studied Chapter 4.

There are only Section A and Section B questions for this chapter. The material does not lend itself to applied questions.

You will need some math skills in this chapter. Math skills covered in Chapter B are indicated with

Short on time?

The material in this chapter helps everything else you learn in economics make sense. But few professors will test you specifically on the material in this chapter. It is a valuable chapter to study, but if you are cramming for tomorrow's test, Chapter 4 is much more vital.

The concept of circular flow is crucial to understanding macroeconomics: be sure you have a good sense of it before moving on. Being able to distinguish between an equilibrium condition and a behavioral relationship is also crucial to your success in economics. The mathematical skills emphasized in this chapter are also a key part of doing economics. You may find you want to return to this chapter periodically during the course.

A. Basic Definitions

Before you apply knowledge, you need a basic grasp of the fundamentals. In other words, there are some things you just have to know. Knowing the material in this section won't guarantee a good grade in the course, but not knowing it will guarantee a poor or failing grade.

USE THE WORDS OR PHRASES FROM THE LIST BELOW TO COMPLETE THE SENTENCES. SOME ARE USED MORE THAN ONCE; SOME ARE NOT USED AT ALL.

behavioral relationship	*models*
build a model	*natural*
circular flow	*Net National Product*
descriptive	*opportunity cost*
equilibrium	*physical*
Gross Domestic Product	*production function*
market	*representative agent.*
metaphor	*social*

1. Economics is a(n) _____ science, not a natural or physical science.

2. Conditions that must be true for the economy to be in balance are called _____ conditions.

3. Net Domestic Product - net factor income paid abroad = _____ .

4. Economists use mathematical _____ to capture behavioral relationships and equilibrium conditions. The models are expressed with algebra and with graphs.

5. Economics is *not* primarily a(n) _____ science because it does not just describe events but looks for general principles applicable over time or to a variety of situations.

6. To _____ means to restrict attention to a few behavioral relationships and a handful of equilibrium conditions, capture these relationships and conditions mathematically, see how the mathematical system of equations behaves, and then apply it to the real world.

7. The concept of _____ assumes that the behavior of many, many individuals can be described by the behavior of just one individual.

8. Economic activity is like a(n) _____ of purchasing power through the economy.

HINT: Sometimes it is easier to understand abstract principles when you are able to see actual people in your mind's eye. If you find the circular flow concept too abstract, try envisioning the people inside each of the economic units (households, businesses, etc.) and the money and products changing hands.

9. _____ - Net Indirect Taxes + Net Subsidy to Government Enterprises + Statistical Discrepancy = National Income

10. The key concept of the "_____" metaphor is that information flows between all parties in the market.

11. A(n) _____ describes how people behave. It can be expressed with math, graphs, or words.

12. The key concept of the "_____" metaphor is the idea of a point(s) of balance at which some economic quantity is neither rising nor falling.

13. The best alternative you forego in making any choice is the _____.

SELECT THE ONE BEST ANSWER FOR EACH MULTIPLE-CHOICE QUESTION.

14. Some "curves" are actually
   A straight lines.
   B. downward-sloping curves.
   C. a curve that changes slope.
   D. all of the above.

15. Economics cannot do large-scale human experiments because it is
   A. infeasible.
   B. too expensive.
   C. unethical.
   D. not useful.

16. In economics, causality can run
   A. from present to present.
   B. from expectations of the future to the past.
   C. from past to present.
   D. all of the above.

17. Gross Domestic Product - Net Domestic Product =
   A. depreciation.
   B. investment abroad.
   C. taxes.
   D. statistical discrepancy.

B. MANIPULATION OF CONCEPTS AND MODELS

Most instructors expect you to be able to do basic manipulation of the concepts. Being able to do so often means you can earn a C in a course. But if you want a better grade, you'll need to be able to complete this next section easily and move on to Sections C and D.

TO THE CHALKBOARD:

Explaining the Circular Flow

The payments in the circular flow are those that flow between sectors: household to business or business to household. Payments received by households include payments to workers as well as payments to business owners. An example is given here to illustrate the concepts. A furniture company manufactures a new desk which it then sells for $200. The $200 revenue is distributed as follows:

paid to workers for their salaries	$100
paid to lumber supplier for inputs	$80
kept by furniture company as profit	$20

The $80 paid by the furniture company to the lumber supplier is a payment from a business to a business. Because the funds stay completely within the business sector, this payment is not shown in the circular flow. (**Note:** The $80 is payment for an intermediate good. Is it counted in GDP? No. Payments that are not counted in GDP are also not reflected in the circular flow.)

The lumber supplier who receives the $80 from the furniture company distributes it as follows:

paid to workers for their salaries	$70
kept by lumber supplier as profit	$10

To summarize these flows of payments:

HOUSEHOLD - TO - BUSINESS PAYMENTS:

Paid for the desk	$200

BUSINESS - TO - HOUSEHOLD PAYMENTS:

Labor Income

Paid to Furniture Company workers	$100	
Paid to Lumber Supply workers	$70	
Total Labor Income		$170

Profit (Capital Income)

Received by Furniture Company owners	$20	
Received by Lumber Company owners	$10	
Total Profit		$30
Total Income Received by Households		$200

Note that the households have received $200 in total income. They will now spend at least part of the income. The usual assumption is that the marginal propensity to consume is the same, regardless of whether the household is spending labor income or capital income. In the next round of spending there will be household - to - business payments. Suppose the marginal propensity to consume is 80 percent. Households will thus spend 80 percent of the additional $200 income, or $160, on consumer goods and services. The circular flow continues.

1. Categorize each of the following activities, indicating where – if anywhere – it is reflected in the simplest circular flow as illustrated with Figure 3.3. The choices are household expenditure, household income, and "not recorded."

    A. Jin Shaun, a permanent resident of Washington, buys a new CD, manufactured in California, at Tower Records.

    B. The stockholders of Chevron Oil Company are paid stock dividends.

     HINT: Businesses are owned by someone. The people who own businesses – whether they are stockholders or owners of their own businesses – are also members of a household.

    C. Jin Shaun buys a used bookcase at a garage sale.

    D. McDonald's purchases paper napkins that were produced in Washington state.

    E. Jin Shaun receives his paycheck from Washington Paper Products Co.

    F. The owner of a Chevron gas station eats lunch at McDonald's.

     HINT: Everyone in a business – workers, managers, owners – goes home at the end of the day and is then (part of) a household.

2. Categorize each of the following activities, indicating where – if anywhere – it is reflected in the complete circular flow as illustrated with Figure 3.4.

    A. MARTA (Metropolitan Atlanta Rapid Transit Authority, a government agency) purchases new transit cars manufactured in Detroit.

    B. You buy a new Toyota that was manufactured in Kentucky.

    C. A student at University of Massachusetts, Amherst (a public school) pays her fees.

    D. Tower Records, using borrowed money, buys new permanent CD display racks that were manufactured in North Carolina.

    E. Tower Records pays its workers their weekly wages.

    F. Ruth receives her monthly Social Security payment.

G. The parents of a high school student pay for a Kaplan course in a perhaps futile attempt to raise their son's SAT scores.

H. A student from South Africa visiting Indiana University for the summer buys lunch at a local Bloomington hamburger joint.

I. The State of Colorado buys U.S. Treasury bonds with its $5 billion budget surplus.

J. Gaurav, a citizen of Singapore, buys a $1,000 U.S. Treasury bill.

K. Nick, a resident of Los Angeles, after receiving $2000 in take-home pay in March and spending $1500, leaves the remaining $500 in his checking account.

L. A resident of Las Cruces, New Mexico visits Russia and buys trinkets to bring home.

> **NOTE**: There are three measures of circular flow: [1] **expenditure** (consumption by households, investment by businesses, purchases of goods and services by government agencies, and purchases and sales of goods and services by the rest of the world); [2] **income** (all income is ultimately received by households, labor income, property income, interest income, capital income, and so on); and [3] **uses of income** (what households do with their income – spending, saving).

3. Categorize each of the following activities indicating which measure of the circular flow it represents. The choices are expenditure, income, and uses of income.

A. Meredith pays her state income taxes.

B. The local hardware store buys new cash registers.

C. Marshawn is paid 1.0 percent interest on his checking account balance by his bank.

D. Edna pays a $15 check-cashing fee at her local check-cashing company.

E. The City of Jackson, Mississippi, pays the Parks and Recreation Director's salary.

F. Meredith saves $100 out of her paycheck, putting it in a cookie jar in the kitchen.

G. The Parks and Recreation Director of Jackson, Mississippi, receives his paycheck.

NOTE: Use the definitions in textbook Box 3.2 to answer Questions 4, 5, and 6. Note that "Net Factor Incomes Paid Abroad" equals "Factor Incomes Paid Abroad" less "Factor Incomes Received from Abroad."

4. Suppose

Depreciation = 1200	Net Indirect Taxes = 800
Net Domestic Product = 7800	Net Subsidy to Government Enterprises = 25
Net National Product = 7750	National Income = 7075

    A. What is the value of Gross Domestic Product?

    B. What is the value of Net Factor Incomes Paid Abroad?

    C. What is the value of Statistical Discrepancy?

5. Suppose

Gross Domestic Product = 5000	Factor Incomes Received from Abroad = 175
Net Domestic Product = 4500	Net Indirect Taxes = 450
Factor Incomes Paid Abroad = 200	Net Subsidy to Government Enterprises = 15
	National Income = 3990

    A. What is the value of Depreciation?

    B. What is the value of Net National Product?

    C. What is the value of Statistical Discrepancy?

6. Suppose

Gross Domestic Product = 7500	Factor Incomes Received from Abroad = 310
Depreciation = 800	Net Indirect Taxes = 600
Factor Incomes Paid Abroad = 300	Net Subsidy to Government Enterprises = 20
	Statistical Discrepancy = –20

    A. What is the value of Net Domestic Product?

    B. What is the value of Net National Product?

    C. What is the value of National Income?

7. What is your opportunity cost for each of the following activities?

    A. Reading this study guide

    B. Going to your economics class

    C. Going to college

8. For each of the following, indicate whether it is a *behavioral relationship* or an *equilibrium condition*.

    A. $C = f(Y_D)$

    B. $Y = C + I + G + NX$

    C. When the price of a red ink pen is $1.20, the quantity of pens supplied equals the quantity of pens demanded.

    D. When the price of red ink pens rises, the quantity of pens demanded falls.

    E. When I let go of a piece of chalk, it falls.

    F. When the piece of chalk I dropped is on the floor, it does not move.

    G. When layoffs are announced in the news, consumers buy fewer new cars.

    H. If spending is maintained at current levels, then businesses will have no unexpected changes in their inventory holdings.

NOTE: Equations can be expressed in one of three forms:

- **General abstract form** (also known as **general functional form**): States the independent (or exogenous) variables that influence the dependent (or endogenous) variable. For example, $\frac{Y}{L} = f\left(\frac{K}{L}\right)$ tells us generally that output per worker depends upon the capital-labor ratio.

- **Particular algebraic form** (also known as **specific functional form**): States the mathematical form of the relationship between the independent (or exogenous) variables and the dependent (or endogenous) variable. For example, $\frac{Y}{L} = \left(\frac{K}{L}\right)^{\alpha} \times E^{1-\alpha}$ tells us specifically how output per worker depends upon the capital-labor ratio.

- **Estimated form** (also sometimes known as **parameterized form**): States the exact nature of the relationship between the independent (or exogenous) variables and the dependent (or endogenous) variable. For example, $\frac{Y}{L} = \left(\frac{K}{L}\right)^{0.4} \times E^{0.6}$ allows us to calculate specific numeric values of $\frac{Y}{L}$ once we have values of $\frac{K}{L}$ and E.

9. Suppose output per worker depends upon the capital-to-labor ratio and the efficiency of labor according to the following equation:

$$\frac{Y}{L} = \left(\frac{K}{L}\right)^{\alpha} \times E^{1-\alpha}$$

HINT: Be sure you think of $\frac{Y}{L}$ as one variable, not two. The equation has three variables: $\frac{Y}{L}$, $\frac{K}{L}$, and E. It has one parameter, α.

A. Suppose $\alpha = 0.3$. What is the estimated form of the equation?

B. Suppose instead $\alpha = \frac{2}{3}$. What is the estimated form of the equation?

C. Suppose $\dfrac{Y}{L} = \left(\dfrac{K}{L}\right)^{0.3} \times E^{0.7}$ and $E = 1000$. Simplify the output per worker equation so you have a relationship just between $\dfrac{Y}{L}$ and $\dfrac{K}{L}$. Then fill in the middle column of the following table.

| | E = 1000 | E = 3000 |
$\dfrac{K}{L}$	$\dfrac{Y}{L}$	$\dfrac{Y}{L}$
0		
1000		
2000		
3000		
4000		
5000		

D. Now suppose instead that $E = 3000$. Again, simplify the output per worker equation so you have a relationship just between $\dfrac{Y}{L}$ and $\dfrac{K}{L}$. Then complete the last column of the table above.

E. Sketch in the graph of the equation $\dfrac{Y}{L} = \left(\dfrac{K}{L}\right)^{0.3} \times E^{0.7}$ when $E = 1000$.

Sketch in the graph of the equation $\dfrac{Y}{L} = \left(\dfrac{K}{L}\right)^{0.3} \times E^{0.7}$ when $E = 3000$.

Notice that when the value of E changes, the entire curve shifts.

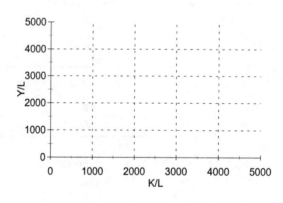

F. Suppose output per worker depends upon the capital-to-labor ratio and the efficiency of labor according to $\frac{Y}{L} = \left(\frac{K}{L}\right)^{\alpha} \times E^{1-\alpha}$. Suppose $E = 1000$ and $\alpha = 0.6$.

What is the simplified version of the output per worker equation? Complete the table at the right.

$\frac{K}{L}$	$\frac{Y}{L}$
0	
1000	
2000	
3000	
4000	
5000	

G. Sketch in the graph of the equation $\frac{Y}{L} = \left(\frac{K}{L}\right)^{0.3} \times E^{0.7}$ when $E = 1000$. Sketch in the graph of the equation $\frac{Y}{L} = \left(\frac{K}{L}\right)^{0.6} \times E^{0.4}$ when $E = 1000$. Notice that when the value of α changes, the entire curve shifts.

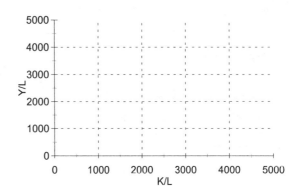

NOTE: Box 3.5 gives an equilibrium condition: $\frac{K}{Y} \equiv \kappa^{*} = \frac{s}{n + g + \delta}$. K measures the stock of capital; Y measures the value of output and income; s measures the saving rate; n measures the rate of growth of the labor force; g measures the rate of growth of the efficiency of the labor force; and δ measures the rate at which capital – machines and buildings – depreciate. *These variables will be explained in Chapter 4.* As you will learn in Chapter 4, when the capital-to-output ratio, $\frac{K}{Y}$ or κ^{*}, equals $\frac{s}{n + g + \delta}$, then we are said to be in a "long-run steady-state balanced-growth equilibrium" because as the economy grows, the capital-to-output ratio will stay the same.

TO THE CHALKBOARD:
Explaining Box 3.6

Boxes 3.6, 3.7, and 3.8 show how to combine a behavioral relationship and an equilibrium condition to derive an interesting economic statement. The behavioral relationship is $\frac{Y}{L} = \left(\frac{K}{L}\right)^{\alpha} \times E^{1-\alpha}$. The equilibrium condition is $\frac{K}{Y} = \kappa^* = \frac{s}{n + g + \delta}$. These two equations can be combined.

Two Tricks You Need in Order to Do the Math

[1] Remember to treat $\frac{Y}{L}$ as one variable, not two. There are three variables in the behavioral relationship, $\frac{Y}{L}$, $\frac{K}{L}$, and E, and one parameter, α. There is one variable in the equilibrium condition, $\frac{K}{Y}$, and four parameters, s, n, g, and δ.

[2] Think creatively about how to reduce the number of variables. This is often the difficult part of doing the math in economics. Try thinking about it as a mystery in which you are trying to assemble clues. You have pieces of information about $\frac{Y}{L}$, $\frac{K}{L}$, $\frac{K}{Y}$, and E, and you need to link the pieces of information together.

How to Reduce the Number of Variables

[1] Remember that we are ultimately interested in how changes in the capital-to-labor ratio, $\frac{K}{L}$, affect output-per-worker, $\frac{Y}{L}$. So we want to wind up with just those two variables.

[2] Remember that we can multiply anything by 1 and that doing so does not change its value ($x \cdot 1 = x$).

[3] Remember that anything divided by itself equals 1. For instance, $\frac{(1/L)}{(1/L)} = 1$.

Can you see how we might proceed? $\frac{K}{Y}$ can be multiplied by 1 and it will still equal $\frac{K}{Y}$. Let's use $\frac{(1/L)}{(1/L)} = 1$. Thus $\frac{K}{Y} = \frac{K}{Y} \times 1 = \frac{K}{Y} \times \frac{1/L}{1/L}$. Simplifying the last term we have $\frac{K}{Y} = \frac{K/L}{Y/L}$, or $\frac{\frac{K}{L}}{\frac{Y}{L}}$.

And now we have reduced the number of variables to three: $\frac{Y}{L}$, $\frac{K}{L}$, and E.

Our behavioral relationship is still $\frac{Y}{L} = \left(\frac{K}{L}\right)^{\alpha} \times E^{1-\alpha}$. But now we can express the equilibrium condition as $\frac{\frac{K}{L}}{\frac{Y}{L}} = \frac{s}{n + g + \delta}$. Next, assume the value of E is fixed so that we can treat E as a constant.

Now we have two equations and two unknowns (variables). That's something we can solve! The variables are $\frac{Y}{L}$ and $\frac{K}{L}$. Everything else – E, α, s, n, g, δ – can be treated as a constant.

And Now We're Ready to Proceed!

Now let's go through Box 3.6. As Prof. DeLong does in Box 3.6, suppose

E = 10,000   n = 1% = 0.01

α = 0.5   g = 1% = 0.01

s = 25% = 0.25   δ = 3% = 0.03

First, simplify both equations by substituting in the values given above:

$$\frac{Y}{L} = \left(\frac{K}{L}\right)^{\alpha} \times E^{1-\alpha} = \left(\frac{K}{L}\right)^{0.5} \times 10000^{1-0.5} = \left(\frac{K}{L}\right)^{0.5} \times 10000^{0.5} = \left(\frac{K}{L}\right)^{0.5} \times 100$$

$$\frac{K}{Y} = \frac{\dfrac{K}{L}}{\dfrac{Y}{L}} = \frac{s}{n + g + \delta} = \frac{0.25}{0.01 + 0.01 + 0.03} = \frac{0.25}{0.05} = 5$$

Rewriting to clarify:

$$\frac{Y}{L} = \left(\frac{K}{L}\right)^{0.5} \times 100 \qquad \text{and} \qquad \frac{\dfrac{K}{L}}{\dfrac{Y}{L}} = 5$$

$$\text{or,} \quad \frac{Y}{L} = \left(\frac{K}{L}\right)^{0.5} \times 100 \qquad \text{and} \qquad \frac{K}{L} = 5 \cdot \frac{Y}{L}$$

We can solve first for either $\frac{Y}{L}$ or $\frac{K}{L}$. Following Box 3.6, let's solve first for $\frac{K}{L}$.

$$\frac{K}{L} = 5 \times \frac{Y}{L} \qquad \textit{equilibrium condition}$$

$$\frac{K}{L} = 5 \times \left(\frac{K}{L}\right)^{0.5} \times 100 \qquad \textit{substituting} \left(\frac{K}{L}\right)^{0.5} \times 100 \textit{ for } \frac{Y}{L}$$

$$\frac{K}{L} = 500 \times \left(\frac{K}{L}\right)^{0.5} \qquad \textit{simplifying}$$

$$\left(\frac{K}{L}\right)^{-0.5} \times \frac{K}{L} = 500 \times \left(\frac{K}{L}\right)^{0.5} \times \left(\frac{K}{L}\right)^{-0.5} \qquad \textit{multiplying both sides by} \left(\frac{K}{L}\right)^{-0.5}$$

$$\left(\frac{K}{L}\right)^{0.5} = 500 \qquad \textit{simplifying}$$

$$\left(\left(\frac{K}{L}\right)^{0.5}\right)^{2} = (500)^{2} \qquad \textit{squaring both sides}$$

$$\frac{K}{L} = 250,000 \qquad \textit{simplifying}$$

Now we can solve for the equilibrium value of $\frac{Y}{L}$. We can use either equation.

$$\frac{K}{L} = 5 \times \frac{Y}{L} \qquad\qquad \text{or,} \qquad\qquad \frac{Y}{L} = \left(\frac{K}{L}\right)^{0.5} \times 100$$

$$250,000 = 5 \times \frac{Y}{L} \qquad\qquad\qquad\qquad \frac{Y}{L} = (250,000)^{0.5} \times 100$$

$$\frac{250,000}{5} = \frac{Y}{L} = 50,000 \qquad\qquad\qquad \frac{Y}{L} = 500 \times 100 = 50,000$$

MATH: Solving two equations in two unknowns is a math skill that is covered in Chapter B.

10. Suppose

E = 900	s = 10%	g = 1%
α = 0.5	n = 2%	δ = 3%

Follow the method shown in Box 3.6. Use separate sheets of paper for your work.

A. What is the equilibrium level of the capital-to-output ratio, $\left(\dfrac{K}{Y}\right)^*$?

B. What is the equilibrium level of output per worker?

11. Suppose

E = 5,000	s = 15%	g = 3%
α = 0.4	n = 2%	δ = 4%

Follow the method shown in Box 3.6. Use separate sheets of paper for your work.

A. What is the equilibrium level of the capital-to-output ratio, $\left(\dfrac{K}{Y}\right)^*$?

B. What is the equilibrium level of output per worker?

TO THE CHALKBOARD:
Explaining Box 3.7

In Box 3.7, Prof. DeLong solves the two-equation, two-unknown equation system algebraically. Specific numerical answers can then be derived by substituting in values for the parameters E, α, s, n, g, δ.

$\frac{y}{L} = \left(\frac{K}{L}\right)^{\alpha} \times E^{1-\alpha}$ is the behavioral relationship; $\frac{K}{y} = \frac{s}{n+g+\delta}$ is the equilibrium condition. Here again, we want to reduce the number of variables from three – $\frac{y}{L}$, $\frac{K}{L}$, and $\frac{K}{y}$ – to two. In Box 3.7, Prof. DeLong chooses to transform $\frac{K}{L}$ so that he winds up with two variables: $\frac{y}{L}$ and $\frac{K}{y}$. (We would derive the same result even if we transformed $\frac{K}{y}$ to wind up with $\frac{y}{L}$ and $\frac{K}{L}$.)

$\frac{K}{L}$ can be multiplied by 1 and it will still equal $\frac{K}{L}$. Let's use $\frac{(1/y)}{(1/y)}$ as 1. Why that expression for 1? Because we know where we are heading: to a place where we will have $\frac{K}{y}$ as one of our variables. Multiplying by $\frac{(1/y)}{(1/y)}$, we have

$$\frac{K}{L} = \frac{K}{L} \times 1 = \frac{K}{L} \times \frac{1/y}{1/y} = \frac{\frac{K}{y}}{\frac{L}{y}}$$

But $\frac{L}{y}$ is not the variable we want; we want to end up with $\frac{y}{L}$. So again multiplying the last term by 1, where this time $\frac{y/L}{y/L} = 1$, we have

$$\frac{K}{L} = \frac{\frac{K}{y}}{\frac{L}{y}} = \frac{\frac{K}{y} \cdot \frac{y}{L}}{\frac{L}{y} \cdot \frac{y}{L}} = \frac{\frac{K}{y} \cdot \frac{y}{L}}{1} = \frac{K}{y} \times \frac{y}{L}$$

Starting with the behavioral relationship, we have

$$\frac{y}{L} = \left(\frac{K}{L}\right)^{\alpha} \times E^{1-\alpha} \qquad \textit{behavioral relationship}$$

$$\frac{y}{L} = \left(\frac{K}{y} \times \frac{y}{L}\right)^{\alpha} \times E^{1-\alpha} \qquad \textit{substituting for } \frac{K}{L}$$

$$\frac{y}{L} = \left(\frac{K}{y}\right)^{\alpha} \times \left(\frac{y}{L}\right)^{\alpha} \times E^{1-\alpha} \qquad \textit{applying exponent rule}$$

$$\left(\frac{y}{L}\right)\cdot\left(\frac{y}{L}\right)^{-\alpha} = \left(\frac{K}{y}\right)^{\alpha} \times \left(\frac{y}{L}\right)^{\alpha} \times \left(\frac{y}{L}\right)^{-\alpha} \times E^{1-\alpha} \qquad \textit{multiplying both sides by} \left(\frac{y}{L}\right)^{-\alpha}$$

$$\left(\frac{y}{L}\right)^{1-\alpha} = \left(\frac{K}{y}\right)^{\alpha} \times E^{1-\alpha} \qquad \textit{simplifying by applying exponent rule}$$

$$\left(\left(\frac{y}{L}\right)^{1-\alpha}\right)^{\frac{1}{1-\alpha}} = \left(\left(\frac{K}{y}\right)^{\alpha}\right)^{\frac{1}{1-\alpha}} \times \left(E^{1-\alpha}\right)^{\frac{1}{1-\alpha}} \qquad \textit{raising both sides to } \frac{1}{1-\alpha} \textit{ power}$$

$$\left(\frac{y}{L}\right) = \left(\frac{K}{y}\right)^{\frac{\alpha}{1-\alpha}} \times E \qquad \textit{simplifying}$$

Now substitute in the information from the equilibrium condition, $\dfrac{K}{Y} = \dfrac{s}{n + g + \delta}$

$$\left(\frac{Y}{L}\right) = \left(\frac{K}{Y}\right)^{\frac{\alpha}{1-\alpha}} \times E$$

$$\left(\frac{Y}{L}\right) = \left(\frac{s}{n + g + \delta}\right)^{\frac{\alpha}{1-\alpha}} \times E$$

Given values for the parameters $E, \alpha, s, n, g, \delta$, we can now solve for the long-run equilibrium level of $\dfrac{Y}{L}$. Then we could use the equilibrium condition to solve for $\dfrac{K}{L}$.

12. Suppose

E = 6,000	s = 20%	g = 2%
α = 2/3	n = 3%	δ = 5%

Follow the method in Box 3.7. Use separate sheets of paper for your work.

A. What is the equilibrium level of output per worker?

B. What is the equilibrium level of capital per worker?

13. Suppose

E = 8,000	s = 12%	g = 1.3%
α = 0.6	n = 1.5%	δ = 2%

Follow the method in Box 3.7. Use separate sheets of paper for your work.

A. What is the equilibrium level of the output per worker?

B. What is the equilibrium level of capital per worker?

TO THE CHALKBOARD:
Explaining Box 3.8

Box 3.8 shows how to determine the long-run equilibrium (steady state level) of output per worker. Someone with a very careful hand would derive the same answer with the graphical method presented in Box 3.8 as they would with the arithmetic method of Box 3.6 or the algebraic method of Box 3.7.

Most of us do not have a careful hand; we need to use the arithmetic or algebraic methods to derive exact answers. But the graphical approach is still quite useful. The graphical approach is best for giving us an intuitive sense of how variables and parameters relate to each other.

Here, let's review the example presented in Box 3.8. The behavioral relationship, $\frac{y}{L} = \left(\frac{K}{L}\right)^{\alpha} \times E^{1-\alpha}$, can be presented in a two-dimensional graph with $\frac{y}{L}$, the dependent variable, on the vertical axis and $\frac{K}{L}$, an independent variable, on the horizontal axis. In general, the graph will look as shown at the right.

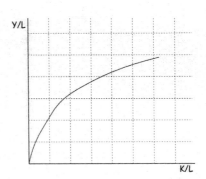

The equilibrium condition, $\frac{K}{y} = \frac{\frac{K}{L}}{\frac{y}{L}} = \frac{s}{n + g + \delta}$, can be transformed to $\frac{K}{L} = \left(\frac{s}{n + g + \delta}\right) \cdot \frac{y}{L}$, or $\frac{y}{L} = \left(\frac{n + g + \delta}{s}\right) \cdot \frac{K}{L}$. This condition can also be presented in a two-dimensional graph, again with $\frac{y}{L}$ on the vertical axis and $\frac{K}{L}$ on the horizontal axis. In general, the graph will look as shown at the right: a straight line with a slope of $\left(\frac{n + g + \delta}{s}\right)$.

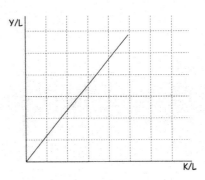

Combining these two curves onto one graph gives us the graph at the right. The point where the two curves cross is the one combination of output per worker, $\frac{y}{L}$, and capital per worker, $\frac{K}{L}$, that satisfies both the behavioral relationship and the equilibrium condition.

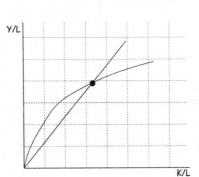

The graphical approach allows us to easily see the impact of a change in, for instance, the efficiency of labor, E. As you saw in Question 9, Part E, a higher value of labor efficiency shifts up the production function, $\frac{y}{L} = \left(\frac{K}{L}\right)^\alpha \times E^{1-\alpha}$. A higher production function (the curved line) would intersect the equilibrium condition (the straight line) at a higher level of capital per worker, $\frac{K}{L}$, and output per worker, $\frac{y}{L}$. Economically: greater efficiency of labor translates to higher levels of output per worker in long-run equilibrium – just the result we would intuitively expect!

14. A. Suppose that the production function is $\frac{Y}{L} = \left(\frac{K}{L}\right)^\alpha \times E^{1-\alpha}$, where E = 500 and α = 0.6. Graph the production function in the space at the right.

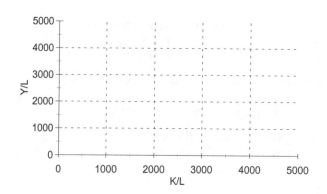

B. Suppose the equilibrium condition is $\frac{K}{Y} = \frac{s}{n + g + \delta}$, where s = 0.15, n = 0.02, g = 0.02, and δ = 0.03. Graph the equilibrium condition in the space above.

C. Based on the graph, what are the approximate values of the capital per worker ratio, $\frac{K}{L}$, and the output per worker ratio, $\frac{Y}{L}$?

D. Suppose the production function instead has α = 4/11. E still equals 500. What effect does the change in α have on the graph of the production function? On the equilibrium values of the capital per worker ratio, $\frac{K}{L}$, and the output per worker ratio, $\frac{Y}{L}$?

15. A. Suppose that the production function is $\frac{Y}{L} = \left(\frac{K}{L}\right)^{\alpha} \times E^{1-\alpha}$ where $E = 1000$ and $\alpha = 0.6$. Graph the production function in the space at the right.

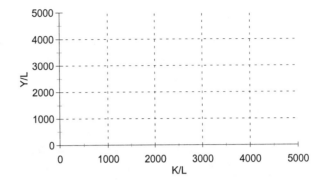

B. Suppose the equilibrium condition is $\frac{K}{Y} = \frac{s}{n + g + \delta}$ where $s = 0.15$, $n = 0.02$, $g = 0.02$, and $\delta = 0.03$. Graph the equilibrium condition in the space above.

C. Based on the graph, what are the approximate values of the capital per worker ratio, $\frac{K}{L}$, and the output per worker ratio, $\frac{Y}{L}$?

D. Suppose instead $E = 500$. The value of α is still 0.6. What effect does the change in E have on the graph of the production function? On the equilibrium values of the capital per worker ratio, $\frac{K}{L}$, and the output per worker ratio, $\frac{Y}{L}$?

SOLUTIONS   SOLUTIONS   SOLUTIONS   SOLUTIONS

A. BASIC DEFINITIONS

* indicates there are notes below related to this question.

1. social
2. equilibrium
3. Net National Product
4. models
5. descriptive

6. build a model.
7. representative agent.
8. circular flow
9. Net National Product
10. market

11. behavioral relationship*
12. equilibrium
13. opportunity cost

*11.   The answer here could also be "model."

---

14. D. All of the above. Economists are sloppy with the word "curve."

15. C. According to Prof. DeLong, it would be unethical to conduct large-scale human experiments. There is a branch of economics known as "experimental economics" that conducts human experiments, but they are in a laboratory-type setting and are not what one would call "large scale."

16. D. All of the above. The one thing economic causality cannot do is run from the future to the present or the past. It can run from our *expectations* of the future to the present or the past, though, since those expectations are themselves formed in the present or the past.

17. A. Depreciation.

B. MANIPULATION OF CONCEPTS AND MODELS

1. Did you notice that many of these questions are identical to those in Chapter 2, Section B, Question 18? That's because the concepts of circular flow and of gross domestic product are intricately related.

    A. Household expenditure. Jin Shaun is a member of a household, buying a final good from a business.

    B. Household income. Stockholders are people, too. The payments they receive from businesses are income.

    C. Not recorded. Buying items at a garage sale is a household-to-household transaction.

    D. Not recorded. Napkins are an intermediate good, so this is a business-to-business transaction.

    E. Household income.

    F. Household expenditure. Business owners are people, too. When they spend money in their role as "households," it is household expenditure. The only exception to this case would be if the company had paid for lunch. In that case, lunch at McDonald's would have been an intermediate good in the production of gassed-up cars and would not show in the circular flow nor be recorded in GDP.

2. Again, notice that many of these questions are identical to those in Chapter 2, Section B, Question 18.

    A. Government Purchases (government-to-business transaction).

    B. Consumption spending (household-to-business transaction).

    C. Net taxes (household-to-government transaction). Because the University of Massachusetts is a public school, payment of fees is treated as a tax.

    D. Investment spending (financial markets-to-business transaction). This aspect of the circular flow can be a little confusing. If Tower Records had paid for the new display racks with retained earnings, they would have bypassed the financial markets. In that case, the transaction would have been a business-to-business transaction and would not show in the circular flow of Figure 3.4. Regardless of how the purchase is financed, however, it is recorded as investment spending in GDP accounting.

    E. Incomes (business-to-household transaction).

    F. Net taxes (government-to-household transaction). In this case, the payment is actually a "transfer payment," which reduces the value of "net taxes." Or, you can think of it as a "negative tax payment."

    G. Consumption spending (household-to-business transaction). Kaplan is a business selling a service.

    H. Net imports (rest-of-the-world-to-business transaction). Purchasing lunch is an export from the U.S. even though it is consumed in the U.S. Exports are a negative entry in "net imports"; they decrease the value of net imports.

    I. Government Surplus (government-to-financial markets transaction). The State of Colorado is providing funds to the financial markets.

J. Net inflow of capital (rest-of-the-world-to-financial markets transaction). Funds are flowing into U.S. financial markets from Singapore.

K. Private saving (households-to-financial markets transaction). Savings can be put into any financial instrument – cash, checking, savings, mutual funds, stocks, bonds, and so on – and will still be represented as a flow of funds from households to the financial markets.

L. Net imports (households-to-rest-of-the-world transaction). Purchasing Russian trinkets is an import into the U.S.

3. It is important to pay attention to the subject and the verb in these questions. Who is doing what? The answer to that question is what largely determines the correct categorization of each activity.

A. Uses of income. Paying her state income taxes is one of the uses of Meredith's income.

B. Expenditure. Buying new cash registers is investment expenditure by a business.

C. Income. Marshawn is being paid interest income for allowing the bank to use his funds to make loans to others.

D. Expenditure. Paying a check-cashing fee is consumption expenditure by a household.

E. Expenditure. When a government agency, in this case a city, pays a salary, it is recorded as government expenditure.

F. Uses of income. Saving, regardless of where the funds are saved, is one of the ways households use their income.

G. Income. The Parks and Recreation Director is receiving income for his services.

4. For Questions 4, 5, and 6, use the formulas that are implicit in Box 3.2, and calculate the missing value.

A. Gross domestic product = depreciation + net domestic product = 1200 + 7800 = 9000

B. Net Factor Incomes Paid Abroad = net domestic product - net national product = 7800 - 7750 = 50

C. Statistical Discrepancy = −Net National Product + net indirect taxes − net subsidy to government enterprises + national income = −(7750 - 800 + 25 - 7075) = 100

5. A. Depreciation = Gross Domestic Product - Net Domestic Product = 5000 - 4500 = 500

B. Net National Product = Net Domestic Product - Factor Incomes Paid Abroad + Factor Incomes Received from Abroad = 4500 - (200 - 175) = 4475

C. Statistical Discrepancy = −Net National Product + net indirect taxes − net subsidy to government enterprises + national income = −(4475 - 450 + 15 - 3990) = −50

6. A. Net Domestic Product = Gross Domestic Product - Depreciation = 7500 - 800 = 6700

B. Net National Product = Net Domestic Product - Factor Incomes Paid Abroad + Factor Incomes Received from Abroad = 6700 - 300 + 310 = 6710

C. National Income = Net National Product - Net Indirect Taxes + Net Subsidy to Government Enterprises + Statistical Discrepancy = 6710 - 600 + 20 + (−20) = 6110

7. In general, the opportunity cost of an activity is the next-best alternative that was not pursued (foregone) in order to undertake the activity. Because each minute in life can only be lived once, there is an opportunity cost to everything we do. Answers to the questions will vary.

A. If you weren't reading this study guide, what would you be doing instead? That's your opportunity cost.

B. If you didn't go to your economics class, what would you do instead? That's your opportunity cost.

C. If you weren't in college, what would you be doing instead? That's your opportunity cost.

8. A *behavioral relationship* describes how one thing changes (effect) when something else happens (cause). An *equilibrium condition* describes the conditions under which a system is balanced or at rest.

A. Behavioral relationship. $C = f(Y_D)$ tells us that if disposable income changes, consumption spending changes.

B. Equilibrium condition. $Y = C + I + G + NX$ tells us what must be true of the relationship between output and income (Y) and aggregate demand ($C + I + G + NX$) for the economy to be "balanced" or in equilibrium.

C. Equilibrium condition. A market is said to be in equilibrium when the quantity supplied equals the quantity demanded.

D. Behavioral relationship. A change in price (cause) changes quantity demanded (effect).

E. Behavioral relationship. Actually, it's a physical relationship, used here to illustrate what economists mean by these metaphors. Things fall (effect) when we let go of them (cause).

Notice that the reason things fall – gravity – is not explicitly mentioned. In the behavioral relationships in economics, we also do not always mention the reason that one thing leads to another. For instance, why does consumption rise when disposable income rises? You could say "because the marginal propensity to consume is greater than 0," and be correct. But that is not *really* answering the question. Why is the marginal propensity to consume greater than zero? For consumers, the reason one thing leads to another ultimately relies on utility maximization. For businesses, the reason one thing leads to another ultimately relies on profit maximization.

F. Equilibrium condition. Most of us first learned the concept of equilibrium in high school physics: equal and opposing forces leave a body at rest. Here, the force of gravity is offset by the floor, so the chalk is at rest. The rhetoric of economics, especially the use of "equilibrium," borrows heavily from the physical sciences.

G. Behavioral relationship. Layoffs are the cause; reduced spending is the effect.

H. Equilibrium condition.

9.

A. $\dfrac{Y}{L} = \left(\dfrac{K}{L}\right)^{0.3} \times E^{0.7}$

B. $\dfrac{Y}{L} = \left(\dfrac{K}{L}\right)^{\frac{2}{3}} \times E^{\frac{1}{3}}$

C. Because $1000^{0.7} = 125.89$, we have $\dfrac{Y}{L} = 125.89 \cdot \left(\dfrac{K}{L}\right)^{0.3}$

$\dfrac{K}{L}$	E = 1000 $\dfrac{Y}{L}$	E = 3000 $\dfrac{Y}{L}$
0	0	0
1000	1000.00	2157.67
2000	1231.14	2656.40
3000	1390.39	3000.00
4000	1515.72	3270.42
5000	1620.66	3496.84

D. Because $3000^{0.7} = 271.63$, we have $\dfrac{Y}{L} = 271.63 \cdot \left(\dfrac{K}{L}\right)^{0.3}$.

E.

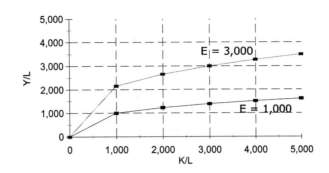

F. Because $1000^{0.4} = 15.85$, we have $\dfrac{Y}{L} = 15.85 \cdot \left(\dfrac{K}{L}\right)^{0.6}$

$\dfrac{K}{L}$	$\dfrac{Y}{L}$
0	0
1000	1000.00
2000	1515.72
3000	1933.18
4000	2297.40
5000	2626.53

G.

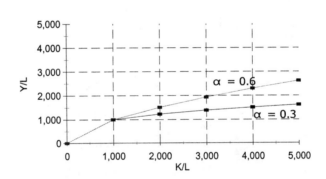

10. A. $(K/Y)^* = 1.667$ B. $Y/L = 1{,}500.$

$$\frac{K}{Y} = \frac{\dfrac{K}{L}}{\dfrac{Y}{L}} = \frac{s}{n+g+\delta} = \frac{0.10}{0.02+0.01+0.03} = \frac{0.10}{0.06} = 1.667$$

$$\frac{Y}{L} = \left(\frac{K}{L}\right)^{\alpha} \times E^{1-\alpha} = \left(\frac{K}{L}\right)^{0.5} \times 900^{1-0.5} = \left(\frac{K}{L}\right)^{0.5} \times 900^{0.5} = \left(\frac{K}{L}\right)^{0.5} \times 30$$

$$\frac{K}{L} = 1.667 \times \frac{Y}{L} \qquad \textit{equilibrium condition}$$

$$\frac{K}{L} = 1.667 \times \left(\frac{K}{L}\right)^{0.5} \times 30 \qquad \textit{substituting}$$

$$\frac{K}{L} = 50 \times \left(\frac{K}{L}\right)^{0.5} \qquad \textit{simplifying}$$

$$\left(\frac{K}{L}\right)^{0.5} = 50 \qquad \textit{simplifying}$$

$$\frac{K}{L} = \left(\left(\frac{K}{L}\right)^{0.5}\right)^2 = (50)^2 = 2500 \qquad \textit{squaring both sides}$$

Substituting to solve for Y/L:

$$\frac{Y}{L} = \left(\frac{K}{L}\right)^{0.5} \times 30$$

$$\frac{Y}{L} = (2500)^{0.5} \times 30$$

$$\frac{Y}{L} = 50 \times 30 = 1{,}500$$

11. A. $(K/Y)^* = 1.667$ 　　　　　 B. $\quad Y/L = 7{,}028.61$

$$\frac{K}{Y} = \frac{\frac{K}{L}}{\frac{Y}{L}} = \frac{s}{n + g + \delta} = \frac{0.15}{0.02 + 0.03 + 0.04} = \frac{0.15}{0.09} = 1.667$$

$$\frac{Y}{L} = \left(\frac{K}{L}\right)^{\alpha} \times E^{1-\alpha} = \left(\frac{K}{L}\right)^{0.4} \times 5000^{(1-0.4)} = \left(\frac{K}{L}\right)^{0.4} \times 5000^{0.6} = \left(\frac{K}{L}\right)^{0.4} \times 165.7227$$

$$\frac{K}{L} = 1.667 \times \frac{Y}{L} \qquad \textit{equilibrium condition}$$

$$\frac{K}{L} = 1.667 \times \left(\frac{K}{L}\right)^{0.4} \times 165.7227 \qquad \textit{substituting}$$

$$\frac{K}{L} = 276.204 \times \left(\frac{K}{L}\right)^{0.4} \qquad \textit{simplifying}$$

$$\left(\frac{K}{L}\right)^{0.6} = 276.204 \qquad \textit{simplifying}$$

$$\frac{K}{L} = \left(\left(\frac{K}{L}\right)^{0.6}\right)^{\frac{1}{0.6}} = (276.204)^{\frac{1}{0.6}} = 11{,}714.342 \qquad \textit{raising both sides to } \frac{1}{0.6} \textit{ power}$$

Substituting to solve for Y/L:

$$\frac{Y}{L} = \left(\frac{K}{L}\right)^{0.4} \times 165.7227$$

$$\frac{Y}{L} = (11{,}714.342)^{0.4} \times 165.7227$$

$$\frac{Y}{L} = 42.4118 \times 165.7227 = 7{,}028.6055$$

12. A. Y/L = 24,000 　　　　　　　 B. K/L = 48,000

$$\frac{Y}{L} = \left(\frac{s}{n + g + \delta}\right)^{\frac{\alpha}{1-\alpha}} \times E$$

$$\frac{Y}{L} = \left(\frac{0.20}{0.03 + 0.02 + 0.05}\right)^{\frac{2/3}{1-2/3}} \times 6000$$

$$\frac{Y}{L} = \left(\frac{0.20}{0.10}\right)^{\frac{2/3}{1/3}} \times 6000 = 2^2 \times 6000 = 24{,}000$$

Solving for K/L

$$\frac{K}{L} = \left(\frac{s}{n + g + \delta}\right) \times \frac{Y}{L}$$

$$\frac{K}{L} = \left(\frac{0.20}{0.03 + 0.02 + 0.05}\right) \times 24{,}000 = 48{,}000$$

13. A.   Y/L = 31,622.777   B.   K/L = 79,056.942

$$\frac{Y}{L} = \left(\frac{s}{n + g + \delta}\right)^{\frac{\alpha}{1-\alpha}} \times E$$

$$\frac{Y}{L} = \left(\frac{0.12}{0.015 + 0.013 + 0.02}\right)^{\frac{0.6}{1-0.6}} \times 8000$$

$$\frac{Y}{L} = \left(\frac{0.12}{0.048}\right)^{\frac{0.6}{0.4}} \times 8000 = 2.5^{1.5} \times 8000 = 31{,}622.777$$

Solving for K/L

$$\frac{K}{L} = \left(\frac{s}{n + g + \delta}\right) \times \frac{Y}{L}$$

$$\frac{K}{L} = \left(\frac{0.12}{0.015 + 0.013 + 0.02}\right) \times 31{,}622.777 = 79{,}056.942$$

14.

C.   K/L ≈ 3000
     Y/L ≈ 1500

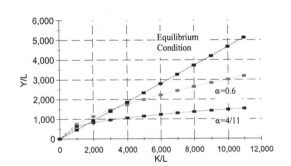

15.

C.   K/L ≈ 6500
     Y/L ≈ 3200

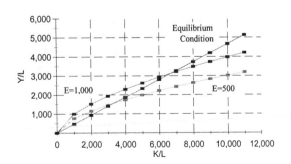

When you have a chance, check out Professor DeLong's personal web site. I guarantee you've never seen anything quite like it.

http://econ161.berkeley.edu

Chapter 4
The Theory of Economic Growth

- The Solow growth model allows us to analyze the long-run equilibrium determinants of standard of living as measured by real output per worker.

- The steady-state balanced-growth equilibrium occurs when the capital-output ratio is constant. Assuming a Cobb-Douglas production function, when the economy is in its steady-state balanced-growth equilibrium, the growth rates of the capital-labor ratio, the output per worker ratio, and labor efficiency will all be equal.

- In steady-state balanced-growth equilibrium and assuming a Cobb-Douglas production function, the level of output per worker (Y/L) depends upon the rate of growth of the labor force (n), the rate of growth of labor efficiency (g), the rate of depreciation of capital (δ), the saving rate (s), the parameter of the production function (α), and the current level of labor efficiency (E).

LEARNING GUIDE

You will probably find this chapter to be one of the most challenging chapters of the text. There is **only one model** in this chapter – the Solow growth model – but it is abstract and the mathematics can be cumbersome. Some of the mathematics used in Chapter 4 were covered in Study Guide Chapter 3.

Some professors believe the material covered in Chapter 4 is the most important material of the course. You will especially want to be able to answer the Section C and Section D questions in this chapter and in Chapter 5.

You will need some math skills in this chapter. Math skills covered in Chapter B are indicated with

Short on time?

If you are short on time, you are in a bind. It is almost impossible to study this chapter quickly. Do not try to save time on Chapter 4.

You must understand the production function and what distinguishes the Cobb-Douglas function from other production functions. The determinants of long-run economic growth and how they combine mathematically to determine steady-state balanced-growth equilibrium are very important. You need to acquire both a technical mastery of the topics and a conceptual one.

BASIC DEFINITIONS

Before you apply knowledge, you need a basic grasp of the fundamentals. In other words, there are some things you just have to know. Knowing the material in this section won't guarantee a good grade in the course, but not knowing it will guarantee a poor or failing grade.

USE THE WORDS OR PHRASES FROM THE LIST BELOW TO COMPLETE THE SENTENCES. SOME ARE USED MORE THAN ONCE; SOME ARE NOT USED AT ALL.

capital stock	investment requirement
capital-labor ratio	investment effort
capital-output ratio	labor force
Cobb-Douglas	output-worker ratio
depreciation	saving rate
efficiency of labor	Solow
growth rate	steady-state balanced-growth
investment	equilibrium

1. _____ occurs when the various forces determining economic growth are balanced so that output per worker is increasing at a constant rate from period to period.

2. The _____ production function is a functional form of the general abstract function $\frac{Y}{L} = F\left(\frac{K}{L}, E\right)$.

3. The _____ describes how much output the typical worker can produce with capital.

4. The _____ production function states $\frac{Y}{L} = \left(\frac{K}{L}\right)^{\alpha} \cdot E^{1-\alpha}$.

5. _____ is the amount of investment needed to replace worn out or obsolete capital, plus that needed to provide capital to the new workers joining the labor force.

6. _____ reduces the amount of capital due to wear-and-tear and obsolescence.

7. Output is produced with two inputs: _____ and _____.

8. _____ is the share of real GDP that is saved and invested in order to increase the stock of capital – machines, buildings, infrastructure, and so on.

9. The growth model is also called the _____ model, named after the economist who received the Nobel Prize for developing the model.

10. _____ increases when people and firms save and invest.

11. _____ is the total amount of machinery, buildings, and infrastructure available for producing goods and services.

12. _____ refers to purchases of machinery, buildings, and infrastructure.

13. The _____ is the average amount of physical capital available to workers for production.

14. The _____ is the share of real output (GDP) that is saved.

CIRCLE THE CORRECT WORD OR PHRASE IN EACH OF THE FOLLOWING SENTENCES.

15. Government spending plays a role / no role in the Solow growth model.

16. The economy is / is not in steady-state balanced-growth equilibrium when $\%\Delta(Y/L) = \%\Delta(K/L) = \%\Delta(E)$.

17. The economy is / is not in steady-state balanced-growth equilibrium when K/Y is constant.

18. Output per worker increases / decreases when capital per worker increases.

19. Output per worker increases / decreases when technology improves.

20. Output per worker increases / decreases when efficiency of labor increases.

21. The growth rate of the labor force is endogenous / exogenous to the growth model.

22. The growth rate of labor efficiency is endogenous / exogenous to the growth model.

23. The growth rate of the output is endogenous / exogenous to the growth model.

24. The growth rate of capital stock is endogenous / exogenous to the growth model.

SELECT THE ONE BEST ANSWER FOR EACH MULTIPLE-CHOICE QUESTION.

25. In steady-state balanced-growth equilibrium,
    A. the amount of capital per worker is constant.
    B. investment per worker is constant.
    C. the amount of output per worker is constant.
    D. the capital-to-output ratio is constant.

TO THE CHALKBOARD:
Explaining Figure 4.15

Textbook Figure 4.15 shows how steady-state output per worker $\left(\frac{Y}{L}\right)_{ss}$ and efficiency of labor (E) grow over time when the economy is in steady-state balanced-growth equilibrium. **Remember that in that equilibrium, $\frac{Y}{L}$ and $\frac{K}{L}$ will grow at the same rate as labor efficiency, g.** A constant rate of growth provides smooth growth but is **not** graphed as a straight line. A straight line would depict increases that were the same amount each period (such as, $5,000 per month) but would then be a declining rate of growth (percentage change) each period. In **steady state**, the **rate of growth** (percentage change) is **constant** from period to period, which means the amount of growth is increasing from period to period. The graphical result is at the right: a smooth curve whose slope continually increases.

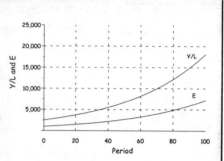

If we were to use a **logarithmic scale** to depict how steady-state output per worker $\left(\frac{Y}{L}\right)_{ss}$ and efficiency of labor (E) grow over time when the economy is in **steady-state balanced-growth equilibrium**, then we would have a **straight line graph**. A constant percentage change over time produces a constant slope when $\log\left(\frac{Y}{L}\right)$ is shown. The graphical result is at the right: a curve with a constant slope. In steady state, the slopes of the two curves will be equal.

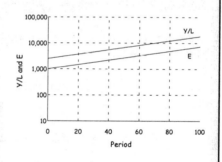

26. The production function tells us
    A. how a firm combines its inputs to produce its output.
    B. how the economy's total labor force, capital, and technology can be used to produce output.
    C. the steady-state balanced-growth equilibrium.
    D. the rate of diminishing returns.

27. To determine the steady-state balanced-growth equilibrium, the Solow growth model requires information about all of the following variables EXCEPT
    A. the rate of growth of the labor force.
    B. the size of the labor force.
    C. the saving rate.
    D. the rate of depreciation of capital.

28. The efficiency of labor can increase when
  A. workers choose to work harder or faster.
  B. employers force their employees to increase the work effort.
  C. scientific discoveries make machines more productive.
  D. all of the above.

TO THE CHALKBOARD:
Organizing All Those Equations

There are a number of equations in this chapter. Here is a list of them, with a brief description of each. Check other "To The Chalkboard" boxes for derivations of some of these equations.

[1] $\frac{Y}{L} = F\left[\left(\frac{K}{L}\right), E\right]$ The general production function. Output per worker depends upon the capital-labor ratio (also known as capital per worker) and the efficiency of labor.

[2] $\frac{Y}{L} = \left(\frac{K}{L}\right)^{\alpha} \cdot (E)^{(1-\alpha)}$ The Cobb-Douglas production function, which specifies the functional form of the relationship between output per worker, capital per worker, and labor efficiency.

[3] $L_{t+1} = (1+n) \cdot (L_t)$ How the labor force changes from one period to the next. Labor force increases at rate n [that is, by (n)·(100) percent] between period t and period t + 1. Also stated as: The growth rate of the labor force is n.

[4] $E_{t+1} = (1+g) \cdot (E_t)$ How labor efficiency changes from one period to the next. Labor efficiency increases at rate g [that is, by (g)·(100) percent] between period t and period t + 1. Also stated as: The growth rate of labor efficiency is g.

[5] $K_{t+1} = K_t + (s) \cdot (Y_t) - (\delta) \cdot (K_t)$ How capital stock changes from one period to the next. Capital stock at the beginning of period t + 1 equals capital stock at the beginning of the previous period plus the saving rate (s) times last period's output (Y_t) minus the depreciation rate (δ) times capital stock at the beginning of period t.

[6] $g(k_t) = g\left(\frac{K}{L}\right) = \dfrac{s}{\left(\frac{K}{Y}\right)} - \delta - n$ The growth rate of the capital-labor ratio (also called capital per worker). Capital per worker grows at the rate $g\left(\frac{K}{L}\right)$ [that is, by (g(K/L))·(100) percent] between any two periods. The growth rate of capital per worker equals the saving rate divided by the capital-output ratio minus the depreciation rate minus the labor force growth rate.

NOTE: The textbook uses the shorthand κ to stand for the capital-output ratio, $\frac{K}{Y}$.

But as you take notes in class, as you write answers in exam books, and as you read the study guide, it is difficult to see the difference between the Greek letter kappa and the Roman letter K: κ and K. To avoid confusion, in the study guide we will always use $\frac{K}{Y}$ for the capital-output ratio.

[7] $\quad g(y_t) = g\left(\dfrac{Y}{L}\right) = g + \alpha\left[\dfrac{s}{\left(\dfrac{K}{Y}\right)} - (n + g + \delta)\right]$ The growth rate of output per worker. Output per worker grows at rate $g\left(\dfrac{Y}{L}\right)$ [that is, by

$(g(Y/L))\cdot(100)$ percent] between any two periods. The growth rate of output per worker equals the growth rate of labor efficiency (g) plus α times the difference between the saving rate divided by the capital-output ratio and the sum of the labor force growth rate (n), the labor efficiency growth rate (g), and the depreciation rate (δ).

[8] $\quad g\left(\dfrac{K}{Y}\right) = (1 - \alpha)\cdot\left[\dfrac{s}{\left(\dfrac{K}{Y}\right)} - (n + g + \delta)\right]$ The growth rate of the capital-output ratio. The capital-output ratio grows at rate $g\left(\dfrac{K}{Y}\right)$ [that is, by

$(g(K/Y))\cdot(100)$ percent] between any two periods. The growth rate of the capital-output ratio equals (1 minus α) times the difference between the saving rate divided by the capital-output ratio and the sum of the labor force growth rate (n), the labor efficiency growth rate (g), and the depreciation rate (δ).

[9] **Equilibrium condition**: "when everything grows at the same proportional rate." That is, when output per worker, capital per worker, and labor efficiency all grow at the same rate between any two periods. Also therefore when the capital-output ratio, K/Y, is constant from one period to the next.

[10] $\quad \left(\dfrac{K}{Y}\right)_{ss} = \kappa^* = \dfrac{s}{n + g + \delta}$ The steady-state balanced-growth value of the capital-output ratio. The steady-state balanced-growth value of the capital-output ratio equals the saving rate (s) divided by the sum of the labor force growth rate (n), the labor efficiency growth rate (g), and the depreciation rate (δ).

[11] $\quad$ *At steady state*, $g(y_t) = g(k_t) = g$ When the capital-output ratio is at its steady state value, then output per worker (y_t), capital per worker (k_t) and labor force efficiency (E_t), will all grow at the same rate.

[12] $\quad y_{ss} = \left(\dfrac{Y}{L}\right)_{ss} = \left[\left(\dfrac{s}{n + g + \delta}\right)^{\left(\frac{\alpha}{1-\alpha}\right)}\right] \times (E_t)$ The steady-state balanced-growth value of output per worker. When the economy is in steady-state, the value of output per worker, given that labor efficiency is some value E_t, equals the saving rate (s) divided by the sum of the labor force growth rate (n), the labor efficiency growth rate (g), and the depreciation rate (δ), all raised to the power (α divided by one minus α), and then multiplied by the value of labor efficiency, E_t.

Equation 12 is a bit cumbersome to type or write, so in the text several shorthand substitutions are made. K* is the shorthand for the steady-state balanced-growth value of the capital-output ratio. Another symbol, λ, is used to stand for the ratio α divided by (one minus α). The result is a shorter equation, but otherwise the same statement as equation [12]: $y_{ss} = \left(\kappa^*\right)^\lambda \cdot (E_t)$.

B. MANIPULATION OF CONCEPTS AND MODELS

Most instructors expect you to be able to do basic manipulation of the concepts. Being able to do so often means you can earn a C in a course. But if you want a better grade, you'll need to be able to complete this section easily and move on to sections C and D.

 NOTE: The distinguishing feature of a **Cobb-Douglas production function** is that the exponents sum to one (1). For instance, $Y = AK^{\beta}L^{(1-\beta)}$ is also Cobb-Douglas because $\beta + (1 - \beta) = 1$. The Cobb-Douglas production function is convenient to use because it has some very nice mathematical properties. A Cobb-Douglas production function exhibits **constant returns to scale**: if you double all of the inputs, output will also double. Mathematically, the function exhibits constant returns to scale because the exponents sum to 1.

1. The Cobb-Douglas production function is $\dfrac{Y}{L} = \left(\dfrac{K}{L}\right)^{\alpha} E^{1-\alpha}$

   A. Suppose labor efficiency, E, is 10,000. Graph the Cobb-Douglas production function when $\alpha = 0.2$. (You might find it easier to do the graph using a spreadsheet package such as Quattro Pro or Excel, or using a graphing calculator.)

   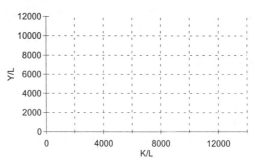

   B. Suppose labor efficiency, E, is 10,000. Graph the Cobb-Douglas production function when $\alpha = 0.8$.

   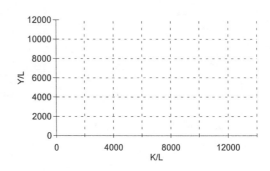

   C. When does a change in the capital to labor ratio generate the larger change in output per worker, when $\alpha = 0.2$ or when $\alpha = 0.8$? Explain your answer, using the economic concept of diminishing returns.

> **NOTE**: Many students are tempted to ask, "Is the Cobb-Douglas production function realistic?" That's the wrong question. The right question is, "Is the Cobb-Douglas production function a good enough approximation of reality to allow us to do reasonable analysis and come up with useful conclusions?" Yes.

2. A. Suppose $E = 10,000$ and $\alpha = 0.4$. Assume production can be described by the Cobb-Douglas production function. Compute the value of output per worker at each level of capital per worker shown at the right.

K/L	Y/L
5000	
10000	
20000	

B. When K/L doubles, does Y/L double? Why or why not?

> **NOTE**: In Questions 3, 4, and 5, you will work with the definitions of labor force, labor efficiency, and capital stock, and see how their values change over time.

3. Compute the average value of n, the growth rate of the labor force, by decade, 1950-2000. Consult the *Economic Report of the President* to locate labor force data.

	Labor Force	Average Annual Growth Rate
1950		
1960		
1970		
1980		
1990		
2000		

HINT: The "efficiency of labor" is sometimes thought of as simply "technology." In general, E is telling us how much output each worker is able to produce with capital. If someone invents a faster or more reliable computer (a piece of capital), a worker will probably be able to produce more output with the same number of computers. Is the worker really more "efficient" in the usual sense of the word? Does he spend less time on the phone? Does she organize her work space so it is more productive? No. The "efficiency of labor" rises in this case not because of any "efficient" action by the worker, but because a technological advance that affected capital increased the worker's productivity.

4. Suppose that the labor force is initially 50,000,000 and labor efficiency is initially 10,000. Suppose g = 0.025 and n = 0.03. Complete the following table.

Period	L_t (in thousands)	E_t
1		10000
2		
3		
4		
5		

5. Use the relationship describing changes in the capital stock, $K_{t+1} = K_t + sY_t - \delta K_t$, to answer the following questions.

 HINT: The **capital stock equation** used in this question is the basis of most of the remaining equations in Chapter 4. **You must know it.**

A. Suppose $K_t = 2,500$, $\delta = 4$ percent, the saving rate is 15 percent, and $Y_t = 1,000$. What is the value of the capital stock at the end of year t + 1?

B. Suppose $K_{t+1} = 8,000$, $K_t = 7,000$, s = 10 percent, and $\delta = 0.03$. What is the value of output in year t?

C. Suppose $Y_t = 300$, s = 0.20, $K_{t+1} = 1,000$, and the depreciation rate is 4 percent. What is the value of K_t?

MATH: The proportional growth rules mentioned below and in Textbook Chapter 4 work only when the changes considered are very small. For a review of the rules, see Chapter B.

TO THE CHALKBOARD:
Deriving $g(k_t) = (s / (K/Y)_t) - \delta - n$

$g(k_t)$ is the expression for the rate of change (or growth rate) of the capital stock. Here is a step-by-step explanation of its derivation.

In the textbook, we are reminded that a growth rate is the same as the percentage change, so

$$g(k_t) = \frac{k_{t+1} - k_t}{k_t}.$$ But k_t is just shorthand for $\frac{K_t}{L_t}$, so $g(k_t) = \frac{\left(\frac{K_{t+1}}{L_{t+1}}\right) - \left(\frac{K_t}{L_t}\right)}{\left(\frac{K_t}{L_t}\right)}.$

To derive the expression for the growth rate of the capital stock, we will use one of the **proportional growth rules**: $g(X/Y) = g(X) - g(Y)$.

Remember: It matters whether you use lower case or upper case letters – k and K are different variables!

Remember: Because it is hard to see the difference between κ (kappa) and K (upper case K), in the study guide we will always use (K/Y) even when the text uses κ (kappa).

$$g(k_t) = g\left(\frac{K_t}{L_t}\right) \qquad \textit{remembering definition of } k_t$$

$$g\left(\frac{K_t}{L_t}\right) = g(K_t) - g(L_t) \qquad \textit{applying proportional growth rule}$$

$$g\left(\frac{K_t}{L_t}\right) = \frac{K_{t+1} - K_t}{K_t} - g(L_t) \qquad \textit{definition of growth rate of } K_t$$

$$g\left(\frac{K_t}{L_t}\right) = \frac{\left(K_t + sY_t - \delta K_t\right) - K_t}{K_t} - g(L_t) \qquad \textit{substituting definition of } K_{t+1}$$

$$g\left(\frac{K_t}{L_t}\right) = \frac{sY_t - \delta K_t + K_t - K_t}{K_t} - g(L_t) \qquad \textit{rearranging terms}$$

$$g\left(\frac{K_t}{L_t}\right) = \frac{sY_t}{K_t} - \frac{\delta K_t}{K_t} - g(L_t) \qquad \textit{simplifying}$$

$$g\left(\frac{K_t}{L_t}\right) = \frac{sY_t}{K_t} - \delta - n \qquad \textit{simplifying and substituting definition of } g(L_t)$$

$$g\left(\frac{K_t}{L_t}\right) = \frac{s}{\left(\frac{K_t}{Y_t}\right)} - \delta - n \qquad \textit{substituting } \frac{1}{\left(\frac{K_t}{Y_t}\right)} \textit{ for } \frac{Y_t}{K_t}$$

NOTE: In Questions 6 through 9, you will work with the capital-labor ratio, K/L, and with its growth rate. In Question 6, you will calculate the rate at which K/L grows. In Questions 7 and 8, you again calculate the growth rate of K/L, and then compare it with the growth rate, g(k), calculated from the formula for g(k). In Question 9, you work with the formula for g(k) to try to gain a conceptual understanding of the equation.

6. Based on the data in the table below, calculate the growth rate of the capital-to-labor ratio. Do not use the growth rule in Textbook Section 4.3; instead, calculate the growth rate by determining the percentage change in K/L.

	K	L	K/L	%Δ(K/L)
year 1	1,500	125		
year 2	1,600	130		
year 3	1,750	140		
year 4	1,800	150		

7. In this question, you are asked to compute the growth rate of K/L first by computing the percentage change, $\%\Delta\left(\dfrac{K}{L}\right)$, and then by calculating $g(k_t) = \dfrac{s}{\left(\dfrac{K_t}{Y_t}\right)} - \delta - n$.

Suppose $\dfrac{Y}{L} = \left(\dfrac{K}{L}\right)^{0.6} E^{0.4}$ and

$g = 0$	$n = 0.025$	$K_1 = 7{,}500$
$s = 0.20$	$E_1 = 50$	$L_1 = 100$
$\delta = 0.04$		

A. Complete the following table.

Period	K	L	$\dfrac{K}{L}$	$\%\Delta\left(\dfrac{K}{L}\right)$	$\dfrac{Y}{L}$	Y	g(k) computed using formula
1	7,500	100		▮			
2							
3							
4							
5							

B. Does the $\%\Delta\left(\dfrac{K}{L}\right)$ equal g(k) in each period? Why or why not?

8. In this question, you are again asked to compute the growth rate of K/L first by computing the percentage change $\%\Delta\left(\dfrac{K}{L}\right)$, and then by calculating

$$g(k_t) = \frac{s}{\left(\dfrac{K_t}{Y_t}\right)} - \delta - n.$$

Suppose $\dfrac{Y}{L} = \left(\dfrac{K}{L}\right)^{0.6} E^{0.4}$ and

$g = 0$	$n = 0.025$	$K_1 = 83{,}000$
$s = 0.20$	$E_1 = 50$	$L_1 = 100$
$\delta = 0.04$		

A. Complete the following table.

Period	K	L	$\dfrac{K}{L}$	$\%\Delta\left(\dfrac{K}{L}\right)$	$\dfrac{Y}{L}$	Y	g(k) computed using formula
1	83,000	100					
2							
3							
4							
5							

B. Does $\%\Delta\left(\dfrac{K}{L}\right)$ equal g(k) in each period? Why or why not?

C. Is the economy in steady state? Answer the question *without* computing the steady-state value of output per worker.

D. Confirm your answer by computing the steady-state value of output per worker using the formula: $\left(\dfrac{Y_t}{L_t}\right)_{SS} = \left[\left(\dfrac{s}{n+g+\delta}\right)^{\frac{a}{1-a}}\right] \cdot (E_t)$

9. Use the formula for the growth rate of capital per worker, $g(k_t) = \dfrac{s}{\left(\dfrac{K_t}{Y_t}\right)} - \delta - n$, to answer the following questions.

A. Suppose the saving rate is 15 percent, the depreciation rate is 5 percent, the labor force is growing by 3 percent annually, the current level of output is $83,000 billion, and the current amount of capital stock is $140,000 billion. What is the growth rate of capital per worker?

> **HINT**: The best way to remember an equation is not to *memorize* it, but to understand the *economics* behind it. The mathematics of an equation should *confirm* the economic analysis, but it is not the *basis* of the analysis. Answer the second part of Questions 9B - 9F by thinking about the economics of economic growth.

B. Suppose the saving rate is 20 percent and that the other values in part A still apply. Now what is the growth rate of capital per worker? Think about the **economic relationships** that are behind the equation: why does an increase in the saving rate increase the growth rate of capital per worker?

C. Suppose the saving rate is 15 percent, the depreciation rate is 3 percent, the labor force is growing by 3 percent annually, the current level of output is $83,000 billion, and the current amount of capital stock is $140,000 billion. (That is, use the figures from part A, but change the depreciation rate to 3 percent.) Now what is the growth rate of capital per worker? Think about the **economic relationships** that are behind the equation: why does a decrease in the depreciation rate increase the growth rate of capital per worker?

D. Suppose the saving rate is 15 percent, the depreciation rate is 5 percent, the labor force is growing by 2 percent annually, the current level of output is $83,000 billion, and the current amount of capital stock is $140,000 billion. (That is, use the figures from part A, but change the labor force growth rate to 2 percent.) Now what is the growth rate of capital per worker? Think about the **economic relationships** that are behind the equation: why does a decrease in the labor force growth rate increase the growth rate of capital per worker?

E. Suppose the saving rate is 15 percent, the depreciation rate is 5 percent, the labor force is growing by 3 percent annually, the current level of output is $80,000 billion, and the current amount of capital stock is $140,000 billion. (That is, use the figures from part A, but change the output level to $80,000 billion.) Now what is the growth rate of capital per worker? Think about the **economic relationships** that are behind the equation: why does a decrease in the amount of output decrease the growth rate of capital per worker?

F. Suppose the saving rate is 15 percent, the depreciation rate is 5 percent, the labor force is growing by 3 percent annually, the current level of output is $83,000 billion, and the current amount of capital stock is $150,000 billion. (That is, use the figures from part A, but change the initial amount of capital to $150,000 billion.) Now what is the growth rate of capital per worker? Think about the **economic relationships** that are behind the equation: why does an increase in the amount of capital decrease the growth rate of capital per worker?

TO THE CHALKBOARD:

Explaining Figure 4.9

Textbook Figure 4.9 shows how the growth rate of the capital-labor ratio, $g\left(\dfrac{K}{L}\right)$, changes when the capital-output ratio changes. Remember: $g\left(\dfrac{K}{L}\right) = \dfrac{s}{\left(\dfrac{K}{y}\right)} - \delta - n$. So as $\dfrac{K}{y}$ increases, the growth rate of $\dfrac{K}{L}$ will decrease. The decrease will be nonlinear because $\dfrac{K}{y}$ is in the denominator. The values of s, δ, and n are constant for any curve. For instance, suppose $s = 0.20$, $\delta = 0.04$, and $n = 0.02$. Then $g\left(\dfrac{K}{L}\right) = \dfrac{0.20}{\left(\dfrac{K}{y}\right)} - 0.04 - 0.02$, which is

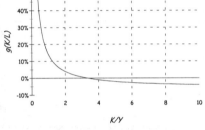

depicted at the right. An increase in the saving rate (s) or a decrease in the depreciation rate (δ) or the labor force growth rate (n) will shift the entire curve up.

---

10. Sketch a graph of the growth rate of the capital-labor ratio, $g\left(\dfrac{K}{L}\right)$, in the space at the right. Label the axes. For each part, sketch in and label a second curve that shows the effect on $g\left(\dfrac{K}{L}\right)$ of

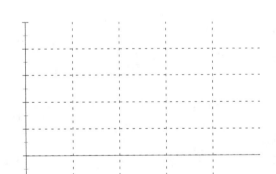

A. an increase in the saving rate.
B. an increase in g.
C. a decrease in the labor force growth rate.
D. a decrease in the depreciation rate.
E. an increase in the Cobb-Douglas parameter, α.

TO THE CHALKBOARD:

Deriving $g(y) = g + (\alpha)\cdot[\ s/(K/Y) - (n + g + \delta)\ ]$

$g(y)$ is the expression for the rate of change of output per worker. Here is a step-by-step explanation of its derivation.

$g(y_t)$ stands for the growth rate of $\dfrac{Y_t}{L_t}$. So $g(y_t) = g\left(\dfrac{Y_t}{L_t}\right)$. The **trick** to remember now is that the production function allows us to express $\dfrac{Y_t}{L_t}$ in terms of $\dfrac{K_t}{L_t}$ and E_t. *How do you remember to use that trick*, rather than the trick we used in deriving $g(k_t)$? Tell yourself: **first, try finding $\dfrac{K_t}{L_t}$ in any expression.** In this case, $\dfrac{Y}{L} = \left(\dfrac{K}{L}\right)^{\alpha}(E)^{1-\alpha}$

Now we're set. We already know an expression for the growth rate of $\dfrac{K_t}{L_t}$ and an expression for the growth rate of E_t. And we already know a "proportional growth rule" that we can apply: $g(X^a Y^b) = a\cdot g(X) + b\cdot g(Y)$. And so we derive:

$$g(y_t) = g\left(\frac{Y_t}{L_t}\right) \qquad \text{\textit{remembering the definition of } } y_t$$

$$g\left(\frac{Y_t}{L_t}\right) = g\left[\left(\frac{K}{L}\right)^{\alpha}\cdot(E)^{1-\alpha}\right] \qquad \text{\textit{substituting Cobb--Douglas production function}}$$

$$g\left(\frac{Y_t}{L_t}\right) = \alpha\cdot g\left(\frac{K}{L}\right) + (1-\alpha)\cdot g(E) \qquad \text{\textit{applying proportional growth rule}}$$

$$g\left(\frac{Y_t}{L_t}\right) = \alpha\cdot\left(\frac{s}{\left(\frac{K_t}{Y_t}\right)} - \delta - n\right) + (1-\alpha)\cdot g \qquad \text{\textit{substituting } } g\left(\frac{K}{L}\right) \text{ \textit{and} } g(E)$$

$$g\left(\frac{Y_t}{L_t}\right) = \alpha\cdot\left(\frac{s}{\left(\frac{K_t}{Y_t}\right)} - \delta - n\right) + g - \alpha\cdot g \qquad \text{\textit{distributing }}(1-\alpha)\cdot g$$

$$g\left(\frac{Y_t}{L_t}\right) = g + \alpha\cdot\left(\frac{s}{\left(\frac{K_t}{Y_t}\right)} - \delta - n\right) - \alpha\cdot g \qquad \text{\textit{rearranging terms}}$$

$$g\left(\frac{Y_t}{L_t}\right) = g + \alpha\cdot\left(\frac{s}{\left(\frac{K_t}{Y_t}\right)} - \delta - n - g\right) \qquad \text{\textit{gathering terms with }}\alpha$$

$$g\left(\frac{Y_t}{L_t}\right) = g + \alpha\cdot\left(\frac{s}{\left(\frac{K_t}{Y_t}\right)} - n - g - \delta\right) \qquad \text{\textit{rearranging terms to match text}}$$

$$g\left(\frac{Y_t}{L_t}\right) = g + \alpha\cdot\left(\frac{s}{\left(\frac{K_t}{Y_t}\right)} - (n + g + \delta)\right) \qquad \text{\textit{inserting parentheses to match text}}$$

HINT: Don't memorize every equation. Remember only one or two equations, plus some rules for manipulating equations. To remember the formula for the growth rate of output per worker, g(y), remember three things:

- The production function: $\frac{Y}{L} = \left(\frac{K}{L}\right)^{\alpha} (E)^{1-\alpha}$

- The growth rate of capital per worker: $g(k_t) = \frac{s}{\left(\frac{K_t}{Y_t}\right)} - \delta - n$

- The proportional growth rule: $g\left(X^a Y^b\right) = a \cdot g(X) + b \cdot g(Y)$

That's all you need to remember. Three things. From those three things, you can derive the growth rate of output per worker.

$g\left(\frac{Y}{L}\right)$ is then equal to

$$g(y) = \alpha \cdot g\left(\frac{K}{L}\right) + (1-\alpha) \cdot g(E) = \alpha \cdot \left(\frac{s}{\left(\frac{K_t}{Y_t}\right)} - \delta - n\right) + (1-\alpha) \cdot g$$

which the text simplifies to $g(y_t) = g + \left[\alpha \cdot \left(\frac{s}{\left(\frac{K_t}{Y_t}\right)} - (n + g + \delta)\right)\right]$

11. In this question, you are asked to work with the equation for the growth rate of output per worker, and also to try to develop a conceptual understanding of the equation. Use

$$g(y_t) = \alpha \cdot \left(\frac{s}{\left(\frac{K_t}{Y_t}\right)} - \delta - n\right) + (1-\alpha) \cdot g \qquad or \qquad g(y_t) = g + \left[\alpha \cdot \left(\frac{s}{\left(\frac{K_t}{Y_t}\right)} - (n + g + \delta)\right)\right]$$

to answer the following questions.

A. Suppose the labor force is growing by 1.5 percent per year, labor efficiency is increasing 0.8 percent annually, the depreciation rate is 3 percent, the production function is $\frac{Y}{L} = \left(\frac{K}{L}\right)^{2/3} E^{(1-2/3)}$, the saving rate is 25 percent, the current value of capital is £6,000 million, and the current value of output is £2,000 million. What is the growth rate of output per worker?

B. Suppose the labor force is growing by 3 percent per year, labor efficiency is increasing 0.8 percent annually, the depreciation rate is 3 percent, the production function is $\frac{Y}{L} = \left(\frac{K}{L}\right)^{2/3} E^{(1-2/3)}$, the saving rate is 25 percent, the current value of capital is £6,000 million, and the current value of output is £2,000 million. (That is, use the figures from part A, but change the labor force growth rate to 3 percent.) Now what is the growth rate of output per worker? Think about the **economic relationships** that are behind the equation: why does an increase in the labor force growth rate decrease the growth rate of output per worker?

C. Suppose the labor force is growing by 1.5 percent per year, labor efficiency is increasing 1.6 percent annually, the depreciation rate is 3 percent, the production function is $\frac{Y}{L} = \left(\frac{K}{L}\right)^{2/3} E^{(1-2/3)}$, the saving rate is 25 percent, the current value of capital is £6,000 million, and the current value of output is £2,000 million. (That is, use the figures from part A, but change the labor efficiency growth rate to 1.6 percent.) Now what is the growth rate of output per worker? Think about the **economic relationships** that are behind the equation: why does an increase in the labor efficiency growth rate increase the growth rate of output per worker?

D. Suppose the labor force is growing by 1.5 percent per year, labor efficiency is increasing 0.8 percent annually, the depreciation rate is 5 percent, the production function is $\frac{Y}{L} = \left(\frac{K}{L}\right)^{2/3} E^{(1-2/3)}$, the saving rate is 25 percent, the current value of capital is £6,000 million, and the current value of output is £2,000 million. (That is, use the figures from part A, but change the depreciation rate to 5 percent.) Now what is the growth rate of output per worker? Think about the **economic relationships** that are behind the equation: why does an increase in the depreciation rate decrease the growth rate of output per worker?

E. Suppose the labor force is growing by 1.5 percent per year, labor efficiency is increasing 0.8 percent annually, the depreciation rate is 3 percent, the production function is $\frac{Y}{L} = \left(\frac{K}{L}\right)^{2/3} E^{(1-2/3)}$, the saving rate is 20 percent, the current value of capital is £6,000 million, and the current value of output is £2,000 million. (That is, use the figures from part A, but change the saving rate to 20 percent.) Now what is the growth rate of output per worker? Think about the **economic relationships** that are behind the equation: why does a decrease in the saving rate decrease the growth rate of output per worker?

TO THE CHALKBOARD:
Deriving $g(K/Y) = (1 - \alpha) \cdot [\, s/(K/Y) - (n + g + \delta)\,]$

$g(K/Y)$ is the expression for the rate of change of the capital-output ratio. Here is a step-by-step explanation of its derivation.

Remember the trick: **manipulate the expression until it contains K/L.** In this case, just divide both

K and Y by L: $\dfrac{K}{Y} = \dfrac{(K) \cdot \left(\frac{1}{L}\right)}{(Y) \cdot \left(\frac{1}{L}\right)} = \dfrac{\left(\frac{K}{L}\right)}{\left(\frac{Y}{L}\right)}$.

Because we already have expressions for the growth rate of $\dfrac{K}{L}$ and the growth rate of $\dfrac{Y}{L}$, and because we have a "proportional growth rule" that states $g(X/Y) = g(X) - g(Y)$, we can now derive $g(K/Y)$.

$$g\left(\frac{K}{Y}\right) = g\left[\frac{\left(\frac{K}{L}\right)}{\left(\frac{Y}{L}\right)}\right] \qquad \textit{dividing both K and Y by L}$$

$$g\left(\frac{K}{Y}\right) = g\left(\frac{K}{L}\right) - g\left(\frac{Y}{L}\right) \qquad \textit{applying proportional growth rule}$$

$$g\left(\frac{K}{Y}\right) = \left(\frac{s}{\left(\frac{K_t}{Y_t}\right)} - \delta - n\right) - \left[\alpha \cdot \left(\frac{s}{\left(\frac{K_t}{Y_t}\right)} - \delta - n\right) + (1 - \alpha) \cdot g\right] \qquad \textit{substituting } g\left(\frac{K}{L}\right) \textit{ and } g\left(\frac{Y}{L}\right)$$

$$g\left(\frac{K}{Y}\right) = \left(\frac{s}{\left(\frac{K_t}{Y_t}\right)} - \delta - n\right) - \alpha \cdot \left(\frac{s}{\left(\frac{K_t}{Y_t}\right)} - \delta - n\right) - (1 - \alpha) \cdot g \qquad \textit{distributing negative sign}$$

$$g\left(\frac{K}{Y}\right) = (1 - \alpha) \cdot \left(\frac{s}{\left(\frac{K_t}{Y_t}\right)} - \delta - n\right) - (1 - \alpha) \cdot g \qquad \textit{collecting } \left(\frac{s}{\left(\frac{K_t}{Y_t}\right)} - \delta - n\right) \textit{ terms}$$

$$g\left(\frac{K}{Y}\right) = (1 - \alpha) \cdot \left(\frac{s}{\left(\frac{K_t}{Y_t}\right)} - \delta - n - g\right) \qquad \textit{collecting } (1 - \alpha) \textit{ terms}$$

$$g\left(\frac{K}{Y}\right) = (1 - \alpha) \cdot \left(\frac{s}{\left(\frac{K_t}{Y_t}\right)} - n - g - \delta\right) \qquad \textit{rearranging terms to match text}$$

$$g\left(\frac{K}{Y}\right) = (1 - \alpha) \cdot \left(\frac{s}{\left(\frac{K_t}{Y_t}\right)} - (n + g + \delta)\right) \qquad \textit{inserting parentheses to match text}$$

HINT: To remember the formula for the growth rate of the capital-output ratio, just remember the same three things as before:

- **The production function:** $\dfrac{Y}{L} = \left(\dfrac{K}{L}\right)^{\alpha} E^{1-\alpha}$

- **The growth rate of capital per worker:** $g(k_t) = \dfrac{s}{\left(\dfrac{K_t}{Y_t}\right)} - \delta - n$

- **The proportional growth rule:** $g\!\left(X^a Y^b\right) = a \cdot g(X) + b \cdot g(Y)$

And add one more:

- **The other proportional growth rule:** $g\!\left(\dfrac{X}{Y}\right) = g(X) - g(Y)$

And remember the trick: *play with ratios until you have an expression with $\dfrac{K}{L}$ in it.*

The growth rate of the capital-output ratio, $\dfrac{K}{Y}$, is the same as the growth rate of $\dfrac{\left(\dfrac{K}{L}\right)}{\left(\dfrac{Y}{L}\right)} = \dfrac{k}{y}$. Use the proportional growth rule: $g\!\left(\dfrac{k}{y}\right) = g(k) - g(y)$.

And then substitute in what we already have for g(k) and g(y):

$$g\!\left(\frac{k}{y}\right) = g(k) - g(y) = \left(\frac{s}{\left(\frac{K_t}{Y_t}\right)} - \delta - n\right) - \left[\alpha \cdot \left(\frac{s}{\left(\frac{K_t}{Y_t}\right)} - \delta - n\right) + (1-\alpha) \cdot g\right]$$

$$= (1 - \alpha) \cdot \left(\frac{s}{\left(\frac{K_t}{Y_t}\right)} - \delta - n - g\right)$$

which the text writes as $g(\kappa_t) = (1 - \alpha) \cdot \left(\dfrac{s}{\kappa_t} - (n + g + \delta)\right)$.

12. In this question, you will work with the equation for the growth rate of capital-output ratio, $g\!\left(\dfrac{K}{Y}\right) = (1-\alpha) \cdot \left(\dfrac{s}{\left(\dfrac{K_t}{Y_t}\right)} - \delta - n - g\right)$.

A. Suppose the labor force is growing by 1.5 percent per year, labor efficiency is increasing 0.8 percent annually, the depreciation rate is 3 percent, the production function is $\dfrac{Y}{L} = \left(\dfrac{K}{L}\right)^{2/3} E^{(1-2/3)}$, the saving rate is 25 percent, the current value of capital is £6,000 million, and the current value of output is £2,000 million. What is the growth rate of the capital-output ratio?

B. Suppose the labor force is growing by 3 percent per year, labor efficiency is increasing 0.8 percent annually, the depreciation rate is 3 percent, the production function is $\frac{Y}{L} = \left(\frac{K}{L}\right)^{2/3} E^{(1 - 2/3)}$, the saving rate is 25 percent, the current value of capital is £6,000 million, and the current value of output is £2,000 million. (That is, use the figures from part A, but change the labor force growth rate to 3 percent.) Now what is the growth rate of the capital-output ratio? Think about the **economic relationships** that are behind the equation: why does an increase in the labor force growth rate decrease the growth rate of the capital-output ratio?

C. Suppose the labor force is growing by 1.5 percent per year, labor efficiency is increasing 1.6 percent annually, the depreciation rate is 3 percent, the production function is $\frac{Y}{L} = \left(\frac{K}{L}\right)^{2/3} E^{(1 - 2/3)}$, the saving rate is 25 percent, the current value of capital is £6,000 million, and the current value of output is £2,000 million. (That is, use the figures from part A, but change the labor efficiency growth rate to 1.6 percent.) Now what is the growth rate of the capital-output ratio? Think about the **economic relationships** that are behind the equation: why does an increase in the labor efficiency growth rate decrease the growth rate of the capital-output ratio?

D. Suppose the labor force is growing by 1.5 percent per year, labor efficiency is increasing 0.8 percent annually, the depreciation rate is 5 percent, the production function is $\frac{Y}{L} = \left(\frac{K}{L}\right)^{2/3} E^{(1 - 2/3)}$, the saving rate is 25 percent, the current value of capital is £6,000 million, and the current value of output is £2,000 million. (That is, use the figures from part A, but change the depreciation rate to 5 percent.) Now what is the growth rate of the capital-output ratio? Think about the **economic relationships** that are behind the equation: why does an increase in the depreciation rate decrease the growth rate of the capital-output ratio?

E. Suppose the labor force is growing by 1.5 percent per year, labor efficiency is increasing 0.8 percent annually, the depreciation rate is 3 percent, the production function is $\frac{Y}{L} = \left(\frac{K}{L}\right)^{2/3} E^{(1 - 2/3)}$, the saving rate is 20 percent, the current value of capital is £6,000 million, and the current value of output is £2,000 million. (That is, use the figures from part A, but change the saving rate to 20 percent.) Now what is the growth rate of the capital-output ratio? Think about the **economic relationships** that are behind the equation: why does a decrease in the saving rate decrease the growth rate of the capital-output ratio?

HINT: Having trouble remembering all those symbols? Maybe this table will help:

Variable Name	Symbol	Symbol for its growth rate
Capital Stock	K	$\%\Delta K$
Labor Force	L	$\%\Delta L = n$
Capital per Worker (or, Capital-Labor Ratio)	$\dfrac{K}{L} = k$	$\%\Delta k = g(k)$
Labor Efficiency	E	$\%\Delta E = g$
Output	Y	$\%\Delta Y$
Output per Worker	$\dfrac{Y}{L} = y$	$\%\Delta y = g(y)$
Capital-Output Ratio	$\dfrac{K}{Y} = \kappa$ (*kappa*)	$\%\Delta\left(\dfrac{K}{Y}\right) = g\left(\dfrac{K}{Y}\right)$

TO THE CHALKBOARD:
Explaining Figure 4.11

Textbook Figure 4.11A shows how the growth rates of the capital-labor ratio, $g\left(\dfrac{K}{L}\right)$, and of output per worker, $g\left(\dfrac{Y}{L}\right)$, change when the capital-output ratio, $\dfrac{K}{Y}$, changes. Remember: $g\left(\dfrac{K}{L}\right) = \dfrac{s}{\left(\dfrac{K}{Y}\right)} - \delta - n$

and $g\left(\dfrac{Y}{L}\right) = g + (\alpha)\cdot\left[\dfrac{s}{\left[\dfrac{K}{Y}\right]} - (n + g + \delta)\right]$. As $\dfrac{K}{Y}$ increases, both $g\left(\dfrac{K}{L}\right)$ and $g\left(\dfrac{Y}{L}\right)$ decrease. The decreases are non-linear because $\dfrac{K}{Y}$ is in the denominator.

The values of s, δ, n, g, and α are constant for any curve. Suppose s = 0.20, δ = 0.04, n = 0.02, g = 0.02, and α = 0.5. The lighter of the two curves at the right is the same $g\left(\dfrac{K}{L}\right)$ curve that was depicted in Figure 4.9. The darker curve is $g\left(\dfrac{Y}{L}\right) = 0.02 + 0.5\cdot\left[\dfrac{0.20}{\left(\dfrac{K}{Y}\right)} - (0.02 + 0.02 + 0.04)\right]$.

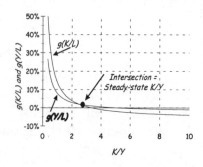

An **increase** in the saving rate (s), an **increase** in the labor efficiency growth rate (g), a **decrease** in the labor force growth rate (n), or a **decrease** in the depreciation rate (δ), **shifts** the $g\left(\frac{Y}{L}\right)$ curve **up**.

An **increase** in the Cobb-Douglas production function parameter α **rotates** the curve: for values of K/Y below the steady-state level, $g\left(\frac{Y}{L}\right)$ shifts up; for values of K/Y above the steady state, $g\left(\frac{Y}{L}\right)$ shifts down. At steady state, $g\left(\frac{Y}{L}\right)$ is independent of the value of α.

Note that the two curves **intersect at the steady-state level of K/Y**. At steady state, the growth rates of K/L and of Y/L are the same; they equal the growth rate of labor efficiency. So the two curves intersect when $g\left(\frac{K}{L}\right) = g\left(\frac{Y}{L}\right) = g$. In this case, $g\left(\frac{K}{L}\right) = g\left(\frac{Y}{L}\right) = g$ when $\frac{K}{Y} = 2.5$.

Steady state is also defined as occurring **when the capital-output ratio is constant**; that is, when $g\left(\frac{K}{Y}\right) = 0$.

Remember the proportional growth rules: g(K/Y) = g(K/L) - g(Y/L). So graphing the vertical difference between the curves $g\left(\frac{K}{L}\right)$ and $g\left(\frac{Y}{L}\right)$ at each value of $\frac{K}{Y}$ gives us the relationship between the capital-output ratio, $\frac{K}{Y}$, and its growth rate, $g\left(\frac{K}{Y}\right)$. That relationship is depicted at the right and in Textbook Figure 4.11B. Note that $g\left(\frac{K}{Y}\right) = 0$ when $\frac{K}{Y} = 2.5$, which is of course also the level of $\frac{K}{Y}$ where $g\left(\frac{K}{L}\right) = g\left(\frac{Y}{L}\right) = g$.

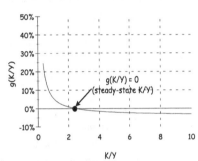

13. Sketch graphs of the growth rates of the capital-labor ratio, $g\left(\frac{K}{L}\right)$, and the output-worker ratio, $g\left(\frac{Y}{L}\right)$, in the space at the right. Label the axes and the steady-state value of the capital-output ratio. For each part, sketch in and label a second set of curves that show the effect on $g\left(\frac{K}{L}\right)$ and $g\left(\frac{Y}{L}\right)$ of

A. an increase in the saving rate.

B. an increase in g.

C. a decrease in the labor force growth rate.

D. a decrease in the depreciation rate.

E. an increase in the Cobb-Douglas parameter, α.

14. Sketch a graph of the growth rate of the capital-output ratio, $g\left(\dfrac{K}{Y}\right)$, in the space at the right. Label the axes and the steady-state value of the capital-output ratio. For each part, sketch in and label a second curve that shows the effect on $g\left(\dfrac{K}{Y}\right)$ of

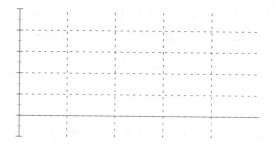

A. an increase in the saving rate.
B. an increase in g.
C. a decrease in the labor force growth rate.
D. a decrease in the depreciation rate.
E. an increase in the Cobb-Douglas parameter, α.

 NOTE: In Questions 12, 13, and 14, you will see how capital, labor, and output change over time as the economy moves toward a steady-state balanced-growth equilibrium. In Question 12, we begin with the capital-output ratio below its steady-state level. In Question 13, we begin with the capital-output ratio above its steady-state level. In Question 14, we begin with the capital-output ratio at its steady-state level.

15. Suppose n = 0.015, g = 0.008, δ = 0.03, s = 0.25, E_1 = 100, K_1 = 75,000, L_1 = 15, and the production function is Cobb-Douglas, with α = 2/3. Complete the following table. Use a separate sheet of paper for your calculations.

Period	K	L	E	Y/L	Y	K/Y
1						
2						
3						
4						
5						

Is the economy at its steady-state balanced-growth equilibrium? Why or why not? Answer the question *without* computing the steady-state value of the capital-output ratio.

16. Suppose n = 0.015, g = 0.008, δ = 0.03, s = 0.25, E_1 = 100, K_1 = 75,000, L_1 = 5, and the production function is Cobb-Douglas, with α = 2/3. Complete the following table. Use a separate sheet of paper for your calculations.

Period	K	L	E	Y/L	Y	K/Y
1						
2						
3						
4						
5						

Is the economy at its steady-state balanced-growth equilibrium? Why or why not? Answer the question *without* computing the steady-state value of the capital-output ratio.

17. Suppose n = 0.015, g = 0.008, δ = 0.03, s = 0.25, E_1 = 100, K_1 = 75,000, L_1 = 7.14, and the production function is Cobb-Douglas, with α = 2/3. Complete the following table. Use a separate sheet of paper for your calculations.

Period	K	L	E	Y/L	Y	K/Y
1						
2						
3						
4						
5						

Is the economy at its steady-state balanced-growth equilibrium? Why or why not? Answer the question *without* computing the steady-state value of the capital-output ratio.

TO THE CHALKBOARD:
Explaining Figure 4.12

Textbook Figure 4.12 illustrates that the steady-state equilibrium, where $g\left(\frac{K}{Y}\right) = 0$, is a "stable" equilibrium. To be stable, $\frac{K}{Y}$ must move to its steady-state level if it is not already there, and if $\frac{K}{Y}$ is already at steady state, it must stay there.

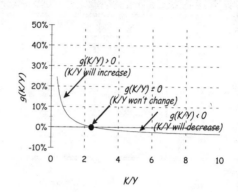

$g\left(\frac{K}{Y}\right) > 0$ means $\frac{K}{Y}$ will increase. $g\left(\frac{K}{Y}\right) < 0$ means $\frac{K}{Y}$ will decrease. $g\left(\frac{K}{Y}\right) = 0$ means $\frac{K}{Y}$ will not change. Take a look at the figure to the right. When the capital-output ratio is below steady state, $g\left(\frac{K}{Y}\right) > 0$, so $\frac{K}{Y}$ will increase toward steady state. When the capital-output ratio is above steady-state, $g\left(\frac{K}{Y}\right) < 0$, so $\frac{K}{Y}$ will decrease toward steady state. And when $g\left(\frac{K}{Y}\right) = 0$, $\frac{K}{Y}$ is at steady state. The steady-state equilibrium is therefore **a stable equilibrium.**

18. Using the data in Questions 15, 16, and 17, create a graph of g(K/Y) at the right. Label your axes. Show that the economy is in a steady-state balanced growth equilibrium when the conditions in Question 17 hold.

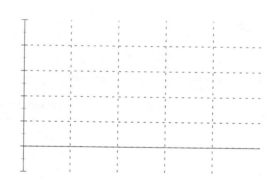

TO THE CHALKBOARD:

Deriving $(K/Y)_{ss} = s/(n + g + \delta)$

and $(Y/L)_{ss} = [(s/(n + g + \delta))^{(\alpha/1-\alpha)}] \cdot E_t$

$(K/Y)_{ss}$ is the expression for the steady-state balanced-growth equilibrium value of the capital-output ratio. Given values for s, n, g, and δ, it is a number.

$(Y/L)_{ss}$ is the expression for the steady-state balanced-growth equilibrium value of output per worker **given a value for labor efficiency, E_t.**

Given values for s, n, g, δ, and α, $(Y/L)_{ss}$ is a constant proportion of labor efficiency, E. Given a value for E as well, $(Y/L)_{ss}$ is a number.

To derive $(K/Y)_{ss}$ requires only that we **remember a definition:** the economy is in equilibrium when K/Y is constant. That is, equilibrium is when g(K/Y) = 0.

$$g\left(\frac{K}{Y}\right) = (1 - \alpha)\cdot\left(\frac{s}{\left(\frac{K_t}{Y_t}\right)} - (n + g + \delta)\right) \quad \text{\textit{definition of growth rate of }} \frac{K}{Y}$$

$$(1 - \alpha)\cdot\left(\frac{s}{\left(\frac{K_t}{Y_t}\right)} - (n + g + \delta)\right) = 0 \quad \text{\textit{definition of equilibrium, }} g\left(\frac{K}{Y}\right) = 0$$

$$\frac{s}{\left(\frac{K_t}{Y_t}\right)} - (n + g + \delta) = 0 \quad \text{\textit{dividing both sides of equation by }} (1-\alpha)$$

$$\frac{s}{\left(\frac{K_t}{Y_t}\right)} = (n + g + \delta) \quad \text{\textit{adding }} (n + g + \delta) \text{\textit{ to both sides of equation}}$$

$$s = (n + g + \delta)\cdot\left(\frac{K_t}{Y_t}\right) \quad \text{\textit{multiplying both sides of equation by }}\left(\frac{K_t}{Y_t}\right)$$

$$\frac{s}{(n + g + \delta)} = \left(\frac{K_t}{Y_t}\right)_{ss} \quad \text{\textit{dividing both sides of equation by }} (n + g + \delta)$$

To derive $(Y/L)_{ss}$ then requires that we **remember two things:** [1] manipulate K/Y until you have an expression with K/L in it and [2] use the Cobb-Douglas production function.

$$\frac{K}{Y} = \frac{s}{n + g + \delta} \quad \text{\textit{definition of steady-state balanced-growth equilibrium}}$$

$$\frac{K}{Y} = \frac{\left(\frac{K}{L}\right)}{\left(\frac{Y}{L}\right)} = \frac{s}{n + g + \delta} \quad \text{\textit{dividing both K and Y by L}}$$

$$\left(\frac{K}{L}\right) = \frac{s}{n + g + \delta}\cdot\left(\frac{Y}{L}\right) \quad \text{\textit{multiplying both sides of equation by }}\left(\frac{Y}{L}\right)$$

Now we will substitute this last expression into the production function.

$$\frac{Y}{L} = \left(\frac{K}{L}\right)^{\alpha} \cdot E^{(1-\alpha)} \quad \text{\textit{Cobb-Douglas production function}}$$

$$\frac{Y}{L} = \left(\frac{s}{n+g+\delta} \cdot \left(\frac{Y}{L}\right)\right)^{\alpha} \cdot E^{(1-\alpha)} \quad \text{\textit{substituting from above for}} \left(\frac{K}{L}\right)$$

$$\frac{Y}{L} = \left(\frac{s}{n+g+\delta}\right)^{\alpha} \cdot \left(\frac{Y}{L}\right)^{\alpha} \cdot E^{(1-\alpha)} \quad \text{\textit{applying exponent rule}}$$

$$\left(\frac{Y}{L}\right)^{(1-\alpha)} = \left(\frac{s}{n+g+\delta}\right)^{\alpha} \cdot E^{(1-\alpha)} \quad \text{\textit{combining }} \frac{Y}{L} \text{ \textit{terms}}$$

$$\left(\frac{Y}{L}\right) = \left(\frac{s}{n+g+\delta}\right)^{\frac{\alpha}{1-\alpha}} \cdot (E)^{\frac{1-\alpha}{1-\alpha}} \quad \text{\textit{raising both sides of equation to}} \frac{1}{(1-\alpha)} \text{ \textit{power}}$$

$$\left(\frac{Y}{L}\right) = \left(\frac{s}{n+g+\delta}\right)^{\frac{\alpha}{1-\alpha}} \cdot (E) \quad \text{\textit{simplifying}}$$

19. This question asks you to work with the equations for the steady-state balanced-growth equilibrium values of the capital-output ratio and output per worker. Use the formula for the steady-state balanced-growth equilibrium value of the capital-output ratio,

$$\left(\frac{K}{Y}\right)_{ss} = \frac{s}{n+g+\delta}.$$

A. Suppose the saving rate is 20 percent, the labor force is increasing 3 percent annually, labor efficiency is increasing by 2 percent each year, and capital depreciates 3.5 percent annually. What is the steady-state balanced-growth value of the capital-output ratio? Suppose $\alpha = 0.6$ and $E_t = 100$. What is the steady-state value of output per worker?

B. Suppose the saving rate is 25 percent, the labor force is increasing 3 percent annually, labor efficiency is increasing by 2 percent each year, and capital depreciates 3.5 percent annually. (That is, use the values from part A, but change the saving rate to 25 percent.) Now what is the steady-state balanced-growth value of the capital-output ratio? Suppose $\alpha = 0.6$ and $E_t = 100$. What is the steady-state value of output per worker?

C. Suppose the saving rate is 20 percent, the labor force is increasing 4 percent annually, labor efficiency is increasing by 2 percent each year, and capital depreciates 3.5 percent annually. (That is, use the values from part A, but change the growth rate of the labor force to 4 percent.) Now what is the steady-state balanced-growth value of the capital-output ratio? Suppose $\alpha = 0.6$ and $E_t = 100$. What is the steady-state value of output per worker?

D. Suppose the saving rate is 20 percent, the labor force is increasing 3 percent annually, labor efficiency is increasing by 2.5 percent each year, and capital depreciates 3.5 percent annually. (That is, use the values from part A, but change the growth rate of labor efficiency to 2.5 percent.) Now what is the steady-state balanced-growth value of the capital-output ratio? Suppose $\alpha = 0.6$ and $E_t = 100$. What is the steady-state value of output per worker?

E. Suppose the saving rate is 20 percent, the labor force is increasing 3 percent annually, labor efficiency is increasing by 2 percent each year, and capital depreciates 5.5 percent annually. (That is, use the values from part A, but change the depreciation rate to 5.5 percent.) Now what is the steady-state balanced-growth value of the capital-output ratio? Suppose $\alpha = 0.6$ and $E_t = 100$. What is the steady-state value of output per worker?

TO THE CHALKBOARD:
Explaining Figure 4.14

Textbook Figure 4.14 shows how to find the steady-state level of output per worker $\left(\dfrac{Y}{L}\right)_{ss}$ when labor efficiency, E, and the steady-state value of $\dfrac{K}{Y}$ are known. The graph of $\dfrac{Y}{L}$ is straightforward; given a value of E, it is just the Cobb-Douglas production function. But which value of $\dfrac{Y}{L}$ is the steady-state value? It is the value of $\dfrac{Y}{L}$ where $\dfrac{K}{Y}$ equals its steady-state value. Suppose in steady state, $\dfrac{K}{Y} = 2.5$. Remember $\dfrac{K}{Y} = \dfrac{K/L}{Y/L}$. Therefore,

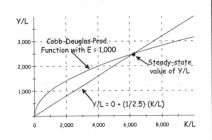

$\dfrac{K/L}{Y/L} = 2.5$, or rearranging slightly, $\dfrac{Y}{L} = \left(\dfrac{1}{2.5}\right) \cdot \dfrac{K}{L}$. Graphing that equation gives us a straight line with intercept 0 and slope $\left(\dfrac{1}{2.5}\right) = 0.4$. Where the two curves intersect, we have the steady-state level of output per worker.

20. Using the values in Question 19 part A, use the graphical method to find the steady-state level of output per worker.

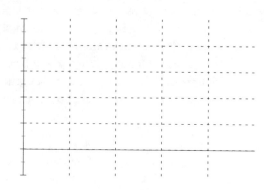

21. This question asks you to compute the change in the steady-state level of output per worker as a result of changes in the parameters. Use the equations $\left(\dfrac{K}{Y}\right)_{ss} = \dfrac{s}{n + g + \delta}$

and $\left(\dfrac{Y}{L}\right)_{ss} = \left(\left(\dfrac{K}{Y}\right)_{ss}^{\left(\frac{\alpha}{1-\alpha}\right)}\right) \cdot (E_t)$

A. Suppose the saving rate is 20 percent, the depreciation rate is 2.7 percent, the labor force is growing by 1.9 percent annually, and labor efficiency is growing by 2 percent a year. Suppose the production function is Cobb-Douglas with $\alpha = 0.7$. Suppose E currently equals 4,000. What is the value of output per worker if the economy is in steady-state equilibrium?

B. Suppose the saving rate is 21 percent, and the remainder of the parameters have the same values as in part A. What is the new value of output per worker in steady state? What is the percentage change in steady-state equilibrium value of output per worker when the saving rate increases by one percentage point?

C. Suppose the depreciation rate is 3.7 percent, and the remainder of the parameters have the same values as in part A. What is the new value of output per worker in steady state? What is the percentage change in steady-state equilibrium value of output per worker when the depreciation rate increases by one percentage point?

D. Suppose the labor force is growing by only 0.9 percent annually and the remainder of the parameters have the same values as in part A. What is the new value of output per worker in steady state? What is the percentage change in steady-state equilibrium value of output per worker when the labor force growth rate decreases by one percentage point?

TO THE CHALKBOARD:
Explaining Figure 4.16

Textbook Figure 4.16 depicts the change in the steady-state level of output per worker when the saving rate increases. At right, the saving rate rises from 20 percent to 24 percent. The result is the steady-state value of capital-output ratio rises from 2.5 to 3, rotating the K/L vs Y/L steady-state line down and to the right. When the saving rate increases, at a given level of output per worker, Y/L, there will be more saving and thus more investment and thus more capital per worker in the subsequent round. The increase in capital per worker will result in an increase in output per worker for a given level of labor efficiency, E. In

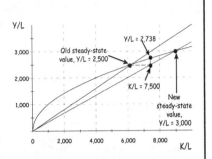

the graph at the right, this first set of changes is depicted with the horizontal line from the old steady-state values (K/L = 6,250 and Y/L = 2,500) to the new higher level of K/L (K/L = 7,500 at Y/L = 2,500). The increase in K/L yields more output per worker, shown as the vertical line at K/L = 7,500 rising from Y/L = 2,500 to Y/L = 2,738. After subsequent rounds of change in Y/L and K/L, the economy will eventually wind up at the new steady-state value of output per worker where Y/L = 3,000 and K/L = 9,000.

C. APPLYING CONCEPTS AND MODELS

Now we're getting to the good stuff. Being able to apply a specific concept or model to a real world situation — where you are told which model to apply but you have to figure out how to apply it — is often what you need to earn a B in a course. This is where macroeconomics starts to become interesting and the world starts to make more sense.

1. The personal saving rate in the United States averaged 8.3 percent in the 1960s but only 5.9 percent in the 1990s. According to the Solow growth model, what is the long-run effect on output per worker?

2. Total savings in the Solow model as presented in Textbook Chapter 4 includes saving by government agencies. When the government runs a budget surplus – when government revenues exceed government outlays – government is increasing the nation's total savings. When the government runs a budget deficit, government is decreasing the nation's total savings. During the Clinton Administration, the federal government budget changed from a deficit of $290 billion (about 4.7 percent of GDP) to a surplus of $230 billion (about 2.4 percent of GDP). Assuming the surplus is not subsequently eliminated, what is the long-run effect on standards of living?

3. If engineers were to develop a way to make machines last much longer, that would dramatically lower depreciation rates. According to the Solow growth model, what is the long-run effect on output per worker?

D. EXPLAINING THE REAL WORLD

Most instructors are delighted when you are able to figure out which concept or model to apply to a real world situation. Being able to do so means you thoroughly understand the material and is often what you need to do to earn an A in a course. This is where you experience the power of macroeconomic theory.

1. What is the long-run effect of the increase in women's labor force participation on output per worker? On output per capita?

2. The United Nations sponsors several programs aimed at helping women in poor nations gain reproductive control. If fertility is lowered, what will be the long-run effect on standards of living in those nations?

3. In the mid-1800s, steam power replaced water power in New England manufacturing. What should have been the long-run impact of this development on standards of living? Why?

4. In the late 1990s, everyone worried that the "Y2K Bug" would lead to collapse of computer-driven systems on January 1, 2000. As a result, most businesses replaced their computer equipment. What effect would the computer purchases have had on standards of living in the long run?

5. The government is choosing between spending $100 billion on funding scientific research and lowering personal taxes by $100 billion. Which action will increase long-run standards of living? Why?

6. A $1.3 trillion tax cut was approved by Congress in 2001. Consider three possible uses of the tax cut: [1] the recipients spend all of the tax cut, purchasing consumer goods and services; [2] the recipients save the entire tax cut, placing the funds into various financial assets; [3] the recipients save half of the tax cut and use the other half to pay off their credit card debt and other loans. In each case, what is the long-run effect of the tax cut? Are there long-run economic benefits of the tax cut?

E. POSSIBILITIES TO PONDER

The more you learn, the more you realize you have more to learn. These questions go beyond the material in the text. They are the sort of questions that distinguish A+ or A work from A- work. Some of them may even serve as decent starting points for junior or senior year research papers.

1. If America and India share knowledge regarding production methods, technology, and organization of the workplace, will Indian standards of living equal American standards of living in the long run?

2. Suppose you were to modify the Solow growth model to include a government sector. The government taxes workers and firms, lowering disposable income relative to income. Since the personal saving rate is usually expressed as a percentage of *disposable* income, government taxation would lower personal saving. The government also spends money, some of which is for transfer payments, which increase disposable income, some of which is for government investment in infrastructure, which contributes to the ability of workers to produce output, and the rest of which is for consumable items which do not contribute to infrastructure. How would you modify the model? What impact would an increase in government spending for infrastructure have on long-run standards of living? What impact would an increase in government spending for consumables have on long-run standards of living? If you are advising the government on how it spends money and you want to increase long-run standards of living, what advice do you give regarding which projects the government should fund?

3. In the 1940s, many economic historians thought that a country had to have a railroad sector to experience economic growth. After all, the United States economy had boomed at the same time that the railroad was being constructed throughout and across America, replacing dirt roads and waterways. According to the Solow model, what aspects of railroad development might have been key to increasing economic growth? Would a railroad be necessary today for an industrializing nation to experience economic growth?

4. The AIDS epidemic is killing thousands of people each day in sub-Saharan Africa. If the standard by which government decides whether to address a problem is "Does this government action contribute to economic growth?," will the government establish programs to end or at least reduce the number of deaths by AIDS?

SOLUTIONS   SOLUTIONS   SOLUTIONS   SOLUTIONS

A. BASIC DEFINITIONS

* indicates there are notes below related to this question.

1. Steady-state balanced-growth equilibrium
2. Cobb-Douglas
3. Efficiency of labor
4. Cobb-Douglas

5. Investment requirements
6. Depreciation
7. Capital stock; labor force*
8. Investment effort
9. Solow

10. Capital stock
11. Capital stock
12. Investment*
13. Capital-labor ratio
14. Saving rate

*7. Note that efficiency of labor, E, is not an **input** to the production function.

*12. Remember: In economics, **investment** is **not** purchasing stocks and bonds. Investment always refers to purchases by business that add to the capital stock.

15. No role*
16. Is
17. Is*
18. Increases

19. Increases*
20. Increases
21. Exogenous*

22. Exogenous
23. Endogenous
24. Endogenous*

*15. As presented in Textbook Chapter 4, government **spending** plays no role. However, as implied by the policy questions at the end of Textbook Chapter 4 and by some of the Section C, D, and E questions in Study Guide Chapter 4, government **saving** does play a role. When the government saves by running a budget surplus, its action contributes to total national saving, increasing the saving rate.

*17. The two definitions of steady-state balanced-growth equilibrium in questions 16 and 17 are equivalent.

*19. Technology is synonymous with labor efficiency in the Solow model as developed in Textbook Chapter 4.

*21. The growth rate of the labor force, n, is not determined by any of the factors that are part of the Solow growth model. Therefore, n is exogenous to the model.

*24. The growth rate of the capital stock depends upon two exogenous factors – s and δ – and upon one endogenous factor – output. Therefore the growth rate of K is itself endogenous.

25. D. The definition of "steady-state balanced-growth equilibrium" is that this is the point where the capital-output ratio is constant, which is equivalent to stating that capital per worker, output per worker, and labor efficiency are all growing at the same rate.

26. B. The production function is usually expressed as $\frac{Y}{L} = F\left(\left(\frac{K}{L}\right), E\right)$. It is a statement about production

of *total* output for the entire economy, *not* about production within one firm.

27. B. The steady-state balanced-growth equilibrium occurs when $\frac{K}{Y} = \frac{s}{n + g + \delta}$. We need information

about the saving rate (s), the labor force growth rate (n), the growth rate of labor efficiency (g), and
the depreciation rate (δ) only.

28. D. The efficiency of labor refers only to how much output per worker is produced with a given amount
of capital per worker. "Efficiency" can be thought of in its usual sense, as an action that someone takes
to accomplish a goal with fewer resources. But in the context of the production function, anything that
increases output given capital is said to increase "efficiency" of labor. So forcing additional labor effort
increases "efficiency," as does technological improvement in physical capital.

B. MANIPULATION OF CONCEPTS AND MODELS

1.

A. $\frac{Y}{L} = \left(\frac{K}{L}\right)^{0.2} \cdot E^{0.8}$ appears as shown at the

right. Notice that at low levels of $\frac{K}{L}$, the

returns to additional capital per worker are
quite large; the curve is nearly vertical
between K/L = 0 and K/L = 1000. But as
capital per worker rises, the returns become
smaller and smaller.

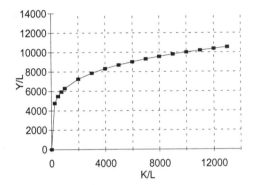

B. $\frac{Y}{L} = \left(\frac{K}{L}\right)^{0.8} \cdot E^{0.2}$ appears as shown at right.

Notice that the returns to additional capital
per worker do not change much as capital
per worker changes. That is, the slope of
the production function is nearly constant.

C. At very low levels of K/L, a change in the
capital to labor ratio generates a larger
change in output per worker when $\alpha = 0.2$;
but at moderate and high levels of K/L, a
change in the capital to labor ratio generates
a larger change in output per worker when α
= 0.8. Regardless of the value of α,

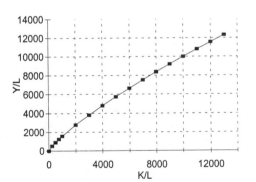

increases in the amount of capital per worker generate additional output per worker (returns are
positive), but the amount of additional output per worker gets smaller with each increase in the
amount of capital per worker (returns are diminishing as K/L rises). When $\alpha = 0.2$, diminishing
returns to inputs set in quickly. When $\alpha = 0.8$, diminishing returns are slow to appear. So over
most of the range of K/L, increases in capital per worker generates a larger change in output per
worker when $\alpha = 0.8$.

2. A. $\dfrac{Y}{L} = (5{,}000)^{0.4} \cdot (10{,}000)^{0.6} = 7578.58$

$\dfrac{Y}{L} = (10{,}000)^{0.4} \cdot (10{,}000)^{0.6} = 10{,}000.$

$\dfrac{Y}{L} = (20{,}000)^{0.4} \cdot (10{,}000)^{0.6} = 13195.08$

K/L	Y/L
5,000	7,579
10,000	10,000
20,000	13,195

B. When K/L doubles, Y/L does not double. With the Cobb-Douglas production function, additions to capital per worker do increase output per worker, but the size of increases in output per worker is not a constant proportion of additions to capital per worker. When K/L doubles, Y/L increases by 32 percent. If both E and K/L doubled, then Y/L would double.

3. In the *Economic Report of the President 2001,* the data for Labor Force are found in Table B35. The average annual growth rate is found by taking the 10th root of the ratio of, for instance, the 1960 to 1950 value, and subtracting 1 from that value. That is, $\left(\dfrac{69{,}628}{62{,}208}\right)^{\frac{1}{10}} - 1 = 0.0113.$

	Labor Force	Average Annual Growth Rate
1950	62,208	
1960	69,628	1.13
1970	82,771	1.74
1980	106,940	2.60
1990	125,840	1.64
2000	141,489	1.18

4.

Period	L_t (in thousands)	E_t
1	50,000.00	10,000.00
2	51,500.00	10,250.00
3	53,045.00	10,506.25
4	54,636.35	10,768.91
5	56,275.44	11,038.13

5.

A. $K_{t+1} = 2{,}550$

$K_{t+1} = K_t + sY_t - \delta K_t$
$K_{t+1} = 2500 + 0.15(1000) - 0.04(2500)$
$K_{t+1} = 2500 + 150 - 100 = 2550$

B. $Y_t = 12{,}100$

$K_{t+1} = K_t + sY_t - \delta K_t$
$\dfrac{K_{t+1} - K_t + \delta K_t}{s} = Y_t$
$\dfrac{8000 - 7000 + 0.03(7000)}{0.10} = Y_t = 12{,}100$

C. $K_t = 979.17$

$$K_{t+1} = K_t + sY_t - \delta K_t$$
$$K_{t+1} - sY_t = K_t - \delta K_t$$
$$K_{t+1} - sY_t = (1-\delta)K_t$$
$$\frac{K_{t+1} - sY_t}{(1-\delta)} = K_t$$
$$\frac{1,000 - 0.20(300)}{1-0.04} = K_t = 979.17$$

6. Note that when you express a growth rate in percentage terms, the value of %Δ(K/L) must first be multiplied by 100. To be complete, you might want to express your answer both ways; for instance, %Δ(K/L) = 0.026 = 2.6 percent.

period	K	L	K/L	%Δ(K/L)
1	1,500	125	12	
2	1,600	130	12.31	0.026 = 2.6 %
3	1,750	140	12.5	0.016 = 1.6 %
4	1,800	150	12	-0.04 = -4.0 %

For example, for period 2, g(k) = (12.31 - 12) / 12 = 0.31/12 = 0.026 or 2.6 percent.

7.

period	K	L	K/L	%Δ(K/L)	Y/L	Y	g(k)
1	7,500	100	75		63.77	6,377.12	
2	8,475.42	102.5	82.69	0.10	67.62	6,930.66	0.099
3	9,522.54	105.06	90.64	0.096	71.44	7,506.18	0.093
4	10,642.87	107.69	98.83	0.090	75.25	8,103.86	0.087
5	11,837.93	110.38	107.25	0.085	79.03	8,723.92	0.082

The answers in row 2 were calculated as follows:

$$\frac{K}{L} = \frac{8475.42}{102.5} = 82.69$$

$$\%\Delta\left(\frac{K}{L}\right) = \frac{82.69 - 75}{75} = 0.10$$

$$\frac{Y}{L} = \left(\frac{K}{L}\right)^a (E)^{1-a} = (82.69)^{0.6}(50)^{0.4} = 67.62$$

$$Y = \left(\frac{Y}{L}\right) \cdot L = 67.62 \cdot 102.5 = 6930.66$$

$$g(k) = \frac{s}{\dfrac{K_t}{Y_t}} - \delta - n = \frac{0.2}{\left(\dfrac{8475.42}{6930.66}\right)} - 0.04 - 0.025 = 0.099$$

B. The % change in $\frac{K}{L}$ does not equal g(k) because the changes in K, L, and $\frac{K}{L}$ are not "small."

8.

period	K	L	K/L	%Δ(K/L)	Y/L	Y	g(k)
1	83,000	100	830		269.80	26,979.56	
2	85,075.91	102.5	830.01	.0000107	269.80	27,654.23	.0000107
3	87,203.72	105.06	830.02	.0000104	269.80	28,345.76	.0000104
4	89,384.72	107.69	830.03	.0000102	269.80	29,054.58	.0000102
5	91,620.25	110.38	830.03	.0000099	269.80	29,781.12	.000099

The answers in row 2 were calculated as follows:

The answers in row 2 were calculated as follows:

$$\frac{K}{L} = \frac{85075.91}{102.5} = 830.01$$

$$\%\Delta\frac{K}{L} = \frac{830.01 - 830}{830} = 1.07E\text{-}05 = 0.0000107$$

$$\frac{Y}{L} = \left(\frac{K}{L}\right)^\alpha (E)^{1-\alpha} = (830.01)^{0.6}(50)^{0.4} = 269.80$$

$$Y = \left(\frac{Y}{L}\right)\cdot L = 269.80\cdot102.5 = 27654.23$$

$$g(k) = \frac{s}{\dfrac{K_t}{Y_t}} - \delta - n = \frac{0.2}{\left(\dfrac{85075.91}{27654.23}\right)} - 0.04 - 0.025 = 1.07E\text{-}05 = 0.0000107$$

B. The % change in $\frac{K}{L}$ equals g(k) because the changes in K, L, and $\frac{K}{L}$ are very "small."

C. The economy is in (or at least very near) a steady state; E, $\frac{K}{L}$ and $\frac{Y}{L}$ are all growing at the same (or almost the same) rate. In this case, E is constant (g = 0), so steady state is when $\frac{K}{L}$ and $\frac{Y}{L}$ are also constant.

D. The steady-state balanced-growth value of $\frac{Y}{L}$ is 269.86.

$$\left(\frac{Y_t}{L_t}\right)_{ss} = \left(\frac{s}{n + g + \delta}\right)^{\frac{\alpha}{1-\alpha}}\cdot E_t = \left(\frac{0.2}{0.025 + 0 + 0.04}\right)^{\frac{0.6}{1-0.6}}\cdot 50 = 269.86$$

9. A. $$g(k) = \frac{s}{\dfrac{K_t}{Y_t}} - \delta - n = \frac{0.15}{\left(\dfrac{140,000}{83,000}\right)} - 0.05 - 0.03 = 0.0089 = 0.89\ percent$$

B. $$g(k) = \frac{0.20}{\left(\dfrac{140,000}{83,000}\right)} - 0.05 - 0.03 = 0.039 = 3.9\ percent$$

An increase in the saving rate means that at every level of output per worker, there will be more investment in capital than when the saving rate was 15 percent. The rate of growth of capital will be greater, and so the rate of growth of capital per worker will also be greater.

NOTE: The question asks about changes in the *growth rate* of capital per worker. If your answer only mentions the initial change in capital, you haven't answered the question. You need to think about what is happening *over time* – the rate of growth – to capital per worker.

C. $$g(k) = \frac{0.15}{\left(\dfrac{140,000}{83,000}\right)} - 0.03 - 0.03 = 0.029 = 2.9\ percent$$

A decrease in the depreciation rate means that every piece of capital will last longer. For example, an average depreciation rate of 5 percent means that the typical piece of capital has a 20-year life (assuming straight line depreciation, a qualification added for those who are also taking accounting.) But a depreciation rate of 3 percent means that the typical piece of capital has a 33 year life. Because capital lasts longer, there is more capital available per worker. More capital per worker will mean more output per worker, and more output per worker will mean more savings, and more savings means more investment in capital – an increase in the rate of growth of capital. An increase in the growth rate of capital means the growth rate of capital per worker increases too.

D. $g(k) = \dfrac{0.15}{\left(\dfrac{140,000}{83,000}\right)} - 0.05 - 0.02 = 0.019 = 1.9$ *percent*

A decrease in the labor force growth rate means that over time, there will be an increase in the amount of capital per worker. More capital per worker will mean more output per worker, and more output per worker will mean more savings, and more savings means more investment in capital – an increase in the rate of growth of capital. An increase in the growth rate of capital means the growth rate of capital per worker increases too.

E. $g(k) = \dfrac{0.15}{\left(\dfrac{140,000}{80,000}\right)} - 0.05 - 0.03 = 0.0057 = 0.57$ *percent*

A decrease in the amount of output means less saving, which means less investment in capital – a decrease in the rate of growth of capital and thus a decrease in the rate of growth of capital per worker.

F. $g(k) = \dfrac{0.15}{\left(\dfrac{150,000}{83,000}\right)} - 0.05 - 0.03 = 0.003 = 0.30$ *percent*

An increase in the amount of capital means that there will be more depreciation in every period, which decreases the rate at which capital grows. This will produce a decrease in the rate of growth of capital and thus a decrease in the growth rate of capital per worker.

10. A. Shifts g(K/L) up
    B. No effect on g(K/L)
    C. Shifts g(K/L) up
    D. Shifts g(K/L) up
    E. No effect on g(K/L)

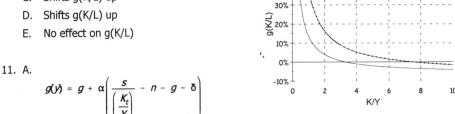

11. A.

$$g(y) = g + \alpha\left(\dfrac{s}{\left(\dfrac{K_t}{Y_t}\right)} - n - g - \delta\right)$$

$$= 0.008 + \dfrac{2}{3}\cdot\left(\dfrac{0.25}{\left(\dfrac{6,000}{2,000}\right)} - 0.015 - 0.008 - 0.03\right) = 0.028 = 2.8 \text{ } percent$$

B. $g(y) = 0.008 + \dfrac{2}{3}\cdot\left(\dfrac{0.25}{\left(\dfrac{6,000}{2,000}\right)} - 0.03 - 0.008 - 0.03\right) = 0.018 = 1.8$ *percent*

Faster growth of the labor force means that over time capital per worker will increase at a slower rate, which means output per worker will increase more slowly, decreasing the rate of growth of output per worker.

C. $g(y) = = 0.016 + \dfrac{2}{3}\cdot\left(\dfrac{0.25}{\left(\dfrac{6,000}{2,000}\right)} - 0.015 - 0.016 - 0.03\right) = 0.031 = 3.1$ *percent*

Faster growth of labor efficiency means that over time the ability of labor to produce output with a given amount of capital is increasing at a faster rate than when g = 0.8 percent, increasing the rate of growth of output per worker.

D. $g(y) = 0.008 + \dfrac{2}{3}\cdot\left(\dfrac{0.25}{\left(\dfrac{6,000}{2,000}\right)} - 0.015 - 0.008 - 0.05\right) = 0.015 = 1.5$ *percent*

A larger depreciation rate means that capital is wearing out more rapidly. The amount of capital available per worker is therefore growing at a slower rate than when the depreciation rate was 3 percent, and thus output per worker is growing at a slower rate as well.

E. $g(y) = 0.008 + \dfrac{2}{3}\cdot\left(\dfrac{0.20}{\left(\dfrac{6,000}{2,000}\right)} - 0.015 - 0.008 - 0.03\right) = 0.017 = 1.7$ *percent*

A lower saving rate means that there is less saving and therefore less investment in capital at every level of output. Less investment in capital means the capital stock, and thus the amount of capital per worker, will increase more slowly than when the saving rate is 25 percent. Slower increases in capital per worker mean slower increases in output per worker, decreasing the growth rate of output per worker.

12. A. $g\left(\dfrac{K}{Y}\right) = (1 - \alpha)\cdot\left(\dfrac{s}{\left(\dfrac{K_t}{Y_t}\right)} - \delta - n - g\right)$

$= \left(1 - \dfrac{2}{3}\right)\cdot\left(\dfrac{0.25}{\left(\dfrac{6,000}{2,000}\right)} - 0.03 - 0.015 - 0.008\right) = 0.010 = 1.0$ *percent*

B. $g\left(\dfrac{K}{Y}\right) = \left(1 - \dfrac{2}{3}\right)\cdot\left(\dfrac{0.25}{\left(\dfrac{6,000}{2,000}\right)} - 0.03 - 0.03 - 0.008\right) = 0.0051 = 0.51$ *percent*

Faster growth of the labor force means that the capital per worker ratio will grow more slowly over time. The slower growth of capital per worker means slower growth of output per worker. Because of the nature of the production function (and in particular, that $\alpha<1$), growth of capital per worker will slow faster than growth of output per worker, so overall, the growth of the capital-output ratio – which equals the growth of capital per worker divided by output per worker – will be slower. The growth rate of the capital-output ratio will decrease.

C. $g\left(\dfrac{K}{Y}\right) = \left(1 - \dfrac{2}{3}\right)\cdot\left(\dfrac{0.25}{\left(\dfrac{6,000}{2,000}\right)} - 0.03 - 0.015 - 0.016\right) = 0.0074 = 0.74$ *percent*

Faster growth of labor efficiency means that for a given growth rate of capital per worker, output per worker will grow more quickly than it did when labor efficiency was growing by 0.8 percent annually. An increase in the rate of growth of output per worker relative to the rate of growth of capital per worker means the growth of the capital-output ratio – which equals the growth of capital per worker divided by output per worker – will be slower. The growth rate of the capital-output ratio will decrease.

D. $g\left(\dfrac{K}{Y}\right) = \left(1 - \dfrac{2}{3}\right)\cdot\left(\dfrac{0.25}{\left(\dfrac{6,000}{2,000}\right)} - 0.05 - 0.015 - 0.008\right) = 0.0034 = 0.34$ *percent*

A higher depreciation rate means that capital wears out more quickly, decreasing the rate of growth of capital and of capital per worker. The slower growth of capital per worker means slower growth of output per worker. Because of the nature of the production function (and in particular, that $\alpha<1$), growth of capital per worker will slow faster than growth of output per worker, so overall, the growth of the capital-output ratio – which equals the growth of capital per worker divided by output per worker – will be slower. The growth rate of the capital-output ratio will decrease.

E. $g\left(\dfrac{K}{Y}\right) = \left(1 - \dfrac{2}{3}\right)\cdot\left(\dfrac{0.20}{\left(\dfrac{6,000}{2,000}\right)} - 0.03 - 0.015 - 0.008\right) = 0.0046 = 0.46$ *percent*

A decrease in the saving rate means that the capital stock and thus the amount of capital per worker will grow more slowly than it did when the saving rate was 25 percent. The slower growth of capital per worker means slower growth of output per worker. Because of the nature of the production function (and in particular, that $\alpha < 1$), growth of capital per worker will slow down faster than growth of output per worker, so overall, the growth of the capital-output ratio – which equals the growth of capital per worker divided by output per worker – will be slower. The growth rate of the capital-output ratio will decrease.

13. A. Shifts g(K/L) up and shifts g(Y/L) up, increasing steady-state K/Y
    B. No effect on g(K/L) and shifts g(Y/L) up, decreasing steady-state K/Y
    C. Shifts g(K/L) up and shifts g(Y/L) up, increasing steady-state K/Y
    D. Shifts g(K/L) up and shifts g(Y/L) up, increasing steady-state K/Y
    E. No effect on g(K/L); rotates g(Y/L) up at levels of K/Y below steady-state and down at levels of K/Y above steady-state, leaving steady-state K/Y unchanged

14. A. Shifts g(K/Y) up
    B. Shifts g(K/Y) down
    C. Shifts g(K/Y) up
    D. Shifts g(K/Y) up
    E. Rotates g(K/Y) down at levels of K/Y below steady-state and up at levels of K/Y above steady-state, leaving steady-state K/Y unchanged

15.

Period	K	L	E	Y/L	Y	K/Y
1	75,000	15	100	1,357.21	20,358.13	3.68
2	77,839.52	15.22	100.8	1,381.18	21,028.39	3.70
3	80,761.45	15.45	101.61	1,405.27	21,716.22	3.72
4	83,767.66	15.69	102.42	1,429.50	22,422.01	3.74
5	86,860.13	15.92	103.24	1,453.86	23,146.19	3.75

Sample calculations are for period 2.

$$K_2 = K_1 + s Y_1 - \delta \cdot K_1 = 75,000 + (0.25)\cdot(20,358.13) - (0.03)\cdot(75,000) = 77,839.53$$
$$L_2 = (L_1)\cdot(1 + n) = (15)\cdot(1 + 0.015) = 15.22$$
$$E_2 = (E_1)\cdot(1 + g) = (100)\cdot(1 + 0.008) = 100.8$$
$$\left(\frac{Y}{L}\right)_2 = \left(\frac{K_2}{L_2}\right)^\alpha \cdot (E_2)^{(1-\alpha)} = \left(\frac{77,839.53}{15.22}\right)^{\frac{2}{3}}\cdot(100.8)^{\frac{1}{3}} = 1,381.18$$
$$Y_2 = \left(\frac{Y_2}{L_2}\right)\cdot L_2 = (1,381.18)\cdot(15.22) = 21,028.39$$
$$\left(\frac{K}{Y}\right)_2 = \frac{K_2}{Y_2} = \frac{77,839.53}{21,028.39} = 3.70$$

The economy is not at its steady-state balanced-growth equilibrium; K/Y is increasing. If the economy was at its steady-state balanced growth equilibrium, K/Y would be constant.

16.

Period	K	L	E	Y/L	Y	K/Y
1	75,000.00	5	100	2,823.11	1,415.54	5.31
2	76,278.89	5.08	100.80	2,834.43	14,384.73	5.30
3	77,586.70	5.15	101.61	2,845.97	14,659.95	5.29
4	78,924.09	5.23	102.42	2,857.73	14,941.34	5.28
5	80,291.70	5.31	103.24	2,869.71	15,229.04	5.27

Sample calculations are for period 2.

$$K_2 = K_1 + s Y_1 - \delta \cdot K_1 = 75,000 + (0.25) \cdot (14,115.54) - (0.03) \cdot (75,000) = 76,278.89$$
$$L_2 = (L_1) \cdot (1 + n) = (5) \cdot (1 + 0.015) = 5.08$$
$$E_2 = (E_1) \cdot (1 + g) = (100) \cdot (1 + 0.008) = 100.8$$
$$\left(\frac{Y}{L}\right)_2 = \left(\frac{K_2}{L_2}\right)^\alpha \cdot (E_2)^{(1-\alpha)} = \left(\frac{76,278.89}{5.08}\right)^{\frac{2}{3}} \cdot (100.8)^{\frac{1}{3}} = 2,834.43$$
$$Y_2 = \left(\frac{Y_2}{L_2}\right) \cdot L_2 = (2,834.43) \cdot (5.08) = 14,384.73$$
$$\left(\frac{K}{Y}\right)_2 = \frac{K_2}{Y_2} = \frac{76,278.89}{14,384.73} = 5.30$$

The economy is not at its steady-state balanced-growth equilibrium; K/Y is decreasing. If the economy was at its steady-state balanced growth equilibrium, K/Y would be constant.

17.

Period	K	L	E	Y/L	Y	K/Y
1	75,000.00	7.14	100	2,226.26	15,895.48	4.72
2	76,723.87	7.25	100.80	2,243.87	16,261.55	4.72
3	78,487.54	7.36	101.61	2,261.63	16,636.08	4.72
4	80,291.93	7.47	102.42	2,279.52	17,019.26	4.72
5	82,137.99	7.58	103.24	2,297.57	17,411.29	4.72

Sample calculations are for period 2.

$$K_2 = K_1 + s Y_1 - \delta \cdot K_1 = 75,000 + (0.25) \cdot (15,895.48) - (0.03) \cdot (75,000) = 76,723.87$$
$$L_2 = (L_1) \cdot (1 + n) = (7.14) \cdot (1 + 0.015) = 7.25$$
$$E_2 = (E_1) \cdot (1 + g) = (100) \cdot (1 + 0.008) = 100.8$$
$$\left(\frac{Y}{L}\right)_2 = \left(\frac{K_2}{L_2}\right)^\alpha \cdot (E_2)^{(1-\alpha)} = \left(\frac{76,723.87}{7.25}\right)^{\frac{2}{3}} \cdot (100.8)^{\frac{1}{3}} = 2,243.87$$
$$Y_2 = \left(\frac{Y_2}{L_2}\right) \cdot L_2 = (2,243.87) \cdot (7.25) = 16,261.55$$
$$\left(\frac{K}{Y}\right)_2 = \frac{K_2}{Y_2} = \frac{76,723.87}{16,261.55} = 4.72$$

The economy is at its steady-state balanced-growth equilibrium; K/Y is constant. Notice that at the steady-state balanced-growth equilibrium, capital, labor, labor efficiency, the capital per worker ratio, and the output per worker ratio are all increasing. Further calculations would show you that output per worker and capital per worker are both increasing at a constant rate of about 0.8 percent per period.

18. In Question 15, K/Y begins at 3.68, which is below steady state; K/Y is rising so g(K/Y) is positive. In Question 16, K/Y begins at 5.31, which is above steady-state; K/Y is falling so g(K/Y) is falling. In Question 17, K/Y is constant at 4.72; that is the steady-state level of the capital-output ratio so g(K/Y) is 0.

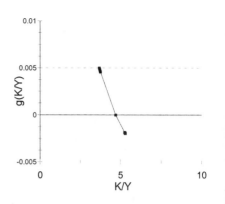

19. A. $\left(\dfrac{K}{Y}\right)_{ss} = 2.35$ and $\left(\dfrac{Y}{L}\right)_{ss} = 360.92$.

$$\left(\frac{K}{Y}\right)_{ss} = \frac{s}{(n+g+\delta)} = \frac{0.2}{(0.03+0.02+0.035)} = 2.35$$

$$\left(\frac{Y}{L}\right)_{ss} = \left[\left(\frac{K}{Y}\right)_{ss}^{\frac{\alpha}{1-\alpha}}\right]\cdot(E_t) = \left[2.35^{\left(\frac{0.6}{0.4}\right)}\right]\cdot 100 = 360.92$$

B. $\left(\dfrac{K}{Y}\right)_{ss} = 2.94$ and $\left(\dfrac{Y}{L}\right)_{ss} = 504.41$

C. $\left(\dfrac{K}{Y}\right)_{ss} = 2.11$ and $\left(\dfrac{Y}{L}\right)_{ss} = 305.46$

D. $\left(\dfrac{K}{Y}\right)_{ss} = 2.22$ and $\left(\dfrac{Y}{L}\right)_{ss} = 331.27$

E. $\left(\dfrac{K}{Y}\right)_{ss} = 1.90$ and $\left(\dfrac{Y}{L}\right)_{ss} = 262.88$

20. The graph depicts the production function and a straight line with slope of 1/2.35. The two curves intersect when Y/L = 360.92, the steady-state level of output per worker.

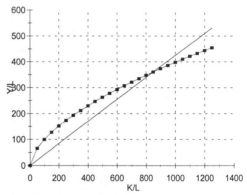

21. A. Steady-state output per worker is 53,153.0.

$$\left(\frac{K}{Y}\right)_{ss} = \frac{s}{(n+g+\delta)} = \frac{0.2}{(0.019+0.02+0.027)} = 3.03$$

$$\left(\frac{Y}{L}\right)_{ss} = \left[\left(\frac{K}{Y}\right)_{ss}^{\frac{\alpha}{1-\alpha}}\right]\cdot(E_t) = \left[3.03^{\left(\frac{0.7}{0.3}\right)}\right]\cdot 4{,}000 = 53{,}152.96$$

B. Steady-state output per worker is now 59,562, an increase of 12.1 percent.

$$\left(\frac{K}{Y}\right)_{ss} = \frac{s}{(n+g+\delta)} = \frac{0.21}{(0.019+0.02+0.027)} = 3.18$$

$$\left(\frac{Y}{L}\right)_{ss} = \left[\left(\frac{K}{Y}\right)_{ss}^{\frac{\alpha}{1-\alpha}}\right]\cdot(E_t) = \left[3.18^{\left(\frac{0.7}{0.3}\right)}\right]\cdot 4{,}000 = 56{,}561.98$$

$$\%\Delta\left(\frac{Y}{L}\right)_{ss} = \frac{\left(\frac{Y}{L}\right)_{ss}^{new}}{\left(\frac{Y}{L}\right)_{ss}^{old}} - 1 = \frac{56{,}561.98}{53{,}152.96} - 1 = 0.121 = 12.1 \ percent$$

C. Steady-state output per worker is now 38,244, a decrease of 28.0 percent.

$$\left(\frac{K}{Y}\right)_{ss} = \frac{s}{(n + g + \delta)} = \frac{0.2}{(0.019 + 0.02 + 0.037)} = 2.63$$

$$\left(\frac{Y}{L}\right)_{ss} = \left[\left(\frac{K}{Y}\right)_{ss}^{\frac{\alpha}{1-\alpha}}\right] \cdot (E_t) = \left[2.63^{\left(\frac{0.7}{0.3}\right)}\right] \cdot 4{,}000 = 38{,}244.14$$

$$\%\Delta\left(\frac{Y}{L}\right)_{ss} = \frac{\left(\frac{Y}{L}\right)_{ss}^{new}}{\left(\frac{Y}{L}\right)_{ss}^{old}} - 1 = \frac{38{,}244.14}{53{,}152.96} - 1 = -0.280 = -28.0 \; percent$$

D. Steady-state output per worker is now 77,987, an increase of 46.7 percent.

$$\left(\frac{K}{Y}\right)_{ss} = \frac{s}{(n + g + \delta)} = \frac{0.2}{(0.009 + 0.02 + 0.027)} = 3.57$$

$$\left(\frac{Y}{L}\right)_{ss} = \left[\left(\frac{K}{Y}\right)_{ss}^{\frac{\alpha}{1-\alpha}}\right] \cdot (E_t) = \left[3.57^{\left(\frac{0.7}{0.3}\right)}\right] \cdot 4{,}000 = 77{,}987.43$$

$$\%\Delta\left(\frac{Y}{L}\right)_{ss} = \frac{\left(\frac{Y}{L}\right)_{ss}^{new}}{\left(\frac{Y}{L}\right)_{ss}^{old}} - 1 = \frac{77{,}987.43}{53{,}152.96} - 1 = 0.467 = 46.7 \; percent$$

C. APPLYING CONCEPTS AND MODELS

1. A lower saving rate lowers K/Y in steady state, lowering Y/L, given E at steady state. But in steady-state balanced-growth equilibrium, Y/L and K/L will grow at the rate g which is unchanged. So the value of Y/L for any value of E will be lower, but at steady state, standards of living will continue to grow at the rate g.

2. The increase in savings will increase the steady-state balanced-growth value of the capital-output ratio. For a given value of labor efficiency, E, output per worker (standard of living) will also increase. The steady-state rate of growth of standards of living will not change, however, unless there is a change in the growth rate of labor efficiency.

3. A fall in the depreciation rate increases the steady-state capital-output ratio. Given the level of labor efficiency, E, steady-state levels of output per worker will rise.

D. EXPLAINING THE REAL WORLD

1. The question is asking about the effect of a change in the labor force growth rate on steady-state output per worker.

   The increase in women's labor force participation provides a period when the labor force is growing at a faster rate. For example, if women's labor force participation began at 20 percent and grew to 70 percent over a 50-year period, but then remained steady at 70 percent, then during those 50 years the labor force will be growing at a higher rate than before women's participation began to grow. After the 50-year period, labor force growth would fall back to the rate of growth of the population. During the 50-year period, faster labor force growth lowers K/Y in steady state, lowering Y/L given E at steady state. Increased labor force participation increases the worker-population ratio – the number of workers per capita. So even though output per worker will be lower (given E), output per capita will be higher.

2. The question is asking about the impact of changes in population growth and thus in labor force growth on steady-state output per worker.

   A decrease in population growth rates should also lower labor force growth rates, with a lag of about 15 years. A decrease in labor force growth rates will increase the steady-state capital-output ratio, increasing the steady-state level of output per worker given efficiency.

3. The question is asking about the effect of a change in labor efficiency on steady-state output per worker.

   All else constant, the development of steam power should increase standards of living in the long run because it would increase labor efficiency. Whether or not the growth rate of output per worker increased permanently would depend upon the continuation of technological developments that subsequently increased labor efficiency further.

4. The question is asking about the effect of a change in depreciation on steady-state output per worker.

   All else constant, replacing computer equipment because of the Y2K Bug did not increase the usable capital stock. The Y2K Bug essentially increased the rate of depreciation of computer equipment, rendering existing computer systems obsolete. That is, it increased the depreciation rate. An increase in the depreciation rate would lower steady-state capital-output ratio and, given a level of E, would lower output per worker. However if labor efficiency continued to grow at the same rate, g, then in the long run, equilibrium output per worker and capital per worker would also continue to grow at rate g. On the other hand, if the new computer equipment not only corrected the Y2K Bug but also enabled workers to produce more output with the same quantity of capital, it would have increased labor efficiency. The increase in labor efficiency would increase output per worker in steady state.

5. The question is asking about the different impacts of increasing labor efficiency and decreasing saving.

   Funding scientific research has the better chance of increasing standards of living in the long run if the research increases labor efficiency. Lowering taxes will lower government saving. All else constant, lower government saving decreases the steady-state capital-output ratio and, given labor efficiency, lowers steady-state output per worker. If consumers save the entire tax cut, then personal saving will rise to offset the drop in government saving, leaving total saving unchanged. In this case, however, there is still no long-run increase in the standard of living.

6. The question is asking about the long-run steady-state effect of changes in saving.

   In case [1], total saving declines, so the steady-state capital-output ratio declines, as does the steady-state level of output per worker. In case [2], total saving remains the same, so the steady-state capital-output ratio and the steady-state level of output per worker also remain the same. Case [3] is the same as case [2]! When consumers pay off debt, they are saving. Saving is simply "not spending on currently produced goods and services" so whether consumers put funds into their savings account or pay off their credit card bills, they are saving. In case [1], there are no long-run economic benefits. In cases [2] and [3], there are long-run *economic* benefits of the tax cut only if you assume that the government will lower its spending commensurate with the tax cut and that investment spending by the private sector is economically better than spending by the government. For instance, if investment spending by the private sector has a lower depreciation rate than government spending on infrastructure or other investment, then transferring funds from the government to the private sector can raise steady-state levels of the capital-output ratio and output per worker. It all depends upon the types of spending cuts imposed by Congress and the type of new spending undertaken by the private sector.

E. POSSIBILITIES TO PONDER

No solutions are given to these questions. The questions are designed to be somewhat open ended. Each question draws on your understanding of the concepts covered in this chapter.

Chapter 5

The Reality of Economic Growth: History and Prospect

- Modern patterns of economic growth began in about 1800 when the industrial revolution ended the Malthusian age.

- Worldwide distribution of standards of living is more unequal today than at any time in history.

LEARNING GUIDE

This chapter is primarily an application of the material in Chapter 4. There are no new models. There is much food for thought, however; this chapter addresses some of the most interesting "big think" questions in macroeconomics.

Be sure you keep the Solow growth model in mind as you read the chapter. Know when the model is applicable and when it is not. It might even be helpful to keep the steady-state equations in front of you as you read. That way you can see when Prof. DeLong is simply applying the model to real world dilemmas.

There are no Section C questions in this chapter.

Short on time?

 Before you study this chapter, find out what you are expected to learn from it. Some teachers will want you to be able to write thoughtful essay answers on the topics raised in this chapter; others may limit their testing to a few multiple-choice questions.

If you are not short on time, give yourself plenty of time to ponder the issues raised in this chapter. The material in this chapter can generate many fascinating late-night conversations.

A. BASIC DEFINITIONS

Before you apply knowledge, you need a basic grasp of the fundamentals. In other words, there are some things you just have to know. Knowing the material in this section won't guarantee a good grade in the course, but not knowing it will guarantee a poor or failing grade.

USE THE WORDS OR PHRASES FROM THE LIST BELOW TO COMPLETE THE SENTENCES. SOME ARE USED MORE THAN ONCE; SOME ARE NOT USED AT ALL.

1500	*industrial revolution*
agriculture	*Malthusian age*
China	*manufacturing*
convergence	*Mexico*
demographic transition	*patent*
divergence	*Russia*
education	*services*
India	*United States*

1. Sustained increases in both population and productivity of labor began about

   _____ .

2. A(n) _____ is characterized by a cycle of rising standards of living and rising population followed by declining standards of living and declining population.

3. A(n) _____ exists when natural resource scarcity imposes limits on growth.

4. A(n) _____ is characterized by an initial rise in birth rates and fall in death rates, followed by a decline in birth rates.

5. Modern economic growth is characterized by structural change – a shift in what is produced from _____ to _____ and then to

   _____ .

6. The countries in the G-7 organization are Canada, _____ , Japan, France, Germany, Italy, and Britain. The G-8 includes these 7 countries plus

   _____ .

7. A(n) _____ protects the property rights to an invention.

8. The widening of the worldwide distribution of standard of living is referred to as

_____ .

9. The most important factor in raising an economy's standard of living is

_____ .

CIRCLE THE CORRECT WORD OR PHRASE IN EACH OF THE FOLLOWING SENTENCES.

10. In the United States today, we <u>do / do not</u> live in a Malthusian age.

11. The Solow growth model <u>does / does not</u> explain 2000 years of economic history.

12. Official twentieth century GDP estimates for the United States are believed to <u>overstate / understate</u> inflation rates and <u>overstate / understate</u> real economic growth.

13. During the productivity growth slowdown, the American distribution of income <u>widened / narrowed.</u>

14. The worldwide distribution of the standard of living is <u>more / less</u> equal today than in the past.

15. In poor countries, capital equipment is <u>expensive / inexpensive</u> relative to its price in industrialized and prosperous economies.

16. Privately-funded research and development is a <u>public / private</u> good.

17. Without patent laws, profit-maximizing firms would conduct <u>more / less</u> research and development.

SELECT THE ONE BEST ANSWER FOR EACH MULTIPLE-CHOICE QUESTION.

18. Worldwide standards of living over the past 7000 years
    A. rose quickly and steadily.
    B. rose slowly and steadily.
    C. were constant.
    D. rose slowly until 1800 and quickly since then.

19. World population growth exploded in
    A. 1000.
    B. 1500.
    C. 1800.
    D. 1950.

20. A demographic transition is characterized by
    A. increasing birth rates and increasing death rates, followed by decreasing death rates.
    B. increasing birth rates and decreasing death rates, followed by decreasing birth rates.
    C. decreasing birth rates and decreasing death rates, followed by increasing death rates.
    D. decreasing birth rates and increasing death rates, followed by decreasing death rates.

21. A good rule-of-thumb as to whether people feel good about the economy is if they
    A. are able to buy a house.
    B. are better off financially than their households were when they were growing up.
    C. can afford to buy everything they want.
    D. are saving enough for retirement.

22. What variable has the strongest correlation with output per worker?
    A. schooling
    B. investment
    C. depreciation
    D. labor force growth

B. MANIPULATION OF CONCEPTS AND MODELS

Most instructors expect you to be able to do basic manipulation of the concepts. Being able to do so often means you can earn a C in a course. But if you want a better grade, you'll need to be able to complete this next section easily and move on to Sections C and D.

1. Why did higher standards of living lead to faster population growth in Malthus's era?

2. What is a "Malthusian age"?

3. What is a "demographic transition"? Name two countries that have experienced their demographic transition and two that have not.

4. What are the basic characteristics of the "industrial revolution"?

5. Describe the pattern of U.S. economic growth from about 1890 on. When was growth relatively rapid? When was it relatively slow?

6. Do official GDP estimates for the United States properly measure standards of living? Why or why not?

7. What are the three major characteristics contributing to rapid U.S. economic growth since 1890?

8. When did the twentieth-century productivity growth slowdown begin? Was it confined to the United States? What are the four factors usually offered as an explanation for the productivity growth slowdown? Are these explanations widely accepted? Explain.

9. Using the *Economic Report of the President (ERP),* look up the nonfarm business sector labor productivity growth rates. Calculate the average productivity growth rates for five-year periods from 1960 on. Write the data in the table at the right. Is the productivity growth slowdown over? According to Professor DeLong, in the 1990s what seemed to have ended the slowdown?

Years	Labor Productivity Growth Rate
1960-1964	
1965-1969	
1970-1974	
1975-1979	
1980-1984	
1985-1989	
1990-1994	
1995-1999	
past five years	

10. What is the "East Asian miracle"? What factors seem to account for this miracle?

11. What policies can increase investment, given limited personal saving, in poor countries?

12. What are the three most important benefits of increasing education?

13. Why is privately-funded research and development considered a public good, but other private investment spending is considered a private good?

NOTE: There are no Section C questions in this chapter.

D. EXPLAINING THE REAL WORLD

Most instructors are delighted when you are able to figure out which concept or model to apply to a real world situation. Being able to do so means you thoroughly understand the material and is often what you need to do to earn an A in a course. This is where you experience the power of macroeconomic theory.

1. The United Nations tries to decrease births and population growth by distributing birth control to women in poor countries. Will the policy hasten the demographic transition in those countries? Will it increase living standards?

2. Using the growth model presented in Chapter 4, what are the principal causes of divergence between countries in their standards of living?

3. The government of a poor country has a choice: fund education or fund road development. Which choice has greater long-run economic benefits? Why?

E. POSSIBILITIES TO PONDER

The more you learn, the more you realize you have more to learn. These questions go beyond the textbook material. They are the sort of questions that distinguish A+ or A work from A- work. Some of them may even serve as starting points for junior or senior year research papers.

1. What are the limits to growth today? Is the answer different for an industrialized country such as the United States than it is for a poor country such as Nigeria?

2. Do we need to know the causes of the productivity growth slowdown? Does the answer depend upon whether or not the slowdown has ended?

3. According to Textbook Table 5.4, countries that were behind the Iron Curtain have substantially lower GDP per capita than do non-Communist countries. What role did communism itself play in keeping incomes low?

4. What is the most sensible policy for a government to impose if it wants to maximize growth: strong patent laws or generous government funding of research and development? Why?

5. What are the connections between democracy and economic growth?

6. A letter to the editor of the San Francisco Chronicle stated, "Aren't we missing something here? The world's population is growing every day yet our research and development is aimed at 'labor-saving machines.' Machines don't buy goods, workers buy goods – when they have jobs to pay for them." How would you reply to the letter writer?

> **SOLUTIONS   SOLUTIONS   SOLUTIONS   SOLUTIONS**

A. BASIC DEFINITIONS

1. 1500
2. Malthusian age
3. Malthusian age
4. demographic transition

5. agriculture, manufacturing, service
6. United States; Russia

7. Patent
8. Divergence
9. Education

---

10. Do not
11. Does not
12. Overstate; understate

13. Widened
14. Less
15. Expensive

16. Public
17. Less

---

18. D
19. C

20. B
21. B

22. A

B. MANIPULATION OF CONCEPTS AND MODELS

1. Higher standards of living led to faster population growth for four major reasons.
   - Increased standards of living caused women to ovulate more frequently.
   - Women miscarried less often.
   - Increased nourishment of both women and children meant they were more resistant to disease, lowering mortality.
   - Increased standards of living made it easier to accumulate the financial resources needed to marry, leading women and men to marry at younger ages, increasing fertility within marriage.

2. A Malthusian age is a period of time when a population experiences the following cycle. Rising living standards lead to faster population growth. But faster population growth eventually results in fewer natural resources per person. This resource scarcity ultimately lowers labor productivity and living standards, rendering the population poor and malnourished. Increased mortality results. Over long stretches of time, population growth is thus approximately zero.

3. A demographic transition is a period of time characterized by an initial rise in birth rates and decline in death rates, followed by a decline in birth rates. During the initial period, the natural increase in the population is quite high; at the end of the transition, the natural population increase is minimal. See Textbook Figure 5.3 for lists of countries that have and have not experienced the demographic transition.

4. The industrial revolution was characterized by a burst of inventions (steam engine, spinning jenny, power loom, hydraulic press, railroad locomotive, water turbine, electric motor, and more). The industrial revolution marks the beginning of an era when it is expected that new technological developments will routinely revolutionize industries, and that these new developments will generate substantial increases in standards of living.

5. See Textbook Figure 5.5 and surrounding text. Output per worker rose about 1.6 percent annually from 1870 to 1929 and about 1.4 percent per year from 1929 to 1950. From 1950 to 1973 growth was about

2.1 percent per year. Growth rates slowed to almost zero from about 1970 to the early 1980s, and then increased rapidly in the past 20 years of the twentieth century.

6. No, official estimates do not properly measure changes in standard of living. It is difficult to measure changes in productivity and in standards of living generated by the invention of new goods and services and new types of goods and services. As a result, many economists believe official estimates overstate inflation and understate real economic growth, perhaps by as much as 1.0 percentage point annually.

7. The three major characteristics contributing to rapid U.S. economic growth since 1890 are that
   • public provision of education increased labor efficiency.
   • the U.S. economy is so large, it could take advantage of potential economies of scale.
   • the United States has a plentiful supply of natural resources, especially energy.

8. The productivity growth slowdown began in 1973 and appeared to end in about 1995. It was not confined to the United States, but affected all major industrialized economies. The four factors usually offered as explanation are
   • oil prices.
   • the baby boom.
   • increased problems of economic measurement.
   • environmental protection expenditures.

   There is no agreement as to the "correct" explanation(s) of the productivity growth slowdown.

9. In the *2001 Economic Report of the President*, the data are in Table B50: "output per hour of all persons: nonfarm business sector." It appears the productivity growth slowdown *may* be over, though this conclusion is based on less than a decade of data. According to Prof. DeLong, the slowdown ended due to technological revolution in computers and communications.

Years	Labor Productivity Growth Rate
1960-1964	3.38
1965-1969	2.30
1970-1974	2.12
1975-1979	1.76
1980-1984	1.40
1985-1989	1.36
1990-1994	1.56
1995-1999	2.14
past five years	

10. The East Asian miracle is discussed in Textbook Box 5.4. The so-called miracle is the very rapid increase in standards of living in the 50 years after World War II in South Korea, Hong Kong, Singapore, and Taiwan. Their successes seem to be attributable to
    • market-determined decisions about resource allocation.
    • encouragement of entrepreneurship and enterprise as a major government goal.
    • government policies that encourage high saving and investment rates.
    • government pursuance of industrial policy, including subsidizing corporations that are seen as strategic for economic development.

11. Investment in poor countries can be increased by policies that
    • welcome foreign investors' money, if the foreign-funded capital is used wisely.
    • encourage free trade.
    • subsidize investment spending by successful businesses.

12. Increasing education is good for an economy because
    • investment will increase, because any given investment in physical capital is more likely to be productive with a better educated work force.

- birth rates will decrease, because educated women are likely to want their children to be educated and are likely to have more attractive economic opportunities outside of the home.
- labor efficiency will increase, because more skills will be directly taught and because a better educated work force has an easier time generally at advancing and adapting technological change.

13. Not all the benefits from new discoveries that result from research and development (R&D) can be captured by the company that funded the R&D; other companies can copy the discovery and thus enjoy the benefits as well. But when a company purchases a new machine or constructs a building, it can exclude others from using those items.

D. EXPLAINING THE REAL WORLD

1. A policy of distributing birth control to women in poor countries *may* work to increase living standards, but it may fail. A country that has gone through its demographic transition and industrialized its economy is more likely to conform to the Solow model. In such cases, decreased birth rates can eventually lower labor force growth rates (n) and increase the standard of living, all else constant. However, in poor countries if there is not commensurate improvement in the standard of living, distribution of birth control may be less likely to hasten a demographic transition. In very poor countries where malnourishment is extensive and childhood mortality rates are high, a large number of births may be a family's strategy for ensuring that enough children live to adulthood to care for the parents in their old age.

2. Differences in standards of living result from differences in capital per worker and thus output per worker. Using the growth model of Chapter 4, the steady-state level of capital per worker is
$\frac{K}{Y_{ss}} = \frac{s}{n + g + \delta}$. So differences between countries could be due to differences in their saving rates, labor force growth rates, rate of growth of labor efficiency, or average rate of depreciation of existing the capital stock. [The textbook notes that two secondary causes of divergence are differences in creation and adaptation of technological change, and differences in the level of education.]

3. The question is asking you to think beyond the Solow growth model.

   Whether the government should choose to fund education or roads depends upon the current state of the transportation system. Increasing educational attainment has the potential to increase long-run economic growth through a number of means: increasing investment, lowering birth rates, and increasing labor efficiency. Educated workers can specialize in producing goods or services in which they have a comparative advantage and trade for other goods, thus enjoying the gains from trade. But if the country does not have roads that allow relatively inexpensive transportation of goods between producers and consumers, then the gains from trade will be limited.

E. POSSIBILITIES TO PONDER

No solutions are given to these questions. The questions are designed to be somewhat open ended. Each question draws on your understanding of the concepts covered in this chapter.

Chapter 6

Building Blocks of the Flexible-Price Model

- In the short run, the amounts of labor, capital, and other productive resources available for production are fixed. If we assume prices and wages are fully flexible, then the amount of resources that are actually employed will equal the amount of resources available.

- Total spending for output is the sum of consumption, investment, government, and net export spending. Different factors determine each of these four types of spending.

LEARNING GUIDE

This chapter begins a new section of the text in which we consider the economy in the short run. There is one important model in the chapter, one that allows for the determination of the actual amount of output when we assume prices and wages are fully flexible. There are several additional but more minor models, each of which will be components of comprehensive models in the future. Those models are the determination of consumption spending, investment spending, and net exports.

This chapter lays the groundwork for the model that is built in Chapter 7. In this chapter and the next, we assume that prices and wages are fully flexible. The assumption will lead us to the conclusion that the economy is always at full employment, a conclusion clearly not a reflection of the real world. Nonetheless we can gain some important insights into the functioning of the real world's economy even with this unrealistic assumption.

Short on time?

Find out from your instructor if you need to learn the material in the Appendices. Be sure you understand the determinants of consumption, investment, and net exports.

You want to learn how a full-employment economy works. You also want to learn the determinants of the components of total spending: consumption, investment, government purchases, gross exports, and gross imports.

A. BASIC DEFINITIONS

Before you apply knowledge, you need a basic grasp of the fundamentals. In other words, there are some things you just have to know. Knowing the material in this section won't guarantee a good grade in the course, but not knowing it will guarantee a poor or failing grade.

USE THE WORDS OR PHRASES FROM THE LIST BELOW TO COMPLETE THE SENTENCES. SOME ARE USED MORE THAN ONCE; SOME ARE NOT USED AT ALL.

appreciation	*investment*
buildings	*labor*
change	*machinery*
Cobb-Douglas	*marginal propensity to consume*
consumption	*nominal interest rates*
depreciation	*production function*
disposable	*productive resources*
foreign exchange traders	*real interest rates*
imports	*transfer payments*

1. The _____ is the change in consumption in response to a $1 change in disposable income.

2. The two sets of factors that determine the short-run levels of potential output and real wages are the _____ and the balance of supply and demand in the _____ market.

3. _____ income is what households have after they pay taxes and receive transfer payments.

4. The investment function is baseline investment minus the responsiveness of investment to changes in _____ times the real interest rate.

5. Retired workers' Social Security checks are examples of government _____.

6. A production function of the form $Y^* = (K)^{\alpha}(L \cdot E)^{1-\alpha}$ is a(n) _____ production function.

7. The amount of _____ spending depends on two sources: the real interest rate and business managers' and investors' confidence.

8. In the short run, the level of _____ is fixed.

9. Three types of purchases are included in investment spending: purchases of new business _____, new construction of _____, and _____ in business inventories.

> **NOTE:** Investment spending has a very specific meaning in economics. To understand, it might help to envision what someone is buying. You should visualize a <u>person</u> – perhaps a business owner, or a maintenance supervisor, or an ordering clerk. And you should see them buying <u>something durable</u> that was <u>produced</u> by another person in the <u>current</u> time period. For example, when the owner of the local McDonald's buys a new frying machine, that's investment. But when she buys napkins, that is *not* investment because napkins are not durable. When a self-employed lawyer buys law reference books, that's investment. When he hires an accountant to prepare his income taxes, that's not investment because services are never durable.

10. _____ spending is transactions that add to capital stock and increase potential output.

11. Labor, capital, land, and technology are all examples of the sorts of _____ that are fixed in quantity in the short run.

12. Exchange rates are determined by the actions of _____.

13. Government spending equals the sum of government purchases of goods and services plus _____.

14. Net taxes, T, equal taxes minus government _____.

15. We subtract _____ when computing total spending for GDP because some consumption, investment, and government purchases are for goods and services produced in other countries.

16. An decrease in the exchange rate is equivalent to a(n) _____ of the dollar.

17. Household saving is equal to _____ income minus _____ spending.

CIRCLE THE CORRECT WORD OR PHRASE IN EACH OF THE FOLLOWING SENTENCES.

18. An increase in expected profits causes investment spending to <u>increase / decrease.</u>

19. An increase in gross domestic product causes gross imports to <u>increase / decrease</u>.

20. Investment projects are undertaken if they are profitable; that is, if the discounted return on the investment is <u>greater / less</u> than the investment's cost.

21. An increase in interest rates causes a(n) <u>increase / decrease</u> in the discounted return on an investment project.

22. The classical assumption is that wages and prices are <u>flexible / inflexible</u>.

23. Government purchases of goods and services <u>include / exclude</u> transfer payments.

24. When the dollar <u>appreciates / depreciates</u>, the exchange rate increases.

25. When interest rates increase, investment spending <u>increases / decreases</u>.

26. An increase in foreign income causes gross exports to <u>increase / decrease</u>.

27. The model presented in Chapter 6 is sometimes called the <u>classical / Keynesian</u> model.

28. An increase in the real exchange rate causes gross exports to <u>increase / decrease</u>.

29. The values for real GDP found in the *Economic Report of the President* measure <u>actual / potential</u> output.

> **HINT:** The distinction between actual and potential output is important. Potential output is the amount of output that can be produced using all of the resources available. Actual output is what is recorded in the National Income and Product Accounts as "Real GDP." It is the amount of output actually produced with the resources available. Real GDP can be below potential output if some resources are left idle (unemployed) or are not used to their full potential (underemployment).

30. The marginal propensity to consume is always <u>less / more</u> than one (1).

31. Transfer payments are <u>excluded from / included in</u> GDP because no currently produced good or service is given to the government in exchange.

SELECT THE ONE BEST ANSWER FOR EACH MULTIPLE-CHOICE QUESTION.

32. Making the "classical assumption" of wage and price flexibility implies
    A. actual output equals potential output.
    B. there is full employment.
    C. there are no unintended inventory changes.
    D. all of the above.

 NOTE: Is the flexible price assumption realistic? Obviously not. But we can gain some useful insights by using the assumption. We will drop the assumption in Chapter 9.

33. Which of the following is investment spending?
    A. buying 100 shares of General Electric stock
    B. buying 100 shares of stock at an IPO (initial public offering)
    C. buying a new filing cabinet for the office
    D. buying a larger building for the office
    E. all of the above

34. Which of the following is subtracted from U.S. GDP to obtain total spending?
    A. a household's purchase of a Toyota Camry that was assembled in Kentucky
    B. a business's purchase of software that was produced in Taiwan
    C. a Brazilian tourist's purchase of dinner at a San Antonio restaurant
    D. all of the above

TO THE CHALKBOARD
Explaining the Production Function

The production function in Chapter 6 is equivalent to that in Chapter 4. Divide both sides of Chapter 6's production function by L, and you get Chapter 4's production function.

$$Y^* = (K)^\alpha (L \cdot E)^{1-\alpha}$$ Chapter 6 production function

$$\frac{Y^*}{L} = \frac{(K)^\alpha (L \cdot E)^{1-\alpha}}{L}$$ dividing both sides by L

$$\frac{Y^*}{L} = (K)^\alpha (L \cdot E)^{1-\alpha} (L)^{-1}$$ expressing 1/L in exponent form

$$\frac{Y^*}{L} = (K)^\alpha (L)^{1-\alpha} (E)^{1-\alpha} (L)^{-1}$$ distributing $(1-\alpha)$ exponent

$$\frac{Y^*}{L} = (K)^\alpha (L)^{1-\alpha-1} (E)^{1-\alpha}$$ gathering exponent terms for L

$$\frac{Y^*}{L} = (K)^\alpha (L)^{-\alpha} (E)^{1-\alpha}$$ simplifying exponent term for L

$$\frac{Y^*}{L} = \left(\frac{K}{L}\right)^\alpha (E)^{1-\alpha}$$ combining terms raised to α power, yielding

Chapter 4 production function

$\mathcal{B}$. MANIPULATION OF CONCEPTS AND MODELS

Most instructors expect you to be able to do basic manipulation of the concepts. Being able to do so often means you can earn a C in a course. But if you want a better grade, you'll need to be able to complete this next section easily and move on to Sections C and D.

1. Suppose the production function is
$Y = (K)^{\alpha}(L \cdot E)^{1-\alpha}$ and $\alpha = 0.6$, L = 250, and E = 10.

   A. Graph the relationship between capital stock and output in the space at the right. Let K range from 0 to 7,000.

   B. Suppose instead $\alpha = 0.8$. Graph a new production function. In words in the space below, describe what happens to the shape of the production function as α increases.

NOTE: Suppose the economy-wide production function is
$Y = (K)^{\alpha}(L \cdot E)^{1-\alpha}$. Assume the value of E is the same for all firms (or companies). Assume the production function applies to each individual firm. Assume each firm has one (1) unit of capital. Then for each firm,
$$Y_{firm} = (1)^{\alpha} [(L_{firm}) \cdot (E)]^{1-\alpha}$$
where Y_{firm} is the output produced by a firm and L_{firm} is the amount of labor employed by that firm. Since $1^{\alpha} = 1$, after distributing the exponent $(1 - \alpha)$ we have
$$Y_{firm} = (L_{firm})^{1-\alpha} \cdot (E)^{1-\alpha}$$

2. Suppose the production function is $Y^* = (K)^{0.6}(L \cdot E)^{1-0.6}$. Suppose each firm (or company) has one unit of capital, K. Suppose labor efficiency, E, equals 100 for each firm.

   A. At Lee's Construction Firm, employment L_{Lee} is 1,000. What is the level of output at Lee's Construction, Y_{Lee}?

   B. At Jarrel's Consulting Firm, employment L_{Jarrel} is 500. What is the level of output at Jarrel's Consulting, Y_{Jarrel}?

C. At a typical firm, employment L_{firm} is 850. What is the level of output at the typical firm, Y_{firm}?

TO THE CHALKBOARD:
Deriving MPL = [(1 - α) · (E)$^{1-\alpha}$] / [L$^{\alpha}$]

The MPL equation is the expression for the marginal product of labor. Here is a step-by-step explanation of its derivation. The MPL is the additional output, Y, that can be produced from one additional unit of labor, L. If you know calculus, you can see that the MPL is just the derivative of the production function with regard to labor. If you do not know calculus, you'll see that the derivation of MPL is a little more roundabout.

Method 1: With calculus

For an individual firm with K = 1, the production function is $Y = (L)^{1-\alpha} \cdot (E)^{1-\alpha}$. Taking the derivative yields

$$MPL = \frac{\partial Y}{\partial L} = \frac{\partial}{\partial L}\left[(L)^{1-\alpha} \cdot (E)^{1-\alpha}\right] \qquad \text{MPL is partial derivative of output}$$

$$MPL = (E)^{1-\alpha} \cdot \frac{\partial L^{1-\alpha}}{\partial L} \qquad \text{isolating constant term, } (E)^{1-\alpha}$$

$$MPL = (E)^{1-\alpha} \cdot \left[(1-\alpha)L^{1-\alpha-1}\right] \qquad \text{derivative of } x^a \text{ with regard to x is } ax^{a-1}$$

$$MPL = (E)^{1-\alpha} \cdot (1-\alpha) \cdot L^{-\alpha} \qquad \text{simplifying}$$

$$MPL = \frac{(1-\alpha) \cdot E^{1-\alpha}}{L^{\alpha}} \qquad \text{rearranging terms to match text}$$

Method 2: Without calculus

To derive the expression for MPL without using calculus, we proceed as follows. The MPL is the additional output produced with one additional unit of labor, so we have

$$MPL = F(K, L+1) - F(K, L) \qquad \text{applying definition of MPL}$$

$$MPL = F(1, L+1) - F(1, L) \qquad \text{by assumption, K = 1 for each firm}$$

$$MPL = (1)^{\alpha} \cdot (L+1)^{1-\alpha} \cdot (E)^{1-\alpha} - (1)^{\alpha} \cdot (L)^{1-\alpha} \cdot (E)^{1-\alpha} \qquad \text{applying Cobb–Douglas production function}$$

$$MPL = (E)^{1-\alpha} \cdot \left[(L+1)^{1-\alpha} - (L)^{1-\alpha}\right] \qquad \text{simplifying}$$

To go further, we need to use a proportional growth rule. The application may not be obvious.

$$g\left(L^{(1-\alpha)}\right) = (1-\alpha) \cdot g(L) \qquad \text{application of proportional growth rule}$$

$$\frac{(L+1)^{(1-\alpha)} - L^{(1-\alpha)}}{L^{(1-\alpha)}} = (1-\alpha)\frac{(L+1)-L}{L} \qquad \text{expanding } g(\cdot) \text{ terms}$$

$$(L+1)^{(1-\alpha)} - L^{(1-\alpha)} = (1-\alpha) \cdot \frac{L+1-L}{L} \cdot L^{(1-\alpha)} \qquad \text{multiplying both sides of equation by } L^{(1-\alpha)}$$

$$(L+1)^{(1-\alpha)} - L^{(1-\alpha)} = (1-\alpha) \cdot \frac{1}{L} \cdot L^{(1-\alpha)} \qquad \text{simplifying } L+1-L$$

$$(L+1)^{(1-\alpha)} - L^{(1-\alpha)} = (1-\alpha) \cdot L^{-1} \cdot L^{(1-\alpha)} \qquad \text{applying exponent rule to } \frac{1}{L}$$

$$(L+1)^{(1-\alpha)} - L^{(1-\alpha)} = (1-\alpha) \cdot L^{(-1+1-\alpha)} \qquad \text{using exponent rule to combine L terms}$$

$$(L+1)^{(1-\alpha)} - L^{(1-\alpha)} = (1-\alpha) \cdot L^{(-\alpha)} \qquad \text{simplifying } L^{(-1+1-\alpha)}$$

$$(L+1)^{(1-\alpha)} - L^{(1-\alpha)} = (1-\alpha) \cdot \frac{1}{L^{\alpha}} \qquad \text{applying exponent rule to } L^{(-\alpha)}$$

Now we can substitute this last term into our MPL equation:

$$MPL = (E)^{1-\alpha} \cdot \left[(L+1)^{1-\alpha} - (L)^{1-\alpha} \right] \quad \text{from above}$$

$$MPL = (E)^{1-\alpha} \cdot \left[(1-\alpha) \cdot \frac{1}{L^\alpha} \right] \quad \text{substituting for } \left[(L+1)^{1-\alpha} - (L)^{1-\alpha} \right]$$

$$MPL = \frac{(1-\alpha) \cdot E^{1-\alpha}}{L^\alpha} \quad \text{rearranging terms to match text}$$

3. Suppose the production function is $Y^* = (K)^{0.6}(L \cdot E)^{1-0.6}$. Suppose each firm (or company) has one unit of capital, K. Suppose labor efficiency, E, equals 100 for each firm.

   A. At Lee's Construction Firm, employment L_{Lee} is 1,000. What is the marginal product of labor at Lee's Construction, MPL_{Lee}?

   B. At Jarrel's Consulting Firm, employment L_{Jarrel} is 500. What is the marginal product of labor at Jarrel's Consulting, MPL_{Jarrel}?

   C. At a typical firm, employment L_{firm} is 850. What is the marginal product of labor at the typical firm, MPL_{firm}?

TO THE CHALKBOARD:
Deriving the Individual Firm's Labor Demand Equation

The profit-maximizing firm will hire labor up to the point where the value of labor's marginal product, $P \cdot MPL$, equals the wage rate. Starting from that point, we can derive the equation for a firm's labor demand.

$$P \cdot MPL = W \quad \text{profit- maximizing condition}$$

$$P \cdot \frac{(1-\alpha) \cdot E^{1-\alpha}}{L^\alpha} = W \quad \text{substituting expression for MPL}$$

$$P \cdot \frac{(1-\alpha) \cdot E^{1-\alpha}}{W} = L^\alpha \quad \text{multiplying by } L^\alpha \text{ and dividing by } W$$

$$\frac{(1-\alpha) \cdot E^{1-\alpha}}{\frac{W}{P}} = L^\alpha \quad \text{multiplying by } \frac{\frac{1}{P}}{\frac{1}{P}}$$

$$\left(\frac{(1-\alpha) \cdot E^{1-\alpha}}{\frac{W}{P}} \right)^{\frac{1}{\alpha}} = L \quad \text{raising both sides of equation to the } \frac{1}{\alpha} \text{ power}$$

4. Suppose the production function is $Y^* = (K)^{0.6}(L \cdot E)^{1-0.6}$. Suppose each firm (or company) has one unit of capital, K. Suppose labor efficiency, E, equals 100 for each firm.

A. At Lee's Construction Firm, current employment L_{Lee} is 1,000. Suppose the firm can sell its product for $250. Suppose the market wage faced by the firm is $10. What is the profit-maximizing demand for labor at Lee's Construction, D_{Lee}? Are they at profit-maximizing equilibrium? If not, do they need to increase or decrease employment?

B. At Jarrel's Consulting Firm, current employment L_{Jarrel} is 500. Suppose the firm can sell its product for $100. Suppose the market wage faced by the firm is $10. What is the profit-maximizing demand for labor at Jarrel's Consulting, D_{Jarrel}? Are they at profit-maximizing equilibrium? If not, do they need to increase or decrease employment?

C. At a typical firm, current employment L_{firm} is 850. Suppose the firm can sell its product for $300. Suppose the market wage faced by the firm is $10. What is the profit-maximizing demand for labor at the typical firm, D_{firm}? Is the firm at profit-maximizing equilibrium? If not, does the firm need to increase or decrease employment?

NOTE: Assuming that each firm charges the same price for its product and faces the same wage rate for workers may be unrealistic, but it makes the rest of the math easier, and is consistent with the model as presented in Textbook Chapter 6. In the next question, we make those two assumptions.

5. Suppose the production function is $Y^* = (K)^{0.6}(L \cdot E)^{1-0.6}$. Suppose each firm (or company) has one unit of capital, K. Suppose labor efficiency, E, equals 100 for each firm. Suppose each firm can sell its product for $250. Suppose the market wage faced by each firm is $10.

A. At Lee's Construction Firm, current employment L_{Lee} is 1,000. What is the profit-maximizing demand for labor at Lee's Construction, D_{Lee}? Are they at profit-maximizing equilibrium? If not, do they need to increase or decrease employment?

B. At Jarrel's Consulting Firm, current employment L_{Jarrel} is 500. What is the profit-maximizing demand for labor at Jarrel's Consulting, D_{Jarrel}? Are they at profit-maximizing equilibrium? If not, do they need to increase or decrease employment?

C. At a typical firm, current employment L_{firm} is 850. What is the profit-maximizing demand for labor at the typical firm, D_{firm}? Is the firm at profit-maximizing equilibrium? If not, does the firm need to increase or decrease employment?

6. If the efficiency of labor, E, increases, what is the effect on a firm's labor demand? Answer the question by thinking about the economics of the relationship.

7. If the real wage is higher, what is the effect on a firm's labor demand? Answer the question by thinking about the economics of the relationship.

8. If α increases, what is the effect on a firm's labor demand? Answer the question by thinking about the economics of the relationship.

TO THE CHALKBOARD:
Deriving the Economy-wide Labor Demand Equation

The profit-maximizing firm will hire labor up to the point where the value of labor's marginal product, P·MPL, equals the wage rate. Assume each firm is hiring one unit of capital. Following the textbook, assume the number of firms in the economy is K. Economy-wide demand for labor, L, will thus be K times each firm's labor demand.

$$K \cdot \left(\frac{(1-\alpha) \cdot (E)^{1-\alpha}}{\frac{W}{P}} \right)^{\frac{1}{\alpha}} = L \qquad \textit{K times individual firm's labor demand}$$

$$(K)^{\alpha} \cdot \left(\frac{(1-\alpha) \cdot (E)^{1-\alpha}}{\frac{W}{P}} \right) = (L)^{\alpha} \qquad \textit{raising both sides of equation to } \alpha \textit{ power}$$

$$\frac{(K)^{\alpha}}{(L)^{\alpha}} \cdot (1-\alpha) \cdot (E)^{1-\alpha} = \frac{W}{P} \qquad \textit{dividing both sides by W/P and } (L)^{\alpha}$$

$$(1-\alpha)\left[\left(\frac{K}{L} \right)^{\alpha} \cdot (E)^{1-\alpha} \right] = \frac{W}{P} \qquad \textit{rearranging terms and add brackets}$$

$$(1-\alpha)\left(\frac{Y}{L} \right) = \frac{W}{P} \qquad \textit{substituting for definition of Y/L}$$

9. Suppose there are 2,000 firms in an economy. Suppose each firm owns one unit of capital. Suppose the real wage, W/P, is $0.50. Suppose that for each firm labor efficiency, E, is 100 and the Cobb-Douglas parameter, α, is 0.6.

   A. What is each firm's labor demand? What is each firm's actual output?

   B. What is the economy-wide actual output? What is the economy-wide potential output?

TO THE CHALKBOARD:
Demonstrating that Actual and Potential Output Are Equal

When wages and prices are flexible, workers will be hired up to the point where the value of their marginal product (P·MPL) equals the wage (W). In this case, the actual amount of output produced in the economy will equal the potential amount of output that the economy could produce if all resources were fully employed. In other words, in an economy where wages and prices are flexible, there will always be full employment. Here is a step-by-step demonstration of this conclusion.

$$Y_{firm} = K_{firm}^{\alpha} \cdot (L_{firm} \cdot E)^{1-\alpha} \qquad \text{individual firm's output}$$

$$Y_{firm} = (K_{firm})^{\alpha} \cdot (E)^{1-\alpha} \cdot (L_{firm})^{1-\alpha} \qquad \text{distributing exponent and rearranging terms}$$

$$Y_{firm} = (1)^{\alpha} \cdot (E)^{1-\alpha} \cdot \left(\frac{L}{K}\right)^{1-\alpha} \qquad \begin{array}{l}\text{for each firm } K_{firm} = 1, \text{ and} \\ L_{firm} = \frac{1}{K} \times \text{economywide labor demand, } L\end{array}$$

- -

$$Y = (\text{number of firms}) \cdot Y_{firm} \qquad \text{definition of total output, } Y$$

$$Y = (K) \cdot Y_{firm} \qquad \text{substituting in number of firms, } K$$

$$Y = (K) \cdot \left[(1)^{\alpha} \cdot (E)^{1-\alpha} \cdot \left(\frac{L}{K}\right)^{1-\alpha} \right] \qquad \text{substituting in expression for } Y_{firm}$$

$$Y = (K) \cdot (E)^{1-\alpha} \cdot \frac{(L)^{1-\alpha}}{(K)^{1-\alpha}} \qquad \text{simplifying and distributing exponent}$$

$$Y = (K)^{1-(1-\alpha)} \cdot (E)^{1-\alpha} \cdot (L)^{1-\alpha} \qquad \text{gathering } K \text{ terms}$$

$$Y = (K)^{\alpha} \cdot (E)^{1-\alpha} \cdot (L)^{1-\alpha} \qquad \text{simplifying } K^{1-(1-\alpha)}$$

$$Y = (K)^{\alpha} \cdot (L \cdot E)^{1-\alpha} \qquad \text{rearranging terms and gathering } L \text{ and } E \text{ terms}$$

$$Y = \text{potential output} \qquad \text{definition of potential output is } (K)^{\alpha} \cdot (L \cdot E)^{1-\alpha}$$

---

10. A. Using the *Economic Report of the President*, look up values for nominal GDP and nominal national income for 1990.

   B. In the textbook, we assume GDP = national income, and we use Y to stand for both GDP and national income. Is the assumption realistic? Why do we make the assumption?

11. Using the *Economic Report of the President*, look up values for nominal GDP, federal and state and local government receipts, and federal and state and local expenditures for transfer payments. Then calculate net taxes, T, and the tax rate, t. Write your answers in the table below.

	Nominal GDP (billion $)	Government receipts (billion $)	Government transfer payments (billion $)	Net taxes, T (billion $)	Tax rate, t (percent)
1960	527.4	131.2	26.3		
1965				139.4	19.4 %
1970					
1975					
1980					
1985					
1990					
1995					
last year available					

HINT: We assume that net taxes equal the average tax rate times income: T = t·Y. For example, if Y = $9,000 billion and T = $900 billion, then t = 0.10 or 10 percent. This is the **average** tax rate, computed as T ÷ Y. The more familiar tax rates – often called tax brackets – are **marginal** tax rates. For example, Amit earns $40,000 per year. Suppose he is taxed 10 percent on the first $15,000 of earnings, 20 percent on the next $20,000, and 30 percent on the last $5,000. Amit might say, "I'm in the 30 percent tax bracket." He may even think to himself that he is paying 30 percent of his income to the government in taxes. But 30 percent is just his *marginal* tax rate – the rate paid on the last dollar of earnings. In fact, Amit's total tax bill is (0.10)·(15,000) + (0.20)·(20,000) + (0.30)·(5,000) = $5,950. Amit's *average* tax rate, t, is therefore 5,950 ÷ 40,000 = 0.149 or 14.9 percent.

Describe the tax rate pattern since 1960.

12. Suppose income is 50,000, tax payments are 10,000, and transfer payments are 1,000.
    A. What is the value of the tax rate, t?

    B. What is the value of disposable income, Y^D?

    C. Suppose consumption spending is 39,000. What is the value of household saving, S^H?

> **HINT**: It is important to remember which symbols represent constants and which ones represent variables. Consider the consumption function, $C = C_0 + C_Y(1 - t)Y$. The constants in the equation are C_0, C_Y, and t. The variables are Y and C. When the value of Y changes (varies), then the value of C will also change (vary). For example, the consumption function could be $C = 100 + 0.8(1 - 0.2)Y$. If $Y = 1,000$, then $C = 100 + 0.8(1 - 0.2)(1,000) = 740$.

13. Suppose the consumption function is $C = C_0 + C_Y \cdot (1 - t) \cdot Y$.
    A. Suppose $C_0 = 500$, $C_Y = 0.8$, and $t = 0.2$. Complete the table at the right.

Y	C
0	
1,000	
5,000	

    B. What is the value of income, Y, at which household saving, S^H, equals zero (0)?

    C. Graph the consumption function in the space at the right. Label your curve and your axes.

> **NOTE:** The consumption function refers to total Consumption *for the economy as a whole.* Not everyone may – or probably does – behave this way. But one person's quirky saving behavior is offset by another person's penchant for overspending. So on average, for the economy as a whole, one consumption function does describe our behavior.

14. Using the *Economic Report of the President*, look up nominal values for personal consumption expenditures, personal saving, disposable personal income, and the saving rate, for the years in the table below. Describe the pattern of the saving rate since 1960.

	Disposable Income (billion $)	Consumption Expenditure (billion $)	Household Saving (billion $)	Saving Rate (percent)
1960	366.2	332.3		
1965			42.7	
1970				
1975				
1980				
1985				
1990				
1995				
last year available				

15. Suppose the consumption function is $C = C_0 + C_Y \cdot (1 - t)Y$. Suppose that

Baseline consumption	400
Marginal propensity to consume	0.75
Average tax rate	0.15

A. Suppose in 1990, an economy's real GDP was $10,000 million. What was that economy's total consumption spending?

B. Suppose in 1991, national income increased by $1,000 million. What is the change in the economy's value of disposable income? What is the change in its value of consumption? Calculate your answers **without** using the consumption function, $C = C_0 + C_Y \cdot (1 - t)Y$.

16. Keshia owns a beauty supply store. She is considering buying a new display rack for hair care supplies. She hopes the new rack will increase her sales of supplies. Keshia estimates the rack will last five years, after which time she will need to throw it out and buy a new one.

    A. What interest rate should Keshia use to determine if her investment will be profitable?

    B. The rack costs $795. Keshia estimates the discounted present value of the future supply sales is $700. Should she buy the rack?

    C. A few months later, interest rates fall as the Fed tries to avert a possible recession. Keshia reconsiders her decision regarding the display rack. Why?

17. Sum Yee is a manager for a large real estate developer. She is preparing a report for the board of directors regarding potential projects. They are considering the Trilon project, a 300-home subdivision that will take four years to design and build. Homes will be offered for sale in 3 years. They expect most of the homes will be sold before the last home is completed. If they undertake the project, the corporation needs to borrow $30 million now to cover its costs. The best interest rate that Sum Yee can obtain from lenders is 12 percent. What additional information does Sum Yee need to determine if the Trilon project will be profitable?

18. When the interest rate is 8 percent, total investment spending is $1,600 billion per quarter. When interest rates decrease to 6 percent, some previously unprofitable investment projects become profitable. What is the likely effect on investment spending in the economy?

19. Using the *Economic Report of the President*, look up values for nominal investment spending given in the table below. Describe trends in the distribution of investment spending over time.

	Private Fixed Investment (billion $)	Non-residential Buildings (billion $)	Information Processing Equipment & Software (billion $)	Industrial Equipment (billion $)	Transportation Equipment (billion $)	Residential Buildings (billion $)
1960	75.7	12.0				26.3
1965			8.5			
1970						
1975						
1980						
1985						
1990						
1995						
last year available						

20. Using the *Economic Report of the President*, look up values for nominal private fixed investment spending and nominal GDP and write them into the table below. Describe the pattern of investment spending as a share of GDP over time.

	Private Fixed Investment (billion $)	Nominal GDP (billion $)	Investment as a share of GDP (percent)
1960	75.7	527.4	
1965			
1970			
1975			
1980			
1985			
1990			
1995			
last year available			

21. Suppose investment spending can be described by $I = I_0 - I_r \cdot r$. Suppose $I_0 = 2000$ and $I_r = 4000$.

    A. Complete the table at the right.

       (**HINT**: If the interest rate is 5 percent, express it in the equation as 0.05.)

r	I
2	
4	
6	
8	

    B. Graph the investment equation in the space at the right. Label your axes. Label your curve I_1.

    C. Suppose business optimism increases, leading business people to increase the amount of revenue they think they will earn from investment projects. What is the effect on baseline investment, I_0? Draw a second investment curve in the graph above. Label this new curve I_2.

22. Using the *Economic Report of the President*, look up nominal values for GDP and government spending, as indicated in the table below. The data for transfer payments are in a different table than the rest of the data. Describe the pattern of government spending over time.

	Nominal GDP (billion $)	Total Government Purchases (billion $)	Federal Defense Purchases (billion $)	Federal Nondefense Purchases (billion $)	State & Local Purchases (billion $)	Transfer Payments (billion $)	Government Spending as a Share of GDP (percent)
1960	527.4	65.9	55.2	10.7	47.9	26.3	
1965							
1970							
1975							
1980						275.0	
1985							
1990							
1995							
last year available							

> **HINT**: It is again important to remember which symbols represent constants and which ones represent variables. Consider the gross export function, $GX = X_f \cdot Y^f + X_\varepsilon \cdot \varepsilon$. The constants in the equation are X_f and X_ε. The variables are Y^f and ε. When the value of Y_f changes (varies), then the value of GX will also change (vary). When the value of ε changes (varies), then the value of GX will also change (vary). For example, the gross export function could be $GX = 10 \cdot Y^f + 80 \cdot \varepsilon$. If $Y_f = 1,000$ and $\varepsilon = 40$, then $GX = 10(1,000) + 80(40) = 13,200$.

23. Suppose the gross exports function is $GX = \left(X_f \cdot Y^f\right) + \left(X_\varepsilon \cdot \varepsilon\right)$. Suppose the responsiveness of gross exports to changes in foreign income is 40. Suppose the responsiveness of gross exports to changes in the real exchange rate is 20. Calculate the values of gross exports in the table at the right.

Y^f	ε	GX
100	300	
100	400	
200	400	

24. A. When foreign income increases, gross exports increase. Why?

    B. When real exchange rates increase, gross exports increase. Why?

25. Give two reasons why it takes time for a change in the real exchange rate to affect gross exports.

26. The gross imports function is $IM = IM_y \cdot Y$. Suppose the responsiveness of gross imports to a change in gross domestic product is 6. Complete the table at the right.

Y	IM
4000	
6000	
8000	

27. Using the *Economic Report of the President*, look up nominal values for GDP, gross imports, and gross exports for the years shown in the table below. Calculate the ratios of imports to GDP and exports to GDP. Describe trends over time in imports into the United States and exports out of the United States.

	Nominal GDP (billion $)	Gross Exports (billion $)	Exports as a share of GDP (percent)	Gross Imports (billion $)	Imports as a share of GDP (percent)
1960	527.4			22.8	
1965					
1970		57.0			
1975					
1980					
1985					
1990					
1995					
last year available					

28. The exchange rate is determined by foreign exchange traders responding to changes in real interest rates. The determinants of the real exchange rate, ε, can be expressed as

$$\varepsilon = \varepsilon_0 - \varepsilon_r \cdot (r - r^f)$$

r	r^f	ε
10	8	
10	12	
12	12	

A. Suppose $\varepsilon_0 = 20$ and $\varepsilon_r = 6$. Complete the table above.

B. When domestic real interest rates increase, do real exchange rates increase or decrease? Explain.

C. When foreign real interest rates increase, do real exchange rates increase or decrease? Explain.

> **NOTE:** By assuming that exchange rates depend upon the confluence of fear and greed and their impact on the actions of foreign exchange traders, we have implicitly assumed that changes in the domestic demand for foreign goods and services and in the foreign demand for domestic goods and services do not have a perceptible impact on the foreign exchange rate. In the current economic and financial environment, that is probably a good assumption to make. In Chapter 15 we consider how the models change when we assume instead that exchange rates depend as well on domestic demand for foreign goods and service and foreign demand for domestic goods and services.

29. The equation for net exports is

    $$NX = (X_f \cdot Y^f) + (X_\varepsilon \cdot \varepsilon) - (IM_y \cdot Y)$$

    A. Suppose $X_f = 300$, $X_\varepsilon = 50$, and $IM_y = 200$. Complete the table at the right.

Y^f	ε	Y	NX
250	20	300	
250	20	400	
250	25	400	
300	25	400	

    B. When domestic income increases, do net exports increase or decrease? Explain.

    C. When the real exchange rate increases, do net exports increase or decrease? Explain.

    D. When foreign income increases, do net exports increase or decrease? Explain .

30. The real exchange rate depends upon real interest rates according to the equation

    $$\varepsilon = \varepsilon_0 - \varepsilon_r \cdot (r - r^f)$$

    Substituting this equation into the net exports equation yields

    $$NX = (X_f \cdot Y^f) + (X_\varepsilon \cdot \varepsilon_0) - (X_\varepsilon \cdot \varepsilon_r \cdot r) + (X_\varepsilon \cdot \varepsilon_r \cdot r^f) - (IM_y \cdot Y)$$

    A. When domestic interest rates increase, do net exports rise or fall? Why?

    B. When foreign interest rates increase, do net exports rise or fall? Why?

31. What is the difference between a permanent and a transitory change in income?

32. Stanley has the chance to purchase an annuity that pays $1,000 annually for his lifetime. When he dies, the annuity will be received by his son, who is currently just 3 years old. He estimates that the average interest rate over this almost-indefinite period will be 5 percent. What is the present value of the annuity? What is the maximum price Stanley should pay for the annuity?

C. APPLYING CONCEPTS AND MODELS

Now we're getting to the good stuff. Being able to apply a specific concept or model to a real world situation — where you are told which model to apply but you have to figure out how to apply it — is often what you need to earn a B in a course. This is where macroeconomics starts to become interesting and the world starts to make more sense.

1. When diminishing returns to investment set in quickly, real incomes are low. Use the equation from the labor demand and supply model to explain why.

2. Stock values increase, making everyone who owns stock feel wealthier. What is the effect on the consumption function? Why?

3. Tax rebate checks of $300 are used to pay off $300 worth of credit card debt. What is the value of the marginal propensity to consume in this case?

4. Tax rebate checks of $300 are used to buy $300 worth of new clothes. What is the value of the marginal propensity to consume in this case?

5. In reference to the Great Depression, President Franklin Delano Roosevelt once said, "All we have to fear is fear itself." What is the impact of fear on consumption spending?

6. Give two examples of events that might change baseline consumption, C_0. Give two examples of events that might change the marginal propensity to consume, C_Y.

7. A lottery official argues a new rule should be established: all lottery winners should be forced to take their winnings in annual checks over a 30-year period. No one would be allowed to take a lump sum payment. He argues this new rule will increase consumption spending and benefit the state's economy. Do you agree with his argument? Why or why not?

8. Federal Reserve Chairman Alan Greenspan hopes to keep businesspeople calm when the economy seems to be chaotic. Use the investment function to explain why calm businesspeople buy more business equipment than panicky ones.

9. The government faces a choice between lowering taxes by $100 billion and increasing its purchases by $100 billion. Which action has a larger effect on total spending, C + I + G + NX? Using the concept of the marginal propensity to consume, explain why.

10. To lower its budget deficit, the government faces a choice between decreasing government purchases by $300 billion and lowering transfer payments by $300 billion. Which action will have a smaller effect on total spending, C + I + G + NX? Using the concept of the marginal propensity to consume, explain why.

11. Recession hits Japan. What is the effect on gross exports from the United States to Japan?

12. The rate of price inflation in Brazil is greater than the rate of price inflation in Guatemala. What is the effect on gross exports from Guatemala to Brazil?

13. International transportation costs fall and flows of information increase between the United States and Mexico. What effect will this have on Mexico's gross export function?

14. If NAFTA, the North American Free Trade Agreement, truly decreased trade barriers between the United States, Mexico, and Canada, what should have been the effect of NAFTA on the U.S. responsiveness of imports to changes in domestic income?

15. The Disney ride "Pirates of the Caribbean" has some historical validity. In the 1600s and early 1700s, piracy was such a serious threat to merchant ships traveling between Europe and America that insurance rates were extremely high. The British Royal Navy undertook a campaign to rid the seas of pirates and was largely successful. The threat of piracy dropped dramatically and so did insurance rates. What effect do you think the Brit's successful campaign had on exports to and imports from America? How would you express your answer using the equation for net exports?

16. Suppose that for the past year, real interest rates in the United States have been 5 percent but real interest rates in South Korea have been 3 percent. After this year of stability, real interest rates in the United States begin to increase while real interest rates in South Korea remain unchanged. What effect would this change have on the exchange rate between U.S. dollars and the Korean won? Why?

17. Kelsey will receive $10,000 for tuition from her grandmother when she starts graduate school. Kelsey is trying to decide whether to begin grad school immediately after college in 2 years, or to put it off for a couple of years and start grad school in 4 years. Grandma thinks Kelsey should live a little before going back to school, so offers her a $500 bonus if she starts grad school in 4 years. Interest rates are currently 8 percent. Grad school tuition is expected to increase by 5 percent a year. Which offer from Grandma is worth more: $10,000 in 2 years or $10,500 in 4 years?

D. EXPLAINING THE REAL WORLD

Most instructors are delighted when you are able to figure out which concept or model to apply to a real world situation. Being able to do so means you thoroughly understand the material and is often what you need to do to earn an A in a course. This is where you experience the power of macroeconomic theory.

1. Roland, an economics major, asserts, "Everyone would be better off if the economy had flexible wages and prices. The labor market would always clear." What is one argument in favor of his assertion? What is one argument against his assertion?

2. Household saving rates fell to near and sometimes below zero in the late 1990s when the economy was booming. Household saving rates were also at or below zero in the 1930s when the economy was experiencing the Great Depression. How can saving rates approach zero in both good and bad times?

3. In the summer of 2001, U.S. taxpayers received tax rebate checks of up to $600 per household. When the rebate was announced, President George W. Bush stated that people needed the tax rebate in order to pay off their credit card bills and stimulate the economy. What is wrong with his statement?

4. Consider two economies alike in most respects. In one economy, 90 percent of the population has little wealth and low income and the remaining 10 percent of the population has much wealth and high income. In the second economy, 20 percent of the population has little wealth and low income, 70 percent of the population has moderate wealth holdings and moderate income, and the remaining 10 percent of the population has much wealth and high income. In which economy is a tax rebate of a flat amount, say $300 per person, likely to have the greatest effect on consumption spending?

5. Managers at nonprofit organizations such as Girl Scouts, Southern Poverty Law Center, and AmFAR make decisions about purchases of business equipment. In most respects, these organizations appear to be businesses making investment decisions. But the National Income and Product Accounts treats nonprofit organizations as households, not businesses, and counts their spending as consumption spending, not investment. Why do you suppose this is so?

6. In 2000 and 2001, the Federal Reserve decreased short-term interest rates markedly. By comparison, long-term interest rates did not change much at all. What effect do you think the interest rate policy had on investment spending? Why?

7. An economist says, "Government should never cut taxes and never cut government purchases." Why might that be good economic advice?

8. Long-term interest rates increase. People in their 60s do not change their saving much, if at all. People in their 30s increase their saving. Why do these two groups of people respond to the change in interest rates differently?

E. POSSIBILITIES TO PONDER

The more you learn, the more you realize you have more to learn. These questions go beyond the textbook material. They are the sort of questions that distinguish A+ or A work from A- work. Some of them may even serve as starting points for junior or senior year research papers.

1. In the textbook, Professor DeLong writes

$$C = Y - T - S^H$$

rather than the alternative

$$S^H = Y - T - C$$

These statements are equivalent mathematically, but have different implications about household economic behavior. The first implies that households make saving decisions and then consume what is left over. The second statement implies that households make consumption decisions, and then save what is left over. A third behavioral possibility is, of course, that households simultaneously determine both consumption and saving. Which statement about economic behavior do you think is more realistic? Does your answer depend upon the demographic characteristics of households?

2. Consider two economies that are alike in most respects. In one economy, 40 percent of the population is either retired or too young to work. In the other economy, only 20 percent of the population is retired or too young to work. Why would the long-run growth rate of the first economy be lower than the long-run growth rate of the second economy?

3. What is the best price index to use when calculating real interest rates?

SOLUTIONS   SOLUTIONS   SOLUTIONS   SOLUTIONS

A. BASIC DEFINITIONS

1. marginal propensity to consume
2. production function; labor
3. Disposable
4. real interest rates
5. transfer payments
6. Cobb-Douglas
7. investment
8. productive resources
9. machinery; buildings; changes
10. Investment
11. productive resources
12. foreign exchange traders.
13. transfer payments
14. transfer payments.
15. imports
16. appreciation
17. disposable; consumption

---

18. increase
19. increase
20. greater
21. decrease
22. flexible
23. exclude
24. depreciates
25. Decreases
26. increase
27. classical
28. increase
29. actual
30. less
31. excluded from

---

32. D. All three conclusions follow from the assumption of wage and price flexibility.

33. C. Buying stock, whether or not it is an initial public offering, is a change in the way we hold wealth; it is not investment spending. Buying a larger building for the office is not investment spending unless the building is a newly constructed building.

34. B. A Toyota may be a Japanese car, but if it was built in the United States it is not an import. When a tourist from another country is in the United States, the United States is exporting services to that other country.

B. MANIPULATION OF CONCEPTS AND MODELS

1. The graphs are shown at the right. A greater value of α causes the production function to rotate. At low levels of capital, output falls. At high levels of capital, output rises.

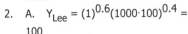

2. A. $Y_{Lee} = (1)^{0.6}(1000 \cdot 100)^{0.4} = 100$

   B. $Y_{Jarrel} = (1)^{0.6}(500 \cdot 100)^{0.4} = 75.79$

   C. $Y_{firm} = (1)^{0.6}(850 \cdot 100)^{0.4} = 93.71$

3. A. $MPL_{Lee} = [(1-0.6) (100)^{0.4}] / [1000^{0.6}] = 0.040$

   B. $MPL_{Jarrel} = [(1-0.6) (100)^{0.4}] / [500^{0.6}] = 0.061$

   C. $MPL_{firm} = [(1-0.6) (100)^{0.4}] / [850^{0.6}] = 0.044$

4. A. $D_{Lee} = [[(1-0.6) (100)^{0.4}] / (10/250)]^{(1/0.6)} = 1000$. Lee's Construction is at profit-maximizing equilibrium.

   B. $D_{Jarrel} = [[(1-0.6) (100)^{0.4}] / (10/100)]^{(1/0.6)} = 217.15$. Jarrel's Consulting is employing more than its profit-maximizing equilibrium. The firm needs to lay off workers to reach equilibrium. Laying off workers without changing the firm's use of capital will increase the capital-labor ratio within the firm, increasing the average productivity of workers, raising the marginal product of the last worker employed.

   C. $D_{firm} = [[(1-0.6) (100)^{0.4}] / (10/300)]^{(1/0.6)} = 1355.09$. The typical firm is employing fewer workers than its profit-maximizing equilibrium. The firm needs to hire additional workers. Adding workers without changing the firm's use of capital will decrease the capital-labor ratio within the firm, decreasing the marginal product of the last worker employed.

5. A. $D_{Lee} = [[(1-0.6) (100)^{0.4}] / (10/250)]^{(1/0.6)} = 1000$. Lee's Construction is at profit-maximizing equilibrium.

   B. $D_{Jarrel} = [[(1-0.6) (100)^{0.4}] / (10/250)]^{(1/0.6)} = 1000$. Jarrel's Consulting is employing fewer workers than its profit-maximizing equilibrium. The firm needs to hire additional workers. Adding workers without changing the firm's use of capital will decrease the capital-labor ratio within the firm, decreasing the marginal product of the last worker employed.

   C. $D_{firm} = [[(1-0.6) (100)^{0.4}] / (10/250)]^{(1/0.6)} = 1000$. The typical firm is employing fewer workers than its profit-maximizing equilibrium. The firm needs to hire additional workers. Adding workers without changing the firm's use of capital will decrease the capital-labor ratio within the firm, decreasing the marginal product of the last worker employed.

6. Demand for labor increases. As efficiency increases there is an increase in the marginal product of labor. At the initial level of employment, MPL will now exceed the real wage. Due to the law of diminishing returns, increased employment will decrease the MPL. Firms therefore can and will increase their demand for labor until the MPL of the last unit of labor hired falls to the real wage.

7. Demand for labor is lower when the real wage is higher. A greater real wage calls for a greater MPL at profit-maximizing equilibrium. To increase MPL, firms must decrease employment.

8. Demand for labor decreases when α increases. A larger α means that diminishing returns to investment set at lower levels of capital stock. As a result, MPL will be lower at every possible level of employment. Firms will need to decrease employment, thus raising the marginal product of the last worker hired, in order to reach profit-maximizing equilibrium.

9. A. $L_{firm} = 14.85$. $Y_{firm} = 18.57$.

$$L_{firm} = \left(\frac{(1 - 0.6) \cdot (100)^{1 - 0.6}}{0.50} \right)^{\frac{1}{0.6}} = 14.85$$

$$Y_{firm} = (1)^{0.6} \cdot (14.85 \cdot 100)^{1 - 0.6} = 18.57$$

B. Actual output $= 2000 \cdot 18.57 = 37,132.71$.

Potential output $= 2000^{0.6} \cdot ((2000 \cdot 14.85) \cdot 100)^{(1 - 0.6)} = 37,132.71$.

10. A. GDP = \$5,803.2 billion. National income = \$4,642.1 billion.

B. No, the assumption that GDP = national income is not realistic. We use the assumption anyway because the differences between GDP and national income are unimportant to the story we want to tell about the determinants of actual output and employment.

11.

	Nominal GDP (billion \$) (Table B-1)	Government receipts (billion \$) (Table B-83)	Government transfer payments (billion \$) (Table B-83)	Net taxes, T (billion \$)	Tax rate, t
1960	527.4	131.2	26.3	104.9	19.9 %
1965	720.1	175.4	36.0	139.4	19.4 %
1970	1,039.7	279.6	73.5	206.1	19.8 %
1975	1,635.2	430.5	166.4	264.1	16.2 %
1980	2,795.6	767.1	275.0	492.1	17.6 %
1985	4,213.0	1,135.8	414.2	721.6	17.1 %
1990	5,803.2	1,607.7	583.1	1,024.6	17.7 %
1995	7,400.5	2,117.1	869.9	1,247.2	16.8 %
last year available (1999)	9,299.2	2,788.0	998.1	1,789.9	19.2 %

From 1960 to the middle of the 1990s, the average tax rate in the U.S. declined. But by the end of the 1990s, the tax rate was almost as high as it had been in 1960. If you assemble every year of data in *ERP* Tables B-1 and B-83, you can derive the graph at right. It shows more clearly that the average tax rate peaked in 1969, was lower on average in the 1970s and 1980s than it had been in the 1960s, and then started to increase in 1992.

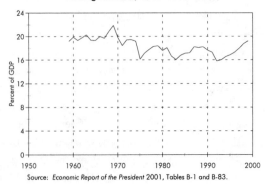

Average tax rate, 1959-1999

Source: *Economic Report of the President* 2001, Tables B-1 and B-83.

12. A. $t = (10,000 - 1,000) / 50,000 = 9,000 / 50,000 = 0.18 = 18\%$

B. Y^D = 50,000 - (10,000 - 1,000) = 50,000 - 9,000 = 41,000

C. S^H = 50,000 - (10,000 - 1,000) - 39,000 = 2,000

13. A. For example, when Y = 1,000,

   C = 500 + 0.8·(1 - 0.2)·1,000 = 500 + (0.64)(1,000) = 1,140

B. S^H = 0 when Y = 3125.

Y	C
0	500
1,000	1,140
5,000	3,700

$S^H = Y - T - C$	*definition of household savings*
$0 = Y - 0.2Y - (500 + 0.8·(1 - 0.2)·Y)$	*substituting for S^H, T, and C*
$0 = Y - 0.2Y - 500 - 0.8·(0.8)·Y$	*simplifying*
$0 = (1 - 0.2 - 0.64)·Y - 500$	*gathering Y terms*
$0 = (0.16)Y - 500$	*simplifying*
$500 = (0.16)Y$	*adding 500 to both sides of equation*
$\dfrac{500}{0.16} = Y$	*dividing both sides of equation by 0.16*
$3125 = Y$	*value of income where saving = 0*

C. The consumption function is graphed with Consumption (C) on the vertical axis and Income (Y) on the horizontal axis. The graph is a straight line, with intercept of 500 and slope of 0.64, which equals mpc · (1 - tax rate).

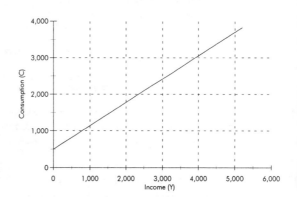

14.

	Nominal Disposable Income (billion $)	Personal Consumption Expenditure (billion $)	Household Saving (billion $)	Saving Rate (percent)
1960	366.2	332.3	26.4	7.2
1965	498.9	444.3	42.7	8.6
1970	736.5	648.9	69.5	9.4
1975	1,181.4	1,030.3	125.2	10.6
1980	2,019.8	1,762.9	205.6	10.2
1985	3,086.5	2,712.6	282.6	9.2
1990	4,293.6	3,831.5	334.3	7.8
1995	5,422.6	4,969.0	302.4	5.6
last year available (1999)	6,637.7	6,268.7	147.6	2.2

The data are all from *ERP*, Table B-30. The household saving rate ranged between 9 and 11 percent in the 1970s and 1980s, then began to fall in the 1990s. If you assemble every year of data in *ERP* Table B-30, you can derive the graph at right. It shows more clearly that the saving rate peaked in the early 1980s, and declined precipitously in the 1990s.

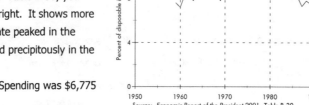

Household Saving Rate, 1959-1999

Source: *Economic Report of the President 2001*, Table B-30.

15. A. Total Consumption Spending was $6,775 million.

C = 400 + 0.75 (1 - 0.15) 10,000

= 400 + 6,375 = 6,775

B. Change in disposable income, ΔY^D, was $850 million. Change in consumption spending, ΔC, was 637.5 million.

$$\Delta Y^D = \Delta Y - \Delta T \qquad \textit{definition of disposable income}$$
$$\Delta Y^D = \Delta Y - t \cdot \Delta Y \qquad \textit{definition of net taxes}$$
$$\Delta Y^D = (1 - t) \cdot \Delta Y \qquad \textit{gathering } \Delta Y \textit{ terms}$$
$$\Delta Y^D = 0.85(1,000) = 850 \qquad \textit{substituting values and computing}$$

- -

$$\Delta C = C_Y \cdot (1 - t) \Delta Y \qquad \textit{definition of } \Delta C$$
$$\Delta C = C_Y \cdot \Delta Y^D \qquad \textit{substituting } \Delta Y^D$$
$$\Delta C = 0.75(850) = 637.5 \qquad \textit{substituting values and computing}$$

16. A. She should use a 5-year interest rate because the display rack has a 5-year estimated life. She should use a "risky" interest rate, because the amount of additional sales of hair care supplies is uncertain. She should either use a real interest rate, adjusting the nominal interest rate by expected inflation over the next 5 years, and then use today's prices of hair care supplies to form her stream of expected revenues; or use nominal interest rates and adjust her estimates of future revenues from sales of hair care supplies to allow for increased prices over the 5-year life of the display rack.

B. If Keshia's goal is to maximize profit, she should not buy the display rack. The discounted present value of the investment project, $700, is less than the investment cost, $795.

C. Keshia should reconsider her decision. The decrease in interest rates, if it is projected to continue in the future and not be accompanied by a matching decrease in the inflation rate, increases the discounted present value of the future stream of revenues from sales of hair care supplies. Previously unprofitable projects, such as purchase of the display rack, may now be profitable.

17. She needs to be able to compute the discounted present value of the net gains from selling the homes. So she needs estimates of the sale prices of the homes, as well as estimates of the other costs of construction. She needs to estimate inflation in building construction costs and in home prices.

18. Assuming there is no change in expected future revenues, investment spending should now be more than $1,600 billion per quarter.

19.   Data are in *ERP* Table B-18.

	Private Fixed Investment (billion $)	Nonresidential Buildings (billion $)	Information Processing Equipment & Software (billion $)	Industrial Equipment (billion $)	Transportation Equipment (billion $)	Residential Buildings (billion $)
1960	75.7	12.0	4.9	9.3	8.5	26.3
1965	109.0	19.5	8.5	13.6	13.2	34.2
1970	150.4	25.4	16.7	20.2	16.2	41.4
1975	236.5	35.6	28.2	31.1	25.2	62.7
1980	484.2	73.7	69.6	60.4	48.4	123.2
1985	714.5	128.0	130.8	71.9	69.7	186.9
1990	847.2	149.1	176.1	91.5	75.7	216.8
1995	1,110.7	144.3	262.0	128.7	126.1	285.6
last year available (1999)	1,606.8	208.5	433.0	150.7	193.5	403.8

Computers and software purchases rise faster than any other category of investment spending. Over time, an increasing share of private fixed investment spending is for computers and software (information processing equipment and software). In 1960, just 6.5 percent of private fixed investment was spent for computers and software; this share had risen to 26.9 percent today.

20.

	Private Fixed Investment (billion $)	Nominal GDP (billion $)	Investment as a share of GDP (percent)
1960	75.7	527.4	14.4
1965	109.0	720.1	15.1
1970	150.4	1,039.7	14.5
1975	236.5	1,635.2	14.5
1980	484.2	2,795.6	17.3
1985	714.5	4,213.0	17.0
1990	847.2	5,803.2	14.6
1995	1,110.7	7,400.5	15.0
last year available (1999)	1,606.8	9,299.2	17.3

Fixed private investment as a share of GDP has ranged between 14 and 17 percent since 1960. Surprisingly, in the 1990s, when investment spending for computers was rising rapidly (see the previous question), investment as a share of GDP was not at relatively high levels.

21. A. For example, when r = 2, I = 2,000 − 4,000·(0.02) = 1,920.
    B. The graph will have an intercept of 2000 and a slope of −4000, where the vertical axis measure the amount of investment spending (I) and the horizontal axis measures the real interest rate (r), with r expressed in decimal form.

r	I
2	1,920
4	1,840
6	1,760
8	1,680

C. Optimism that increases expected future revenue from investment projects leads to an increase in the expected return from investment. At every interest rate, more investment projects will therefore be profitable. This would be shown as an increase in baseline investment, I_0, and a shift to the right of the investment function as shown at the right.

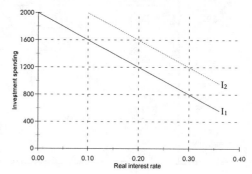

22.

	Nominal GDP (billion $)	Total Government Purchases (billion $)	Federal Defense Purchases (billion $)	Federal Nondefense Purchases (billion $)	State & Local Purchases (billion $)	Transfer Payments (billion $)	Government Spending as a Share of GDP (percent)
1960	527.4	65.9	55.2	10.7	47.9	26.3	21.6
1965	720.1	153.7	62.4	19.7	71.6	36.0	21.3
1970	1,039.7	237.1	90.9	25.5	120.7	73.5	22.8
1975	1,635.2	361.1	107.9	44.2	209.0	166.4	22.1
1980	2,795.6	569.7	169.6	75.6	324.4	275.0	20.4
1985	4,213.0	878.3	312.4	101.0	464.9	414.2	20.8
1990	5,803.2	1,181.4	374.9	133.6	673.0	583.1	20.4
1995	7,400.5	1,372.0	350.6	170.9	850.5	869.9	18.5
last year available (1999)	9,299.2	1,634.4	365.0	203.5	1,065.8	998.1	17.6

Government purchases (G) as a share of GDP fell in the 1990s, after having held steady in the 1960s, 1970s, and 1980s at about 20 to 22 percent. The annual pattern is seen more clearly in the graph at the right, which shows that government purchases (G) as a share of GDP held steady from about 1978 to 1991, then began a secular decline in 1992.

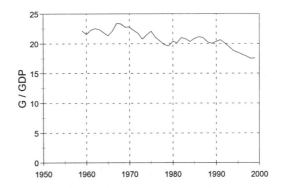

23. The answers are in the table at the right. The gross exports function is $GX = 40 \cdot Y^f + 20 \cdot \varepsilon$. For example, $GX = 40 \cdot (100) + 20 \cdot (300) = 10{,}000$.

Y^f	ε	GX
100	300	10,000
100	400	12,000
200	400	16,000

24. A. It is probably easier to use specific country names when answering the question. Gross exports from India increase when income in England increases because higher income in England means more spending by all sectors of the English economy – households, businesses, and government agencies. Some of their spending will be for goods and services produced in countries other than England. If one of those countries from which they purchases goods and services is England, then gross exports from England will rise when incomes increase in India.

   B. Again, use specific country names so that your answer is clear. When the real exchange rate increases in England, gross exports from England will increase. When the real exchange rate in England increases, the English face higher prices for Indian goods. Equivalently, those in India face lower prices for English goods. Indian demand for English goods will therefore increase. As a result, gross exports from England to India will increase.

25. Answers will vary. One possibility, for instance, is that many contracts for importing or exporting goods are long-term contracts set many months in advance. Toys produced in Taiwan that are sold in U.S. toy stores in December are ordered 10 to 12 months in advance. The orders are received at U.S. importers, forwarded to a factory abroad, produced, packaged for shipment, shipped by rail or other means to a seaport, placed into containers with other goods destined for the United States, loaded onto a freighter, shipped across the ocean, unloaded at a container port, placed onto a freight train, transported to a regional distribution site, stored in a warehouse, placed into a truck, transported by truck to a local store, and finally placed on the shelves for sale. All of that takes time.

26. The answers are given in the table at the right. The gross imports function is $IM = IM_y \cdot Y$. For example, $IM = 6 \cdot 4{,}000 = 24{,}000$.

Y	IM
4,000	24,000
6,000	36,000
8,000	48,000

27. The answers are found in Table B-1 of the *Economic Report of the President*.

	Nominal GDP (billion $)	Gross Exports (billion $)	Exports as a share of GDP (percent)	Gross Imports (billion $)	Imports as a share of GDP (percent)
1960	527.4	25.3	4.8	22.8	4.3
1965	720.1	35.4	4.9	31.5	4.4
1970	1,039.7	57.0	5.5	55.8	5.4
1975	1,635.2	136.3	8.3	122.7	7.5
1980	2,795.6	278.9	10.0	293.8	10.5
1985	4,213.0	303.0	7.2	417.2	9.9
1990	5,803.2	557.2	9.6	628.6	10.8
1995	7,400.5	818.6	11.1	902.8	12.2
last year available (1999)	9,299.2	990.2	10.6	1,244.2	13.4

Over time, imports and exports as a share of GDP have increased sharply. The increase was most pronounced in the 1970s. The full pattern of change can be seen in the graph at the right. Only the ratio of imports to gross domestic product is shown. The pattern for exports is similar.

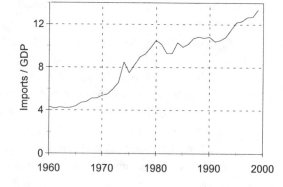

28. A. The answers are in the table at the top of the next page. The real exchange rate is determined by the equation $\varepsilon = 20 - 6 \cdot (r - r^f)$. For example, $\varepsilon = 20 - 6 \cdot (10 - 8) = 8$.

B. When domestic real interest rates increase, real exchange rates fall. For example, when domestic real interest rates increased from 10 to 12 percent, the real exchange rate fell from 32 to 20. Real exchange rates fall because the increase in domestic real interest rates leads to an increase in demand for dollar-denominated assets and a decrease in demand for assets denominated in other currencies. The resulting increase in the supply of foreign currency offered in exchange for dollars leads to a decrease in the dollar-price of foreign currency (that is, a decrease in the nominal exchange rate) and thus to a decrease in the real exchange rate.

C. When foreign real interest rates increase, real exchange rates rise. For example, when foreign real interest rates increased from 8 to 12 percent, the real exchange rate rose from 8 to 32. Real exchange rates rise because the increase in foreign real interest rates leads to an increase in demand for assets denominated in other currencies and a decrease in demand for dollar-denominated assets. The resulting increase in the demand for foreign currency offered in exchange for dollars leads to an

r	r^f	ε
10	8	8
10	12	32
12	12	20

increase in the dollar-price of foreign currency (that is, an increase in the nominal exchange rate) and thus to an increase in the real exchange rate.

29. A. For example, NX = 300 ·250 + 50 ·20 - 200 ·300 = 16,000

Y^f	ε	Y	NX
250	20	300	16,000
250	20	400	- 4,000
250	25	400	- 3,750
300	25	400	11,250

   B. When domestic income increases, net exports fall. An increase in domestic income leads to a rise in imports, which decreases net exports.

   C. When the real exchange rate increases, net exports rise. An increase in the real exchange rate is an increase in the price of foreign goods relative to domestically-produced goods. This change leads to an increase in exports, which increases net exports

   D. When foreign income increases, net exports rise. An increase in foreign income leads to an increase in gross exports, which increases net exports.

30. A. When domestic interest rates increase, net exports fall. Even though you can see this from the equation without having to calculate real exchange rates, the explanation includes real exchange rates. When domestic real interest rates increase, real exchange rates fall. The resulting decrease in the relative price of foreign goods means that gross exports fall. A decrease in gross exports causes a decrease in net exports.

   B. When foreign interest rates increase, net exports rise. Even though you can see this from the equation without having to calculate real exchange rates, the explanation includes real exchange rates. When foreign real interest rates increase, real exchange rates rise. The resulting increase in the relative price of foreign goods means that gross exports rise. An increase in gross exports causes an increase in net exports.

31. A permanent change in income is something like an increase in salary. It is a change that is expected to continue into the future. A transitory change in income is something like unexpected gambling winnings. It is a change that is not expected to be repeated in the future.

32. The present value of an annuity that pays $1,000 annually over an indefinite period, when interest rates are 5 percent, is 1,000 / 0.05 = $20,000. If Stanley can purchase the annuity for $20,000 or less, it is a good financial opportunity.

C. APPLYING CONCEPTS AND MODELS

1. In equilibrium, real wages equal $(1 - \alpha) \times Y/L$. If diminishing returns to investment set in quickly, then α is large. In this case, real wages will be low. Diminishing returns setting in quickly means that as additional capital is added to the production process, the additional output produced with the additional capital, while existent, is quite small. As a result, workers do not benefit much from the addition of capital to the production process. Real wages are low.

2. Consumption spending would increase, as the baseline consumption amount, C_0, increased. As a result of the increased value of stock holdings, households can save less and still achieve the same wealth-accumulation goals. Consumption spending increases.

3. The mpc = 0. Paying off debt is *not* current consumption. When we pay off credit card debt, we are paying for consumption that took place in a previous period when the credit card debt was accumulated. For example, if you buy school books in August but don't pay the bill until December, the

consumption spending took place in August. In December, you are counted as "saving" the amount you send to the credit card company.

4. The mpc = 1. Buying newly produced goods or services *is* consumption spending.

5. When people are fearful about the economy's future, they tend to spend less and save more. This change is reflected as a shift down of the consumption function due to a decrease in baseline consumption, C_0.

6. Answers will vary.

7. The lottery official will probably lose the argument – and probably should. A transitory change in income – a change that was unexpected and is not expected to be repeated, such as a one-time lottery winning – typically faces a lower marginal propensity to consume than does a permanent change in income – a change that is expected to be repeated, such as a raise. The lottery official probably thinks that the state will benefit more if the lottery payments are spread over 30 years because then the lottery winnings will be a permanent change in income and will face a higher marginal propensity to consume. But the benefit to the state's economy from spreading the payments over 30 years would come in future years, not in the years immediately following establishment of the new rule. For the state's economy to benefit right away, the marginal propensity to consume out of permanent income would need to be at least 30 times greater than the marginal propensity to consume out of transitory income. That's unlikely.

8. Calm businesspeople may buy more business equipment than panicky ones because their assessment of future risk is lower, and therefore they are able to use a less risky interest rate when determining the discounted present value of investment returns. Less risky interest rates are lower than more risky interest rates. Lower interest rates increase the present discounted value, increasing the number of potential investment projects that are profitable, increasing investment spending.
A second possible explanation for greater spending on business equipment by calm businesspeople could be that calm businesspeople have a more optimistic view of future expected sales than do panicky businesspeople. This again would increase the value of an investment project, increasing its profitability and thus increasing investment spending.

9. Increasing government purchases by $100 billion has a larger effect on total spending than does decreasing taxes. When taxes are lowered, disposable income increases. When disposable income increases, consumption spending increases. The marginal propensity to consume (mpc) tells us the change in consumption for a change in disposable income. Because the mpc is typically less than one, the change in consumption will be smaller than the change in disposable income. Therefore, if the government lowers taxes by $100 billion, increasing disposable income by $100 billion, consumption spending will rise by some amount less than $100 billion. On the other hand, if the government increases its purchases by $100 billion, the full $100 billion contributes to total spending.

10. Lowering transfer payments will have a smaller effect on total spending than would decreasing government purchases. The explanation is similar to that in Question 9. When transfer payments are decreased, disposable income decreases. As a result, consumption spending decreases. But because the mpc is less than one, the drop in consumption spending will be less than the decrease in disposable income. On the other hand, every penny of a decrease in government purchases shows up as a decrease in total spending.

11. Gross exports from the United States to Japan will probably fall. Recession in Japan means that incomes in Japan have fallen. Lower income means lower spending. Some of that decreased spending by households, businesses, and government agencies will be decreased spending for goods and services

produced outside of Japan. Japanese spending for goods and services produced in the United States will therefore fall, decreasing U.S. exports to Japan.

12. The higher rate of price inflation in Brazil than in Guatemala means that Guatemala's real exchange rate with Brazil has increased. That is, for Guatemalans, the price of Brazilian goods and services relative to Guatemalan goods and services has increased. For Brazilians, the price of Guatemalan goods and services relative to Brazilian goods and services has decreased. Brazilians will therefore increase their demand for Guatemalan goods and services. Gross exports from Guatemala to Brazil will increase.

13. If it is less costly to transport goods between the United States and Mexico, and if there is more information flowing between the two economies about the goods and services available, then there should be an increase in trade between the two countries. The gross export function should shift out. Mathematically, this could be shown as an increase in the responsiveness of gross exports to changes in foreign income, X_f, and possibly also an increase in the responsiveness of gross exports to changes in the real exchange rate, X_ε.

14. Lower trade barriers should have translated to easier exchange of goods and services across the Mexico-U.S. and Canada-U.S. borders. It is likely that imports could then respond more to any change in U.S. income. The responsiveness of imports to changes in domestic income, IM_y, probably increased.

15. Decreased insurance rates and increased likelihood of trade routes being secure would be expected to – and did – increase trade. We could show this as an increase in any of the parameters of the net export equation.

16. The exchange rate between dollars and won – more specifically, the dollar-price of won – will decrease. Foreign exchange traders will want to sell won-denominated securities and buy dollar-denominated securities. This increases the supply of won being offered in exchange for dollars, decreasing the dollar-price of won, which is equivalent to decreasing the nominal exchange rate for won. When the nominal exchange rate decreases, the real exchange rate also decreases.

17. The question draws on the material in the Appendix to Chapter 6. Kelsey needs to calculate the discounted present value of each offer. The real interest rate she should use is 3 percent – the nominal interest rate of 8 percent minus the expected tuition inflation rate of 5 percent. She needs to discount $10,000 over a 2-year period, and $10,500 over a 4-year period, and then compare.

Go to school in 2 years: $\$PV = \dfrac{\$10,000}{(1 + 0.03)^2} = \$9,425.96$.

Go to school in 4 years: $\$PV = \dfrac{\$10,500}{(1 + 0.03)^4} = \$9,334.46$

The offer of $10,000 in 2 years is worth more than the offer of $10,500 in 4 years.

D. EXPLAINING THE REAL WORLD

1. In favor: full employment. Against: potentially low wages for all.

2. In the late 1990s, stock values soared. Many people felt wealthier, so decreased how much of their current income that they saved. As a result, the saving rate fell to zero. This is an example of the consumption function shifting due to a change in C_0. In the 1930s, incomes decreased dramatically when the unemployment rate soared to near 25 percent. As income fell, people reduced both their consumption *and* their saving. Income fell so far that household saving fell below zero. In order to cover even the baseline consumption amount, households had to deplete their savings or go into debt. This is an example of a movement along the consumption function due to a change in Y.

3. Paying off credit card bills is not consumption spending; it is paying for consumption spending that took place in some previous period. When people pay off their credit card bills, it is considered saving.

Saving does not stimulate the economy in the short run. The tax rebate is an economic stimulus only if it is used for current consumption.

4. The tax rebate of $300 per person will have the greatest effect on spending in the first economy, where 90 percent of the population is poor. The poor are likely to have a much higher marginal propensity to consume than the moderate income group. And the rich are likely to have a quite low marginal propensity to consume since they are already able to pay for everything they want.

5. Nonprofit organizations are not considered businesses in the National Income and Product Accounts because their investment decisions are not primarily guided by a goal of maximizing profit. Investment spending is a profit-maximizing decision by a business that is comparing the expected costs and benefits of an expenditure.

6. Because short-term rates fell more than long-term rates, then investment spending for goods with a short life probably increased more than did investment spending for goods with a long life. For example, purchases of computers and printers that were expected to contribute to business productivity for 2 or 3 years probably responded more to the Fed policy than did purchases of newly-constructed structures.

7. Never cutting taxes and never cutting government purchases is good advice if the government's goal is always to choose the policy with the most beneficial short-term effect on the economy. If the government is increasing its budget surplus, it can cut taxes or increase purchases. Because the marginal propensity to consume is less than one, increasing purchases will have a larger effect on total spending, $C + I + G + NX$, than cutting taxes. Similarly, if the government is decreasing its budget surplus or deficit, it can increase taxes or cut government purchases. In this case, increasing taxes will have a smaller contractionary effect on total spending than will decreasing purchases.

8. The question draws on the material in the Appendix to Chapter 6. People in their 60s have low future income relative to current income. Soon they will retire, at which time their income will probably fall markedly and they will enter a period of dissaving. Because their future income is low relative to their current income, the change in interest rates hardly affects their evaluation of the tradeoff between consumption now and consumption in the future, and thus has very little if any effect on saving. On the other hand, people in their 30s have potentially quite high future income relative to current income. Most of their working years lie ahead of them. The people in this group are likely to increase their saving. The discounted value of future consumption decreases when interest rates rise, so utility-maximizing consumers will shift some consumption from the present to the future in order to maximize lifetime utility. The way to shift consumption from the present to the future is by decreasing consumption now.

E. POSSIBILITIES TO PONDER

No solutions are given to these questions. The questions are designed to be somewhat open ended. Each question draws on your understanding of the concepts covered in this chapter.

Chapter 7

Equilibrium in the Flexible-Price Model

- In an economy with fully flexible wages and prices, output is always equal to potential output. Equilibrium is constantly maintained by the real interest rate, which adjusts to balance the flow-of-funds through financial markets.

- The flexible-price full-employment classical model can be use to assess the effect of changes in any component of aggregate demand or in aggregate supply.

LEARNING GUIDE

A new model is presented in this chapter: the flexible-price full-employment classical model. The components of the model were presented in Chapter 6. The model is straightforward but may not be immediately intuitive because some of the assumptions of the model are not consistent with "real life."

You will need some math skills in this chapter. Math skills covered in Chapter B are indicated with

Don't let the equations alarm you. Deriving the equations you will need requires only algebra (though the derivations are quicker with calculus). What may look like lots of math is really just several different but related applications of the same basic model. There are fewer equations to memorize than you might think, and the symbols used in the ones you do need to memorize are very logically chosen. There is one basic graph in the chapter, redrawn for each application.

Short on time?

Find out what you are expected to learn before you begin. Some teachers will want you to be able to derive and manipulate the equations. Some will want you to understand the economics behind the equations but won't expect you to derive them. Don't spend all your time agonizing over the math if you will be expected to write economic explanations of the relationships illustrated by the model.

You want to learn the components of the flow-of-funds through financial markets, and how interest rates adjust to clear those markets. You want to understand when and why the various components of aggregate demand change. You want to be able to do all of the comparative statics examples in the chapter so that you are comfortable with new examples.

A. BASIC DEFINITIONS

Before you apply knowledge, you need a basic grasp of the fundamentals. In other words, there are some things you just have to know. Knowing the material in this section won't guarantee a good grade in the course, but not knowing it will guarantee a poor or failing grade.

USE THE WORDS OR PHRASES FROM THE LIST BELOW TO COMPLETE THE SENTENCES. SOME ARE USED MORE THAN ONCE; SOME ARE NOT USED AT ALL.

aggregate demand	*potential output*
comparative statics	*real business cycle*
government bonds	*real exchange rate*
investment goods	*real interest rate*
involuntary	*recession*
loanable funds	*voluntary*

1. The real interest rate is a price determined in the market for _____.

2. If supply of and demand for loanable funds are equal, then real output will equal _____.

3. When we use a model to see how an equilibrium value changes in response to changes in policy, we are using an analytical method called _____.

4. In real business cycle theory, all unemployment is _____.

> **CAREFUL:** The model in Chapter 7 is the flexible-price full-employment classical model. You probably learned the Keynesian model in your principles course. Some of the conclusions of the Keynesian model do not apply to the flexible-price full-employment classical model. In particular, in the Keynesian model, there can be unemployment. But in the flexible-price full-employment classical model, the real interest rate adjusts to clear markets so that there is **no** unemployment.

5. In the flexible-price full-employment classical model, changes in the _____ bring the economy to equilibrium.

6. A(n) _____ is a business cycle driven by the fundamental technological dynamic of the economy.

7. In the flexible-price full-employment classical model, total output always equals _____.

8. When the financial markets are in equilibrium, the supply of and demand for
    _____ are equal.

CIRCLE THE CORRECT WORD OR PHRASE IN EACH OF THE FOLLOWING SENTENCES.

9. The real business cycle approach does a better job of explaining <u>booms / busts</u> than it
    does of explaining <u>booms / busts</u>.

10. <u>Inflows into / outflows from</u> the market for loanable funds include loans to firms
    purchasing business equipment.

11. Total expenditure, E, and real output, Y, <u>are / are not</u> the same thing.

12. In the flexible-price full-employment classical model of Chapter 7, when government
    purchases increase, total output <u>increases / stays the same / decreases</u>.

13. <u>Inflows into / outflows from</u> the market for loanable funds include household saving
    and other forms of saving.

> **NOTE:** Several phrases are used in Chapter 7, all of which have the same
> meaning.
> - Household saving
> - Personal saving
> - Private savings
>
> All three phrases mean Y - T - C, the difference between disposable
> income and consumption spending.

14. In the flexible-price full-employment classical model of Chapter 7, when government
    purchases increase, investment spending <u>increases / stays the same / decreases</u>.

15. In equilibrium, the value of total expenditure, E, is <u>less than / equal to / greater than</u>
    output, Y.

16. In the flexible-price full-employment classical model of Chapter 7, when any component
    of aggregate demand changes, total output <u>changes / stays the same.</u>

17. In the flexible-price full-employment classical model of Chapter 7, when government
    purchases increase, gross export spending <u>increases / stays the same / decreases</u>.

18. In the flexible-price full-employment classical model of Chapter 7, when aggregate
    supply changes, total output <u>changes / stays the same.</u>

SELECT THE ONE BEST ANSWER FOR EACH MULTIPLE-CHOICE QUESTION.

19. In the flexible-price full-employment classical model, what variable plays the role of making sure the economy reaches equilibrium?
    A. Real interest rates, r.
    B. Output, Y.
    C. Total expenditure, E.
    D. Inventory holdings.

> **NOTE:** It is **very** important that you understand the role of real interest rates, r, in bringing the economy to equilibrium in the flexible-price full-employment classical model.

20. When the real interest rate changes, the loanable funds market moves into equilibrium because the following quantities change in response to the change in real interest rates:
    A. I and GX and IM.
    B. I and IM.
    C. I and GX.
    D. I and C and G and GX and IM.

B. MANIPULATION OF CONCEPTS AND MODELS

Most instructors expect you to be able to do basic manipulation of the concepts. Being able to do so often means you can earn a C in a course. But if you want a better grade, you'll need to be able to complete this next section easily and move on to Sections C and D.

1. Suppose that in the second quarter of last year, gross exports from the United States were $400 billion and imports into the United States were $300 billion.
   A. What was the value of net exports?

   B. What was the value of –NX, the term in the flow of funds equation?

   C. What was the value of funds flowing into U.S. financial markets from abroad?

2. Suppose that in a certain month, the value of imports from Mexico into the United States was $600 billion. Suppose in the same month, companies in the United States sold goods and services to consumers and businesses in Mexico, who paid a total of 5,000 billion Mexican pesos. Suppose the exchange rate was 1 peso = $0.11.

    A. What was the value in dollars of U.S. net exports to Mexico?

    B. Did funds flow from Mexico to the United States or from the United States to Mexico for the funding of investment spending? Explain.

3. Suppose government purchases of goods and services exceed net government tax receipts. On net, are government funds flowing into or out of financial markets? Is this called an "inflow" or an "outflow" of funds?

TO THE CHALKBOARD:
Deriving the Flow-of-Funds Equation

In the textbook, Professor DeLong derives the equation for the flow of funds. This equation shows the inflows of loanable funds and outflows of loanable funds. It is a very important equation. Be sure you understand the equation and can derive it. Here is a step-by-step explanation of its derivation.

$$Y^* = Y \quad \text{by definition, potential output equals actual real output}$$
$$Y = E \quad \text{in equilibrium, actual output equals aggregate demand}$$
$$E = C + I + G + NX \quad \text{the definition of aggregate demand}$$

- -

$$Y^* = C + I + G + NX \quad \text{substituting from the equations above}$$
$$Y^* - C - G - NX = I \quad \text{subtracting } C, G, \text{ and } NX \text{ from both sides of equation}$$
$$Y^* - C - T + T - G - NX = I \quad \text{adding and subtracting } T \text{ from the left-hand side}$$
$$(Y^* - C - T) + (T - G) - NX = I \quad \text{adding parentheses to emphasize economic concepts}$$
$$(Y^* - T - C) + (T - G) - NX = I \quad \text{rearranging terms}$$

The equation emphasizes that the flows of funds into the financial markets are from three sources:

1. Household saving: $S^H = Y^* - T - C$
2. Government saving: Budget Surplus = $T - G$
3. Foreign Funds: $-NX = IM - GX$

The flow of funds out of financial markets is due to one activity:

1. Investment spending: I

---

4. Suppose

Y = 8,000	C = 5,500	GX = 1,000
T = 2,000	G = 1,500	IM = 1,100

    A. What is the value of household saving, S^H?

    B. What is the value of the government's budget surplus, BS?

C. What is the value of "minus net exports," –NX?

D. What is the total inflow of funds into the financial markets?

5. Suppose

Y = 8,000	C = 5,500	GX = 1,300
T = 2,000	G = 2,200	IM = 1,100

A. What is the value of household saving, S^H?

B. What is the value of the government's budget surplus, BS?

C. What is the value of "minus net exports," –NX?

D. What is the total inflow of funds into the financial markets?

6. Using the *Economic Report of the President (ERP)*, look up the nominal values of personal saving, total government budget surplus (or deficit), and net exports for the years given in the table below. (Note: You will need to use several different tables of *ERP* to answer the question.) Use these values to compute the inflow of funds into financial markets. Describe the pattern of inflow of funds since 1960.

	Personal Saving (billion $)	Budget Surplus (billion $)	Net Exports (billion $)	Total Inflow of Funds (billion $)
1960	26.4		2.4	
1965		9.7		
1970				61.0
1975				
1980				
1985				
1990				
1995				
last year available				

7. Give an example of a case where an individual *indirectly* funds private investment spending. Give an example of a case where an individual *directly* funds private investment spending.

TO THE CHALKBOARD:
Explaining Figure 7.3

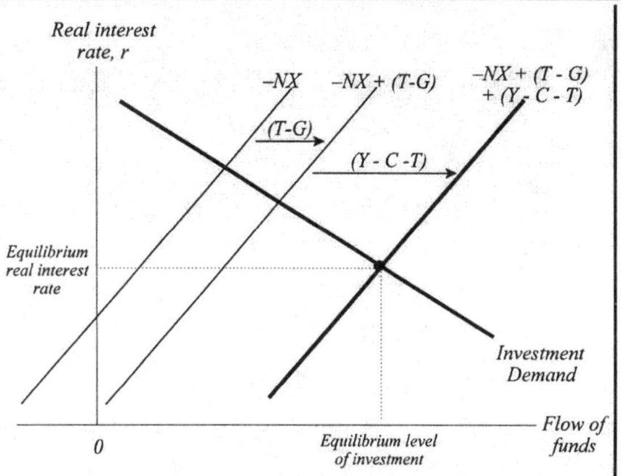

Figure 7.3 illustrates equilibrium in the flow-of-funds. A slightly different version of the graph is shown at the right. As in the text, the real interest rate is on the vertical axis and dollar amounts are on the horizontal axis.

The demand for loanable funds is straightforward. It is just investment demand. We already know that investment spending increases when the real interest rate declines, so it is a downward-sloping curve.

The supply of loanable funds is the sum of international savings (–NX = IM - GX), private savings (Y - C - T), and government savings (T - G). The only component of the supply of loanable funds that changes when the real interest rate changes is gross exports, GX. When the real interest rate rises, gross exports decline so international savings rise. The relationship between real interest rates and international savings will thus be depicted by an upward-sloping curve. Because international savings can be negative as well as positive, the –NX curve as shown above crosses the vertical axis.

Government savings do not change when the real interest rate changes. So adding government savings to international savings simply shifts the –NX curve to the right by the amount of the budget surplus, T- G. (If the total government budget was in deficit, then we would be shifting the –NX curve to the left by the amount of the deficit.) Private savings also do not change when the real interest rate changes. So again, adding private savings to the sum of international savings and government savings simply shifts the –NX + (T - G) curve to the right by the amount of private savings, Y - T - C. The resulting curve, –NX + (T - G) + (Y - T - C), is total savings, which is the supply of loanable funds.

(Note that the only difference between this version and the textbook version of this graph is that the textbook begins with government savings and private savings, and then adds in international savings. The study guide version begins with international savings and then adds in government savings and private savings.)

When the demand for loanable funds (the dark downward-sloping line) equals the supply of loanable funds (the dark upward-sloping line), the market for loanable funds is in equilibrium. At the intersection point of the demand and supply curves, we then have the equilibrium level of investment (shown on the horizontal axis), and the equilibrium real interest rate (shown on the vertical axis).

8. A. Suppose household saving is 500, government budget surplus is 200, imports exceed gross exports by 300, and investment spending is 1,200. What is the supply of loanable funds? What is the demand for loanable funds? Is the market for loanable funds in equilibrium? If not, will real interest rates rise or fall in response to the absence of equilibrium? What quantities – saving, budget surplus, gross exports, imports, or investment spending – will change in response to the change in interest rates in order to bring the market for loanable funds into equilibrium?

B. Suppose that in response to the conditions in Part A, net exports fall by 50 and investment spending falls by 150. Now what is the supply of loanable funds? What is the demand for loanable funds? Is the market for loanable funds now in equilibrium? If not, will real interest rates rise or fall in response to the absence of equilibrium? What quantities – saving, budget surplus, gross exports, imports, or investment spending – will change in response to the change in interest rates in order to bring the market for loanable funds into equilibrium?

C. Suppose that the conditions in Part B exist. Suddenly business people become pessimistic about the economy's future. Investment spending falls to 900. Now what is the supply of loanable funds? What is the demand for loanable funds? Is the market for loanable funds now in equilibrium? If not, will real interest rates rise or fall in response to the absence of equilibrium? What quantities – saving, budget surplus, gross exports, imports, or investment spending – will change in response to the change in interest rates in order to bring the market for loanable funds into equilibrium?

TO THE CHALKBOARD:
Deriving the Equation for the Equilibrium Real Interest Rate

In the textbook, Professor DeLong derives the equation for the equilibrium real interest rate. Here is a step-by-step explanation of the derivation.

First, we derive the expression for private (household) savings.

$S^H = Y^* - C - T$	definition of household savings
$S^H = Y^* - [C_0 + C_y \cdot Y^D] - t \cdot Y^*$	substituting equation for consumption
$S^H = Y^* - C_0 - C_y \cdot Y^D - t \cdot Y^*$	distributing minus sign
$S^H = Y^* - t \cdot Y^* - C_y \cdot Y^D - C_0$	rearranging terms to match text
$S^H = Y^* - t \cdot Y^* - C_y \cdot (1 - t) \cdot Y^* - C_0$	substituting definition of disposable income
$S^H = Y^* - t \cdot Y^* - (1 - t) \cdot C_y \cdot Y^* - C_0$	rearranging terms to match text
$S^H = [1 - t - (1 - t) \cdot C_y] \cdot Y^* - C_0$	collecting Y^* terms

Next, we derive the expression for public (government) savings.

$$BS = T - G \qquad \textit{definition of budget surplus}$$
$$BS = t \cdot Y^* - G \qquad \textit{substituting definition of T}$$

Finally, we derive the expression for international (foreign) savings:

$$- NX = - (GX - IM) \qquad \textit{definition of net exports}$$
$$- NX = IM - GX \qquad \textit{distributing minus sign and simplifying}$$
$$- NX = IM_y \cdot Y^* - \left[X_f \cdot Y^f + X_\varepsilon \cdot \varepsilon_0 - X_\varepsilon \cdot \varepsilon_r \cdot r + X_\varepsilon \cdot \varepsilon_r \cdot r^f \right] \qquad \textit{substituting defintions of IM and GX}$$
$$- NX = IM_y \cdot Y^* - X_f \cdot Y^f - X_\varepsilon \cdot \varepsilon_0 + X_\varepsilon \cdot \varepsilon_r \cdot r - X_\varepsilon \cdot \varepsilon_r \cdot r^f \qquad \textit{distributing minus sign}$$
$$- NX = IM_y \cdot Y^* + X_\varepsilon \cdot \varepsilon_r \cdot r - X_f \cdot Y^f - X_\varepsilon \cdot \varepsilon_0 - X_\varepsilon \cdot \varepsilon_r \cdot r^f \qquad \textit{rearranging terms to match text}$$

Now we can proceed. We simply set the supply of loanable funds equal to the demand for loanable funds; that is, we set the sum of private, public, and international savings equal to investment demand. Investment demand, I, is equal to $I_0 - I_r r$. We then solve for the real interest rate.

$$\textit{Supply of loanable funds = Demand for loanable funds} \qquad \textit{definition of equilibrium}$$

$$\left[1 - t - (1 - t) \cdot C_y \right] Y^* - C_0 + t \cdot Y^* - G + IM_y \cdot Y^*$$
$$+ X_\varepsilon \cdot \varepsilon_r \cdot r - X_f \cdot Y^f - X_\varepsilon \cdot \varepsilon_0 - X_\varepsilon \cdot \varepsilon_r \cdot r^f = I_0 - I_r \cdot r \qquad \textit{substituting from above}$$

$$\left[1 - t - (1 - t) \cdot C_y \right] Y^* + t \cdot Y^* + IM_y \cdot Y^* - C_0 - G$$
$$+ X_\varepsilon \cdot \varepsilon_r \cdot r - X_f \cdot Y^f - X_\varepsilon \cdot \varepsilon_0 - X_\varepsilon \cdot \varepsilon_r \cdot r^f = I_0 - I_r \cdot r \qquad \textit{rearranging } Y^* \textit{ terms}$$

$$\left[1 - t - (1 - t) \cdot C_y + t + IM_y \right] Y^* - C_0 - G$$
$$+ X_\varepsilon \cdot \varepsilon_r \cdot r - X_f \cdot Y^f - X_\varepsilon \cdot \varepsilon_0 - X_\varepsilon \cdot \varepsilon_r \cdot r^f = I_0 - I_r \cdot r \qquad \textit{gathering } Y^* \textit{ terms}$$

$$\left[1 - (1 - t) \cdot C_y + IM_y \right] Y^* - C_0 - G + X_\varepsilon \cdot \varepsilon_r \cdot r - X_f \cdot Y^f - X_\varepsilon \cdot \varepsilon_0 - X_\varepsilon \cdot \varepsilon_r \cdot r^f$$
$$= I_0 - I_r \cdot r \qquad \textit{simplifying } Y^* \textit{ terms}$$

$$\left[1 - (1 - t) \cdot C_y + IM_y \right] Y^* - C_0 - I_0 - G + X_\varepsilon \cdot \varepsilon_r \cdot r - X_f \cdot Y^f - X_\varepsilon \cdot \varepsilon_0 - X_\varepsilon \cdot \varepsilon_r \cdot r^f$$
$$= - I_r \cdot r \qquad \textit{subtracting } I_0 \textit{ from both sides}$$

$$\left[1 - (1 - t) \cdot C_y + IM_y \right] Y^* - C_0 - I_0 - G - X_f \cdot Y^f - X_\varepsilon \cdot \varepsilon_0 - X_\varepsilon \cdot \varepsilon_r \cdot r^f$$
$$= - I_r \cdot r - X_\varepsilon \cdot \varepsilon_r \cdot r \qquad \textit{subtracting } X_\varepsilon \cdot \varepsilon_r \cdot r \textit{ from both sides}$$

$$\left[1 - (1 - t) \cdot C_y + IM_y \right] Y^* - C_0 - I_0 - G - X_f \cdot Y^f - X_\varepsilon \cdot \varepsilon_0 - X_\varepsilon \cdot \varepsilon_r \cdot r^f$$
$$= - \left(I_r + X_\varepsilon \cdot \varepsilon_r \right) \cdot r \qquad \textit{gathering r terms}$$

$$\left[1 - (1 - t) \cdot C_y + IM_y \right] Y^* - \left(C_0 + I_0 + G \right) - \left(X_f \cdot Y^f + X_\varepsilon \cdot \varepsilon_0 + X_\varepsilon \cdot \varepsilon_r \cdot r^f \right)$$
$$= - \left(I_r + X_\varepsilon \cdot \varepsilon_r \right) \cdot r \qquad \textit{gathering terms}$$

$$\frac{\left[1 - (1 - t) \cdot C_y + IM_y \right] Y^* - \left(C_0 + I_0 + G \right) - \left(X_f \cdot Y^f + X_\varepsilon \cdot \varepsilon_0 + X_\varepsilon \cdot \varepsilon_r \cdot r^f \right)}{- \left(I_r + X_\varepsilon \cdot \varepsilon_r \right)}$$
$$= r \qquad \textit{dividing both sides by } - \left(I_r + X_\varepsilon \cdot \varepsilon_r \right)$$

$$\frac{\left(C_0 + I_0 + G \right) + \left(X_f \cdot Y^f + X_\varepsilon \cdot \varepsilon_0 + X_\varepsilon \cdot \varepsilon_r \cdot r^f \right) - \left[1 - (1 - t) \cdot C_y + IM_y \right] Y^*}{\left(I_r + X_\varepsilon \cdot \varepsilon_r \right)}$$
$$= r \qquad \textit{simplifying minus signs and rearranging terms to match text}$$

It is important to remember which terms are constants and which are variables. **Every** term on the left-hand side of the above equation for the equilibrium real interest rate is a constant! In that equation, only the real interest rate, r, is a variable.

Should you memorize this equation? **Absolutely not**. Your brain cells have better things to do. Remember how to derive it. The equation is messy, but the derivation was just simple algebra. Trust your ability to do algebra, remember you are trying to isolate the real interest rate, be sure you know the component equations (household saving, government saving, international saving, investment demand, and loanable funds market equilibrium) – and that's all.

9. Suppose that the following equations describe spending in the economy.

Consumption: $C = C_0 + C_y Y^D$ Net Taxes: $T = tY$

Investment: $I = I_0 - I_r r$ Imports: $IM = IM_y Y$

Government Purchases: $G = G$ Gross Exports: $GX = X_f Y^f + X_\varepsilon \varepsilon$

Real Exchange Rate: $\varepsilon = \varepsilon_0 - \varepsilon_r(r - r^f)$

On a separate sheet of paper, derive the equation for the equilibrium level of the real interest rate. Try to do the derivation without looking at the "To The Chalkboard" box on the previous page.

HINT: The next question illustrates why it is a bad idea to memorize the expression for the real interest rate. Because the equations expressing any of the components of spending can be changed, thus changing the expression for the real interest rate, you need to be able to **derive** the equation.

10. Suppose that the equations from Question 9 describe spending in the economy, except that gross exports is now equal to $GX = X_0 + X_f Y^f + X_\varepsilon \varepsilon$. On a separate sheet of paper, derive the equation for the equilibrium level of the real interest rate.

HINT: The answer to the next question can be derived either by plugging values into the equation for the real interest rate, or by algebraically solving the equilibrium condition for the equilibrium value of the real interest rate. The disadvantage to the "plug and chug" method is that it requires memorizing, or at least having handy, the equation for the real interest rate. The advantage to the algebraic method is that you need to know only one piece of information in addition to the equations given in Question 11: the equation describing equilibrium in financial markets.

11. Suppose that the following equations describe spending in the economy.

   Consumption: $C = 100 + 0.7Y^D$ Net Taxes: $T = 0.2Y$

   Investment: $I = 1500 - 2000r$ Imports: $IM = 0.15Y$

   Government Purchases: $G = 1600$ Gross Exports: $GX = 2Y^f + 10\varepsilon$

   Real Exchange Rate: Foreign Income: $Y^f = 600$

   $\quad \varepsilon = 300 - 800(r - 0.06)$ Potential Domestic Output $= 12,000$

   What is the equilibrium value of the real interest rate? What is the equilibrium value of investment spending? What are the equilibrium values of private savings, government savings, and international savings? Check to be sure that the total value of funds flowing into the financial markets equals the total flow of funds out of the markets.

12. Suppose the following values pertain to an economy:

   Baseline consumption, $C_0 = 1,000$

   Baseline investment, $I_0 = 1,000$

   Government purchases, $G = 1,600$

   The sensitivity of exports to foreign income, $X_f = 0.2$

   Foreign income, $Y^f = 6,000$

   The sensitivity of exports to changes in the exchange rate, $X_\varepsilon = 0.2$

   Foreign exchange speculators' long-run view of the real exchange rate, $\varepsilon_0 = 30$

   The sensitivity of the exchange rate to changes in the interest rate, $\varepsilon_r = 8,000$

   Foreign interest rates, $r^f = 0.12$

   Tax rate, $t = 0.25$

   Marginal propensity to consume, $C_y = 0.8$

   Marginal propensity to import, $IM_y = 0.2$

   Potential output, $Y^* = 8,000$

   Sensitivity of investment to changes in the real interest rate, $I_r = 2,000$

   Sensitivity of exchange rates to changes in the real interest rate, $\varepsilon_r = 8,000$

   What is the equilibrium value of the real interest rate? Confirm your answer by calculating the following values and then checking to be sure total inflows equal total outflows: private savings, government savings, international savings, and investment spending.

13. Suppose the values from Question 12 pertain to an economy, with one exception: suppose that baseline consumption, C_0, equals 1,072.

   A. Now what is the equilibrium value of the real interest rate? Confirm your answer by calculating the following values and then checking to be sure total inflows equal total outflows: private savings, government savings, international savings, and investment spending.

   B. Explain why real interest rates increase when consumption spending increases. Explain why international savings increase and investment spending declines.

14. Suppose the values from Question 12 pertain to an economy, with one exception: suppose that government spending, G, equals 1,870.

   A. Now what is the equilibrium value of the real interest rate? Confirm your answer by calculating the following values and then checking to be sure total inflows equal total outflows: private savings, government savings, international savings, and investment spending.

   B. Explain why real interest rates increase when government spending increases. Explain why international savings increase and investment spending declines.

HINT: When government spending changes in the flexible-price full-employment classical model, there is **no change** in the amount of output produced. In the flexible-price full-employment classical model, the amount of output produced is always the full-employment potential output. Real interest rates adjust in this model so that there is never a gap between actual and potential output. As a result, when government spending increases, resulting adjustments in the real interest rate lead to changes in the components of spending that are sensitive to changes in the domestic real interest rate: investment spending and gross exports. A change in government spending therefore does **not** change total output. It simply redistributes that output among the four sectors of the economy: households, businesses, government agencies, and the rest of the world.

15. Suppose the values from Question 12 pertain to an economy, with one exception: suppose that potential output, Y*, equals 8,180.

   A. Now what is the equilibrium value of the real interest rate? Confirm your answer by calculating the following values and then checking to be sure total inflows equal total outflows: private savings, government savings, international savings, and investment spending.

   B. Explain why real interest rates decrease when potential output increases. Explain why international savings decrease and investment spending increases.

TO THE CHALKBOARD:

Deriving the Equations for the Effect of a Change in Government Spending

In the textbook, Prof. DeLong derives the equation for the change in real interest rates, Δr, when there is a change in government spending, ΔG. Here is a step-by-step explanation of the derivation.

Method One: Using Calculus

It is not mentioned in the text, but the quickest and easiest way to derive the equation is with calculus. Don't panic if you have not had calculus – though you really should take it if you want to major in economics – because we can derive the equation without calculus, too. But with calculus, we just take the partial derivative of the equilibrium equation with regard to government spending. Everything but G is treated as a constant. The derivative of G times a constant equals the constant, regardless of how messy the constant is. And because the derivative of a constant is 0, all the other terms drop out. We thus have

$$\frac{\partial r}{\partial G} = \frac{\partial}{\partial G}\left(\frac{\left(C_0 + I_0 + G\right) + \left(X_f \cdot Y^f + X_\varepsilon \cdot \varepsilon_0 + X_\varepsilon \cdot \varepsilon_r \cdot r^f\right) - \left[1 - (1 - t)\cdot C_y + IM_y\right]\cdot Y^*}{\left(I_r + X_\varepsilon \cdot \varepsilon_r\right)}\right)$$

$$= \frac{\partial}{\partial G}\left(\frac{\left(C_0 + I_0\right) + \left(X_f \cdot Y^f + X_\varepsilon \cdot \varepsilon_0 + X_\varepsilon \cdot \varepsilon_r \cdot r^f\right) - \left[1 - (1 - t)\cdot C_y + IM_y\right]\cdot Y^*}{\left(I_r + X_\varepsilon \cdot \varepsilon_r\right)}\right) + \frac{\partial}{\partial G}\left(\frac{G}{\left(I_r + X_\varepsilon \cdot \varepsilon_r\right)}\right)$$

$$= 0 + \frac{1}{\left(I_r + X_\varepsilon \cdot \varepsilon_r\right)}$$

$$= \frac{1}{\left(I_r + X_\varepsilon \cdot \varepsilon_r\right)}$$

Mathematicians would shudder, but economists are happy to use the following approximation: the change in real interest rates equals this derivative times the change in government spending.

$$\Delta r = \frac{\partial r}{\partial G}\cdot(\Delta G) = \left(\frac{1}{I_r + X_\varepsilon \cdot \varepsilon_r}\right)\cdot(\Delta G) = \frac{\Delta G}{I_r + X_\varepsilon \cdot \varepsilon_r}$$

Method Two: Without Calculus

We can derive the same equation without calculus. To do so requires two things: (1) we must remember which symbols stand for constants and which ones stand for variables and (2) we must think about which variables change value when government spending changes.

Consumption spending is $C_0 + C_y(1 - t)Y$. The only variable in this equation is Y. But because we are using the flexible-price full-employment classical model, output (Y) never changes. So when government spending changes, nothing changes in the consumption spending equation.

$$\Delta C = 0 \text{ when government spending changes.}$$

Investment spending is $I_0 - I_r r$. The only variable in this equation is r. When government spending changes, real interest rates will change. The change in real interest rates is how the economy adjusts in the flexible-price full-employment model. Use Δr to stand for the change in interest rates. The change in investment spending will then be

$$\Delta I = -I_r \cdot \Delta r \text{ when government spending changes.}$$

Government spending is G. There is no variable in this equation, but we are considering the effect of a change in government spending, so

$$\Delta G = \Delta G \text{ when government spending changes}$$

Gross export spending is $X_f Y^f + X_\varepsilon \varepsilon_0 - X_\varepsilon \varepsilon_r r + X_\varepsilon \varepsilon_r r^f$. The only variable in this equation is r. Everything else is a constant. When government spending changes, real interest rates will change, changing gross exports. The change in gross exports will be

$$\Delta GX = -X_\varepsilon \varepsilon_r \Delta r \text{ when government spending changes}$$

Import spending is $IM_y Y$. Again, the only variable in this equation is Y. But because we are using the flexible-price full-employment classical model, output (Y) never changes. So when government spending changes, nothing changes in the import spending equation.

$$\Delta IM = 0 \text{ when government spending changes.}$$

Finally, to repeat again, because we are using the flexible-price full-employment classical model, output (Y) never changes. So when government spending changes, there is no change in output.

$$\Delta Y = 0 \text{ when government spending changes.}$$

Output, Y, equals total spending, $C + I + G + GX - IM$. So when government spending changes, the change in output must equal the change in total spending.

$$\Delta Y = \Delta C + \Delta I + \Delta G + \Delta GX - \Delta IM$$

Now we simply substitute into this last equation, and solve algebraically.

$$\Delta Y = \Delta C + \Delta I + \Delta G + \Delta GX - \Delta IM \quad \text{\textit{definition of equilibrium in goods markets}}$$
$$0 = 0 - I_r \Delta r + \Delta G - X_\varepsilon \varepsilon_r \Delta r - 0 \quad \text{\textit{substituting from above}}$$
$$I_r \Delta r + X_\varepsilon \varepsilon_r \Delta r = \Delta G \quad \text{\textit{adding } } I_r \Delta r + X_\varepsilon \varepsilon_r \Delta r \text{ \textit{to both sides}}$$
$$[I_r + X_\varepsilon \varepsilon_r] \Delta r = \Delta G \quad \text{\textit{factoring out } } \Delta r$$
$$\Delta r = \frac{\Delta G}{I_r + X_\varepsilon \varepsilon_r} \quad \text{\textit{dividing both sides by } } I_r + X_\varepsilon \varepsilon_r$$

Last Steps: Using Δr

Now we can use the equation for the change in real interest rates, Δr, to derive the equations that tell us how the components of aggregate demand and the real exchange rate change when government spending changes.

We already determined that $\Delta C = 0$ when government spending changes.

The change in investment spending is $\Delta I = -I_r \cdot \Delta r$ when government spending changes. Substituting

$$\Delta I = -I_r \cdot \Delta r = -I_r \cdot \left(\frac{\Delta G}{I_r + X_\varepsilon \cdot \varepsilon_r} \right)$$

The change in government spending is just ΔG.

The change in net exports equals the difference between the change in gross exports and the change in imports. We already determined that $\Delta GX = -X_\varepsilon \varepsilon_r \Delta r$ and $\Delta IM = 0$ when government spending changes. Substituting

$$\Delta NX = -X_\varepsilon \cdot \varepsilon_r \cdot \left(\frac{\Delta G}{I_r + X_\varepsilon \cdot \varepsilon_r} \right) - 0 = -X_\varepsilon \cdot \varepsilon_r \cdot \left(\frac{\Delta G}{I_r + X_\varepsilon \cdot \varepsilon_r} \right)$$

Finally, the real exchange rate equation is $\varepsilon = \varepsilon_0 - \varepsilon_r (r - r^f)$. The constants in the equation are ε_0, ε_r, and r^f. The variable in the equation is r. A change in the real interest rate, r, will lead to a change in the real exchange rate, ε: $\Delta \varepsilon = -\varepsilon_r \cdot \Delta r$. Substituting

$$\Delta \varepsilon = -\varepsilon_r \cdot \Delta r = -\varepsilon_r \cdot \left(\frac{\Delta G}{I_r + X_\varepsilon \cdot \varepsilon_r} \right)$$

It's probably more important – check with your instructor – that you know the direction of change in real interest rates, consumption, investment, government spending, net exports, and the real exchange rate than that you know the precise size of the change. The graphical approach is most useful for assessing the direction of change. For example, an decrease in government spending increases government saving, **shifting** the total savings curve to the right. The real interest rate will decrease. Investment demand will increase, **moving along** the investment curve. Remember that the total savings curve is upward sloping only because gross exports respond to a change in real interest rates. Gross exports will increase when real interest rates fall, decreasing international savings, **moving** us **along** the total savings curve as shown at the right.

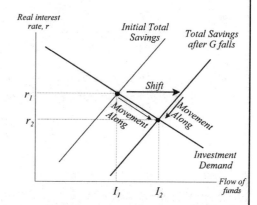

 NOTE: In Questions 16, 17, 18, and 19, you should use the equations for a change in real interest rates, Δr, and for changes in the components of total spending, ΔC, ΔI, ΔG, and ΔNX. The equations are derived in the textbook and in "To The Chalkboard" boxes below.

16. Suppose the following values initially pertain to an economy:

   Baseline consumption, $C_0 = 1,000$

   Baseline investment, $I_0 = 2,200$

   Government purchases, $G = 1,600$

   The sensitivity of exports to foreign income, $X_f = 0.2$

   Foreign income, $Y^f = 6,000$

   The sensitivity of exports to changes in the exchange rate, $X_\varepsilon = 0.2$

   Foreign exchange speculators' long-run view of the real exchange rate, $\varepsilon_0 = 30$

   The sensitivity of the exchange rate to changes in the interest rate, $\varepsilon_r = 5,000$

   Foreign interest rates, $r^f = 9\%$

   Tax rate, $t = 0.25$

   Marginal propensity to consume, $C_y = 0.8$

   Marginal propensity to import, $IM_y = 0.2$

   Potential output, $Y^* = 9,800$

   Sensitivity of investment to changes in the real interest rate, $I_r = 2,000$

   Sensitivity of exchange rates to changes in the real interest rate, $\varepsilon_r = 5,000$

   A. Now suppose that government purchases increase by 60. What is the resulting change in the real interest rate, Δr? Answer the question using the equation for Δr.

   B. When government purchases increase by 60, what are the resulting changes in consumption, investment, government purchases, and net exports, ΔC, ΔI, ΔG, and ΔNX?

TO THE CHALKBOARD:
Deriving the Equations for the Effect of a Change in Baseline Investment Spending

In the textbook, Prof. DeLong derives the equation for the change in real interest rates, Δr, when there is a change in baseline investment spending, ΔI_0. Because the derivation here is very similar to that for government spending, be sure you read "TO THE CHALKBOARD: Deriving the Equations for the Effect of a Change in Government Spending" which begins on page 173 before reading this box.

Method One: Using Calculus

With calculus, we just take the partial derivative of the equilibrium equation with regard to investment spending. Everything but I_0 is treated as a constant. We thus have

$$\frac{\partial r}{\partial I_0} = \frac{\partial}{\partial I_0}\left(\frac{(C_0 + I_0 + G) + (X_f Y^f + X_\varepsilon \cdot \varepsilon_0 + X_\varepsilon \cdot \varepsilon_r \cdot r^f) - [1 - (1 - t) \cdot C_y + IM_y] \cdot Y^*}{(I_r + X_\varepsilon \cdot \varepsilon_r)}\right)$$

$$= \frac{\partial}{\partial I_0}\left(\frac{(C_0 + G) + (X_f Y^f + X_\varepsilon \cdot \varepsilon_0 + X_\varepsilon \cdot \varepsilon_r \cdot r^f) - [1 - (1 - t) \cdot C_y + IM_y] \cdot Y^*}{(I_r + X_\varepsilon \cdot \varepsilon_r)}\right) + \frac{\partial}{\partial I_0}\left(\frac{I_0}{(I_r + X_\varepsilon \cdot \varepsilon_r)}\right)$$

$$= \frac{1}{(I_r + X_\varepsilon \cdot \varepsilon_r)}$$

Thus the change in real interest rates equals this derivative times the change in investment spending.

$$\Delta r = \frac{\partial r}{\partial I_0} \cdot (\Delta I_0) = \left(\frac{1}{I_r + X_\varepsilon \cdot \varepsilon_r}\right) \cdot (\Delta I_0) = \frac{\Delta I_0}{I_r + X_\varepsilon \cdot \varepsilon_r}$$

Method Two: Without Calculus

Consumption spending is $C_0 + C_y(1 - t)Y$. Using the flexible-price full-employment classical model, output (Y) never changes. So

$$\Delta C = 0 \text{ when baseline investment spending changes.}$$

Investment spending is $I_0 - I_r r$. When baseline investment spending changes, both I_0 and real interest rates will change. The change in investment spending will then be

$$\Delta I = \Delta I_0 - I_r \cdot \Delta r \text{ when baseline investment spending changes.}$$

Government spending is G. There is no variable in this equation, so

$$\Delta G = 0 \text{ when baseline investment spending changes.}$$

Gross export spending is $X_f Y^f + X_\varepsilon \varepsilon_0 - X_\varepsilon \varepsilon_r r + X_\varepsilon \varepsilon_r r^f$. When baseline investment spending changes, real interest rates will change, changing gross exports. The change in gross exports will be

$$\Delta GX = -X_\varepsilon \varepsilon_r \Delta r \text{ when baseline investment spending changes.}$$

Import spending is $IM_y Y$. Because output (Y) never changes,

$$\Delta IM = 0 \text{ when baseline investment spending changes.}$$

Finally, to repeat, output (Y) never changes, so

$$\Delta Y = 0 \text{ when baseline investment spending changes.}$$

Output, Y, equals total spending, $C + I + G + GX - IM$. So when baseline investment spending changes, the change in output must equal the change in total spending.

$$\Delta Y = \Delta C + \Delta I + \Delta G + \Delta GX - \Delta IM$$

Now we simply substitute into this last equation, and solve algebraically.

$\Delta Y = \Delta C + \Delta I + \Delta G + \Delta GX - \Delta IM$	*definition of equilibrium in goods markets*
$0 = 0 + I_0 - I_r \Delta r + 0 - X_\varepsilon \varepsilon_r \Delta r - 0$	*substituting from above*
$I_r \Delta r + X_\varepsilon \varepsilon_r \Delta r = \Delta I_0$	*adding $I_r \Delta r + X_\varepsilon \varepsilon_r \Delta r$ to both sides*
$(I_r + X_\varepsilon \varepsilon_r)\Delta r = \Delta I_0$	*factoring out Δr*
$\Delta r = \dfrac{\Delta I_0}{I_r + X_\varepsilon \varepsilon_r}$	*dividing both sides by $I_r + X_\varepsilon \varepsilon_r$*

Last Steps: Using Δr

Now we can derive the equations that tell us how the components of aggregate demand and the real exchange rate change when baseline investment spending changes. We already determined that $\Delta C = 0$ and $\Delta G = 0$ when baseline investment spending changes.

The change in investment spending is $\Delta I = \Delta I_0 - I_r \cdot \Delta r$ when baseline investment spending changes. Substituting and simplifying,

$$\Delta I = \Delta I_0 - I_r \cdot \Delta r = \Delta I_0 - I_r \cdot \left(\frac{\Delta I_0}{I_r + X_\varepsilon \cdot \varepsilon_r} \right)$$

$$= \Delta I_0 \cdot \left(\frac{I_r + X_\varepsilon \cdot \varepsilon_r}{I_r + X_\varepsilon \cdot \varepsilon_r} \right) - I_r \cdot \left(\frac{\Delta I_0}{I_r + X_\varepsilon \cdot \varepsilon_r} \right)$$

$$= \frac{\left(\Delta I_0 \cdot I_r + \Delta I_0 \cdot X_\varepsilon \cdot \varepsilon_r - I_r \cdot \Delta I_0 \right)}{I_r + X_\varepsilon \cdot \varepsilon_r}$$

$$= \frac{\Delta I_0 \cdot X_\varepsilon \cdot \varepsilon_r}{I_r + X_\varepsilon \cdot \varepsilon_r}$$

We already determined that $\Delta GX = -X_\varepsilon \varepsilon_r \Delta r$ and $\Delta IM = 0$ when baseline investment spending changes. So the change in net exports is

$$\Delta NX = -X_\varepsilon \cdot \varepsilon_r \left(\frac{\Delta I_0}{I_r + X_\varepsilon \cdot \varepsilon_r} \right) - 0 = -X_\varepsilon \cdot \varepsilon_r \left(\frac{\Delta I_0}{I_r + X_\varepsilon \cdot \varepsilon_r} \right)$$

Finally, the change in the real exchange rate equation is $\Delta \varepsilon = -\varepsilon_r \cdot \Delta r$. Substituting

$$\Delta \varepsilon = -\varepsilon_r \cdot \Delta r = -\varepsilon_r \cdot \left(\frac{\Delta I_0}{I_r + X_\varepsilon \cdot \varepsilon_r} \right)$$

The graphical approach is useful for assessing the direction of change. For example, an increase in baseline investment spending **shifts** the investment demand curve to the right. The real interest rate will increase. The part of investment demand that responds to changes in the real interest rate will then decrease, **moving** back **along** the second investment demand curve. Gross exports will decrease when real interest rates rise, increasing international savings, **moving** us **along** the total savings curve.

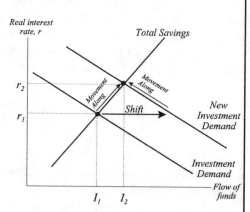

17. Suppose the values of Question 16 (repeated below) pertain to an economy.

Baseline consumption, $C_0 = 1,000$

Baseline investment, $I_0 = 2,200$

Government purchases, $G = 1,600$

The sensitivity of exports to foreign income, $X_f = 0.2$

Foreign income, $Y^f = 6,000$

The sensitivity of exports to changes in the exchange rate, $X_\varepsilon = 0.2$

Foreign exchange speculators' long-run view of the real exchange rate, $\varepsilon_0 = 30$

The sensitivity of the exchange rate to changes in the interest rate, $\varepsilon_r = 5,000$

Foreign interest rates, $r^f = 9\%$

Tax rate, $t = 0.25$

Marginal propensity to consume, $C_y = 0.8$

Marginal propensity to import, $IM_y = 0.2$

Potential output, $Y^* = 9,800$

Sensitivity of investment to changes in the real interest rate, $I_r = 2,000$

Sensitivity of exchange rates to changes in the real interest rate, $\varepsilon_r = 5,000$

A. Now suppose baseline investment spending decreases by 150. What is the resulting change in the real interest rate, Δr? Answer the question using the formula for Δr.

B. When baseline investment spending decreases by 150, what are the resulting changes in consumption, investment, government purchases, and net exports, ΔC, ΔI, ΔG, and ΔNX?

TO THE CHALKBOARD:
Deriving the Equations for the Effect of a Change in Foreign Interest Rates

Be sure you read "TO THE CHALKBOARD: Deriving the Equations for the Effect of a Change in Government Spending" which begins on page 173 before reading this box.

Method One: Using Calculus

With calculus, we just take the partial derivative of the equilibrium equation with regard to foreign interest rates. Everything but r^f is treated as a constant. We thus have

$$\frac{\partial r}{\partial r^f} = \frac{\partial}{\partial r^f}\left(\frac{(C_0 + I_0 + G) + \left(X_f \cdot Y^f + X_\varepsilon \cdot \varepsilon_0 + X_\varepsilon \cdot \varepsilon_r \cdot r^f\right) - \left[1 - (1 - t)\cdot C_y + IM_y\right]\cdot Y^*}{\left(I_r + X_\varepsilon \cdot \varepsilon_r\right)}\right)$$

$$= \frac{\partial}{\partial r^f}\left(\frac{(C_0 + I_0 + G) + \left(X_f \cdot Y^f + X_\varepsilon \cdot \varepsilon_0\right) - \left[1 - (1 - t)\cdot C_y + IM_y\right]\cdot Y^*}{\left(I_r + X_\varepsilon \cdot \varepsilon_r\right)}\right) + \frac{\partial}{\partial r^f}\left(\frac{X_\varepsilon \cdot \varepsilon_r \cdot r^f}{I_r + X_\varepsilon \cdot \varepsilon_r}\right)$$

$$= \frac{X_\varepsilon \cdot \varepsilon_r}{I_r + X_\varepsilon \cdot \varepsilon_r}$$

Thus the change in real interest rates equals this derivative times the change in foreign interest rates.

$$\Delta r = \frac{\partial r}{\partial r^f}\cdot(\Delta r^f) = \left(\frac{X_\varepsilon \cdot \varepsilon_r}{I_r + X_\varepsilon \cdot \varepsilon_r}\right)\cdot(\Delta r^f) = \frac{X_\varepsilon \cdot \varepsilon_r \cdot \Delta r^f}{I_r + X_\varepsilon \cdot \varepsilon_r}$$

Method Two: Without Calculus

Consumption spending is $C_0 + C_y(1 - t)Y$ but output (Y) never changes, so

$$\Delta C = 0 \text{ when the foreign interest rate changes.}$$

Investment spending is $I_0 - I_r r$. When the foreign interest rate changes, real interest rates will change. The change in investment spending will then be

$$\Delta I = I_r \cdot \Delta r \text{ when the foreign interest rate changes.}$$

Government spending is G. There is no variable in this equation, so

$$\Delta G = 0 \text{ when the foreign interest rate changes.}$$

Gross export spending is $X_f Y^f + X_\varepsilon \varepsilon_0 - X_\varepsilon \varepsilon_r r + X_\varepsilon \varepsilon_r r^f$. When the foreign interest rate changes, real interest rates will also change, further changing gross exports. The total change in gross exports is

$$\Delta GX = -X_\varepsilon \varepsilon_r \Delta r + X_\varepsilon \varepsilon_r \Delta r^f = -X_\varepsilon \varepsilon_r(\Delta r - \Delta r^f) \text{ when the foreign interest rate changes.}$$

Import spending is $IM_y Y$. Because output (Y) never changes,

$$\Delta IM = 0 \text{ when the foreign interest rate changes.}$$

Finally, to repeat, output (Y) never changes.

$$\Delta Y = 0 \text{ when the foreign interest rate changes.}$$

Output, Y, equals total spending, $C + I + G + GX - IM$. So when the foreign interest rate changes, the change in output must equal the change in total spending.

$$\Delta Y = \Delta C + \Delta I + \Delta G + \Delta GX - \Delta IM$$

Now we simply substitute into this last equation, and solve algebraically.

$$\Delta Y = \Delta C + \Delta I + \Delta G + \Delta GX - \Delta IM \qquad \textit{definition of equilibrium in goods markets}$$

$$0 = 0 - I_r\Delta r + 0 - X_\varepsilon\varepsilon_r\Delta r + X_\varepsilon\varepsilon_r\Delta r^f - 0 \qquad \textit{substituting from above}$$

$$I_r\Delta r + X_\varepsilon\varepsilon_r\Delta r = X_\varepsilon\varepsilon_r\Delta r^f \qquad \textit{adding } I_r\Delta r + X_\varepsilon\varepsilon_r\Delta r \textit{ to both sides}$$

$$\left(I_r + X_\varepsilon\varepsilon_r\right)\Delta r = X_\varepsilon\varepsilon_r\Delta r^f \qquad \textit{factoring out } \Delta r$$

$$\Delta r = \frac{X_\varepsilon\varepsilon_r\Delta r^f}{I_r + X_\varepsilon\varepsilon_r} \qquad \textit{dividing both sides by } I_r + X_\varepsilon\varepsilon_r$$

Last Steps: Using Δr

Now we can derive the equations that tell us how the components of aggregate demand and the real exchange rate change when the foreign interest rate changes. We already determined that $\Delta C = 0$ and $\Delta G = 0$ when the foreign interest rate changes.

The change in investment spending is $\Delta I = -I_r \cdot \Delta r$ when the foreign interest rate changes. Substituting and simplifying,

$$\Delta I = -I_r \cdot \Delta r = -I_r \cdot \left(\frac{X_\varepsilon \varepsilon_r \Delta r^f}{I_r + X_\varepsilon \varepsilon_r} \right)$$

We already determined that $\Delta GX = -X_\varepsilon \varepsilon_r \Delta r + X_\varepsilon \varepsilon_r \Delta r^f$ and $\Delta IM = 0$ when the foreign interest rate changes. So the change in net exports is

$$\Delta NX = -X_\varepsilon \cdot \varepsilon_r \cdot \left(\frac{X_\varepsilon \varepsilon_r \Delta r^f}{I_r + X_\varepsilon \cdot \varepsilon_r} \right) + X_\varepsilon \varepsilon_r \Delta r^f = -X_\varepsilon \cdot \varepsilon_r \cdot \left(\frac{X_\varepsilon \varepsilon_r \Delta r^f}{I_r + X_\varepsilon \cdot \varepsilon_r} \right) + X_\varepsilon \varepsilon_r \Delta r^f \cdot \left(\frac{I_r + X_\varepsilon \cdot \varepsilon_r}{I_r + X_\varepsilon \cdot \varepsilon_r} \right)$$

$$= \frac{-X_\varepsilon \cdot \varepsilon_r \cdot X_\varepsilon \varepsilon_r \Delta r^f + I_r \cdot X_\varepsilon \varepsilon_r \Delta r^f + X_\varepsilon \cdot \varepsilon_r \cdot X_\varepsilon \varepsilon_r \Delta r^f}{I_r + X_\varepsilon \cdot \varepsilon_r}$$

$$= \frac{I_r X_\varepsilon \varepsilon_r \Delta r^f}{I_r + X_\varepsilon \cdot \varepsilon_r}$$

Finally, the change in the real exchange rate equation is $\Delta \varepsilon = -\varepsilon_r \cdot (\Delta r - \Delta r^f)$. Substituting

$$\Delta \varepsilon = -\varepsilon_r \cdot (\Delta r - \Delta r^f) = -\varepsilon_r \cdot \left(\frac{X_\varepsilon \varepsilon_r \Delta r^f}{I_r + X_\varepsilon \varepsilon_r} - \Delta r^f \right)$$

$$= \frac{-\varepsilon_r \cdot X_\varepsilon \varepsilon_r \Delta r^f}{I_r + X_\varepsilon \varepsilon_r} + \varepsilon_r \Delta r^f \cdot \left(\frac{I_r + X_\varepsilon \varepsilon_r}{I_r + X_\varepsilon \varepsilon_r} \right)$$

$$= \frac{-\varepsilon_r X_\varepsilon \varepsilon_r \Delta r^f + \varepsilon_r \Delta r^f \cdot I_r + \varepsilon_r X_\varepsilon \varepsilon_r \Delta r^f}{I_r + X_\varepsilon \varepsilon_r}$$

$$= \frac{-\varepsilon_r \cdot X_\varepsilon \varepsilon_r \Delta r^f}{I_r + X_\varepsilon \varepsilon_r} + \varepsilon_r \Delta r^f \cdot \left(\frac{I_r + X_\varepsilon \varepsilon_r}{I_r + X_\varepsilon \varepsilon_r} \right)$$

$$= \frac{\varepsilon_r \Delta r^f I_r}{I_r + X_\varepsilon \varepsilon_r}$$

The graphical approach is useful for assessing the direction of change. For example, a decrease in the foreign interest rate decreases the real exchange rate, decreasing gross exports and thus increasing international savings, which **shifts** the total savings curve to the right. The real interest rate will decrease. Investment demand will then increase, **moving along** the investment demand curve. Gross exports will increase when real interest rates fall, partly offsetting the increase in international savings, a **movement along** the second total savings curve.

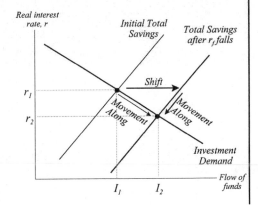

18. Suppose the values of Question 16 (repeated below) pertain to an economy.

Baseline consumption, $C_0 = 1,000$

Baseline investment, $I_0 = 2,200$

Government purchases, $G = 1,600$

The sensitivity of exports to foreign income, $X_f = 0.2$

Foreign income, $Y^f = 6,000$

The sensitivity of exports to changes in the exchange rate, $X_\varepsilon = 0.2$

Foreign exchange speculators' long-run view of the real exchange rate, $\varepsilon_0 = 30$

The sensitivity of the exchange rate to changes in the interest rate, $\varepsilon_r = 5,000$

Foreign interest rates, $r^f = 9\%$

Tax rate, $t = 0.25$

Marginal propensity to consume, $C_y = 0.8$

Marginal propensity to import, $IM_y = 0.2$

Potential output, $Y^* = 9,800$

Sensitivity of investment to changes in the real interest rate, $I_r = 2,000$

Sensitivity of exchange rates to changes in the real interest rate, $\varepsilon_r = 5,000$

A. Now suppose foreign interest rates increase by 3 percentage points to 12%. What is the resulting change in the real interest rate, Δr? Answer the question using the formula for Δr.

B. When foreign interest rates increase by 3 percentage points, what are the resulting changes in consumption, investment, government purchases, and net exports, ΔC, ΔI, ΔG, and ΔNX?

TO THE CHALKBOARD:
Deriving the Equations for the Effect of a Change in Speculators' Confidence, ε_0

Be sure you read "TO THE CHALKBOARD: Deriving the Equations for the Effect of a Change in Government Spending" which begins on page 173 before reading this box.

Method One: Using Calculus

With calculus, we just take the partial derivative of the equilibrium equation with regard to ε_0. Everything but ε_0 is treated as a constant. We thus have

$$\frac{\partial r}{\partial \varepsilon_0} = \frac{\partial}{\partial \varepsilon_0}\left(\frac{\left(C_0 + I_0 + G\right) + \left(X_f \cdot Y^f + X_\varepsilon \cdot \varepsilon_0 + X_\varepsilon \cdot \varepsilon_r \cdot r^f\right) - \left[1 - (1 - t)\cdot C_y + IM_y\right]\cdot Y^*}{\left(I_r + X_\varepsilon \cdot \varepsilon_r\right)} \right)$$

$$= \frac{\partial}{\partial \varepsilon_0}\left(\frac{\left(C_0 + I_0 + G\right) + \left(X_f \cdot Y^f + X_\varepsilon \cdot \varepsilon_r \cdot r^f\right) - \left[1 - (1 - t)\cdot C_y + IM_y\right]\cdot Y^*}{\left(I_r + X_\varepsilon \cdot \varepsilon_r\right)} \right) + \frac{\partial}{\partial \varepsilon_0}\left(\frac{X_\varepsilon \cdot \varepsilon_0}{I_r + X_\varepsilon \cdot \varepsilon_r} \right)$$

$$= \frac{X_\varepsilon}{I_r + X_\varepsilon \cdot \varepsilon_r}$$

Thus the change in real interest rates equals this partial derivative times the change in ε_0,

$$\Delta r = \frac{\partial r}{\partial \varepsilon_0}\cdot (\Delta \varepsilon_0) = \left(\frac{X_\varepsilon}{I_r + X_\varepsilon \cdot \varepsilon_r} \right)\cdot (\Delta \varepsilon_0) = \frac{X_\varepsilon \cdot \Delta \varepsilon_0}{I_r + X_\varepsilon \cdot \varepsilon_r}$$

Method Two: Without Calculus

Consumption spending is $C_0 + C_y(1 - t)Y$ but output (Y) never changes, so

$$\Delta C = 0 \text{ when } \varepsilon_0 \text{ changes.}$$

Investment spending is $I_0 - I_r r$. When foreign exchange speculators' long-run confidence changes, real interest rates will change. The change in investment spending will then be

$$\Delta I = I_r \cdot \Delta r \text{ when } \varepsilon_0 \text{ changes.}$$

Government spending is G. There is no variable in this equation, so

$$\Delta G = 0 \text{ when } \varepsilon_0 \text{ changes.}$$

Gross export spending is $X_f Y^f + X_\varepsilon \varepsilon_0 - X_\varepsilon \varepsilon_r r + X_\varepsilon \varepsilon_r r^f$. When ε_0 changes, real interest rates will also change, further changing gross exports. The total change in gross exports will be

$$\Delta GX = X_\varepsilon \Delta \varepsilon_0 - X_\varepsilon \varepsilon_r \Delta r \text{ when } \varepsilon_0 \text{ changes.}$$

Import spending is $IM_y Y$. Because output (Y) never changes,

$$\Delta IM = 0 \text{ when } \varepsilon_0 \text{ changes.}$$

Output (Y) never changes, by assumption.

$$\Delta Y = 0 \text{ when } \varepsilon_0 \text{ changes.}$$

Output, Y, equals total spending, $C + I + G + GX - IM$. So when ε_0 changes, the change in output must equal the change in total spending, or

$$\Delta Y = \Delta C + \Delta I + \Delta G + \Delta GX - \Delta IM.$$

Now we simply substitute into this last equation, and solve algebraically.

$$\Delta Y = \Delta C + \Delta I + \Delta G + \Delta GX - \Delta IM \qquad \textit{definition of equilibrium in goods markets}$$
$$0 = 0 - I_r \Delta r + 0 + X_\varepsilon \Delta \varepsilon_0 - X_\varepsilon \varepsilon_r \Delta r - 0 \qquad \textit{substituting from above}$$
$$I_r \Delta r + X_\varepsilon \varepsilon_r \Delta r = X_\varepsilon \Delta \varepsilon_0 \qquad \textit{adding } I_r \Delta r + X_\varepsilon \varepsilon_r \Delta r \textit{ to both sides}$$
$$(I_r + X_\varepsilon \varepsilon_r)\Delta r = X_\varepsilon \Delta \varepsilon_0 \qquad \textit{factoring out } \Delta r$$
$$\Delta r = \frac{X_\varepsilon \Delta \varepsilon_0}{I_r + X_\varepsilon \varepsilon_r} \qquad \textit{dividing both sides by } I_r + X_\varepsilon \varepsilon_r$$

Last Steps: Using Δr

Now we can derive the equations that tell us how the components of aggregate demand and the real exchange rate change when ε_0 changes. We already determined that $\Delta C = 0$ and $\Delta G = 0$ when ε_0 changes.

The change in investment spending is $\Delta I = - I_r \cdot \Delta r$ when ε_0 changes. Substituting and simplifying,

$$\Delta I = - I_r \cdot \Delta r = - I_r \cdot \left(\frac{X_\varepsilon \Delta \varepsilon_0}{I_r + X_\varepsilon \varepsilon_r} \right)$$

We already determined that $\Delta GX = X_\varepsilon \Delta \varepsilon_0 - X_\varepsilon \varepsilon_r \Delta r$ and $\Delta IM = 0$ when ε_0 changes. So the change in net exports is

$$\Delta NX = X_\varepsilon \Delta \varepsilon_0 - X_\varepsilon \cdot \varepsilon_r \cdot \left(\frac{X_\varepsilon \Delta \varepsilon_0}{I_r + X_\varepsilon \varepsilon_r} \right) = X_\varepsilon \Delta \varepsilon_0 \cdot \left(\frac{I_r + X_\varepsilon \cdot \varepsilon_r}{I_r + X_\varepsilon \cdot \varepsilon_r} \right) - X_\varepsilon \cdot \varepsilon_r \cdot \left(\frac{X_\varepsilon \Delta \varepsilon_0}{I_r + X_\varepsilon \cdot \varepsilon_r} \right)$$

$$= \frac{I_r \cdot X_\varepsilon \Delta \varepsilon_0 + X_\varepsilon \Delta \varepsilon_0 \cdot X_\varepsilon \varepsilon_r - X_\varepsilon \cdot \varepsilon_r \cdot X_\varepsilon \Delta \varepsilon_0}{I_r + X_\varepsilon \cdot \varepsilon_r}$$

$$= \frac{I_r X_\varepsilon \Delta \varepsilon_0}{I_r + X_\varepsilon \cdot \varepsilon_r}$$

Finally, the change in the real exchange rate equation is $\Delta \varepsilon = \Delta \varepsilon_0 - \varepsilon_r \cdot \Delta r$. Substituting

$$\Delta \varepsilon = \Delta \varepsilon_0 - \varepsilon_r \cdot \Delta r = \Delta \varepsilon_0 - \varepsilon_r \cdot \left(\frac{X_\varepsilon \Delta \varepsilon_0}{I_r + X_\varepsilon \varepsilon_r} \right)$$

$$= \Delta \varepsilon_0 \cdot \left(\frac{I_r + X_\varepsilon \varepsilon_r}{I_r + X_\varepsilon \varepsilon_r} \right) - \frac{\varepsilon_r \cdot X_\varepsilon \Delta \varepsilon_0}{I_r + X_\varepsilon \varepsilon_r}$$

$$= \frac{\Delta \varepsilon_0 \cdot I_r + \varepsilon_r X_\varepsilon \Delta \varepsilon_0 - \varepsilon_r X_\varepsilon \Delta \varepsilon_0}{I_r + X_\varepsilon \varepsilon_r}$$

$$= \frac{I_r \cdot \Delta \varepsilon_0}{I_r + X_\varepsilon \varepsilon_r}$$

The graphical approach is useful for assessing the direction of change. A decrease in ε_0 decreases the real exchange rate, decreasing gross exports and thus increasing international savings, which **shifts** the total savings curve to the right. The real interest rate will decrease. Investment demand will then increase, **moving along** the investment demand curve. Gross exports will increase when real interest rates fall, partly offsetting the increase in international savings, a **movement along** the second total savings curve.

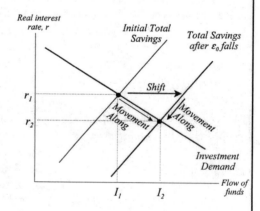

19. Suppose the values of Question 16 (repeated below) pertain to an economy.

Baseline consumption, $C_0 = 1,000$

Baseline investment, $I_0 = 2,200$

Government purchases, $G = 1,600$

The sensitivity of exports to foreign income, $X_f = 0.2$

Foreign income, $Y^f = 6,000$

The sensitivity of exports to changes in the exchange rate, $X_\varepsilon = 0.2$

Foreign exchange speculators' long-run view of the real exchange rate, $\varepsilon_0 = 30$

The sensitivity of the exchange rate to changes in the interest rate, $\varepsilon_r = 5,000$

Foreign interest rates, $r^f = 9\%$

Tax rate, $t = 0.25$

Marginal propensity to consume, $C_y = 0.8$

Marginal propensity to import, $IM_y = 0.2$

Potential output, $Y^* = 9,800$

Sensitivity of investment to changes in the real interest rate, $I_r = 2,000$

Sensitivity of exchange rates to changes in the real interest rate, $\varepsilon_r = 5,000$

A. Now suppose foreign exchange speculators long-term expectation of the real exchange rate, ε_0, decreases by 15. What is the resulting change in the real interest rate, Δr? Answer the question using the formula for Δr.

B. When foreign exchange speculators long-term expectation of the real exchange rate, ε_0, decreases by 15, what are the resulting changes in consumption, investment, government purchases, and net exports, ΔC, ΔI, ΔG, and ΔNX?

TO THE CHALKBOARD:
Deriving the Equations for the Effect of a Change in Potential Output

Be sure you read "TO THE CHALKBOARD: Deriving the Equations for the Effect of a Change in Government Spending" which begins on page 173 before reading this box.

Method One: Using Calculus

With calculus, we just take the partial derivative of the equilibrium equation with regard to potential output. Everything but Y* is treated as a constant. We thus have

$$\frac{\partial r}{\partial Y^*} = \frac{\partial}{\partial Y^*}\left(\frac{\left(C_0 + I_0 + G\right) + \left(X_f \cdot Y^f + X_\varepsilon \cdot \varepsilon_0 + X_\varepsilon \cdot \varepsilon_r \cdot r^f\right) - \left[1 - (1 - t) \cdot C_y + IM_y\right] \cdot Y^*}{\left(I_r + X_\varepsilon \cdot \varepsilon_r\right)}\right)$$

$$= \frac{\partial}{\partial Y^*}\left(\frac{\left(C_0 + I_0 + G\right) + \left(X_f \cdot Y^f + X_\varepsilon \cdot \varepsilon_0 + X_\varepsilon \cdot \varepsilon_r \cdot r^f\right)}{\left(I_r + X_\varepsilon \cdot \varepsilon_r\right)}\right) + \frac{\partial}{\partial Y^*}\left(\frac{-\left[1 - (1 - t) \cdot C_y + IM_y\right] \cdot Y^*}{I_r + X_\varepsilon \cdot \varepsilon_r}\right)$$

$$= \frac{-\left[1 - (1 - t) \cdot C_y + IM_y\right]}{I_r + X_\varepsilon \cdot \varepsilon_r}$$

Thus the change in real interest rates equals this partial derivative times the change in potential output,

$$\Delta r = \frac{\partial r}{\partial Y^*} \cdot (\Delta Y^*) = -\left(\frac{1 - (1 - t) \cdot C_y + IM_y}{I_r + X_\varepsilon \cdot \varepsilon_r}\right) \cdot (\Delta Y^*)$$

Method Two: Without Calculus

Consumption spending is $C_0 + C_y(1 - t)Y$. When output (Y) changes, consumption changes, so

$$\Delta C = C_y(1 - t)\Delta Y \text{ when Y* changes.}$$

Investment spending is $I_0 - I_r r$. When potential output changes, real interest rates will change. The change in investment spending will then be

$$\Delta I = I_r \cdot \Delta r \text{ when Y* changes.}$$

Government spending is G. It is a constant, so

$$\Delta G = 0 \text{ when Y* changes.}$$

Gross export spending is $X_f Y^f + X_\varepsilon \varepsilon_0 - X_\varepsilon \varepsilon_r r + X_\varepsilon \varepsilon_r r^f$. When potential output changes, real interest rates will change. The change in gross exports will be

$$\Delta GX = -X_\varepsilon \varepsilon_r \Delta r \text{ when Y* changes.}$$

Import spending is $IM_y Y$, which changes when potential output changes,

$$\Delta IM = IM_y \Delta Y \text{ when Y* changes.}$$

In this example, potential output (Y) is changing, so

$$\Delta Y = \Delta Y^*$$

Output, Y, equals total spending, $C + I + G + GX - IM$. So when potential output changes, the change in output must equal the change in total spending, so

$$\Delta Y = \Delta C + \Delta I + \Delta G + \Delta GX - \Delta IM.$$

Now we simply substitute into this last equation, and solve algebraically.

$$\Delta Y = \Delta C + \Delta I + \Delta G + \Delta GX - \Delta IM \qquad \textit{definition of equilibrium in goods markets}$$

$$\Delta Y = C_y(1 - t)\Delta Y - I_r \Delta r + 0 - X_\varepsilon \varepsilon_r \Delta r - IM_y \Delta Y \qquad \textit{substituting from above}$$

$$I_r \Delta r + X_\varepsilon \varepsilon_r \Delta r = -\Delta Y + C_y(1 - t)\Delta Y - IM_y \Delta Y \qquad \textit{adding } I_r \Delta r + X_\varepsilon \varepsilon_r \Delta r - \Delta Y \textit{ to both sides}$$

$$\left(I_r + X_\varepsilon \varepsilon_r\right)\Delta r = -\left(1 - C_y(1 - t) + IM_y\right) \cdot \Delta Y \qquad \textit{factoring out } \Delta r \textit{ and } \Delta Y$$

$$\Delta r = -\left(\frac{1 - C_y(1 - t) + IM_y}{I_r + X_\varepsilon \varepsilon_r}\right) \cdot \Delta Y \qquad \textit{dividing both sides by } I_r + X_\varepsilon \varepsilon_r$$

Last Steps: Using Δr

Now we can derive the equations that tell us how the components of aggregate demand and the real exchange rate change when potential output changes.

The change in consumption spending is $\Delta C = C_y(1 - t)\Delta Y$ when Y^* changes.

The change in investment spending is $\Delta I = - I_r \cdot \Delta r$ when Y^* changes. Substituting and simplifying,

$$\Delta I = - I_r \cdot \Delta r = \left(- I_r \cdot \right)\left(-\left(\frac{1 - C_y(1 - t) + IM_y}{I_r + X_\varepsilon \varepsilon_r} \right) \cdot \Delta Y \right) = I_r \cdot \left(\frac{1 - C_y(1 - t) + IM_y}{I_r + X_\varepsilon \varepsilon_r} \right) \cdot \Delta Y$$

There is no change in government spending: $\Delta G = 0$.

We already determined that $\Delta GX = - X_\varepsilon \varepsilon_r \Delta r$ and the change in imports is $\Delta IM = IM_y \Delta Y$ when Y^* changes, so the change in net exports is

$$\Delta NX = \Delta GX - \Delta IM$$

$$= - X_\varepsilon \cdot \varepsilon_r \cdot \left(-\left(\frac{1 - C_y(1 - t) + IM_y}{I_r + X_\varepsilon \varepsilon_r} \right) \cdot \Delta Y \right) - IM_y \Delta Y$$

$$= \left[X_\varepsilon \cdot \varepsilon_r \cdot \left(\frac{1 - C_y(1 - t) + IM_y}{I_r + X_\varepsilon \varepsilon_r} \right) - IM_y \right] \cdot \Delta Y$$

Finally, the change in the real exchange rate equation is $\Delta \varepsilon = - \varepsilon_r \cdot \Delta r$. Substituting

$$\Delta \varepsilon = - \varepsilon_r \cdot \left(-\left(\frac{1 - C_y(1 - t) + IM_y}{I_r + X_\varepsilon \varepsilon_r} \right) \cdot \Delta Y \right)$$

$$= \varepsilon_r \cdot \left(\frac{1 - C_y(1 - t) + IM_y}{I_r + X_\varepsilon \varepsilon_r} \right) \cdot \Delta Y$$

The graphical approach is useful for assessing the direction of change. An increase in potential output increases private savings, which **shifts** the total savings curve to the right. The real interest rate will decrease. Investment demand will then increase, **moving along** the investment demand curve. Gross exports will increase when real interest rates fall, partly offsetting the increase in private savings, a **movement along** the second total savings curve.

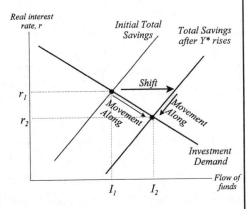

20. Suppose the values of Question 16 (repeated below) pertain to an economy.

   Baseline consumption, $C_0 = 1,000$

   Baseline investment, $I_0 = 2,200$

   Government purchases, $G = 1,600$

   The sensitivity of exports to foreign income, $X_f = 0.2$

   Foreign income, $Y^f = 6,000$

   The sensitivity of exports to changes in the exchange rate, $X_\varepsilon = 0.2$

   Foreign exchange speculators' long-run view of the real exchange rate, $\varepsilon_0 = 30$

   The sensitivity of the exchange rate to changes in the interest rate, $\varepsilon_r = 5,000$

   Foreign interest rates, $r^f = 9\%$

   Tax rate, $t = 0.25$

   Marginal propensity to consume, $C_y = 0.8$

   Marginal propensity to import, $IM_y = 0.2$

   Potential output, $Y^* = 9,800$

   Sensitivity of investment to changes in the real interest rate, $I_r = 2,000$

   Sensitivity of exchange rates to changes in the real interest rate, $\varepsilon_r = 5,000$

   A. Now suppose potential output declines by 60. What is the resulting change in the real interest rate, Δr? Answer the question using the formula for Δr.

   B. When potential output declines by 60, what are the resulting changes in consumption, investment, government purchases, and net exports, ΔC, ΔI, ΔG, and ΔNX?

C. APPLYING CONCEPTS AND MODELS

Now we're getting to the good stuff. Being able to apply a specific concept or model to a real world situation — where you are told which model to apply but you have to figure out how to apply it — is often what you need to earn a B in a course. This is where macroeconomics starts to become interesting and the world starts to make more sense.

1. In 2000 and 2001, the U.S. Congress stipulated that the Social Security surplus had to be used to buy back previously issued federal government bonds. In particular, the Social Security surplus was not to be used to finance other government programs. Would this policy create an inflow of funds into financial markets or an outflow of funds from them? What effect should this policy have on the market for loanable funds?

2. Since he was a child, Eric saved for college by using his birthday gift money to buy U.S. government savings bonds. Now that he is in his first year at the university, he has cashed in all of his bonds to pay tuition and fees. Was his behavior best characterized as a change in the demand for loanable funds or in the supply of loanable funds? When he was buying bonds, was he contributing to the inflow of funds? When he cashed in his bonds, was he contributing to the inflow of funds?

3. David and Ruth saved for retirement by purchasing stock. Now that they are in their 70s, they are selling stock to pay their living expenses. Is their current behavior a change in the demand for or supply of loanable funds?

4. Describe the process by which the loanable funds market moves into equilibrium.

5. Suppose Congress reduces taxes by $1.35 trillion. According to the flexible-price full-employment classical model, what effect will this change have on real interest rates, net exports, and investment spending. What effect will it have on real GDP? Draw a relevant graph in the space at the right. Be sure to label your axes and your curves.

NOTE: A reminder. The flexible-price full-employment classical model is not a good representation of the real world in the short run. However, we are gaining some insights from the model that will be helpful in understanding the interaction between the short-run and long-run effects of policy changes. But it is not a good idea to try to use this model to explain what you read in the newspapers. In the real world, prices and wages do not adjust instantaneously to clear markets.

6. Suppose business people become more optimistic about the future of the economy. As a result, they increase their baseline investment. According to the flexible-price full-employment classical model, what effect will this change have on real interest rates, net exports, and investment spending. What effect will it have on real GDP? Draw a relevant graph in the space at the right. Be sure to label your axes and your curves.

7. Suppose consumers become less optimistic about the future of the economy. As a result, they decrease their baseline consumption According to the flexible-price full-employment classical model, what effect will this change have on real interest rates, net exports, and investment spending. What effect will it have on real GDP? Draw a relevant graph in the space at the right. Be sure to label your axes and your curves.

8. Suppose interest rates in other countries fall. According to the flexible-price full-employment classical model, what effect will this change have on domestic real interest rates, net exports, and investment spending. What effect will it have on real GDP? Draw a relevant graph in the space at the right. Be sure to label your axes and your curves.

D. EXPLAINING THE REAL WORLD

Most instructors are delighted when you are able to figure out which concept or model to apply to a real world situation. Being able to do so means you thoroughly understand the material and is often what you need to do to earn an A in a course. This is where you experience the power of macroeconomic theory.

1. Congress is considering a bill to increase spending on education. Assuming prices and wages in the economy are fully flexible, what will be the short-run effect on the economy?

2. A country's electricity grid becomes unreliable and large regions of the country begin to experience periodic power outages. What will be the short-run effect on the economy, assuming full flexibility of wages and prices?

3. The United Nations funds a water project that removes life-threatening bacteria from the drinking water of various countries, improving the health of all residents. What effect does the water project have on that nation's economy?

4. A level 7.2 earthquake renders most downtown buildings uninhabitable. What is the effect on the region's economy?

5. Foreign exchange speculators become much less responsive to every change in domestic interest rates. The Chairman of the Fed warns members of Congress that they must exercise additional caution in their budgeting and may indeed want to reconsider a proposed increase in government spending for prescription drugs for the elderly. Why does the change in behavior of foreign exchange speculators have any bearing on decisions made by Congress?

E. POSSIBILITIES TO PONDER

The more you learn, the more you realize you have more to learn. These questions go beyond the textbook material. They are the sort of questions that distinguish A+ or A work from A- work. Some of them may even serve as starting points for junior or senior year research papers.

1. If the economy truly conformed to the assumptions of the flexible-price full-employment classical model, there would never be an unemployment problem. Why aren't prices and wages fully flexible?

2. Under the National Income and Product Accounts, government spending for education counts as part of G and household spending for private tuition or school books counts as part of C. Should government and private spending for education count instead as part of investment spending? Explain.

3. The development of the internet has facilitated worldwide trading of stocks and bonds. In the context of the flexible-price full-employment classical model, what are the economic effects of the development of the internet?

4. Should foreign exchange speculators have unlimited power to change exchange rates?

SOLUTIONS   SOLUTIONS   SOLUTIONS   SOLUTIONS

A. BASIC DEFINITIONS

* indicates there are notes below related to this question.

1. loanable funds	4. voluntary	7. potential output
2. aggregate demand	5. real interest rate	8. loanable funds
3. comparative statics	6. real business cycle	

9. booms; busts	11. are not *	13. Inflows into
10. Outflows from	12. stays the same	14. decreases

15. equal to

16. stays the same

17. decreases

18. changes

*11.   Expenditure and output are different concepts. The two concepts have the same numerical value when the economy is in equilibrium, but they are not the same "thing."

---

19. A. Real interest rates carry the burden of adjustment.

20. C. Imports (IM), Consumption (C), and Government Purchases (G) do not change when real interest rates change. Investment spending (I) and Gross Exports (GX) do.

B. MANIPULATION OF CONCEPTS AND MODELS

1. A. NX = GX - IM = 400 - 300 = $100 billion.

    B. −NX = IM - GX = − $100 billion.

    C. $100 billion flows into U.S. financial markets from abroad.

2. A. NX = −$50,000 million.

$$NX = GX - IM = (5{,}000{,}000 \ million \ pesos) \cdot \left(\frac{\$0.11}{1 \ peso} \right) - \$600 \ billion$$
$$= \$550{,}000 \ million - \$600{,}000 \ million = - \$50{,}000 \ million$$

    B. $50,000 million in funds for investment spending flowed from Mexico into the United States. Mexican companies received $600,000 million from the United States. Of that amount, they spent $550,000 million purchasing currently produced goods and services. The remaining $50,000 million will be used to purchase U.S. assets – that is, $50,000 million will flow into U.S. financial markets.

3. If government purchases (G) exceed net tax receipts (T), then on net government funds are flowing out of financial markets. (In fact, funds are flowing both into and out of financial markets, but the amount flowing out exceeds the amount flowing in.) Nevertheless, we call this an "inflow" of funds into financial markets. When G > T, we say there is a *negative* inflow of funds from the government sector. Because the flow of funds model is designed to focus on the availability of funds for private investment, only private investment spending is referred to as an "outflow" of funds from financial markets.

4. A. S^H = Y - T - C = 8000 - 2000 - 5500 = 500

    B. BS = T - G = 2000 - 1500 = 500

    C. −NX = IM - GX = 1100 - 1000 = 100

    D. Total Inflow = S^H + BS - NX = 500 + 500 + 100 = 1100

5. A. S^H = Y - T - C = 8000 - 2000 - 5500 = 500

    B. BS = T - G = 2000 - 2200 = −200

    C. −NX = IM - GX = 1100 - 1300 = −200

    D. Total Inflow = S^H + BS - NX = 500 - 200 - 200 = 100

6. In the 2001 *Economic Report of the President*, the data are from Tables B-30 (personal saving), B-82 or B-83 (total budget surplus), and B-1 (net exports). When computing the total inflow of funds, don't forget to *subtract* (not add) the value of net exports.

	Personal Saving (billion $)	Budget Surplus (billion $)	Net Exports (billion $)	Total Inflow of Funds (billion $)
1960	26.4	11.3	2.4	35.3
1965	42.7	9.7	3.9	48.5
1970	69.5	(7.3)	1.2	61.0
1975	125.2	(66.9)	13.6	44.7
1980	205.6	(44.9)	(14.9)	175.6
1985	282.6	(154.9)	(114.2)	241.9
1990	334.3	(170.3)	(71.4)	235.4
1995	302.4	(176.7)	(84.3)	210.0
last year available (1999)	147.6	174.4	(254.0)	576.0

The flow of funds is given in nominal terms, so the increase from 1960 to 1999 is partly attributable to inflation. To see real changes, we could deflate by a price index. The GDP price index might be a good choice. But no matter what adjustments we made for inflation, we would conclude that the inflow of funds declined in the early 1970s, increased in the late 1970s as personal saving rose, declined slightly between 1985 and 1990 as net exports rose, and increased remarkably in the late 1990s despite the decline in personal saving. The annual pattern is seen more

Inflow of Funds, 1959-1999

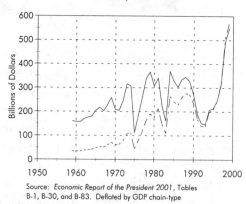

Source: *Economic Report of the President 2001*, Tables B-1, B-30, and B-83. Deflated by GDP chain-type

clearly in the graph at the right, which shows nominal inflow of funds (dashed line) and real inflow of funds, using the GDP price index as a deflator (solid line). The inflow of funds is quite volatile in the 1970s and 1980s, but more than triples between 1992 and 1999.

7. Answers will vary. Almost any time an individual saves, the funds will indirectly fund investment saving. For example, depositing $1,000 in a checking account allows a bank to lend to a business undertaking investment. In a few cases, saving may directly finance investment spending. For example, the funds raised by a company through an Initial Public Offering (IPO) are likely to be used for private investment spending. Another example of personal saving directly financing investment spending is when a family-owned business uses personal funds to buy business machinery.

8. A. The supply of loanable funds, S^H + BS - NX, equals 500 + 200 - (-300), or 1000. The demand for loanable funds, I, equals 1200. The market for loanable funds is therefore not in equilibrium; demand exceeds supply. The price of loanable funds, the real interest rate, will therefore increase. As the real interest rate rises, both gross exports and investment spending will fall. The decline in gross exports increases the supply of loanable funds from abroad. The decline in investment spending decreases the demand for loanable funds. Real interest rates will continue to rise until the supply of loanable funds equals the demand for loanable funds.

B. If net exports fall by 50, then NX now equals -350. The supply of loanable funds, S^H + BS - NX, now equals 500 + 200 - (-350) = 1050. If investment spending falls by 150, then I now equals 1050. So the demand for loanable funds is 1050. The market for loanable funds is therefore in equilibrium; demand equals supply. So long as there are no exogenous changes, there will be no change in real interest rates.

C. A change in business peoples' attitudes is an exogenous change. The supply of loanable funds remains 1050. The demand for loanable funds has declined to 900. The market for loanable funds is not in equilibrium; supply exceeds demand. The real interest rate will therefore fall. As the real interest rate falls, both gross exports and investment spending will increase. The increase in gross exports will reduce the supply of loanable funds; the increase in investment spending will increase the demand for loanable funds. These changes will continue until real interest rates fall to the point where the supply of and demand for loanable funds are equal.

9. The derivation of the equation for the equilibrium level of the real interest rate is given in the "To The Chalkboard" box that begins on page 168. To begin the derivation, remember the following relationships:

- In equilibrium, the inflow of funds equals the outflow of funds. That is, private savings plus government savings plus international savings (the three components of the inflow of funds) equals investment spending.
- Private savings, S^H, equals Y - T - C. Substituting in the expressions for net taxes and consumption, and remembering the definition of disposable income, Y^D, yields
  $$S^H = Y - tY - [C_0 + C_y(1 - t)Y]$$
- Government savings is the budget surplus, T - G.
- International savings is the opposite of net exports, so it is IM - GX. Substituting in the expression for real exchange rate yields
  $$IM - GX = IM_y Y - [X_f Y^f + X_\varepsilon(\varepsilon_0 - \varepsilon_r(r - r^f))]$$
- Investment spending is described by the equation $I_0 - I_r r$

From here, the derivation of the equilibrium equation is just an application of algebra. See the "To The Chalkboard" box that begins on page 168 for the full derivation.

10. The derivation of the equation for the equilibrium real interest rate follows the same steps as in Question 9. The only change is in the expression for gross exports.

$$[1 - t - (1 - t) \cdot C_y] \cdot Y^* - C_0 + t \cdot Y^* - G + IM_y \cdot Y^* - X_0$$
$$+ X_\varepsilon \cdot \varepsilon_r \cdot r - X_f Y^f - X_\varepsilon \cdot \varepsilon_0 - X_\varepsilon \cdot \varepsilon_r \cdot r^f = I_0 - I_r r \qquad \text{definition of equilibrium}$$
$$\overline{\qquad\qquad\qquad\qquad\qquad\qquad\qquad\qquad\qquad\qquad}$$
$$[1 - (1 - t) \cdot C_y + IM_y] \cdot Y^* - C_0 - G - X_0 + X_\varepsilon \cdot \varepsilon_r \cdot r - X_f Y^f - X_\varepsilon \cdot \varepsilon_0 - X_\varepsilon \cdot \varepsilon_r \cdot r^f$$
$$= I_0 - I_r r \qquad \text{rearranging, gathering, and simplifying } Y^* \text{ terms}$$
$$\overline{\qquad\qquad\qquad\qquad\qquad\qquad\qquad\qquad\qquad\qquad}$$
$$[1 - (1 - t) \cdot C_y + IM_y] \cdot Y^* - C_0 - I_0 - G - X_0 - X_f Y^f - X_\varepsilon \cdot \varepsilon_0 - X_\varepsilon \cdot \varepsilon_r \cdot r^f$$
$$= -I_r r - X_\varepsilon \cdot \varepsilon_r \cdot r \qquad \text{subtracting } I_0 \text{ and } X_\varepsilon \cdot \varepsilon_r \cdot r \text{ from both sides}$$
$$\overline{\qquad\qquad\qquad\qquad\qquad\qquad\qquad\qquad\qquad\qquad}$$
$$[1 - (1 - t) \cdot C_y + IM_y] \cdot Y^* - (C_0 + I_0 + G + X_0) - (X_f Y^f + X_\varepsilon \cdot \varepsilon_0 + X_\varepsilon \cdot \varepsilon_r \cdot r^f)$$
$$= -(I_r + X_\varepsilon \cdot \varepsilon_r) \cdot r \qquad \text{gathering terms}$$
$$\overline{\qquad\qquad\qquad\qquad\qquad\qquad\qquad\qquad\qquad\qquad}$$
$$\frac{(C_0 + I_0 + G + X_0) + (X_f Y^f + X_\varepsilon \cdot \varepsilon_0 + X_\varepsilon \cdot \varepsilon_r \cdot r^f) - [1 - (1 - t) \cdot C_y + IM_y] \cdot Y^*}{(I_r + X_\varepsilon \cdot \varepsilon_r)}$$
$$= r \qquad \text{dividing both sides by } -(I_r + X_\varepsilon \cdot \varepsilon_r) \text{ and simplifying}$$

11. In equilibrium, r = 0.08 (8%), investment spending = 1,340, private savings = 2,780, government savings = 800, international savings = −2,240, and total value of funds flowing into financial

markets = 1,340. To find the answers by plugging values into the equation for the equilibrium value of the real interest rate, we have

$$r = \frac{(100 + 1500 + 1600) + (2 \cdot 600 + 10 \cdot 300 + 10 \cdot 800 \cdot 0.06) - (1 - (1 - 0.2) \cdot 0.7 + 0.15) \cdot 12,000}{(2000 + 10 \cdot 800)} = 0.08$$

Use this value of real interest rate to derive the remaining values.

Investment spending = 1500 - 2000 · 0.08 = 1340

Private savings = 12000 - 0.2 · 12000 - (100 + 0.7 · (12000 - 0.2 · 12000)) = 2780

Government savings = 0.2 · 12000 - 1600 = 800

International savings = 0.15 · 12000 - (2 · 600 + 10 · (300 - 800 · (0.08 - 0.06))) = -2240

Total inflows = 2780 + 800 - 2240 = 1340

12. r = 0.055 (5.5%). Private savings = 200. Government savings = 400. International savings = 290. Total inflows = 890. Investment spending = 890.

13. A. r = 0.075 (7.5%). Private savings = 128. Government savings = 400. International savings = 322. Total inflows = 850. Investment spending = 850.

   B. When consumption spending increases by 72, private savings decreases by the same amount. The amount of funds available for investment – the supply of loanable funds – has decreased. As a result, the price of loanable funds – the real interest rate – will increase. Note that when real interest rates increased from 5.5 percent to 7.5 percent, international savings rose and investment spending fell. International savings rose because the higher domestic interest rate led foreign exchange traders to decrease their demand for foreign exchange, decreasing the price of foreign exchange – the exchange rate. When the exchange rate falls, the cost of U.S. goods and services relative to foreign goods and services rises. Gross exports from the United States therefore fall. Looked at from outside the United States, foreign spending for goods and services imported from the United States falls. The amount of dollars that foreigners have on hand and that they are not spending on U.S. goods and services – international savings – rises. Investment spending fell when real interest rates increased because some previously profitable investment projects are now unprofitable and will not be undertaken.

14. A. r = 0.13 (13%). Private savings = 200. Government savings = 130. International savings = 410. Total inflows = 740. Investment spending = 740.

   B. When government spending increases by 270, government savings decreases by the same amount. The remainder of the explanation is exactly the same as in the answer to Question 13. The amount of funds available for investment – the supply of loanable funds – has decreased. As a result, the price of loanable funds – the real interest rate – will increase. Note that when real interest rates increased from 5.5 percent to 7.5 percent, international savings rose and investment spending fell. International savings rose because the higher domestic interest rate led foreign exchange traders to decrease their demand for foreign exchange, decreasing the price of foreign exchange – the exchange rate. When the exchange rate falls, the cost of U.S. goods and services relative to foreign goods and services rises. Gross exports from the United States therefore fall. Looked at from outside the United States, foreign spending for goods and services imported from the United States falls. The amount of dollars that foreigners have on hand and that they are not spending on U.S. goods and services – international savings – rises. Investment spending fell when real interest rates increased because some previously profitable investment projects are now unprofitable and will not be undertaken.

15. A. r = 0.025 (2.5%). Private savings = 227. Government savings = 445. International savings = 278. Total inflows = 950. Investment spending = 950.

B. When potential output increases by 180, both consumption spending and private savings increase. The amount of funds available for investment – the supply of loanable funds – has therefore increased. As a result, the price of loanable funds – the real interest rate – will decrease. When real interest rates decreased from 5.5 percent to 2.5 percent, international savings fell and investment spending rose. International savings fell because the lower domestic interest rate led foreign exchange traders to increase their demand for foreign exchange, increasing the price of foreign exchange – the exchange rate. When the exchange rate rises, the cost of U.S. goods and services relative to foreign goods and services falls. Gross exports from the United States therefore rise. At the same time, import spending rises because of the increase in potential output and income. The increase in import spending partially, but not fully, offsets the rise in gross exports. The net effect is an increase in net exports. The net amount of dollars that foreigners have on hand and that they are not spending on U.S. goods and services – international savings – therefore falls. Investment spending rises when real interest rates increase because some previously unprofitable investment projects are now profitable and will be undertaken.

16. A. $\Delta r = +0.02$.
    B. $\Delta C = 0$. $\Delta I = -40$. $\Delta G = +60$. $\Delta NX = -20$.

> **CAREFUL:** Real GDP does not change. This point is so important, it is worth repeating. In the flexible-price full-employment classical model, real GDP always equals potential output. Therefore real GDP does not change. $\Delta Y = 0$.

17. A. $\Delta r = -0.05$.
    B. $\Delta C = 0$. $\Delta I = -50$. $\Delta G = 0$. $\Delta NX = +50$.
18. A. $\Delta r = +0.01$
    B. $\Delta C = 0$. $\Delta I = -20$. $\Delta G = 0$. $\Delta NX = +20$.
19. A. $\Delta r = -0.001$
    B. $\Delta C = 0$. $\Delta I = +2$. $\Delta G = 0$. $\Delta NX = -2$.
20. A. $\Delta r = +0.012$
    B. $\Delta C = -36$. $\Delta I = -24$. $\Delta G = 0$. $\Delta NX = -12$.

C. APPLYING CONCEPTS AND MODELS

1. If the federal government can stick to this policy, it will create an inflow of funds into financial markets. The supply of loanable funds will increase relative to what would happen if the Social Security surplus was used to finance other government programs. All else constant, real interest rates should decline.

2. Eric's behavior – both as a child and as a first-year student – is part of the supply of loanable funds. When he was buying bonds, he was increasing the supply of loanable funds, albeit by such a small amount that it would not have a perceptible effect on the market. He was contributing to the inflow of funds available for investment. When he cashed in his bonds, he imperceptibly decreased the supply of loanable funds, taking away funds from the total inflow of funds available for private investment. Note that Eric's payment of tuition and fees, even though it can be seen as an investment in human capital, is **not** considered investment spending in the National Income and Product Accounts. Human capital investment is part of consumption spending.

3. Individuals selling shares of stock changes neither the demand for nor supply of loanable funds. If they are selling stock for cash and not using the cash to buy other assets, they are still just changing the form in which they hold their wealth, from stock to cash holdings. But when David and Ruth use the

proceeds of their stock sale to pay their living expenses, they are dissaving. They have decreased the supply of loanable funds.

4. In the textbook, pages 189-190, Prof. DeLong describes the process this way. If "the flow of savings into the financial markets exceeds the demand by corporations and others for purchasing power to finance investment . . . some financial institutions – banks, mutual funds, venture capitalists, insurance companies, whatever – will find purchasing power piling up as more money flows into their accounts than they can find good securities and other investment vehicles to commit it to. They will try to underbid their competitors for the privilege of lending money or buying equity in some particular set of investment projects. How do they underbid? They underbid by saying that they would accept a lower interest rate than the market interest rate r. Thus if the flow of savings exceeds investment, the interest rate r falls. As r falls, the number and value of investment projects firms and entrepreneurs find it worthwhile to undertake rises. The process will stop when the interest rate r adjusts to bring about equilibrium in the loanable funds market."

5. You can answer the question without deriving any equations. When tax revenues decline, the budget surplus shrinks (or, if tax revenues do not exceed government spending, the deficit grows larger). Government saving declines. The decline in government saving is partially offset by an increase in household saving due to the increase in disposable income. The net effect is a shift left of the total savings curve by an amount equal to $Cy \cdot \Delta Tax$. The decrease in total savings leads to an increase in real interest rates.

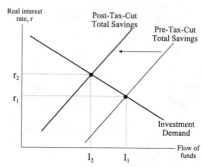

Higher real interest rates lead to a decrease in exchange rates and therefore a decrease in U.S. exports to other countries, increasing international savings. The increase in international savings partially offsets the decrease in saving. The increase in real interest rates leads to a drop in investment spending. Under the flexible-price full-employment classical model, real GDP does not change when taxes are cut. There is a redistribution of spending for output from investment and exports to consumption. But the total amount of spending remains the same.

6. An increase in investment spending increases the demand for loanable funds. As a result, real interest rates increase. Higher real interest rates lead to a decrease in exchange rates and therefore a decrease in U.S. exports to other countries, increasing international savings. The increase in international savings partially meets the increase in demand for funds. The increase in real interest rates leads to a drop in investment spending, partially offsetting the initial increase in baseline investment. Under the flexible-price full-employment

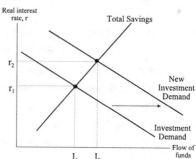

classical model, real GDP does not change when baseline investment rises. There is a redistribution of spending for output from exports to investment. But the total amount of spending remains the same.

Chapter 7 • 199

7. A decrease in consumption spending increases saving, which increases the supply of loanable funds. As a result, real interest rates decrease. Lower real interest rates lead to an increase in exchange rates and therefore an increase in U.S. exports to other countries, decreasing international savings. The decrease in international savings partially offsets the increase in private savings. The decrease in real interest rates leads to a rise in investment spending. Under the flexible-price full-employment classical model, real GDP does not change

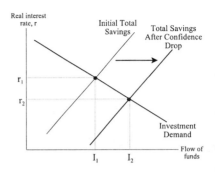

when baseline consumption rises. There is a redistribution of spending for output from consumption to exports and investment. But the total amount of spending remains the same.

8. A decrease in foreign interest rates will lead foreign exchange speculators to increase their demand for dollar-denominated assets and decrease their demand for assets denominated in other currencies. As a result, the dollar price of foreign currency, the exchange rate, will decrease. Lower exchange rates reduce the price of foreign goods and services relative to domestic goods and services, decreasing demand for U.S. exports. The decrease in exports increases international savings. The story this far is shown as a **shift** of the Total Savings

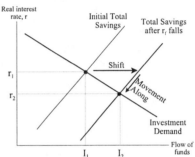

curve to the right. The increase in international savings increases the supply of loanable funds, which leads to a decrease in the real interest rate. Lower domestic real interest rates lead to an increase in exchange rates, partially offsetting the earlier decline in exchange rates and partially offsetting the earlier decrease in U.S. exports. This part of the story is depicted as a **movement along** the second Total Savings curve toward the new equilibrium. The decrease in real interest rates leads to a rise in investment spending. Under the flexible-price full-employment classical model, real GDP does not change. There is a redistribution of spending for output from exports to investment. But the total amount of spending remains the same.

D. EXPLAINING THE REAL WORLD

1. The question is asking you to apply the flexible-price full-employment model. The clue is this phrase: "Assuming prices and wages in the economy are fully flexible. . ."

The National Income and Product Accounts treats all government purchases in the same way, whether or not the purchases are for items that increase the economy's productive capacity. But if we treat any government purchases as part of G, then the short-run effect of an increase in government spending for education will be an increase in real interest rates and thus a decrease in gross exports and in investment spending. Assuming fully flexible wages and prices, total output will remain at potential output. There is a redistribution of output from the private sector to the public sector.

However, most economists would argue that education spending increases human capital, increasing the economy's productive capacity. In this case, it might make just as much sense to consider this form of government spending as a form of investment spending. In that case, we would conclude that the increase in government investment in education will lead to a rise in real interest rates, which decrease both gross exports and other forms of investment spending.

2. The question is asking about the effects of a supply shock.

   Power outages decrease potential output, Y^*. Because less output can and will be produced, incomes fall. As a result, private savings decrease, putting upward pressure on real interest rates. Higher real interest rates lead to decreases in both gross exports and in investment spending.

3. This is another example of a supply shock.

   Improved health usually leads to increased worker productivity. Higher levels of productivity increase potential output, Y^*. Assuming fully flexible wages and prices, more output will be produced and therefore incomes rise. Private savings increase, decreasing real interest rates. As a result, gross exports and investment spending both rise.

4. This is another example of a supply shock.

   Earthquake damage decreases potential output, Y^*. Because less output can and will be produced, incomes fall. As a result, private savings decrease, putting upward pressure on real interest rates. Higher real interest rates lead to decreases in both gross exports and in investment spending.

5. The question is asking you to think about the equations relating a change in government spending to changes in real interest rates, investment spending, and more.

   A decrease in the responsiveness of foreign exchange speculators to changes in domestic interest rates is represented as a decrease in ε_r. Mathematically, a lowering of ε_r will increase Δr for any change in government spending.

> **NOTE**: Some faculty members want you to know how to manipulate equations. Others want you to be able to explain the economics behind the equations. Find out what you are supposed to learn. For some faculty, the answer above to Question 5 would be sufficient. But for others, you must have the next paragraph as well.

Economically, the decrease in responsiveness of foreign exchange speculators to changes in domestic interest rates means that the international sector is less able to offset the impact of changes in government spending. An increase in government spending decreases supply of loanable funds, putting upward pressure on real interest rates. The increase in real interest rates has two effects: it decreases investment spending and it decreases gross exports. But if foreign exchange speculators are less sensitive to changes in domestic real interest rates, then there will be very little change in real exchange rates and thus very little change in gross exports. There will probably still be an increase in international savings, but it will be small. So most of the decline in government savings will have to come from investment spending. The change in behavior of foreign exchange speculators alters the extent to which government spending crowds out investment spending.

E. POSSIBILITIES TO PONDER

No solutions are given to these questions. The questions are designed to be somewhat open ended. Each question draws on your understanding of the concepts covered in this chapter.

Chapter 8
Money, Prices, and Inflation

- The Quantity Theory of Money tells us that the overall level of prices and the rate of inflation in a full-employment flexible-price economy depend upon the rate of growth of the money stock.

- The demand for money is a decision about whether we hold our wealth in liquid or illiquid forms. It depends upon real interest rates, expected inflation rates, and total spending.

LEARNING GUIDE

Chapter 6 explained why real GDP equals potential output in the long run. Chapter 7 explained how national income is divided among consumption, investment, government purchases, and net exports in the long run. In Chapter 8, we learn what determines the price level and inflation rate. There are many new definitions and concepts. The full-employment flexible-price assumption of Chapter 7 is used in this chapter. If you get confused, be sure you are assuming that the economy is at full employment. There is one model introduced in Chapter 8: the Quantity Theory of Money. The model is simple but because it assumes the economy is always at full employment, its implications are not always intuitive.

Economists use the term "money" differently than the rest of the world does. You will be confused throughout the chapter if you are not very clear on what is and is not "money." Spend enough time on the Section A questions until you answer every question in that section correctly.

Short on time?

 If you learn nothing else, you absolutely must be clear on the definition of money. Understanding the role of interest rates in the determination of money demand is also essential.

You will want to learn the definition of money, the determinants of money demand, the Quantity Theory of Money, and how the central bank changes the money stock. Be sure you understand how a change in the money stock causes prices to change.

A. BASIC DEFINITIONS

Before you apply knowledge, you need a basic grasp of the fundamentals. In other words, there are some things you just have to know. Knowing the material in this section won't guarantee a good grade in the course, but not knowing it will guarantee a poor or failing grade.

USE THE WORDS OR PHRASES FROM THE LIST BELOW TO COMPLETE THE SENTENCES. SOME ARE USED MORE THAN ONCE; SOME ARE NOT USED AT ALL.

barter economy	money
central bank	money stock
classical dichotomy	neutral
Federal Reserve	open-market operations
government bonds	opportunity cost
hyperinflation	quantity theory of money
inflation	unit of account
interest rate	U.S. Treasury
medium of exchange	velocity

1. Money is said to be _____ when the determination of real GDP does not depend upon the price level.

2. The _____ of money measures how fast money moves through the economy.

3. A(n) _____ requires coincidence of wants.

4. When the Federal Reserve buys or sells government bonds, this is called

   _____ .

5. _____ exists when prices rise by more than 20 percent per month.

 NOTE: The famous British economist, John Maynard Keynes, is reputed to have advised friends during the 1920s German hyperinflation that when they went to a cabaret they should order two beers at once rather than order the second beer only after consuming the first. Prices were rising so fast, the story goes, that the lost quality of the second beer as its suds became flat was more than offset by the savings of not having to pay a higher price for the second beer than the first.

6. Because money is used to quote prices, we say it is a(n) _____ .

7. The _____ of a country undertakes monetary policy.

8. When real variables can be analyzed without thinking of nominal variables such as the price level, this is called the _____ .

9. The central bank of the United States is the _____ .

10. When the central bank wants to change the monetary base, it buys or sells _____ .

> **NOTE**: In your principles class, you may have learned there are two additional ways that the Federal Reserve can, in theory, change the monetary base: changing the discount rate and changing the required reserve ratio. But in practice, the Fed almost never changes the discount rate or the required reserve ratio as a way to change the monetary base.

11. _____ includes coins, currency, checking account balances, and other very liquid assets.

12. _____ are undertaken at the direction of the Federal Open Market Committee.

13. The _____ states $MV = PY$.

14. A government putting lots of money into circulation is equivalent to its creating a(n) _____ tax.

15. Because money is accepted as payment, we say it is a(n) _____ .

16. The difference between the rate of return on money balances and the rate of return on other assets is the _____ of holding money.

17. The basic task of monetary policy is the determination of the _____ .

> **NOTE**: The process by which money is created is not described in the textbook. The shortest description is this: Money is created by banks making loans with their excess reserves. If you want to review the money creation process, dig out your principles textbook. The process is of course more complicated than how it is portrayed in your principles text – almost everything about the economy is more complicated than how it was portrayed in your principles text – but the explanation in your principles textbook is good enough for now.

CIRCLE THE CORRECT WORD OR PHRASE IN EACH OF THE FOLLOWING SENTENCES.

18. A decrease in nominal interest rates causes the velocity of money to <u>increase / decrease</u> and the demand for money to <u>increase / decrease</u>.

19. If the Fed wants to <u>increase / decrease</u> the monetary base, it will buy government bonds.

20. The most illiquid form of money is included in <u>M1 / M2 / M3 / L</u>.

21. M1, M2, and M3 are different measures of money <u>stock / demand</u>.

22. P·Y represents the <u>real / nominal</u> flow of spending.

23. Because money is an asset that can be used to pay for goods and services, it is called a <u>liquid / illiquid</u> asset.

24. If the central bank wants to increase the monetary base, it will <u>buy / sell</u> government bonds.

25. Inflation raises prices <u>and also / but not</u> wages.

26. The most liquid form of money is <u>M1 / M2 / M3 / L</u>.

27. When the Fed buys bonds, there is a(n) <u>increase / decrease</u> in the amount of money in the hands (or checking accounts) of the public.

28. The <u>nominal / real</u> interest rate is the sum of the <u>nominal / real</u> interest rate and the inflation rate.

SELECT THE ONE BEST ANSWER FOR EACH MULTIPLE-CHOICE QUESTION.

29. When an economist uses the term "money," she or he means.
    A. wealth.
    B. income.
    C. coin and currency only.
    D. liquid wealth such as coin, currency, and checking account balances.

HINT: Will the grocer or your landlord accept it as payment? Is it an asset? If the answer to both questions is "yes," then the item is "money." If the answer to either question is "no," then it is not generally considered "money."

30. The benefit to having money is that doing so
    A. makes you wealthier.
    B. makes it easier to undertake transactions.
    C. allows you to earn interest on your checking account.
    D. gives you a higher income.

31. The cost of having money is
    A. the foregone interest you could earn if you held other assets instead.
    B. money can be stolen.
    C. you are likely to spend more if you have more money.
    D. you will incur bank fees.

 CAREFUL! It is *very* important to be clear on the definition of money. Money is not wealth. Money is not income. Wealth is not money. Income is not money. Don't go on until you understand what is and is not "money."

B. MANIPULATION OF CONCEPTS AND MODELS

Most instructors expect you to be able to do basic manipulation of the concepts. Being able to do so often means you can earn a C in a course. But if you want a better grade, you'll need to be able to complete this next section easily and move on to Sections C and D.

1. "Money" is a common word with special meaning to economists. Give two examples of misuse of the word "money." Give two examples of correct use of "money."

2. Give two examples of liquid assets. Give two examples of illiquid assets. What determines if an asset is liquid or illiquid?

3. Are credit cards "money"? Are debit cards "money"? Explain.

4. Using the *Economic Report of the President (ERP)*, complete the following table. Compute the value of velocity first using M1 as your measure of money, and then using M2 as your measure of money. Describe the pattern of velocity since 1960.

	Nominal GDP (billion $)	Money as measured by M1 (billion $)	Velocity computed using M1	Money as measured by M2 (billion $)	Velocity computed using M2
1960					
1965					
1970					
1975					
1980					
1985					
1990					
1995					
last year available					

TO THE CHALKBOARD:
The Quantity Theory of Money

The Quantity Theory of Money is in many ways the easiest model of economics. Many students are often suspicious of its simplicity. There's no reason to be suspicious.

The Quantity Theory states M·V = P·Y. We can then relate prices to money. Algebraically, we just divide by Y to see how prices (P) depend upon money (M).

$$M \cdot V = P \cdot Y \quad \text{\textit{Quantity Theory of Money}}$$
$$\frac{M \cdot V}{Y} = P \quad \text{\textit{dividing both sides by Y}}$$
$$\left(\frac{V}{Y}\right) \cdot M = P \quad \text{\textit{rearranging terms to match text}}$$

If we assume that velocity, V, is constant, and that output, Y, is constant and equal to potential output, Y*, then changes in the amount of money in the economy, M, translate directly to changes in prices, P.

Really. It's that simple.

NOTE: The Quantity Theory of Money is a different model of how the economy functions than the model we've seen in previous chapters. In the full-employment flexible-price model of Chapter 7, we explained the determination of total spending for goods and services by considering the spending in each of four sectors: consumption spending by households, investment spending by businesses, government purchases by government agencies, and net export spending by the rest of the world. Each of these four components of spending had its own determinants. Consumption spending depended primarily upon disposable income; investment spending depended primarily upon real interest rates; net export spending depended primarily upon domestic real interest rates, foreign real interest rates, domestic income, and foreign income; and government purchases were taken as exogenous.

In the Quantity Theory of Money of Chapter 8, spending is just spending. There are no components to spending. There are no sectors in which spending is determined. Spending for goods and services is total spending for real GDP. And in the Quantity Theory of Money of Chapter 8, total spending depends upon the value of money balances. Spending is the mechanism by which people and businesses adjust their money balances. If real money balances (M/P) increase above desired money balances, then people and businesses spend more in order to reduce their money holdings. If real money balances decrease below their desired level, then people and businesses spend less in order to increase their money holdings.

The irony, of course, is that when one person or business changes his or her spending, doing so changes his or her individual money holdings but does not change the total money holdings in the economy. If I think my money holdings are too high and so I reduce my money holdings by going out for dinner every night this week, I have not lowered the money holdings of the economy as a whole. I have only transferred my money holdings to the restaurant owners. But if everyone in the economy engages in the same behavior – spending more in an attempt to lower their real money balances – we will all eventually be successful. We will not rid the economy of any nominal money balances, but the increases in spending will lead to increases in prices, reducing the real value of our nominal money holdings.

The important thing to remember as you read Chapter 8 is this: do not try to explain **why** spending changes in reaction to changes in money holdings. It just does. Accept it and go on.

5.   Define each term in the Quantity Theory of Money: MV = PY.

6. Suppose prices rise. What immediate effect does the increase in prices have on real money balances? What effect does it have on spending? What ultimate effect does the initial increase in prices have on prices?

NOTE: Remember that the economy we are considering is a full-employment flexible-price economy. When demand for output declines, prices will adjust in order to return demand to its original level, keeping the economy at full employment.

TO THE CHALKBOARD:
Deriving the Equation for Inflation

Starting from the Quantity Theory of Money and using two proportional growth rules, we can relate the inflation rate (π) to the rates of change of money (m), velocity (v), and real GDP (y).

$$M \cdot V = P \cdot Y \qquad \textit{Quantity Theory of Money}$$

$$\frac{M \cdot V}{Y} = P \qquad \textit{dividing both sides by Y}$$

$$P = \left(\frac{V}{Y}\right) \cdot M \qquad \textit{rearranging terms to match text}$$

$$\%\Delta P = \%\Delta\left[\left(\frac{V}{Y}\right) \cdot M\right] \qquad \textit{proportional growth rate of each side}$$

$$\%\Delta P = \%\Delta V - \%\Delta Y + \%\Delta M \qquad \textit{applying proportional growth rules}$$

$$\pi = v - y - m \qquad \textit{using symbols given in text}$$

$$\pi = m + v - y \qquad \textit{rearranging terms to match text}$$

If we have values for the rates of growth of the money stock, velocity, and real GDP, straightforward arithmetic gives us the inflation rate. The inflation equation holds so long as the basic equation of Quantity Theory of Money, $M \cdot V = P \cdot Y$, is satisfied. Because velocity is calculated by dividing real GDP by the money stock, it is pretty much guaranteed that the basic equation of the Quantity Theory will be satisfied.

7. Suppose that the rate of change of the money stock is 6 percent, the rate of change of velocity is constant, and the rate of change of real GDP is 2 percent. What is the inflation rate?

8. Suppose that the money stock is growing at 9 percent annually, velocity is increasing annually by 2 percent, and real GDP is growing at 4 percent a year. What is the inflation rate?

9. Suppose the rate of inflation is 4 percent annually. What is the real rate of return on the coins and currency in your pockets and wallet?

TO THE CHALKBOARD:
Money Demand Terminology

This table might be helpful as you try to follow the terminology introduced in Chapter 8.

Term and Symbol	Nominal or Real	Who Determines	Description
Money stock, M	Nominal	Central bank and banks	The amount of money that is available in the economy.
Money demand (no symbol in Chapter 8; M^d in Chapter 11)	Nominal	People, Businesses, Government Agencies	The amount of wealth that everyone who spends – people, businesses, and government agencies – wishes to hold in the form of the most liquid asset, money.
Relative money demand, $L(r + \pi^e)$	Real	People, Businesses, Government Agencies	The demand for money **relative to** total spending, and taking into account time-trend of velocity, V^L. Nominal money demand equals relative money demand times total spending ($P \cdot Y$), divided by trend velocity, V^L.
Velocity, V	Real	People, Businesses, Government Agencies	The number of times a dollar changes hands in a year. Equivalent to total spending ($P \cdot Y$) divided by money stock (M).
Trend velocity, V^L	Real	Financial Technology	The changes in velocity that are determined by financial technology, and which therefore tend to leave to steady increases in velocity over the long-run.
Money-demand-driven fluctuations in velocity, $V_0 + V_i(i)$	Real	People, Businesses, Government Agencies	The changes in velocity that are determined by the factors which influence relative money demand.

Relative money demand: $L(r + \pi^e) = \dfrac{1}{V_0 + V_i(i)} = \dfrac{1}{V_0 + V_i(r + \pi^e)}$

Nominal money demand: $M^d = L(r + \pi^e) \cdot \left(\dfrac{P \cdot Y}{V^L}\right) = \dfrac{P \cdot Y}{V^L \cdot [V_0 + V_i(r + \pi^e)]}$

10. Suppose nominal interest rates increase. Explain what effect the increase in nominal interest rates has on money demand and on the velocity of money.

HINT: One way to think of velocity – not as a technical definition but as an intuitive explanation – is that velocity is the number of times in a year that someone changes their wealth between money and other assets such as stocks and bonds. When interest rates are low, there is little reason to spend the time and effort and transactions fees to move wealth between money and bonds. Velocity is low when interest rates are low. When interest rates are high, there is good reason to take the time to move wealth between money and bonds, and then to move funds back into the checking account whenever bills must be paid. Velocity is high when interest rates are high.

TO THE CHALKBOARD:
Velocity and the Money Demand Equation

The equation for money demand is given in Chapter 8. Let's review it here. Nominal money demand depends upon the total flow of spending ($P \cdot Y$), upon the time-trend of velocity (V^L), and upon that part of velocity that fluctuates as money demand fluctuates (referred to below as "money-demand-driven fluctuations").

Money-demand-driven fluctuations in velocity depend upon the nominal interest rate, which is the sum of the real interest rate, r, and the expected inflation rate, Π^e. When nominal interest rates rise, the opportunity cost of holding our wealth in the form of money (versus in stocks or bonds, forms of wealth that usually earn a positive return) also increases. For instance, when the rate of return on a stock mutual fund is 3 percent, there is not much loss from keeping most of our funds in a checking account that does not pay interest. It simply is not worth the time and hassle to move balances back and forth between a checking account and stock mutual fund.

But if stock mutual funds are paying 16 percent, as they did in the late 1990s, then people and firms will find it worthwhile to move funds between checking accounts and stock mutual funds, shifting just enough funds into their checking account (converting just enough wealth into money) to pay the bills that need paying that day. When nominal interest rates rise, everyone who uses money will therefore find it profitable to spend more time switching his or her wealth between stock mutual funds and checking accounts. The more often our wealth is moved between money (checking) and non-money (stock mutual fund) accounts, the higher the velocity of money. So an increase in nominal interest rates simultaneously increases velocity and decreases money demand.

One way to capture this story mathematically is to connect this part of money demand and the money-demand-driven fluctuations in velocity. Start with the definition of velocity.

Velocity (V) = (financial technology-driven trend) · (money-demand-driven fluctuations)

The financial technology-driven trend is V^L

The money-demand-driven fluctuations are $V_0 + V_i \cdot (r + \pi^e)$

Thus, $V = (V^L) \cdot (V_0 + V_i \cdot (r + \pi^e))$

V_i is the sensitivity of money-demand-driven fluctuations in velocity to changes in the nominal interest rate, i. $V_i > 0$.

The "relative demand for money," $L(r + \pi^e)$, is equal to the reciprocal of the money-demand-driven fluctuations in velocity. That is,

$$L(r + \pi^e) = \frac{1}{V_0 + V_i \cdot (i)} = \frac{1}{V_0 + V_i \cdot (r + \pi^e)}$$

An increase in the nominal interest rate increases money-demand-driven fluctuations in velocity and thus decreases "relative" money demand.

Nominal money demand then equals the product of "relative" money demand and total spending (P·Y) divided by the time-trend of velocity, V^L. That is,

$$M^d = L(r + \pi^e) \cdot \left(\frac{P \cdot Y}{V^L} \right) = \frac{P \cdot Y}{V^L \cdot \left[V_0 + V_i \cdot (r + \pi^e) \right]}$$

11. Suppose $V^L = 2$, $V_0 = 3$, and $V_i = 0.15$. Complete the table below.

π^e	r	i	V
2	3		
3	3		
10	3		
100	3		

What is the effect of an increase in expected inflation on velocity?

12. Suppose $V_0 = 7.3$, and $V_i = 0.6$. Complete the table that is below.

π^e	r	$V_0 + V_i(r + \pi^e)$	$L(r + \pi^e)$
2	2		
4	2		
10	2		
20	2		

TO THE CHALKBOARD:
Explaining Figure 8.7

Figure 8.7, repeated at the right, shows the relationship between the nominal interest rate and money demand. A lower nominal interest rate corresponds to a decrease in the opportunity cost of holding money, and thus to an increase in the demand for money, $L(r + \pi^e)$, relative to total spending and the time-trend of velocity.

$r + \pi^e$
Nominal interest rate

$L(r + \pi^e)$: Relative Money Demand

To derive the expression along the horizontal axis of Textbook Figure 8.7, $L(r + \pi^e) = M \cdot V^L / P \cdot Y$, start with the Quantity Theory:

$$M \cdot V = P \cdot Y \qquad \text{Quantity Theory of Money}$$

$$M \cdot \left[V^L \cdot \left(V_0 + V_i \cdot (r + \pi^e) \right) \right] = P \cdot Y \qquad \text{substituting definition of } V$$

$$\frac{M \cdot V^L}{P \cdot Y} \cdot \left(V_0 + V_i \cdot (r + \pi^e) \right) = 1 \qquad \text{dividing both sides by } P \cdot Y$$

$$\frac{M \cdot V^L}{P \cdot Y} = \frac{1}{V_0 + V_i \cdot (r + \pi^e)} \qquad \text{dividing both sides by } \left(V_0 + V_i \cdot (r + \pi^e) \right)$$

$$\frac{M \cdot V^L}{P \cdot Y} = L(r + \pi^e) \qquad \text{substituting definition of } L(r + \pi^e)$$

The relative demand for money balances equals the stock of money (M) times the financial-technology-driven trend of velocity (V^L), divided by total spending ($P \cdot Y$).

13. As the expected inflation rate increases, what is the effect on velocity? On money demand? Explain.

14. A. Suppose V_0 increases. What effect will this have on money demand?

   B. Suppose V_i increases. What effect will this have on money demand?

15. Give an example of an event that might increase the interest sensitivity of velocity.

TO THE CHALKBOARD:
Explaining Figure 8.8

Figure 8.8 depicts what happens to prices over time if the central bank increases the rate of growth of the money stock, m. There are two important assumptions to remember when looking at Figure 8.8.

1. Nominal interest rates depend upon **expected** inflation rates.
2. Output always equals potential output (at least, in Chapter 8).

Suppose the economy is initially in equilibrium with $M \cdot V = P \cdot Y$. The inflation rate, as explained in the "To The Chalkboard" box on page 208, is $\Pi = m + v - y$. If there is no change from month to month in the growth rates of the money stock, velocity, or real output, there will be no change in the inflation rate.

Now **suppose the central bank suddenly increases the rate of growth of the money stock.** Two things will happen.

1. *An immediate effect:* higher **expected** inflation rates will immediately increase the nominal interest rate and thus increase velocity.
2. *An ongoing effect:* money stock in excess of money demand will increase spending, which because we are already and always at full employment, will increase prices.

The combination of these two effects is that the price level jumps immediately upon the increase in the money growth rate, and then continues increasing at a higher rate than previously.

The immediate effect: use $M \cdot V = P \cdot Y$ to explain

When the central bank increases the rate of growth of the money stock, everyone believes future inflation rates will increase, for it is known that faster money growth leads to higher inflation. This increase in expected inflation rates makes today's nominal interest rate jump. Higher nominal interest rates increase the opportunity cost of holding money, leading to an increase in velocity and a decrease in money demand. Real output does not change because we are, by assumption, always at full employment, producing the potential level of output. The increase in velocity, V, coupled with no change in real output, Y, means that the price level, P, will jump immediately. This jump is labeled as Point A on the graph at the right.

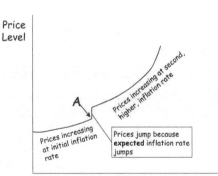

Price Level

A

Prices increasing at second, higher, inflation rate

Prices increasing at initial inflation rate

Prices jump because **expected** inflation rate jumps

Time

The ongoing effect: use $\Pi = m + v - y$ to explain

The central bank's increase in the money stock leads the public to try to rid themselves of the extra money they now find themselves holding. People and businesses with excess money balances increase their spending. But **in the full-employment flexible-price model**, there can be no increase in the amount of output being produced because the economy is already and always producing at full employment. So producers react to the increase in demand for their products by increasing prices. **The inflation rate rises.**

Money demand continues to fall short of money supply. Everyone continues to find themselves with more money than they wish to have, and so they keep trying to rid themselves of excess money balances by increasing spending. But again, because the economy is already and always at full employment, there can be no increase in output. So, again, prices rise. Inflation continues, as seen in the graph at the right. The new inflation rate will be the sum of the new money growth rate and the velocity growth rate less the growth rate of real output.

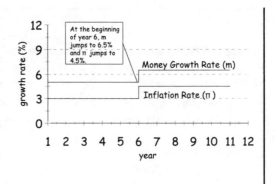

16. What are the costs of inflation?

17. What are the benefits of inflation?

$\mathcal{C}$. APPLYING CONCEPTS AND MODELS

Now we're getting to the good stuff. Being able to apply a specific concept or model to a real world situation — where you are told which model to apply but you have to figure out how to apply it — is often what you need to earn a B in a course. This is where macroeconomics starts to become interesting and the world starts to make more sense.

1. Nausher keeps an average balance of $1,500 in his checking account. From his checking account, he pays rent and utilities, buys groceries, pays bus fares, and takes out cash which he uses for restaurant meals and other entertainment. Over the last few years, he has found that an average balance of $1,500 meets his needs.

    Nausher receives a notice that his rent will increase by 10 percent. What effect will this increase have on his real money demand? On his nominal money demand? On his spending behavior?

2. The Federal Reserve wants to increase the monetary base. What do they do?

> **HINT:** Money held by the Federal Reserve – be it coin, currency, or balances the Fed uses to pay for bonds – is not counted as part of the monetary base.

3. What effect did the emergence of online trading of stocks and bonds have on velocity of money?

> **NOTE:** The demand for money is a tradeoff between holding wealth in liquid form (money) and holding it in illiquid form (here, stocks and bonds).
>
> The advantage to holding wealth in the form of money is its liquidity, which means it can be used to pay for goods and services. This characteristic of money refers to the transactions motive for holding money rather than other assets. The disadvantage to holding wealth in the form of money is that money pays little or no interest, so its nominal rate of return is equal or close to zero. This characteristic of money refers to the profit motive for holding money rather than other assets.
>
> The advantage to holding wealth in the form of stocks or bonds is that stocks and bonds usually have a nominal rate of return greater than zero. This characteristic of assets refers to the profit motive. The disadvantage to holding wealth in the form of stocks or bonds is their illiquidity, which means stocks and bonds cannot be used directly to pay for goods and services. This characteristic of assets refers to the transactions motive.

4. Consumers buy lots of gifts for family and friends between Thanksgiving and the New Year. What happens to money demand in December?

D. EXPLAINING THE REAL WORLD

Most instructors are delighted when you are able to figure out which concept or model to apply to a real world situation. Being able to do so means you thoroughly understand the material and is often what you need to do to earn an A in a course. This is where you experience the power of macroeconomic theory.

1. Velocity as calculated with M1 has increased since 1960. Velocity as calculated with M2 has remained virtually constant since 1960. What do these two statements, taken together, imply?

2. In the 1970s when someone wanted to withdraw funds from a savings account (a nonmoney asset), he or she had to go into the bank, stand in line, talk with a human teller, fill out a withdrawal slip, and then receive the funds. Banks were generally open 10 a.m. to 3 p.m. Monday through Thursday, 10 a.m. to 6 p.m. on Fridays, and closed on weekends. If someone wanted to deposit funds into a savings account, they were limited to those same hours. By the 1990s when someone wanted to withdraw funds from savings, an ATM machine was easy to find and was usually available 24 hours a day, 7 days a week. What effect did the development of ATM machines have on the velocity of money?

3. During the United States Civil War (also sometimes called The War between The States), the government of the South, the Confederacy, paid its bills by printing money called Confederate dollars. What effect did their policy have on prices in the South?

4. In Russia in the late 1990s, inflation was rampant. If the government's goal was to decrease the long-run inflation rate, what advice should have been given to the central monetary authorities of Russia? What would have been the most likely short-run economic effect of that advice?

E. POSSIBILITIES TO PONDER

The more you learn, the more you realize you have more to learn. These questions go beyond the textbook material. They are the sort of questions that distinguish A+ or A work from A- work. Some of them may even serve as starting points for junior or senior year research papers.

1. Would opening the New York Stock Exchange on Saturday change velocity?

2. Is stringent money growth a good policy to implement in an economy that has been experiencing hyperinflation?

3. Should there be just one currency common to every country in the world?

4. If we do not assume prices and wages are fully flexible, what parts of the model that is discussed in Chapter 8 will change?

SOLUTIONS   SOLUTIONS   SOLUTIONS   SOLUTIONS

A. BASIC DEFINITIONS
* indicates there are notes below related to this question.

1. neutral
2. velocity
3. barter economy
4. open-market operations
5. Hyperinflation
6. unit of account
7. central bank
8. classical dichotomy
9. Federal Reserve
10. government bonds
11. Money
12. Open-market operations
13. quantity theory of money
14. inflation
15. medium of exchange
16. opportunity cost
17. money stock

---

18. decrease; increase
19. increase
20. L
21. stock
22.* nominal
23. liquid
24. buy
25. and also
26. M1
27. increase
28. nominal; real

22.* P is the GDP price deflator. Y is real output (real GDP). So P·Y is real GDP times the GDP price deflator, which equals nominal GDP.

---

29. D. Wealth is not money, though money is one component of wealth. Income is not money, though incomes are often received in the form of money (paychecks). Coin and currency are money, but they are a relatively small part of the total value of money.

30. B. Money is not the same as wealth or income. Holding money is a decision about the *form* in which to hold wealth. The benefit to holding money is that it is useful for paying for goods and services; that is, for undertaking transactions. Checking accounts may pay interest, but the rate of return on checking accounts is almost always lower than the rate of return on alternative, less liquid, assets,

31. A. The primary cost of holding your assets in the form of money rather than in less liquid forms is an opportunity cost. Holding money means earning a lower rate of return than is possible when holding wealth in alternative, less liquid, assets.

B. MANIPULATION OF CONCEPTS AND MODELS

1. Answers will vary. Incorrect usage examples may include equating wealth or income with money. Correct usage examples may include "I am going to deposit into my checking account all these pennies in my cookie jar, converting some of my money from coins to checking account balances." Another example of correct usage is "I am going to transfer some of my wealth out of assets and into money, by moving some funds from my stock mutual fund to my checking account."

2. Answers will vary. Liquid assets include coin, currency, and checking account balances. Illiquid assets include houses and other physical property. Whether or not an asset is liquid depends upon the ease and cost of changing it into a form that is accepted as payment by landlords, grocers, and others.

3. Credit cards are not money. Credit cards are not an asset; they create a liability – a debt – for the credit card holder. When you use a credit card, you are not changing one asset – money – into another asset – the item being purchased. When you use a credit card, you are creating a liability – credit card debt – that at least initially equals the value of the item being purchased.
On the other hand, debit cards *are* money. A debit card deducts the amount "charged" directly from your checking account. When you use a debit card, you are changing one asset – part of the balance in your checking account – for another – the item being purchased.

4. In the 2001 *Economic Report of the President*, the data are from Tables B-1 (nominal GDP), and B-69 (M1 and M2).

	Nominal GDP (billion $)	Money as measured by M1 (billion $)	Velocity computed using M1	Money as measured by M2 (billion $)	Velocity computed using M2
1960	527.4	140.7	3.7	312.4	1.7
1965	720.1	167.8	4.3	459.2	1.6
1970	1,039.7	214.3	4.9	626.4	1.7
1975	1,635.2	286.8	5.7	1,015.9	1.6
1980	2,795.6	408.1	6.9	1,599.1	1.7
1985	4,213.0	619.3	6.8	2,495.4	1.7
1990	5,803.2	824.4	7.0	3,277.6	1.8
1995	7,400.5	1,126.8	6.6	3,641.9	2.0
last year available (1999)	9,299.2	1,123.0	8.3	4,643.7	2.0

Velocity as calculated with M1 has risen over time, from 3.7 in 1960 to 8.3 in 1999. Velocity as calculated with M2 has remained relatively constant, with a slight increase in the late 1990s. Velocity (as calculated with M1) increasing means that a dollar held in the form of M1 money is changing hands more often in 1999 than it was in 1960. Velocity (as calculated with M2) staying about the same means that there has been relatively little change since 1960 in the number of times a dollar changes hands in a year. The annual patterns are seen more clearly in Textbook Figure 8.4 and in the graph at the right.

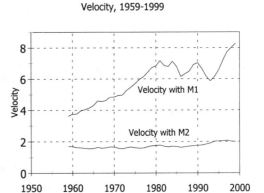

Velocity, 1959-1999

5. M: Money. The amount of money in the economy. Money is an asset that is liquid enough to be used to pay for goods and services. In the United States, money as measured with M1 includes coins, currency, travelers' checks, and balances in checking accounts.

    V: Velocity. Velocity is the number of times a dollar changes hands in one year.

    P: Price. The average price level in the economy, measured by GDP Price Deflator or another price index that is an average price of all goods and services produced.

    Y: Income, which equals Output. Real GDP. The quantity of goods and services produced in the economy in a year.

6. If prices rise, real money balances fall. A $20 bill buys fewer goods and services after prices increase than it did before. Everyone realizes their real money holdings are now lower than they desire. To try to increase their real money holdings, everyone reduces their spending. Sellers do not want everyone to reduce their spending, so sellers decrease their prices in an attempt to spur a return to previous spending levels. In the end, prices wind up where they began.

7. $\pi = m + v - y = 0.06 + 0 - 0.02 = 0.04$, or 4 percent.

8. $\pi = m + v - y = 0.09 + 0.02 - 0.04 = 0.07$, or 7 percent.

9. The real rate of return on coins and currency (cash) is the nominal rate minus the inflation rate. The nominal rate of return is 0. So the real rate of return is 0 - 4, or -4 percent. You are losing 4 percent annually in the real value of your cash balances when the inflation rate is 4 percent.

10. When nominal interest rates rise, the opportunity cost of holding our wealth in the form of money (versus in nonmoney forms of wealth that usually earn a positive nominal return) also increases. People and firms who use money will therefore find it profitable to spend more time switching their wealth between money and nonmoney forms of wealth. That is, their demand for money (versus other assets) will decline. The average amount of time a dollar is held by someone will decrease, which is the same thing as saying the velocity of money will increase.

11. $V = 2 \cdot (3 + 0.15 \cdot (\pi^e + r)) = 2 \cdot (3 + 0.15 \cdot i)$

π^e	r	i	V
2	3	5	7.5
3	3	6	7.8
10	3	13	9.9
100	3	103	36.9

When the expected inflation rate rises, nominal interest rates also rise. As a result, velocity increases as people and firms spend more time changing their wealth between money, nonmoney assets, and back again.

12. Suppose $V_0 = 7.3$, and $V_i = 0.6$.

π^e	r	$V_0 + V_i(r + \pi^e)$	$L(r + \pi^e)$
2	2	9.7	0.103
4	2	10.9	0.092
10	2	14.5	0.069
20	2	20.5	0.049

13. As expected inflation rises, velocity increases. A typical dollar changes hands more often. Money demand falls. At higher inflation rates, everyone wants to hold less wealth in cash because the purchasing power of cash – its real rate of return – is declining as prices rise. Instead, everyone wants to hold more wealth in nonmoney wealth that earns a greater nominal rate of return than money does.

14. A. When V_0 increases, velocity increases. Therefore money demand decreases.
    B. When V_i increases, velocity increases. Therefore money demand decreases.

15. Answers will vary. An increase in V_i represents people and firms being willing and able to change their wealth more often in response to a change in interest rates. A decrease in transactions costs associated with changing wealth is one example of an event that could cause an increase in V_i.

16. The costs of inflation include
    • the need to devote more time and energy to managing cash balances.
    • the costs of changing prices on menus, price tags, computer databases, and so on.
    • perverse tax effects experienced because the U.S. tax system is not designed to deal well with inflation.
    • redistribution of wealth from creditors to debtors.

- an increased likelihood that incumbent politicians will be voted out of office (of course, depending upon your point of view and the politician in question, this effect could certainly be a *benefit* of inflation!)

17. The benefits of inflation include:
    - the ability of the central bank to push the real interest rate below zero
    - avoiding deleterious effects on worker morale if wage cuts are imposed in a slowdown

C. APPLYING CONCEPTS AND MODELS

1. The increase in rent decreases the value of his money holdings, reducing Nausher's real money balances. It does not, however, change his real money demand. Nausher therefore wants to increase his nominal money holdings. That is, he wants to increase his average balance in his checking account. To do so, Nausher reduces his spending where possible – probably by switching to cheaper grocery brands and reducing his entertainment expenses.

2. The Fed should buy bonds from the public. Some households, some businesses, and all banks hold government bonds in their wealth portfolios. If the Fed buys bonds from households, businesses, and banks, the Fed pays for the bonds by directly transferring funds to the sellers. You can think of this as the Fed paying with a check drawn on itself, the Federal Reserve. When the bond seller deposits this check into a checking account, the amount of money in the economy increases. If the bond seller is a household or a business, the bank that receives the household or business's deposit will increase its balance in its reserve account at its Federal Reserve Bank. The bank's balance in its account at the Federal Reserve Bank is part of the monetary base. If the bond seller is a bank, the Fed pays the bank for the bonds by increasing the bank's balance in its account at the Federal Reserve Bank. Again, this is part of the monetary base.

   Remember: The monetary base is defined as the amount of currency in circulation plus the amount of coin in circulation plus the total balances of deposits that banks hold at the central bank (in the United States, the Federal Reserve Banks). Currency and coin in the vaults of banks are **not** counted; they are not in circulation. Balances held in checking deposits at commercial banks are **not** counted; balances that the banks themselves hold at the Federal Reserve Banks are counted.

3. Online trading of stocks and bonds made it easier and less expensive to move wealth between money and stocks or bonds than was the case when it was necessary to have a stockbroker whom you called on the phone during business hours when you wanted to buy or sell stock. Velocity should increase as a result.

4. The increase in spending for gifts means there is an increase in the transactions motive. The demand for money increases every year in December.

D. EXPLAINING THE REAL WORLD

1. M2 includes everything that is in M1 plus balances in savings accounts, in household money-market funds, and in small time-deposits. The implication of M1 velocity increasing while M2 velocity remained constant is that households were changing funds between (most likely) money-market funds and checking account balances much more often by the 1990s than they were in 1960. This implication is consistent with what we know of financial developments between 1960 and 1990. Balances in "retail" (household) money market mutual funds were nonexistent until 1974, increased tenfold between 1979 and 1989, and nearly tripled between 1989 and 1999. (See "Components of Money Stock Measures," Table B-70 in the 2001 *ERP*.) Transferring wealth from a money-market fund to a checking account became as simple as writing a check (technically, a negotiable order of withdrawal) against the balance in the money-market fund and depositing the money-market fund check into a regular checking

account. Relatively small minimum check sizes in most money-market funds meant that many individuals could make rent, mortgage, car loan, and other payments directly out of their money-market funds.

2. The development of ATM machines increased velocity. With an ATM machine it is possible to withdraw funds from savings accounts at any time of day, any day of the week, any place in the country (or the world!). All else constant, people therefore hold smaller money (checking account) balances because the cost of withdrawing funds from savings accounts is smaller than it was before the advent of ATM machines.

3. The Confederacy's policy of paying its bills with newly printed money led to hyperinflation in the south. When the government printed money, this increased the amount of money in the economy. The Confederacy's costs of fighting the war were very large, so the amount of money in the economy increased very rapidly. Hyperinflation resulted.

4. If Russia's goal was to decrease inflation, then they needed to control the growth of the money supply. Some economists therefore recommended a stringent policy of little or no growth in the Russian money supply. But in the real world and the short run, rapid reduction of the growth rate of the money stock, if velocity did not change, probably reduced both output and prices. The short-run effect of rapid reduction in the money growth rate would have been recession.

E. POSSIBILITIES TO PONDER

No solutions are given to these questions. The questions are designed to be somewhat open ended. Each question draws on your understanding of the concepts covered in this chapter.

Chapter 9

The Income-Expenditure Framework: Consumption and the Multiplier

- When prices are sticky, the equilibrium amount of output and income in the macroeconomy depends upon aggregate demand.

- Because aggregate demand depends in part on income, any initial change in autonomous spending creates a much larger total change in income through the multiplier process.

LEARNING GUIDE

This chapter is the first of four chapters in which we develop the short-run model of the economy. One model is introduced: the income-expenditure model that determines equilibrium income. Several important concepts are also introduced, including sticky prices, equilibrium income, and the multiplier.

Be careful as you read through this chapter. The chapter includes a review of the long-run model of Chapters 4 through 8, and it introduces the short-run model of Chapters 9 through 12. It is important to keep the long-run and short-run stories separate. You might want to use two different colors of highlighters—one for passages about the long run and another for passages about the short run.

Short on time?

If you are really in a pinch, begin with Section 9.2. But in general, do not try to study this chapter quickly. The material in Chapters 9 through 12 is cumulative. If you skimp on Chapter 9, you will be lost in Chapter 10. (And if you're lost in Chapter 10, it is good that you are back here, reviewing Chapter 9.)

When you finish Chapter 9, you should be sure to understand what determines equilibrium output in the short run, how the adjustment process brings the economy to equilibrium, how to find equilibrium output and the value of the multiplier algebraically, and why there is a multiplier process. You should also be able to explain how and why a change in any component of autonomous spending changes national income; and how and why a change in the marginal propensity to consume, the tax rate, and the marginal propensity to import change the size of the multiplier.

A. BASIC DEFINITIONS

Before you apply knowledge, you need a basic grasp of the fundamentals. In other words, there are some things you just have to know. Knowing the material in this section won't guarantee a good grade in the course, but not knowing it will guarantee a poor or failing grade.

USE THE WORDS OR PHRASES FROM THE LIST BELOW TO COMPLETE THE SENTENCES. SOME ARE USED MORE THAN ONCE; SOME ARE NOT USED AT ALL.

aggregate demand
automatic stabilizer
business cycles
disposable income
expansion
inventory
menu costs

money illusion
multiplier process
national income
natural rate of unemployment
potential output
price
recession

1. The adjustment process by which real GDP comes to equal aggregate demand is a(n) _____ adjustment process.

2. _____ is said to occur when changes in nominal prices are confused with changes in real prices.

3. The automatic working of the government's tax and transfer payments systems function as a(n) _____.

4. In the _____, an increase in spending causes an increase in production and incomes, which leads to a further increase in spending.

5. Fluctuations in growth of real GDP are called _____.

6. When prices are sticky, income equals _____ in equilibrium, but when prices are flexible, income equals _____ in equilibrium.

7. A business cycle has two phases: a(n) _____ phase when output is growing rapidly and a(n) _____ phase when output is falling.

8. The share of an extra dollar of _____ that is added to import spending is equal to IM_y.

9. The share of an extra dollar of _____ that is added to consumption spending is equal to the marginal propensity to consume (MPC), C_y.

10. The share of an extra dollar of _____ that is added to consumption spending is equal to $(1 - t)C_y$.

11. The costs associated with changing prices are called _____.

12. Because of the _____, an increase in autonomous spending leads to a much larger increase in income in equilibrium.

13. An average level of unemployment that is consistent with stable inflation is called a(n) _____.

CIRCLE THE CORRECT WORD OR PHRASE IN EACH OF THE FOLLOWING SENTENCES.

14. The natural rate of unemployment is constant / changing over time.

15. Investment of C + I + G + NX is planned / actual investment spending.

16. Beginning with Chapter 9, we assume prices are flexible / sticky.

> **NOTE**: Be sure you are clear on sticky versus flexible prices. When do we assume prices are flexible? When do we assume they are sticky? What are the implications of assuming flexible prices? What are the implications of assuming sticky prices?

17. When prices are assumed to be sticky / flexible, we are considering the long run.

18. Aggregate demand and total expenditure are / are not necessarily equal.

19. The larger the marginal propensity to consume, the larger / smaller the multiplier.

20. If production of output is greater than aggregate demand, inventories are rising / falling.

21. In most real world cases, it is more realistic to assume that in the short run, prices are flexible / inflexible.

22. When prices are sticky / flexible, the actual level of real GDP is determined by the level of aggregate demand.

23. When prices are assumed to be sticky, we are considering the short / long run.

24. In a business cycle, potential / actual output fluctuates.

25. If aggregate demand is greater / less than output, inventories will be falling.

26. The larger the marginal tax rate, the <u>larger / smaller</u> the multiplier.

27. The larger the MPE, the <u>larger / smaller</u> the multiplier.

28. When prices are <u>sticky / flexible</u>, the actual level of real GDP is determined by potential output.

29. The more open an economy is to free trade, the <u>larger / smaller</u> the multiplier.

 CAREFUL! Always be clear – especially on exams – whether you are assuming flexible prices or sticky prices. The flexible price story is different than the story you will tell when prices are sticky.

SELECT THE ONE BEST ANSWER FOR EACH MULTIPLE-CHOICE QUESTION.

30. A recession occurs when there is a
    A. slowdown in production.
    B. rise in unemployment.
    C. drop in production.
    D. drop in the stock market.

31. When aggregate demand decreases, producers respond by
    A. always cutting prices.
    B. always cutting output.
    C. cutting prices if prices are flexible.
    D. cutting prices if prices are sticky.

32. In equilibrium,
    A. planned investment spending equals actual investment spending.
    B. output equals aggregate demand.
    C. inventory holdings are constant over time.
    D. all of the above.

 CAREFUL! The material in Chapters 9 to 12 is cumulative. If you don't understand the material in Chapter 9, you'll never understand Chapter 10. Chapter 11 depends upon Chapter 10. Chapter 12 depends upon Chapter 11. Spend lots of time on Chapter 9. From here on the material is like blocks: each block builds on the previous one.

B. MANIPULATION OF CONCEPTS AND MODELS

Most instructors expect you to be able to do basic manipulation of the concepts. Being able to do so often means you can earn a C in a course. But if you want a better grade, you'll need to be able to complete this next section easily and move on to Sections C and D.

1. Before we begin learning the sticky-price model of Chapters 9 to 12, let's review the flexible-price full-employment model of Chapters 6 to 8. If the economy has flexible prices and is always at full employment, what is the effect of a decrease in autonomous consumption spending, C_0, on real output, Y? On the allocation of output among consumers, businesses, government agencies, and the rest of the world? On prices?

2. Using the *Economic Report of the President*, complete the table below.

year	Unemployment Rate	Inflation Rate (GDP deflator)	Rate of Growth of Real GDP
1980			
1981			
1982			
1983			
1984			
1985			
1986			
1987			
1988			
1989			
1990			

Do the assumptions of the models in Chapters 4 through 8 seem consistent with the data in the above table?

3. Describe what happens in a sticky-price economy when government purchases of goods and services decrease.

> **HINT:** There is a big difference between flexible- and sticky-price models in the response to a change in aggregate demand. In a **flexible-price** model, a change in aggregate demand leads to a change in **prices**. In a **sticky-price** model, a change in aggregate demand leads to a change in **output**.

4. Suppose $C = 1000 + 0.8Y^D$. Suppose the tax rate, t, equals 0. Now suppose there is a drop in government purchases, G. Suppose that the drop in government purchases ultimately causes income, Y, to decrease by 500.

    A. Suppose prices are sticky. By how much will consumption spending change? By how much will saving change?

    B. Suppose prices are flexible. Are your answers to Part A the same? Explain.

> **HINT:** If you are having trouble keeping track of what is a short-run effect and what is a long-run effect of some change, try making a table like this one.
>
> When autonomous consumption, C_0, decreases . . .
>
> | Flexible price (long-run) effects | Sticky price (short-run) effects |
> | --- | --- |
> | Consumption, C, decreases | Output, real GDP, decreases |
> | Saving, S, increases | Income, Y, decreases |
> | Real interest rates, r, decrease | Consumption, C, decreases |
> | Investment, I, increases | Saving, S, decreases |
> | Gross and net exports, NX, increase | |
> | Income, Y, does not change | |
> | Output, real GDP, is reallocated away from consumers and toward businesses and the rest of the world | |

5. How many years long is the "long run"? How many years long is the "short run"?

6. Give three reasons why prices are sticky in the short run.

7. Give two real-world examples of "menu costs."

TO THE CHALKBOARD:

Deriving the Consumption Function

The consumption function can be expressed in several ways. We can write simply $C = C_0 + C_y Y^D$, or more fully $C = C_0 + C_y(1 - t)Y$. Here, we see that these two expressions of the consumption function are equivalent.

$C = C_0 + C_y \cdot Y^D$ *consumption is a function of disposable income*

$C = C_0 + C_y \cdot (Y - T)$ *substituting definition of disposable income, Y^D*

$C = C_0 + C_y \cdot (Y - t \cdot Y)$ *substituting definition of net taxes, T*

$C = C_0 + C_y \cdot [(1 - t) \cdot Y]$ *factoring out Y*

$C = C_0 + C_y \cdot (1 - t) \cdot Y$ *dropping parentheses to match text*

HINT: You might want to review Chapter 6. In Chapter 6, we first introduced the consumption, investment, and net exports functions.

8. Suppose the consumption function is
$$C = 1{,}000 + 0.7Y$$

Using the axes at the right, graph this consumption function. Label your axes, curve, and intercept.

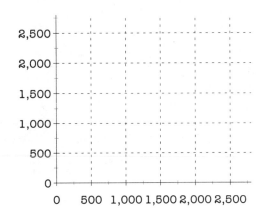

9. Suppose $C_0 = 800$ $C_y = 0.6$ $t = 0.2$

    What is the equation for consumption spending as a function of income?

10. Suppose $C_0 = 1,200$ $t = 0.2$ $C = 6,000$ when $Y = 8,000$

    What is the value of the marginal propensity to consume?

11. Suppose

    $C = 5,000$ when $Y = 8,000$

    $C = 5,400$ when $Y = 8,800$

    $t = 25\%$

    What is the value of the marginal propensity to consume?

12. Suppose $C = 600 + 0.8(1 - 0.2)Y$

    $I = 1,000 - 4,000r$

    $G = 2,000$

    $NX = 40Y^f + 300\varepsilon - 0.15Y$

    What is the value of autonomous spending, A? What is the value of the marginal propensity to spend, the MPE?

NOTE: In the textbook, the equation for aggregate demand is given as

$$E = [\, C_0 + C_y(1 - t)Y \,] + I + G + (GX - IM_y Y)$$

A more complete equation would spell out the determinants of investment spending, I, and gross exports, GX. But spelling out the determinants adds details that are not relevant to what concerns us now: the parts of aggregate demand that are independent of income (A) and the parts that are dependent upon income (MPE·Y).

13. Suppose

$$C = 600 + 0.8(1 - 0.2)Y$$

$$I = 1,000 - 4,000r$$

$$G = 2,000$$

$$NX = 40Y^f + 300\varepsilon - 0.15Y$$

$$r = 0.05$$

$$Y^f = 95$$

$$\varepsilon = 10$$

Using the axes at the right, graph the relationship between income and aggregate demand. Label your axes, curve, and intercept.

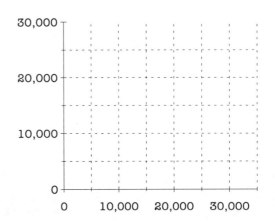

TO THE CHALKBOARD:
Explaining the Income-Expenditure Diagram

Textbook Figure 9.12 presents the Income-Expenditure Diagram. Here is another explanation of the diagram which helps us find the equilibrium level of income.

The first thing to clarify is that the dash between Income and Expenditure is just a dash, not a minus sign. This is not the "Income minus Expenditure Diagram"; it is the "Income and Expenditure Diagram."

Equilibrium income exists, by definition, when aggregate demand equals income. First, graph the aggregate demand line. In general, the aggregate demand line is E = A + MPE·Y. It shows, for every level of income, Y (which is measured on the horizontal axis) and the amount of aggregate demand, E (which is measured on the vertical axis). In the graph at the right, the aggregate demand line is shown.

To find equilibrium income, we want that level of income where income equals aggregate demand. If we try to find equilibrium income from the graph at the right, we have to dig out a ruler, or trust our eye. It is hard – maybe impossible – to tell from looking at the graph which of those points on the Aggregate Demand line is the same distance from both the horizontal and vertical axes.

But we can use a trick. We can add a second line to the graph. The second line can show us every point where income equals aggregate demand. Then to locate the equilibrium level of income, we just need to find the place where that second line intersects the aggregate demand line. That is why we add the second line, which is the income = expenditure line. The point where the two lines intersect is the equilibrium level of income!

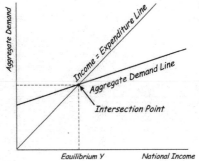

TO THE CHALKBOARD:
Deriving the Income-Expenditure Equilibrium Equation

Equilibrium income exists when aggregate demand equals income. We can derive an algebraic expression for equilibrium income, illustrating how equilibrium income depends upon autonomous levels of spending and the marginal propensity to spend.

First, let's derive the expression for equilibrium income starting from the simplest form of the aggregate demand equation, $E = A + MPE \cdot Y$.

$$E = A + MPE \cdot Y \qquad \textit{definition of aggregate demand}$$
$$E = Y \qquad \textit{definition of equilibrium}$$
$$Y = E = A + MPE \cdot Y \qquad \textit{substituting}$$
$$Y - MPE \cdot Y = A \qquad \textit{subtracting } MPE \cdot Y \textit{ from both sides of equation}$$
$$Y \cdot (1 - MPE) = A \qquad \textit{factoring out } Y$$
$$Y = \frac{A}{(1 - MPE)} \qquad \textit{dividing both sides by } (1 - MPE)$$

This form of the equilibrium income equation illustrates the roles of autonomous spending, A, and the marginal propensity to spend, MPE. But it does not immediately illustrate the roles of factors such as autonomous consumption, foreign income, the marginal propensity to import, and so on. The method of deriving the expression for equilibrium income is the same. The equations look much messier.

$$E = C + I + G + (GX - IM) \qquad \textit{definition of aggregate demand}$$
$$Y = E \qquad \textit{definition of equilibrium}$$
$$Y = E = C + I + G + (GX - IM) \qquad \textit{substituting}$$
$$Y = (C_0 + C_y(1 - t)Y) + (I_0 - I_r r) + G + (X_f y^f + X_\varepsilon \varepsilon_0 - X_\varepsilon {}_r r + X_\varepsilon {}_r r^f - IM_y Y) \qquad \textit{substituting}$$
$$Y = C_0 + I_0 - I_r r + G + X_f y^f + X_\varepsilon \varepsilon_0 - X_\varepsilon {}_r r + X_\varepsilon {}_r r^f + C_y(1 - t)Y - IM_y Y$$
$$\textit{eliminating parentheses and rearranging terms}$$
$$Y - \left(C_y(1 - t)Y - IM_y Y \right) = C_0 + I_0 - I_r r + G + X_f y^f + X_\varepsilon \varepsilon_0 - X_\varepsilon {}_r r + X_\varepsilon {}_r r^f$$
$$\textit{subtracting } \left(C_y(1 - t)Y - IM_y Y \right) \textit{ from both sides}$$
$$Y - C_y(1 - t)Y + IM_y Y = C_0 + I_0 - I_r r + G + X_f y^f + X_\varepsilon \varepsilon_0 - X_\varepsilon {}_r r + X_\varepsilon {}_r r^f$$
$$\textit{simplifying left side}$$
$$Y \cdot \left(1 - C_y(1 - t) + IM_y \right) = C_0 + I_0 - I_r r + G + X_f y^f + X_\varepsilon \varepsilon_0 - X_\varepsilon {}_r r + X_\varepsilon {}_r r^f$$
$$\textit{factoring out } Y$$
$$Y = \frac{C_0 + I_0 - I_r r + G + X_f y^f + X_\varepsilon \varepsilon_0 - X_\varepsilon {}_r r + X_\varepsilon {}_r r^f}{\left(1 - C_y(1 - t) + IM_y \right)}$$
$$\textit{dividing both sides by } \left(1 - C_y(1 - t) + IM_y \right)$$

Messier, much messier, but the story is the same. When autonomous spending increases, equilibrium income increases. When the marginal propensity to spend increases, equilibrium income increases.

14. Suppose the economy can be described by the equations in Question 13. Using algebra, derive the equilibrium level of income. Confirm your answer graphically, using the axes at the right.

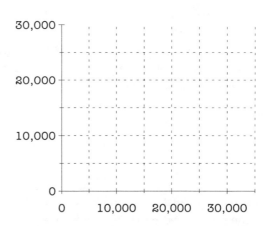

15. Suppose the equations from Question 13 describe the economy initially. Suppose that business optimism increases, so that in the next year autonomous investment spending, I_0, increases by 510. What is the new expression for aggregate demand as a function of income? What is the new value of autonomous spending, A? What is the new value of the marginal propensity to spend, the MPE? What is the new value of equilibrium income, Y? Using the axes at the right, graph the initial aggregate demand relationship from Question 13 and the new aggregate demand relationship, and then show the new equilibrium level of income.

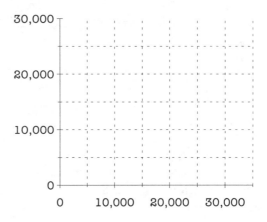

16. Suppose the equations from Question 13 describe the economy initially. Suppose that the need for defense spending increases, so that in the next year autonomous government spending, G, increases by 255. What is the new expression for aggregate demand as a function of income? What is the new value of autonomous spending, A? What is the new value of the marginal propensity to spend, the MPE? What is the new value of equilibrium income, Y?

17. Suppose the equations from Question 13 describe the economy initially. Suppose that in the next year foreign income, Y^f, increases by 25.5. What is the new expression for aggregate demand as a function of income? What is the new value of autonomous spending, A? What is the new value of the marginal propensity to spend, the MPE? What is the new value of equilibrium income, Y?

18. Suppose the equations from Question 13 describe the economy initially. Suppose that in the next year the real exchange rate, ε, increases by 5.1. What is the new expression for aggregate demand as a function of income? What is the new value of autonomous spending, A? What is the new value of the marginal propensity to spend, the MPE? What is the new value of equilibrium income, Y?

19. Suppose the equations from Question 13 describe the economy initially. Suppose that in the next year autonomous consumption, C_0 decreases by 40.8. What is the new expression for aggregate demand as a function of income? What is the new value of autonomous spending, A? What is the new value of the marginal propensity to spend, the MPE? What is the new value of equilibrium income, Y?

20. Suppose the equations from Question 13 describe the economy initially. Suppose that in the next year the tax rate, t, increases to 25 percent. What is the new expression for aggregate demand as a function of income? What is the new value of autonomous spending, A? What is the new value of the marginal propensity to spend, the MPE? What is the new value of equilibrium income, Y?

TO THE CHALKBOARD:
Deriving the Expression for the Multiplier

The expression for the multiplier can be derived several ways. In the textbook, it is given in its simplest form. But sometimes the more complete, messier, form is actually more useful.

The Simplest Form

First, use the simplest expression of aggregate demand: $E = A + MPE \cdot Y$. Remember that in equilibrium, $Y = E$. Solving $Y = A + MPE \cdot Y$ for Y yields the expression for equilibrium income: $Y = \dfrac{A}{1 - MPE}$. The multiplier tells us the change in equilibrium income, ΔY, that results from a change in autonomous spending, ΔA. That is, the multiplier is $\dfrac{\Delta Y}{\Delta A}$.

$$Y = \frac{A}{1 - MPE} \qquad \text{expression for equilibrium income}$$

$$\Delta Y = \Delta \left(\frac{A}{1 - MPE} \right) \qquad \text{an equivalent statement}$$

$$\Delta Y = \frac{\Delta A}{(1 - MPE)} \qquad \text{MPE is a constant}$$

$$\frac{\Delta Y}{\Delta A} = \frac{1}{(1 - MPE)} \qquad \text{expression for multiplier}$$

This expression for the multiplier emphasizes that the multiplier depends upon the size of the marginal propensity to spend. The greater the MPE, the greater the multiplier. But this expression for the multiplier does not immediately help us see how a change in, for instance, the tax rate affects the size of the multiplier.

The More Complete Form

To gain more information about the determinants of the multiplier, we need to begin with the more complete expression for equilibrium income. The quickest way to derive the multipliers is with calculus. It is not the only way, but if you are comfortable with partial derivatives, it is the best approach to take. (Hint: Review the box "To The Chalkboard: Deriving the Income-Expenditure Equilibrium Equation" on page 232 if you do not know where the next expression comes from.) For instance, the government spending multiplier, dY/dG, is

$$Y = \frac{C_0 + I_0 - I_r r + G + X_f Y^f + X_\varepsilon \varepsilon_0 - X_\varepsilon \varepsilon_r r + X_\varepsilon \varepsilon_r r^f}{\left(1 - C_y(1 - t) + IM_y\right)} \qquad \text{equilibrium income}$$

$$dY = \frac{\partial}{\partial G} \left(\frac{C_0 + I_0 - I_r r + G + X_f Y^f + X_\varepsilon \varepsilon_0 - X_\varepsilon \varepsilon_r r + X_\varepsilon \varepsilon_r r^f}{\left(1 - C_y(1 - t) + IM_y\right)} \right) \cdot dG \qquad \text{differential of Y}$$

$$dY = \left(\frac{0 + 0 - 0 + 1 + 0 + 0 - 0 + 0}{\left(1 - C_y(1 - t) + IM_y\right)} \right) \cdot dG \qquad \text{everything but G is a constant}$$

$$dY = \left(\frac{1}{\left(1 - C_y(1 - t) + IM_y\right)} \right) \cdot dG \qquad \text{simplifying}$$

$$\frac{dY}{dG} = \frac{1}{\left(1 - C_y(1 - t) + IM_y\right)} \qquad \text{dividing both sides by dG}$$

If the tax rate, t, increases, then $(1 - t)$ decreases, so $-C_y(1 - t)$ increases, so the multiplier decreases. Behaviorally, the tax rate increases so that more taxes are paid for each dollar of income, then any change in income resulting from a change in spending results in a smaller change in disposable income than was the case before tax rates increased. A smaller change in disposable income means a smaller change in consumption spending, and thus a smaller multiplier effect.

What if instead we want to know the multiplier effect of a change in real interest rates, r? The same process is used.

$$dY = \frac{\partial}{\partial r} \left(\frac{C_0 + I_0 - I_r r + G + X_f y^f + X_\varepsilon \varepsilon_0 - X_\varepsilon \varepsilon_r r + X_\varepsilon \varepsilon_r r^f}{\left(1 - C_y(1 - f) + IM_y\right)} \right) \cdot dr \qquad \textit{differential of Y}$$

$$dY = \left(\frac{0 + 0 - I_r + 0 + 0 + 0 - X_\varepsilon \varepsilon_r + 0}{\left(1 - C_y(1 - f) + IM_y\right)} \right) \cdot dr \qquad \textit{everything but r is a constant}$$

$$dY = \left(\frac{- I_r - X_\varepsilon \varepsilon_r}{\left(1 - C_y(1 - f) + IM_y\right)} \right) \cdot dr \qquad \textit{simplifying}$$

$$\frac{dY}{dr} = \frac{- I_r - X_\varepsilon \varepsilon_r}{1 - C_y(1 - f) + IM_y} \qquad \textit{dividing both sides by dr}$$

The advantage to this more complete approach is that we can see explicitly how each factor influences the extent to which income changes in reaction to a change in some other factor. The disadvantage is only that it is messy.

21. A. Using the equations in Question 13, what is the value of the multiplier?

B. Compare the values of autonomous spending, A, and income, Y, in Question 14 with the values of these two variables in Question 15. Confirm that the change in income that you calculated is equal to the multiplier times the change in autonomous spending.

C. Compare the values of autonomous spending, A, and income, Y, in Question 14 with the values of these two variables in Question 16. Confirm that the change in income that you calculated is equal to the multiplier times the change in autonomous spending.

D. Compare the values of autonomous spending, A, and income, Y, in Question 14 with the values of these two variables in Question 17. Confirm that the change in income that you calculated is equal to the multiplier times the change in autonomous spending.

E. Compare the values of autonomous spending, A, and income, Y, in Question 14 with the values of these two variables in Question 18. Confirm that the change in income that you calculated is equal to the multiplier times the change in autonomous spending.

F. Compare the values of autonomous spending, A, and income, Y, in Question 14 with the values of these two variables in Question 19. Confirm that the change in income that you calculated is equal to the multiplier times the change in autonomous spending.

22. On the axes at the right, should the income = expenditure line be drawn at a 45° angle? Explain.

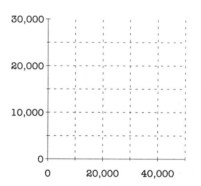

23. Consider the graph at the right.
    A. If real GDP = Y_1, is the economy at equilibrium? Describe what will happen to inventory holdings over time if income initially equals Y_1.

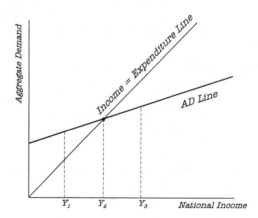

    B. If real GDP = Y_2, is the economy at equilibrium? Describe what will happen to inventory holdings over time if income initially equals Y_2.

C. If real GDP = Y_3, is the economy at equilibrium? Describe what will happen to inventory holdings over time if income initially equals Y_3.

> **HINT:** Review Study Guide Chapter 2, Section B, Question 20, if you do not remember how changes in inventory holdings are recorded in the national income and product accounts.

24. Suppose that income is $5,000 billion and aggregate demand is $5,400 billion. If output increases to $5,400 billion, will the economy then be at equilibrium? Explain.

25. Suppose autonomous spending increases by $400 billion. Will national income increase by more than $400 billion, less than $400 billion, or just $400 billion? Explain.

TO THE CHALKBOARD:
Illustrating the Multiplier Process

Any initial change in autonomous spending leads to round after round of changes in spending, such that the total change in national income far exceeds the initial change in spending. This multiplier process is an important part of the macroeconomy.

An illustration of the multiplier process may make the concept clearer. For the purposes of the illustration, assume

the marginal propensity to consume, C_y, is 80 percent,

the marginal tax rate, t, is 15 percent,

and the marginal propensity to import, IM_y, is 20 percent.

Example 1: An Increase in Autonomous Spending
Suppose autonomous spending, A, increases by $800 billion. The chart on the next page illustrates the multiplier process that results.

Changes in Spending	Changes in Domestic Output and Domestic Income	Changes in Disposable Income
ΔA = +$800 b.	$\Delta GDP = \Delta Y$ = + $800 b.	$\Delta Y^D = \Delta Y - \Delta T = \Delta Y - t\Delta Y$ = 800 - 0.15(800) = + $680 b.
$\Delta C = c_y(\Delta Y^D) = 0.8(680)$ = + $544 b. $\Delta IM = IM_y(\Delta Y) =$ 0.20(800) = + $160 b.	$\Delta GDP = \Delta C - \Delta IM$ = + $544 b. - $160 b. = $384 b. = ΔY	$\Delta Y^D = \Delta Y - t\Delta Y =$ 384 - 0.15(384) = + $326.4 b.
$\Delta C = c_y(\Delta Y^D) = 0.8(326.4)$ = + $261.12 b. $\Delta IM = IM_y(\Delta Y) =$ 0.20(384) = + $76.8 b.	$\Delta GDP = \Delta C - \Delta IM$ = + $261.12 b. - $76.8 b. = + $184.32 b. = ΔY	$\Delta Y^D = \Delta Y - t\Delta Y =$ 184.32 - 0.15(184.32) = + $156.672 b.
And on and on and on		

Envision the people who are behind all those figures. There is an initial increase in autonomous spending of $800 billion when (for instance) the government increases defense spending by $800 billion. The increase in spending by the government leads to an increase in output (jet fuel, jets, military salaries, boots, shoes, computers, paper, and so on). The companies that produce the output purchased by the government, their employees, and the people directly employed by the government experience a collective increase in income of $800 billion. With a tax rate of 15 percent, government tax revenues increase by $120 billion, leaving an increase in disposable income of $680 billion for all those folks to spend. The people who own and are employed by the companies that produce the goods and services that the government purchased plus the people directly employed by the government who received increased income spend 80 percent of their increase in disposable income buying consumer goods and services for themselves and their families. Of this $544 billion increase in consumer spending, $160 billion is spent on goods and services produced in other countries. The net increase in demand for domestically produced goods and services, $384 billion, generates additional domestic income of $384 billion for the firm owners and employees in the businesses that produced and sold the consumer goods and services. Of this $384 billion in income, 15 percent is paid to the government in taxes, leaving $326.4 billion in disposable income for the firm owners and employees. Of this $326.4 billion in disposable income, they choose to spend 80 percent, $261.12 billion, on consumer goods and services. The remaining 20 percent, $65.28 billion, is saved. Of the $261.12 billion that is spent on goods and services, $76.8 billion is used to purchase goods and services produced in other countries. The remaining $184.32 billion is spent on goods and services produced domestically, generating additional income for the firms and employees who produced those goods of $184.32 billion. The process continues, with round after round of increases in spending, increases in output, increases in income, increases in disposable income, and then further increases in spending for domestically produced goods and services. The total amount of income generated as a result of the initial $800 billion in autonomous spending will be the sum of the figures in the middle column in the table that is above: $800 billion + $384 billion + $184.32 billion + . . . = $1,538.5 billion.

Example 2: A Decrease in Autonomous Spending

How does the story change if instead we have a decrease in autonomous spending? The only substantial difference is that instead of firms and employees receiving additional income, they now face a loss of income and even perhaps a loss of their jobs. One round of cuts in spending leads to another round of spending cuts by the people who lose income because their products are no longer purchased by the people who cut back their spending in the first round.

Suppose autonomous spending, A, decreases by $500 billion. We could tell any number of stories that could generate a drop in A of $500 billion: a drop in consumer confidence, a drop in investor confidence, a decline in foreign income, a decline in the real exchange rate, a rise in real interest rates. The next steps of the multiplier process story are the same, regardless of the reason autonomous spending initially declines.

Changes in Spending	Changes in Domestic Output and Domestic Income	Changes in Disposable Income
$\Delta A = -\$500$ b.	$\Delta GDP = \Delta y = -\$500$ b.	$\Delta y^D = \Delta y - \Delta T = \Delta y - t\Delta y$ $= 500 - 0.15(500) = -\$425$ b.
$\Delta C = c_y(\Delta y^D) = 0.8(-425)$ $= -\$340$ b. $\Delta IM = IM_y(\Delta y) =$ $0.20(-500) = -\$100$ b.	$\Delta GDP = \Delta C - \Delta IM$ $= -\$340$ b. $- (-\$100$ b.$)$ $= -\$240$ b. $= \Delta y$	$\Delta y^D = \Delta y - t\Delta y =$ $-240 - (0.15(-240))$ $= -\$204$ b.
$\Delta C = c_y(\Delta y^D) = 0.8(-204)$ $= -\$163.2$ b. $\Delta IM = IM_y(\Delta y) =$ $0.20(-240) = -\$48$ b.	$\Delta GDP = \Delta C - \Delta IM$ $= -\$163.2$ b. $- (-\$48$ b.$)$ $= -\$115.2$ b. $= \Delta y$	$\Delta y^D = \Delta y - t\Delta y =$ $-115.2 - 0.15(-115.2)$ $= -\$97.92$ b.
And on and on and on		

The initial drop in spending of $500 billion means that some firms will see their sales decrease, causing them to decrease their production of output. Some workers will be laid off; some businesses will shut down. The amount of output produced (real GDP) will drop by $500 billion and thus income will also decline by $500 billion. But when workers have no income, they pay no taxes. So tax revenues paid to the government will decrease by $75 billion, resulting in a loss of disposable income of only $425 billion. The people who have lost their jobs and income will need to cut back on their spending. They reduce their consumption spending by 80 percent of the loss in disposable income, $340 billion, and draw down their savings by an amount equal to the other 20 percent of their loss in disposable income, $85 billion. Of the $340 billion in spending they are no longer doing, $100 billion would have been for goods and services produced in other countries and $240 would have been for goods and services produced domestically. Another round of layoffs now occurs: the firms and people who would have produced the no-longer-demanded $240 billion in goods and services will lose income equal to $240 billion. Their disposable income will decline by $204 billion, leading them to reduce consumption spending, some of which would have been for consumer goods produced in other countries. The waves of layoffs would continue in the consumer goods and services sector as the multiplier process continued. The total loss in income resulting from the initial $500 billion decline in autonomous spending would be $500 + $240 + $115.2 + . . . = $961.54 billion.

26. Suppose autonomous spending declines by $300 billion. Will national income decline by more than $300 billion, less than $300 billion, or just $300 billion? Explain.

27. Suppose the MPE = 0.4.
   A. If government purchases increases by $300 billion, what is the size of the effect on national income?

   B. If consumer spending decreases by $600 billion, what is the size of the effect on national income?

28. A. Suppose the MPE = 0.5. What is the value of the multiplier?

   B. Suppose the MPE = 0.6. What is the new value of the multiplier?

   C. Explain why an increase in the marginal propensity to spend causes an increase in the multiplier. Use economic concepts in your explanation, not just mathematics. (That is, an answer of "1 - MPE is in the denominator, so a larger MPE makes the denominator smaller, which makes the fraction – the multiplier – larger" is an answer that uses mathematics, not economic concepts.)

29. Complete the table below.

	(A)	(B)	(C)	(D)
c_y	0.8	0.8	0.8	0.9
t	0.2	0.3	0.2	0.2
IM_y	0.15	0.15	0.25	0.15
multiplier				

$\mathcal{C}$. APPLYING CONCEPTS AND MODELS

Now we're getting to the good stuff. Being able to apply a specific concept or model to a real world situation — where you are told which model to apply but you have to figure out how to apply it — is often what you need to earn a B in a course. This is where macroeconomics starts to become interesting and the world starts to make more sense.

1. Suppose a national disaster causes consumers to reduce their consumption spending. In the short run, when prices are sticky, what is the effect of the drop in consumption on national income, Y? If prices were instead fully flexible, is the effect on national income the same?

2. In the United States in the late twentieth and early twenty-first centuries, were employers willing to cut wages if demand for their products decreased? Explain.

3. Suppose that consumers in the United States respond to a possibly misguided call to reduce their purchases of imported goods as an act of patriotism. What effect will their action have on equilibrium income in the United States?

4. Leon is a stock clerk at a local retail store. His boss tells him there should be twelve cases of their product in the back room. Leon goes into the back and finds only four cases. Leon's experience is common to stock clerks from California to Maine. Is the economy in short-run equilibrium? Explain.

5. The government plans to increase marginal tax rates in order to fund a war on terrorists. What effect will the increase in tax rates have on national income?

6. The airline industry lost thousands of passengers following the terrorist attacks of September 11, 2001. In cities where tourism is a dominant industry, city officials expressed concern that tourists were staying home, leaving hotels and restaurants empty. Is the drop in tourism an example of a multiplier effect? Explain.

7. Suppose consumers in America decide to purchase proportionately more imported goods as a share of their total spending. As a result, will government fiscal policy be more or less effective in altering income?

8. Suppose consumers decide they need to increase their saving, and do so by devoting a larger share of any additional income to saving than they had been doing in the past. As a result, will government fiscal policy be more or less effective in altering income?

D. EXPLAINING THE REAL WORLD

Most instructors are delighted when you are able to figure out which concept or model to apply to a real world situation. Being able to do so means you thoroughly understand the material and is often what you need to do to earn an A in a course. This is where you experience the power of macroeconomic theory.

1. The local Office Depot store has been filling a standing order for 1,000 reams of copy paper per week to the local public university. In an attempt to reduce spending, the University's Business Office announces that all departments are to photocopy announcements only when absolutely necessary and instead to send out all announcements by e-mail. What is the short-run effect of this new policy on the local economy?

2. With widespread availability of the internet, more and more consumers are shopping online. What is the impact of the increase in online shopping on the stickiness of prices?

3. During an economic slowdown in the United States in the second quarter of 2001, inventory holdings declined markedly. In late August 2001, many pundits pointed to the inventory declines as evidence that the economy would turn around soon. Explain how the behavior of inventory holdings in the second quarter of 2001 could be used to predict production in the third quarter of 2001. Were the pundits correct in their prediction?

4. In modern industrialized countries, is government fiscal policy more or less effective in changing national income than it is in relatively closed economies with undeveloped financial systems? Explain.

E. Possibilities to Ponder

The more you learn, the more you realize you have more to learn. These questions go beyond the textbook material. They are the sort of questions that distinguish A+ or A work from A-work. Some of them may even serve as starting points for junior or senior year research papers.

1. What is the impact of the increased availability of credit cards on the propensity of consumers to spend?

2. A typical Boston, Massachusetts, resident in 1700 was a colonist, a resident of America but a subject of the British Crown, purchasing many products that were manufactured in England in addition to products produced locally. Compare the marginal propensity to spend of a typical Boston resident of 1700 to a typical Boston resident today.

3. A change in government transfer payments directly affects only those people who receive that particular payment. A change in government taxes directly affects everyone who pays taxes. Do you think that a $100 billion increase in transfer payments has the same effect on national income as a $100 billion decrease in taxes? Explain.

SOLUTIONS   SOLUTIONS   SOLUTIONS   SOLUTIONS

Solutions Solutions Solutions

A. Basic Definitions

* indicates there are notes below related to this question.

1. inventory
2. money illusion
3. automatic stabilizer
4. multiplier process
5. business cycles

6. aggregate demand; potential output
7. expansion; recession
8. national income
9. disposable income

10. national income
11. menu costs
12. multiplier process
13. natural rate of unemployment

14. changing

15. planned

16. sticky

17. flexible

18.* are not

19. larger

20. rising

21. inflexible

22. sticky

23. short

24. actual

25. greater

26. smaller

27. larger

28. flexible

29. smaller

18.*   Are not. Aggregate demand includes *planned* changes in inventory holdings; total expenditure includes *actual* changes in inventory holdings.

---

30. C. A slowdown in production does occur in recession but can occur at other times too. Similarly, a rise in unemployment does occur in recession but can occur at other times too. The stock market rises and falls at any point in the business cycle. A drop in production, a negative growth rate for real GDP, must occur for a period to be labeled a recession.

31. C.

32. D.

B. MANIPULATION OF CONCEPTS AND MODELS

1. In the flexible-price full-employment model, real output is always equal to potential output. That is, $Y = Y^*$. With total income therefore unchanged, a decrease in autonomous consumption spending, C_0, leads to an increase in personal saving. More personal saving means there is an increase in funds available for investment. That increase in the supply of loanable funds decreases real interest rates. The decrease in real interest rates leads to increases in investment spending. Simultaneously, the decrease in real interest rates leads to a worldwide decrease in demand for dollar-denominated assets and thus to a decrease in the amount of foreign currency offered in exchange for dollars. This decrease in the supply of foreign currency leads to an increase in the nominal exchange rate (the dollar price of foreign currency), increasing the relative price of foreign goods and services. The resulting drop in the relative price of domestically produced goods and services increases foreign demand for domestically produced goods and services, thus increasing gross and net exports. Therefore, as a result of the decrease in autonomous consumption spending, less output will be purchased by consumers, more output will be purchased by businesses and the rest of the world, and there will be no change in the amount of output purchased by government agencies.

   When real interest rates decline, velocity also declines; fewer people and businesses will choose to move their funds between money and nonmoney assets when the advantage to doing so has declined. The decrease in velocity corresponds to an increase in money demand. Everyone tries to increase her or his money holdings by decreasing spending. Firms respond by lowering prices. At lower prices, the existing nominal money stock has a higher real value, satisfying people and businesses' increased demand for money and thus restoring equilibrium in the money market.

2. In *Economic Report of the President 2001*, the data are in Tables B-35 and B-3.

year	Unemployment Rate	Inflation Rate (GDP deflator)	Rate of Growth of Real GDP
1980	7.1	9.2	-0.2
1981	7.6	9.3	2.5
1982	9.7	6.2	-2.0
1983	9.6	4.0	4.3
1984	7.5	3.7	7.3
1985	7.2	3.2	3.8
1986	7.0	2.2	3.4
1987	6.2	3.0	3.4
1988	5.5	3.4	4.2
1989	5.3	3.8	3.5
1990	5.6	3.9	1.8

If the assumptions of the flexible-price full-employment model were satisfied in these data, then the unemployment rate would be the full-employment unemployment rate (about 4 percent), the inflation rate would be low and stable, and real GDP would be growing at the same rate as potential output was growing (about 3.5 to 4 percent). But when we look at the data for the 1980s in the table that is above, we see a very different picture of the U.S. economy. The unemployment rate in the 1980s never fell below 5.3 percent and spent most of the decade above 7 percent, clearly not at full employment. Inflation was relatively stable from 1984 on but the rate had been nearly 10 percent at the beginning of the decade before it declined. Real GDP fell in 1980 and 1982, grew rapidly in 1984, grew only slowly in 1990. This pattern is not the stable, steady growth rate we would expect if real GDP and potential output were growing at the same rate. The assumptions of the models presented in the previous chapters do not seem to be satisfied.

If the assumptions of the flexible-price full-employment model are not satisfied, did we just waste our time in studying Chapters 4 through 8? No. Look back at Chapter 5. Some of the most pressing questions of our age are questions regarding long-run growth. Why are some countries rich and some countries poor? Are there any policy options that can help lead the poor of the world, their children, and grandchildren out of poverty? These vital questions can be addressed with the insights gained from studying the economy in the long run. That is the reason we studied the flexible-price full-employment model. But now we turn to other, equally important questions: In industrialized economies, what can be done to alleviate unemployment during economic downturns? This short-run question cannot be addressed with long-run assumptions of flexible prices and full employment. So now, in Chapter 9, we begin building the short-run model that allows us to understand the determinants of unemployment and inflation in the short run.

3. A decrease in government purchases means that some businesses that had been selling their goods or services to various government agencies now sell less to those agencies. Those businesses reduce their production and lay off some workers. The laid-off workers now have less income coming in each month, and so they reduce their consumption spending. Businesses that had been selling the no-longer-purchased consumer goods and services must reduce their production, so they lay off workers. Those laid-off workers, no longer receiving regular paychecks, must reduce their consumption spending. The total change in output produced, income earned, and aggregate demand will be larger (in absolute size) than the initial drop in government purchases.

4. A. $\Delta C = -400$. $\Delta S = -100$. If $C = 1000 + 0.8Y^D$, then $\Delta C = 0 + 0.8\Delta Y^D$. Because $Y^D = C + S$, $\Delta Y^D = \Delta C + \Delta S$. Because we assumed $t = 0$, $\Delta Y^D = \Delta Y$. Therefore, $\Delta C = 0.8(\Delta Y) = 0.8(-500)$ $= -400$. And $\Delta S = \Delta Y - \Delta C = -500 - (-400) = -100$.

    B. In the flexible-price full-employment model, income never changes. In that model, actual income always equals potential income. Therefore, if government purchases fell, income would not decrease by 500. There would be no change in income, Y. Consumption and saving would thus not change. So, in the flexible-price full-employment model, $\Delta C = 0$ and $\Delta S = 0$.

5. Sorry; it is a trick question. (But it was the first trick question in the study guide!) There is no answer. The "long run" and "short run" are abstract ideas; they cannot be pinned down to a certain number of years. The "long run" is a period of time long enough that prices can fully adjust to any shock. The "short run" is a period of time during which prices can change, but cannot fully adjust to any shock. At any moment in time, we are in a short run period. But when we consider why standards of living in the United States were higher in 2001 than they had been in 1901, we are considering a period of time long enough that prices were able to fully adjust to changes that happened in the early part of the twentieth century.

6. The textbook gives four reasons, so a correct answer would include any three of the following four reasons:
    *   Changing prices is costly.
    *   Information is incomplete, so managers and workers sometimes confuse changes in aggregate demand with changes in demand for their product in particular.
    *   Workers believe a wage cut is "unfair" and so employers avoid wage cuts that may otherwise damage morale to the point that productivity declines.
    *   Managers and workers may have "money illusion." Managers forget that when the nominal price of output rises, costs are likely to rise as well, eliminating any real gains from price increases. Workers forget that when their nominal wages rise, prices they pay are likely to rise as well, eliminating any real gain from the wage increase.

7. Answers will vary. Possible answers include
    *   Restaurants incur costs of layout, design, and printing when they have to reprint menus following price changes.
    *   Retail stores incur labor and supply costs when they have to change prices for products that are already on the shelves.
    *   Online stores incur programming costs when they have to change prices on the products they sell.

8.

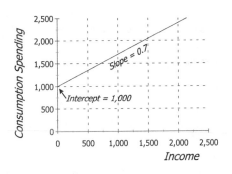

9. $C = 800 + 0.6(1 - 0.2)Y = 800 + 0.48Y$.

10. $C_y = 0.75$. In general, we know that $C = 1,200 + C_y(1 - 0.2)Y$. And in particular we know that $6,000 = 1,200 + C_y(1 - 0.2)(8,000)$. Solving for C_y, we have $C_y = 0.75$.

11. t = 2/3 or 0.67. It is very important to remember that the marginal propensity to consume tells us the change in consumption spending for a change in *disposable* income. If you answered 0.5 rather than 0.67, you probably computed the change in consumption spending (400 = 5,400 - 5,000) from a change in *income* (800 = 8,800 - 8,000) – but that is not the definition of the marginal propensity to consume.

The easier way to derive the answer is to use the definitions of disposable income and of the marginal propensity to consume.

$$\Delta Y^D = \Delta Y - t \cdot \Delta Y \qquad \text{\textit{definition of disposable income}}$$
$$\Delta Y^D = (1 - t) \cdot \Delta Y \qquad \text{\textit{factoring out} } \Delta Y$$
$$\Delta Y^D = (1 - 0.25) \cdot (8,800 - 8,000) \qquad \text{\textit{substituting in known values}}$$
$$\Delta Y^D = 600 \qquad \text{\textit{simplifying}}$$

- -

$$C_y = \frac{\Delta C}{\Delta Y^D} \qquad \text{\textit{definition of marginal propensity to consume}}$$
$$C_y = \frac{(5,400 - 5,000)}{600} \qquad \text{\textit{substituting in known values}}$$
$$C_y = \frac{400}{600} = \frac{2}{3} = 0.67 \qquad \text{\textit{simplifying}}$$

12. $A = 3,600 - 4,000r + 40Y^f + 300\varepsilon$

MPE = 0.49

The answer is found by substituting the information given in the question into the expression for aggregate demand, E = C + I + G + NX.

$E = C + I + G + NX$

$E = 600 + 0.8(1-0.2)Y + 1,000 - 4,000r + 2,000 + 40Y^f + 300\varepsilon - 0.15Y$

$E = [600 + 1,000 + 2,000 - 4,000r + 40Y^f + 300\varepsilon] + 0.8(0.8)Y - 0.15Y$

$E = [3,600 - 4,000r + 40Y^f + 300\varepsilon] + 0.49Y$

13. Substituting and simplifying yields E = 10,200 + 0.49Y. The equations for C, I, G, and NX are the same equations that were used in Question 12, so we can begin with E = $[3,600 - 4,000r + 40Y^f + 300\varepsilon] + 0.49Y$, and then substitute in the values for real interest rate, foreign income, and real exchange rate.

$E = 3,600 - 4,000 \cdot (0.05) + 40 \cdot (95) + 300 \cdot (10) + 0.49Y$

$E = 3,600 - 200 + 3,800 + 3,000 + 0.49Y$

$E = 10,200 + 0.49Y$

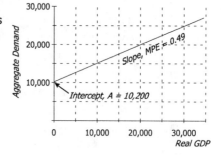

14. Y = 20,000 in equilibrium. Algebraically, the answer is derived by setting output and income, Y, equal to aggregate demand, E, and then solving for Y.

$$Y = 10,200 + 0.49Y \qquad \text{\textit{in equilibrium, output equals aggregate demand}}$$
$$Y - 0.49Y = 10,200 \qquad \text{\textit{subtracting 0.49Y from both sides of the equation}}$$
$$(1 - 0.49)Y = 10,200 \qquad \text{\textit{factoring out Y}}$$
$$0.51 \cdot Y = 10,200 \qquad \text{\textit{simplifying}}$$
$$Y = \frac{10,200}{0.51} \qquad \text{\textit{dividing both sides by 0.51}}$$
$$Y = 20,000 \qquad \text{\textit{simplifying}}$$

Graphically, the answer is derived by finding the intersection point of the aggregate demand line and the income = expenditure (45 degree) line. Again we find the equilibrium value is 20,000.

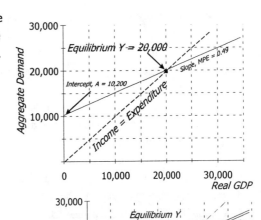

15. E = 10,200 + 510 + 0.49Y = 10,710 + 0.49Y

    A = 10,710

    MPE = 0.49

    Y = 10,710 / 0.51 = 21,000

16. E = 10,200 + 255 + 0.49Y = 10,455 + 0.49Y

    A = 10,455

    MPE = 0.49

    Y = 10,455 / 0.51 = 20,500

17. E = 10,200 + 40·(25.5) + 0.49Y = 11,220 + 0.49Y

    A = 11,220

    MPE = 0.49

    Y = 11,220 / 0.51 = 22,000

18. E = 10,200 + 300(5.1) + 0.49Y = 11,730 + 0.49Y

    A = 11,730

    MPE = 0.49

    Y = 11,730 / 0.51 = 23,000

19. E = 10,200 - 40.8 + 0.49Y = 10,159.2 + 0.49Y

    A = 10,159.2

    MPE = 0.49

    Y = 10,159.2 / 0.51 = 19,920

20. E = 10,200 + 0.8(1 - 0.25)Y - 0.15Y = 10,200 + 0.45Y

    A = 10,200

    MPE = 0.45

    Y = 10,200 / 0.55 = 18,545.45

21. A. Multiplier = 1 / 0.51 = 1.96

    B. ΔA = 510

        ΔY = 1,000 = (ΔA)(1.96) = (500)(1.96) = 1,000

    C. ΔA = 255

        ΔY = 500 = (ΔA)(1.96) = (255)(1.96) = 500

    D. ΔA = (40)(25.5) = 1,020.

        ΔY = 2,000 = (ΔA)(1.96) = (1,020)(1.96) = 2,000

    E. ΔA = (300)(5.1) = 1,530

        ΔY = 3,000 = (ΔA)(1.96) = (1,530)(1.96) = 3,000

    F. ΔA = −40.8

        ΔY = −80 = (ΔA)(1.96) = (−40.8)(1.96) = −80

22. The line where income = expenditure is not drawn at a 45º angle in this case, because the scale of the horizontal axis is different than the scale of the horizontal axis. Instead, in this case the line appears as shown at the right.

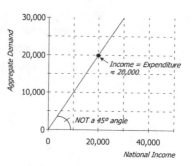

The importance of the income = expenditure line is that it shows us all the points where income and expenditure have the same value. It is a visual trick; without the income = expenditure line, we would have to eyeball the aggregate demand line and guess where is the one point on the aggregate demand line where income = expenditure. With the income = expenditure line, we just find the intersection point of the aggregate demand and income = expenditure lines and there we have equilibrium income.

23. A. If real GDP = Y_1, then the economy is not at equilibrium. Aggregate demand, AD_1, is greater than output, Y_1. Inventories will be depleted as businesses are forced to sell goods out of inventory. Businesses will respond to the unexpected inventory depletion by increasing output, Y.

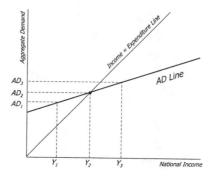

B. If real GDP = Y_2, then the economy is at equilibrium. Aggregate demand, AD_2, equals output, Y_2. Inventories will not change over time. Businesses will continue to produce an amount of output equal in the aggregate to Y_2.

C. If real GDP = Y_3, then the economy is not at equilibrium. Aggregate demand, AD_3, is less than output, Y_3. Inventories will accumulate as businesses cannot sell as much as they expected. Businesses will respond to the unexpected inventory accumulation by decreasing output, Y.

24. No, the economy will not be in equilibrium if output and income increase to $5,400 billion. Aggregate demand will also increase as income increases. In this question, we do not know the equation for aggregate demand. But so long as $C_y(1 - t)$ is greater than IM_y, any increase in income will generate an increase in aggregate demand. So when income increases from $5,000 billion to $5,400 billion, aggregate demand will rise above its former level of $5,400 billion.

25. National income will increase by more than $400 billion due to the multiplier process. The initial increase in autonomous spending will cause an initial increase in output and income of $400 billion. The workers and firm owners who receive that $400 billion in income will, in turn, use part of that additional income to buy goods and services that are produced in the United States. Their spending in the United States will depend upon the marginal propensity to consume, C_y, the marginal tax rate, t, and the marginal propensity to import, IM_y. Suppose their marginal propensity to spend is 40 percent. Then these workers will spend $160 billion on goods and services produced in the United States. Their additional spending of $160 billion will cause an increase in output and income equal to $160 billion. The workers and firm owners who receive this $160 billion in income will, in turn, use part of that additional income to buy goods and services that are produced in the United States, generating further increases in output and income. This multiplier process will continue. The total amount of income and output generated as a result of the initial $400 billion increase in autonomous spending will include not

only the initial change in autonomous spending but also the sum of the spending over time by all the workers and firm owners. The total change in national income will exceed $400 billion.

26. National income will decline by more than $300 billion. The beauty of the multiplier process when national income is rising becomes the ugliness of the multiplier process when national income is declining. The initial decrease in autonomous spending will cause an initial drop in output and income of $300 billion as workers are laid off and some firm owners close their businesses permanently. The workers and firm owners who lose income will, in turn, need to reduce their consumption spending. The amount of their drop in spending for goods and services produced in the United States will depend upon the marginal propensity to consume, C_y, the marginal tax rate, t, and the marginal propensity to import, IM_y. Suppose their marginal propensity to spend is 60 percent. Their spending on goods and services produced in the United States will therefore decline by $180 billion. The firms that experience the loss in demand will need to lay off workers, and some of those firms will go out of business permanently. The loss in income by this set of workers and firm owners will be $180 billion. These people, in turn, will need to reduce their consumption spending, generating further declines in output and income. This multiplier process will continue. The total amount of income and output lost as a result of the initial $300 billion decrease in autonomous spending will include not only the initial change in autonomous spending but also the sum of the lost spending over time by all the workers and firm owners. The total change in national income will exceed $300 billion.

27. A. $\Delta Y = \dfrac{\Delta G}{1 - MPE} = \dfrac{\$300\ billion}{1 - 0.4} = \dfrac{\$300\ billion}{0.6} = \$500\ billion$

B. $\Delta Y = \dfrac{\Delta C}{1 - MPE} = \dfrac{-\$600\ billion}{1 - 0.4} = \dfrac{-\$600\ billion}{0.6} = -\$1,000\ billion$

28. A. Multiplier = 2.

B. Multiplier = 2.5.

C. When the MPE increases, the multiplier increases. In each round of the multiplier process, those workers and firm owners who have received additional income will spend a larger share of their additional income after the MPE increases than they did before. So in every round, the additions to spending, output, and income will be larger than they would have been with a smaller MPE. The total change in income from any initial change in spending – the sum of the changes in income that occur in each round of the multiplier process – will therefore be larger after the MPE increases than they would have been with a smaller MPE.

29.

	(A)	(B)	(C)	(D)
C_y	0.8	0.8	0.8	0.9
t	0.2	0.3	0.2	0.2
IM_y	0.15	0.15	0.25	0.15
multiplier	1.96	1.69	1.64	2.33

C. APPLYING CONCEPTS AND MODELS

1. In the short run, a drop in consumption leads to a drop in national income. But if prices are fully flexible, then a drop in consumption does not cause national income to drop. Instead, with fully flexible prices, output is reallocated away from consumers and toward both businesses and the rest of the world. With fully flexible prices, the drop in consumption results in a rise in saving, increasing the supply of loanable funds, decreasing real interest rates, and thus increasing investment and net exports.

2. In general, employers in the United States were not willing to cut wages in the late twentieth and early twenty-first centuries. Most employers believed that cutting wages would lead to a decrease in worker morale. Employers therefore often used layoffs rather than wage cuts as a means of responding to decreases in demand. The exception to this practice seemed to be in the high-tech sector at the turn of the century. Layoffs were common in some high-tech firms, but wage cuts were also used as a way to avoid further layoffs.

3. The reduction in imports could come in the form of a drop in the autonomous level of imports, or in a drop in the marginal propensity to import. In either case, consumers would be switching their demand from foreign-produced goods and services to domestically-produced goods and services. Their actions will increase income in the United States. If consumers respond by *decreasing* their spending rather than *switching* their spending from foreign-produced to domestically-produced goods and services, there will be no change in U.S. income.

4. No, the economy is not in short-run equilibrium. If stock clerks across the country are finding that the actual inventory in their stores is less than expected inventory, then this unexpected depletion of inventories is the signal that aggregate demand exceeds output. Leon's boss will respond by increasing her order with the manufacturer. Bosses around the country will do the same as Leon's boss. Manufacturers will respond by increasing production. The process will continue until Leon and every other stock clerk in the country find the number of cases in the back room that their bosses expect them to find. Only then will the economy be in equilibrium, with output equal to aggregate demand.

5. The increase in tax rates will have two effects: an immediate effect of decreasing spending and an ongoing effect of decreasing the size of the multiplier. The net effect of the tax rate increase will be a decline in national income. (Presumably there would also be increases in government purchases that would be financed with the increased tax revenues. If the increase in government purchases is sufficiently large, the net effect of conducting a war on terrorists could increase national income.)

6. No, concern about a loss of tourism dollars is not a multiplier effect. The loss of tourism is part of the initial decline in consumer spending. Subsequent declines in consumer spending attributable to cutbacks in spending by people who previously had been employed in the tourism industry are examples of multiplier effects.

7. The more we import, the less effective is fiscal policy. If there is an increase in the marginal propensity to import, then the size of the multiplier is smaller. When the multiplier is smaller, then fiscal policy is relatively less effective in altering income.

8. The more we save out of changes in income, the less effective is fiscal policy. As consumers increase their marginal propensity to save, they are decreasing their marginal propensity to consume. The multiplier is therefore smaller than it was before the change in saving behavior. Because the multiplier is smaller, changes in government purchases have a smaller effect on national income than they did before saving behavior changed.

D. EXPLAINING THE REAL WORLD

1. The policy will lead to a reduction in the university's demand for copy paper. This reduction in spending by a public university is a decrease in government purchases of goods and services, G. Office Depot will in turn reduce its order for copy paper from the supplier. The university's decrease in demand for copy paper will thus lead to a reduction in production of copy paper. Layoffs will occur. At the Office Depot store, it probably took one employee a full day to unload the paper delivery, put it onto an Office Depot truck, and transport it to the university. That worker loses her or his job. At the paper factory, less paper is produced, leading to layoffs at the factory. Those workers who have lost their jobs will have to cut back their spending because they now have no paychecks coming in. Perhaps they go out to dinner

less often, or cancel plans to buy a new washing machine, or polish the old shoes rather than buy a new pair. These reductions in consumption spending begin the *multiplier* process. Producers of consumer goods and services find demand for their products declining, and they in turn lay off workers. Those laid-off workers reduce their consumption spending. The total drop in spending and income in the economy that results from the university's new "e-mail only" policy will be larger in size than just the university's decline in spending.

2. Increased online shopping may decrease menu costs, lowering the stickiness of prices. With online shopping, menu costs depend upon the programming costs of updating the website. If the online store replaces thousands of individual brick-and-mortar stores, it is likely the programming costs are lower than the total costs of changing prices at those thousands of individual stores.

3. A decline in inventory holdings could signal that aggregate demand exceeded production and that producers would therefore be increasing production soon. This argument depends upon assuming that the initial levels of inventory holdings were not above businesses' desired levels. In fact, the pundits were wrong, but not because they misinterpreted the second quarter decline in inventory holdings. The September 11 terrorist attacks in New York City and Washington DC, the resulting suspension of air travel in the United States, the subsequent fear of flying on the part of many Americans, and the uncertainty associated with the political and economic future of the United States led to a dramatic decline in aggregate demand. The economy fell into recession.

4. Government fiscal policy is less effective, dollar for dollar, in modern industrialized countries than in countries with relatively closed economies with undeveloped financial systems. The difference in effectiveness is due to differences in the marginal propensity to spend and thus to differences in the size of the multiplier. In modern industrialized countries in which there is substantial international trade, any change in national income leads to a change in imports. An increase in government purchases will lead to an increase in domestic income. But the increases in domestic income will lead to increases in spending for goods and services produced in other economies, benefitting employment and national income in those other economies but thereby lowering spending for domestically produced goods and services. The higher the propensity to import, IM_y, the lower the domestic spending multiplier and the smaller the effectiveness of government fiscal policy.

The absence of a well-developed financial system also affects the size of the spending multiplier. In the absence of a well-developed financial system – and especially in the absence of means by which consumers can smooth consumption over fluctuations in income – the marginal propensity to consume, C_y, will be relatively large. Without credit cards, household borrowing, or other means to finance consumption in the absence of income, households will tie their consumption spending much more closely to their disposable income. Every dollar change in disposable income, in economies without extensive consumer borrowing systems, will result in a relatively large change in consumption spending. Therefore, an increase in government purchases that leads to an initial increase in national income, will lead to subsequent rounds of consumer spending that are larger in economies without a well-developed financial system than in modern industrialized economies.

E. POSSIBILITIES TO PONDER

No solutions are given to these questions. The questions are designed to be somewhat open ended. Each question draws on your understanding of the concepts covered in this chapter.

Check out the Notation list at the end of the study guide. There you will find a list of every variable symbol used in the text book and its meaning.

But before you look there, have you caught on to the logic of the notation?

- A variable with a '0' subscript is always a "baseline" amount. I_0 is baseline investment; C_0 is baseline consumption; and so on.

- A variable that measures the responsiveness of one variable (such as C) to changes in another variable (such as y) has the form C_y. C_y is the responsiveness of consumption to changes in income; I_r is the responsiveness of investment to changes in the real interest rate; and so on.

Chapter 10

Investment, Net Exports, and Interest Rates

- When interest rates change, investment spending and gross exports both change.

- The IS curve is a graphical way of showing that when interest rates rise, equilibrium income declines.

LEARNING GUIDE

The IS Curve is introduced in this chapter. It is a crucial part of the IS/LM model developed in Chapters 10 and 11. The IS Curve draws upon several models presented in earlier chapters: the determination of stock prices (Chapter 2), the determinants of the components of aggregate demand (Chapter 6), and the income-expenditure model (Chapter 9).

This chapter is the second of four chapters in which the sticky-price model is presented. As we warned in Chapter 9, the material in Chapters 9 to 12 is cumulative. If you tried to skip over Chapter 9, or if you did not understand some part of it, you should probably go back and study Chapter 9 before attempting Chapter 10.

Short on time?

Bad news. If you are short on time, you are sunk. There is no way to understand the material in Chapters 10, 11, and 12 if you do not understand the IS curve.

You need to understand the IS curve: what it is, why it is downward sloped, what determines its slope, what makes it shift, when we are moving along the IS curve and when it is shifting, and what it means to be off of the IS curve. The math is important, but its most important role is to confirm – not replace – the economic intuition. Be sure that you understand the economics of the IS curve.

A. BASIC DEFINITIONS

Before you apply knowledge, you need a basic grasp of the fundamentals. In other words, there are some things you just have to know. Knowing the material in this section won't guarantee a good grade in the course, but not knowing it will guarantee a poor or failing grade.

USE THE WORDS OR PHRASES FROM THE LIST BELOW TO COMPLETE THE SENTENCES. SOME ARE USED MORE THAN ONCE; SOME ARE NOT USED AT ALL.

actual income
consumption spending
equilibrium income
government spending

gross exports
imports
investment spending
opportunity cost

1. The _____ of an investment project is the real interest rate.

2. Two components of aggregate demand change when real interest rates change: _____ and _____ .

3. The IS Curve shows combinations of real interest rates and _____ .

CIRCLE THE CORRECT WORD OR PHRASE IN EACH OF THE FOLLOWING SENTENCES.

4. Reductions in <u>consumption / investment</u> have played a powerful role in every recession and depression.

5. When the real interest rate increases, investment spending <u>increases / decreases</u>.

6. The interest rate that is relevant for determining investment spending is a <u>short / long</u> -term interest rate.

7. We depict a change in income as a <u>shift of / movement along</u> the IS curve.

8. In the <u>sticky-price / flexible-price</u> model, the interest rate is set in the loanable funds market.

9. We depict a change in the real interest rate as a <u>shift of / movement along</u> the IS curve.

10. The interest rate that is relevant for determining investment spending is a <u>safe / risky</u> interest rate.

11. The higher the interest rate, the <u>greater / fewer</u> the number and value of investment projects for which the rate of return is greater than the interest rate.

12. We depict a change in baseline investment spending, I_0, as a <u>shift of / movement along</u> the IS curve.

13. When the Fed wants to decrease interest rates, it <u>buys / sells</u> government bonds.

14. When baseline investment spending increases by $100 billion, the IS curve shifts to the <u>right / left</u> by an amount that is <u>less than / equal to / more than</u> $100 billion.

15. When the real interest rate increases, gross exports <u>increase / decrease</u>.

> **NOTE**: You may want to review Study Guide Chapter 6, where the relationship between real interest rates and exchange rates is explored.

16. We depict a change in government spending as a <u>shift of / movement along</u> the IS curve.

17. The riskier the loan, the <u>higher / lower</u> the interest rate.

SELECT THE ONE BEST ANSWER FOR EACH MULTIPLE-CHOICE QUESTION.

18. A decrease in real interest rates leads to
    A. increased investment spending.
    B. increased gross exports.
    C. increased investment spending and increased gross exports.
    D. increased investment spending and decreased gross exports.

19. The responsiveness of equilibrium income to changes in the real interest rate depends upon the
    A. size of the spending multiplier.
    B. interest sensitivity of investment.
    C. responsiveness of the real exchange rate to changes in the real interest rate.
    D. responsiveness of gross exports to a change in the real exchange rate.
    E. all of the above.

B. MANIPULATION OF CONCEPTS AND MODELS

Most instructors expect you to be able to do basic manipulation of the concepts. Being able to do so often means you can earn a C in a course. But if you want a better grade, you'll need to be able to complete this next section easily and move on to Sections C and D.

1. Suppose the Investment function is I = 2,000 - 300r.

   A. Complete the table at the right.

r	I
6	
4	
2	
0	
-2	

   B. Is it possible for the real interest rate, r, to be negative? Explain.

   C. Using the axes at the right, graph the investment function. Label your axes and your curve.

   CAUTION: In Chapter 10, when r is 6 percent you should use r = 6. This is different than how we expressed interest rates in previous chapters, where we used r = 0.06 when r is 6 percent. Check with your instructor to find out how you should express interest rates for problem sets and exams.

2. What is a yield curve?

3. Suppose the 3-month nominal interest rate is 5 percent and the 30-year nominal interest rate is 8 percent. What does this term structure imply that borrowers and lenders expect will happen to short-term rates in the future?

4. A. Suppose business people become increasingly pessimistic about the economy's future. What effect does their increasing pessimism have on baseline investment? On investment spending?

    B. Suppose business people become uncertain about the economy's future. What effect does their increasing uncertainty have on baseline investment? On investment spending?

NOTE: The real interest rate equals the difference between the nominal interest rate and the future expected inflation rate. When business people consider the profitability of an investment project, they compare the expected net gains in revenue from purchasing and using the investment good with the costs of purchasing the good. For the comparison to make sense, inflation must be taken into account.

Any individual business would probably form careful estimates of expected increases in the prices it charges for its output and that it pays for its inputs, and then compare the expected net gains in revenue with nominal interest rates. Equivalently, the business managers could estimate the inflation they will face in output and in costs, subtract that inflation rate from the nominal interest rate, and compare the resulting real interest rate with the expected net gains in revenue that are computed using today's prices and costs.

When we consider the macroeconomy, we need a way to consider the investment decisions that are made by thousands of businesses across the economy, in hundreds of different industries, producing thousands of different products. Computing firm-specific inflation rates for each of these businesses is impossible. A good simplification is to use an economy-wide inflation rate to compute a real interest rate.

5. A. Why does an increase in real interest rates lead to a decrease in investment spending?

B. Why does an increase in real interest rates lead to a decrease in gross exports?

TO THE CHALKBOARD:

The Algebra of the IS Curve

Deriving the IS curve algebraically is straightforward, but messy. All you need to remember is the condition for equilibrium in the markets for goods and services (Y = AD), and the definitions of the components of aggregate demand. Do not under any circumstances attempt to memorize the equation that we will derive. Your brain cells have much better things to do.

$$Y = AD \qquad \text{equilibrium condition}$$

$$Y = C + I + G + NX \qquad \text{substituting definition of AD}$$

$$Y = \left[C_0 + C_y \cdot (1-t) \cdot Y\right] + \left[I_0 - I_r \cdot r\right] + G + \\ \left[X_f \cdot Y^f + X_\varepsilon \cdot \left(\varepsilon_0 - \varepsilon_r \cdot (r - r^f)\right) - IM_y \cdot Y\right] \qquad \text{substituting definitions}$$

$$Y = \left[C_0 + C_y \cdot (1-t) \cdot Y\right] + \left[I_0 - I_r \cdot r\right] + G + \\ \left[X_f \cdot Y^f + X_\varepsilon \cdot \varepsilon_0 - X_\varepsilon \cdot \varepsilon_r \cdot r + X_\varepsilon \cdot \varepsilon_r \cdot r^f - IM_y \cdot Y\right] \qquad \text{simplifying}$$

$$Y - C_y \cdot (1-t) \cdot Y + IM_y \cdot Y = \\ \left(C_0 + I_0 + G + X_f \cdot Y^f + X_\varepsilon \cdot \varepsilon_0 + X_\varepsilon \cdot \varepsilon_r \cdot r^f\right) - \left(I_r \cdot r + X_\varepsilon \cdot \varepsilon_r \cdot r\right) \qquad \text{gathering terms}$$

$$Y \cdot \left[1 - \left(C_y \cdot (1-t) - IM_y\right)\right] = \\ \left(C_0 + I_0 + G + X_f \cdot Y^f + X_\varepsilon \cdot \varepsilon_0 + X_\varepsilon \cdot \varepsilon_r \cdot r^f\right) - \left(I_r + X_\varepsilon \cdot \varepsilon_r\right) \cdot r \qquad \text{gathering terms}$$

$$Y = \frac{\left(C_0 + I_0 + G + X_f \cdot Y^f + X_\varepsilon \cdot \varepsilon_0 + X_\varepsilon \cdot \varepsilon_r \cdot r^f\right) - \left(I_r + X_\varepsilon \cdot \varepsilon_r\right) \cdot r}{1 - \left(C_y \cdot (1-t) - IM_y\right)} \qquad \text{dividing by 1 - MPE}$$

Equilibrium income depends upon all of those factors. It's a mess. But it actually is only one step more complicated than the equilibrium income expression we had in Chapter 9. In Chapter 9, we did not have an explicit role for the real interest rates, r, to affect autonomous spending (the numerator) and equilibrium income (the entire fraction). Now we show explicitly that an increase in the real interest rate decreases autonomous spending by $(I_r + X_\varepsilon \varepsilon_r) \cdot (\Delta r)$, which then decreases equilibrium income by that amount times the multiplier, $1 / [1 - (C_y(1-t) - IM_y)]$.

---

6. Suppose we can express autonomous spending, A, as the difference between baseline spending, A_0, and interest-rate-dependent spending, $(I_r + X_\varepsilon \varepsilon_r) \cdot r$. Suppose the economy can be described by the following equations.

$$C = 600 + 0.8(1 - 0.2)Y \qquad\qquad NX = 40Y^f + 300\varepsilon - 0.15Y$$
$$I = 1{,}000 - 40r \qquad\qquad\qquad\quad Y^f = 95$$
$$G = 2{,}000 \qquad\qquad\qquad\qquad\quad \varepsilon = 40 - 10(r - r^f)$$
$$\qquad\qquad\qquad\qquad\qquad\qquad\quad r^f = 2$$

A. What is the value of baseline spending, A_0? What is the expression for interest-rate-dependent spending? What is the expression for autonomous spending? What is the expression for aggregate demand?

B. When the real interest rate is 5 percent, what is the expression for aggregate demand as a function of income? What is the equilibrium value of real GDP?

C. When the real interest rate is 6 percent, what is the expression for aggregate demand as a function of income? What is the equilibrium value of real GDP?

D. When the real interest rate increased from 5 to 6 percent, by how much did aggregate demand change? By how much did equilibrium income change?

E. Think about the economics behind the equations. What factors determined the size of the change in aggregate demand when the interest rate increased? What factors determined the size of the change in equilibrium income, given the change in aggregate demand?

F. Using the axes at the right, plot the two combinations of real interest rate and equilibrium income that you calculated in Parts B and C. Connect the two points with a straight line.

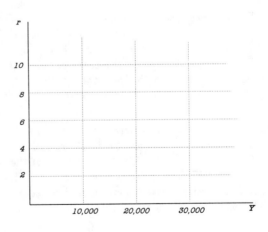

TO THE CHALKBOARD:
Explaining Figure 10.8

Figure 10.8 shows how to derive the IS curve graphically. Let's go through it here.

The graph in the upper right corner shows the determination of equilibrium income. It is the same as Figure 9.12. You may want to review the "To The Chalkboard" box on page 231 in which Figure 9.12 is discussed.

The graph in the lower left corner shows the relationship between the real interest rate and autonomous spending. Because both investment

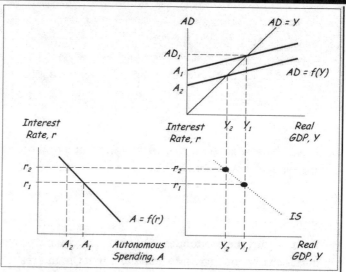

spending and gross exports rise when the real interest rate falls, the relationship between r and A is depicted with a downward-sloping line. We have labeled it A = f(r).

The graph in the lower right corner plots the set of combinations of interest rates, r, and income, Y, that give us equilibrium in the markets for goods and services, that is, which give us Y = AD.

Start in the lower left corner. If the interest rate is r_1, then autonomous spending is A_1. Now go to the upper right corner. The aggregate demand curve will have intercept A_1. Its slope will be the MPE. (We are not given the value of the MPE; we just sketch in an aggregate demand line with a reasonable slope.) The equilibrium level of income, Y_1, is the value of output and income where income equals aggregate demand, determined graphically by the intersection of the aggregate demand line and the AD = Y line. Now go back to the lower left corner and draw a dashed line from the lower left graph to the lower right graph at interest rate r_1. Now go up to the upper right corner and draw a dashed line from the upper right graph to the lower right graph at equilibrium income level, Y_1. Where those two dashed lines intersect in the lower right graph is one combination of interest rates and income – r_1 and Y_1 – that produces equilibrium in the markets for goods and services.

Do it again, starting with a different interest rate. This time, start in the lower left corner at interest rate r_2. Autonomous spending is therefore A_2. Find that same amount, A_2, on the vertical axis in the upper right corner; that is the intercept of the new aggregate demand curve that will have the same slope, MPE. The new equilibrium income is Y_2. Find the combination of interest rate and equilibrium income, r_2 and Y_2, in the lower right graph. That is a second combination of interest rates and income that produces equilibrium in the markets for goods and services.

We could do this exercise over and over again, for every possible interest rate. What we would find is that the set of combinations of interest rates and income that give us equilibrium in the markets for goods and services is described by a downward-sloping line that goes through the two points (r_1, Y_1) and (r_2, Y_2). That curve is the IS curve!

7. The slope of the IS curve depends upon the sizes of the spending multiplier and of the responsiveness of autonomous spending to a change in real interest rates.

A. What is the effect of an increase in the marginal propensity to consume, C_y, on the slope of the IS curve? Explain.

B. What is the effect of an increase in the marginal tax rate, t, on the slope of the IS curve? Explain.

C. What is the effect of an increase in the marginal propensity to import, IM_y, on the slope of the IS curve? Explain.

D. What is the effect of an increase in the responsiveness of investment to changes in the interest rate, I_r, on the slope of the IS curve? Explain.

E. What is the effect of an increase in the responsiveness of gross exports to changes in the real exchange rate, X_ε, on the slope of the IS curve? Explain.

F. What is the effect of an increase in the responsiveness of the real exchange rate to changes in the real interest rate, ε_r, on the slope of the IS curve? Explain.

8. Suppose the economy can be described by the following equations.

$C = 600 + 0.8(1 - 0.2)Y$

$I = 17,200 - 2,740r$

$G = 2,000$

$NX = 40Y^f + 30\varepsilon - 0.15Y$

$Y^f = 95$

$\varepsilon = 40 - 10(r - r^f)$

$r^f = 2$

A. Derive the expression for equilibrium income as a function of the real interest rate.

B. What is the responsiveness of equilibrium income to a change in the real interest rate, $\dfrac{\Delta Y}{\Delta r}$?

C. What is the equilibrium value of income when the real interest rate equals 4 percent? What is the equilibrium value of income when the real interest rate equals 6 percent? Draw in the IS curve on the graph at the right. Also draw this IS curve on the graphs in Questions 9 - 17, labeling it IS_1 each time.

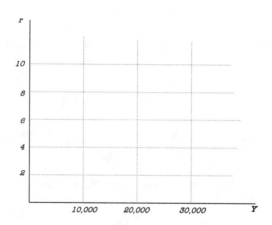

9. Suppose the equations in Question 8 describe the economy, with the following exception: the marginal propensity to consume, C_y, equals 0.9 rather than 0.8.

    A. Derive the expression for equilibrium income as a function of the real interest rate.

    B. What is the responsiveness of equilibrium income to a change in the real interest rate, $\dfrac{\Delta Y}{\Delta r}$?

    C. What is the equilibrium value of income when the real interest rate equals 4 percent? What is the equilibrium value of income when the real interest rate equals 6 percent? Draw in the IS curve on the graph at the right and label it IS_2. Is IS_2 flatter than the IS curve you drew in Question 8?

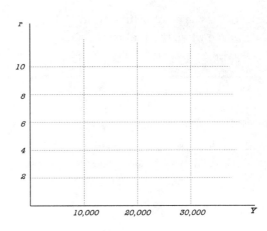

10. Suppose the equations in Question 8 describe the economy, with the following exception: the marginal tax rate, t, equals 0.3 rather than 0.2.

    A. Derive the expression for equilibrium income as a function of the real interest rate.

    B. What is the responsiveness of equilibrium income to a change in the real interest rate, $\dfrac{\Delta Y}{\Delta r}$?

    C. What is the equilibrium value of income when the real interest rate equals 4 percent? What is the equilibrium value of income when the real interest rate equals 6 percent? Draw in the IS curve on the graph at the right and label it IS_2. Is IS_2 steeper than the IS curve you drew in Question 8?

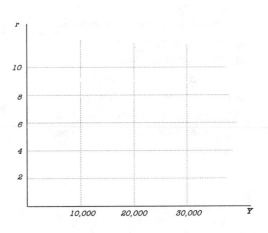

11. Suppose the equations in Question 8 describe the economy, with the following exception: the marginal propensity to import, IM_y, equals 0.2 rather than 0.15.

   A. Derive the expression for equilibrium income as a function of the real interest rate.

   B. What is the responsiveness of equilibrium income to a change in the real interest rate, $\frac{\Delta Y}{\Delta r}$?

   C. What is the equilibrium value of income when the real interest rate equals 4 percent? What is the equilibrium value of income when the real interest rate equals 6 percent? Draw in the IS curve on the graph at the right and label it IS_2. Is IS_2 steeper than the IS curve you drew in Question 8?

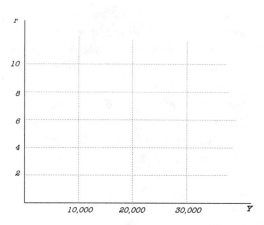

12. Suppose the equations in Question 8 describe the economy, with the following exception: the interest sensitivity of investment, I_r, equals 2,750 rather than 2,740.

   A. Derive the expression for equilibrium income as a function of the real interest rate.

   B. What is the responsiveness of equilibrium income to a change in the real interest rate, $\frac{\Delta Y}{\Delta r}$?

   C. What is the equilibrium value of income when the real interest rate equals 4 percent? What is the equilibrium value of income when the real interest rate equals 6 percent? Draw in the IS curve on the graph at the right and label it IS_2. Is IS_2 flatter than the IS curve you drew in Question 8?

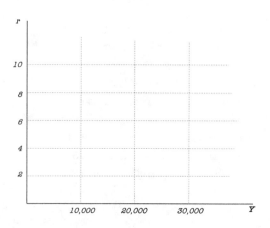

13. Suppose the equations in Question 8 describe the economy, with the following exception: the responsiveness of gross exports to changes in the real exchange rate, X_ε, equals 40 rather than 30.

   A. Derive the expression for equilibrium income as a function of the real interest rate.

   B. What is the responsiveness of equilibrium income to a change in the real interest rate, $\frac{\Delta Y}{\Delta r}$?

   C. What is the equilibrium value of income when the real interest rate equals 4 percent? What is the equilibrium value of income when the real interest rate equals 6 percent? Draw in the IS curve on the graph at the right and label it IS_2. Is IS_2 flatter than the IS curve you drew in Question 8?

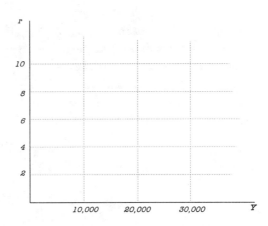

14. Suppose the equations in Question 8 describe the economy, with the following exception: the responsiveness of the real exchange rate to changes in the real interest rate, ε_r, equals 12 rather than 10.

   A. Derive the expression for equilibrium income as a function of the real interest rate.

   B. What is the responsiveness of equilibrium income to a change in the real interest rate, $\frac{\Delta Y}{\Delta r}$?

   C. What is the equilibrium value of income when the real interest rate equals 4 percent? What is the equilibrium value of income when the real interest rate equals 6 percent? Draw in the IS curve on the graph at the right and label it IS_2. Is IS_2 flatter than the IS curve you drew in Question 8?

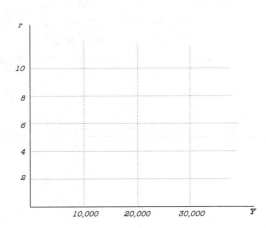

15. Suppose the equations in Question 8 describe the economy, with the following exception: baseline consumption spending, C_0, equals 2,130 rather than 600.

    A. Derive the expression for equilibrium income as a function of the real interest rate.

    B. What is the equilibrium value of income when the real interest rate equals 4 percent? What is the equilibrium value of income when the real interest rate equals 6 percent? Draw in the IS curve on the graph at the right and label it IS_2. Is IS_2 to the right or the left of the IS curve you drew in Question 8?

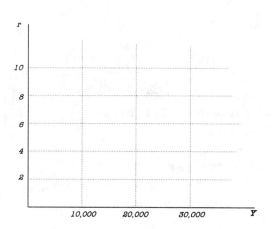

16. Suppose the equations in Question 8 describe the economy, with the following exception: foreign income equals 197 rather than 95.

    A. Derive the expression for equilibrium income as a function of the real interest rate.

    B. What is the equilibrium value of income when the real interest rate equals 4 percent? What is the equilibrium value of income when the real interest rate equals 6 percent? Draw in the IS curve on the graph at the right and label it IS_2. Is IS_2 to the right or the left of the IS curve you drew in Question 8?

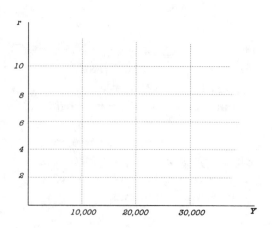

17. Suppose the equations in Question 8 describe the economy, with the following exception: baseline investment spending, I_0, equals 13,120 rather than 17,200.
    A. Derive the expression for equilibrium income as a function of the real interest rate.

    B. What is the equilibrium value of income when the real interest rate equals 4 percent? What is the equilibrium value of income when the real interest rate equals 6 percent? Draw in the IS curve on the graph at the right and label it IS_2. Is IS_2 to the right or the left of the IS curve you drew in Question 8?

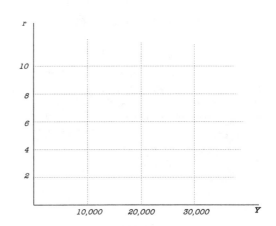

18. Suppose the economy can be described by the equations given in Question 8 (repeated here)

    $C = 600 + 0.8(1 - 0.2)Y$

    $I = 17,200 - 2,740r$

    $G = 2,000$

    $NX = 40Y^f + 30\varepsilon - 0.15Y$

    $Y^f = 95$

    $\varepsilon = 40 - 10(r - r^f)$

    $r^f = 2$

    A. Suppose that when the real interest rate is 4 percent, real GDP = 25,000. What will happen to inventory holdings?

    B. Suppose that when the real interest rate is 4 percent, real GDP = 27,000. What will happen to inventory holdings?

    C. In the graph at the right, sketch in the IS curve you derived in Question 8. Then plot the combination of interest rates and income given in Part A of this question and label it A. Finally, plot the combination of interest rates and income given in Part B of this question and label it B.

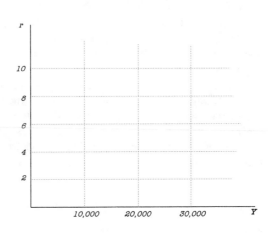

TO THE CHALKBOARD:
The IS Curve

It is important to understand three things about the IS curve:
- why it is downward sloped
- what makes it shift and by how much it shifts
- what it means to be "off of" the IS curve.

Why the IS curve is downward sloped

Suppose that (r_1, Y_1) is a combination of interest rates and income that yields equilibrium in the markets for goods and services; that is, income equals aggregate demand when income equals Y_1 and the real interest rate equals r_1. If instead the interest rate is higher, then what can we conclude about the corresponding equilibrium value of income? At a higher interest rate, r_2, both investment spending and gross exports will decline. Equilibrium income will decline by an amount equal to these initial drops in investment spending and gross exports, multiplied by the spending multiplier. So (r_2, Y_2) will be a second combination of interest rates and income at which $Y = AD$. At a higher interest rate, the level of income that yields equilibrium in the markets for goods and services will be lower. The curve that connects all of the combinations of interest rates and income that yield equilibrium in the markets for goods and services will thus slope downward.

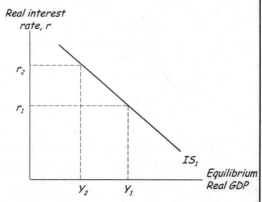

What makes the IS Curve shift and by how much

The position of the IS curve depends upon autonomous spending, the amount of spending that does not depend upon income. If there is a change in autonomous spending, then at every interest rate there will be a different level of income that yields equilibrium in the markets for goods and services. Because the IS curve shows the equilibrium level of income that corresponds to each level of the real interest rate, a change in autonomous spending will shift the IS curve. If autonomous spending increases, the IS curve will shift to the right (see graph at the right). If autonomous spending decreases, the IS curve will shift to the left.

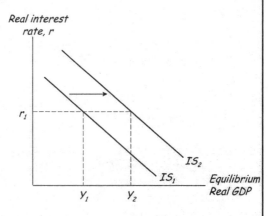

The size of the shift of the IS curve is *greater than* the change in autonomous spending. The IS curve is showing the equilibrium amount of output and income corresponding to each interest rate. Suppose interest rates equal r_1. Suppose there is an increase in autonomous spending. The increase in autonomous spending will initiate a multiplier process. And so, at any interest rate such as r_1, the change in equilibrium income in response to a change in autonomous spending will equal the change in autonomous spending multiplied by the spending multiplier.

What it means to be "off of" the IS Curve

The IS curve does not depict all possible combinations of interest rates and output. It depicts all possible combinations of interest rates and **equilibrium** output. So if the economy is not at equilibrium in the goods and services markets, it will be depicted by a point that is off of the IS curve.

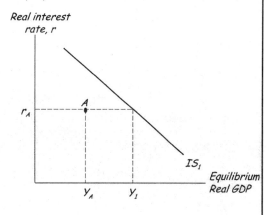

Suppose the economy is operating at point A depicted in the graph at the right. That is, the interest rate is r_A and real GDP is Y_A. Is the economy in equilibrium in the goods and services markets? No. How do we know? Because (r_A, Y_A) is not on the IS curve and if (r_A, Y_A) was an equilibrium combination of interest rates and output, it would be on the IS curve. Are inventories accumulating or being depleted when the economy is at (r_A, Y_A)? Being depleted. How do we know? Because we know from the graph that when interest rates are r_A, the equilibrium amount of output and income equal Y_1. The equilibrium amount of output equals aggregate demand (because that is the definition of equilibrium). And so the actual output, Y_A, is less than aggregate demand, Y_1, implying inventories are being depleted.

19. Suppose baseline consumption increases. What factors determine how far the IS curve shifts to the right?

20. What are three sources of difficulties the Fed faces in its attempts to manipulate the economy by changing interest rates?

C. APPLYING CONCEPTS AND MODELS

Now we're getting to the good stuff. Being able to apply a specific concept or model to a real world situation — where you are told which model to apply but you have to figure out how to apply it — is often what you need to earn a B in a course. This is where macroeconomics starts to become interesting and the world starts to make more sense.

1. Can we use just one IS curve to explain the United States economy of the 1960s, 1970s, 1980s, and 1990s?

2. A. Carmen is considering purchasing a piece of machinery for her business. She expects the machine to last three years, after which time she will probably need to replace it. What interest rate should Carmen consider when making this investment decision? Explain.

    B. Carmen is also considering constructing a new building for her business. She expects to own the building for thirty years. Should she consider the same interest rate in making this decision? Explain.

3. After the September 11 attack, investment spending declined. Using the investment function, explain why.

4. Congress reduced income tax rates during Summer 2001. What effect did this policy action have on the responsiveness of equilibrium income to changes in the interest rate?

D. EXPLAINING THE REAL WORLD

Most instructors are delighted when you are able to figure out which concept or model to apply to a real world situation. Being able to do so means you thoroughly understand the material and is often what you need to do to earn an A in a course. This is where you experience the power of macroeconomic theory.

1. Why do long-term interest rates fluctuate less than do short-term rates?

2. Alan Greenspan, chairman of the Federal Reserve Board, and the members of the Federal Open Market Committee decreased short-term interest rates more than nine times between 1999 and 2002. Long-term rates did not decrease by as much as short-term rates decreased. Why?

3. During Summer 2001, Congress decreased marginal tax rates. During spring, summer, and fall 2001, the Fed decreased short-term interest rates. But policy makers were frustrated because there was relatively little change in real GDP. What economic logic led them to believe that output and income would increase?

E. POSSIBILITIES TO PONDER

The more you learn, the more you realize you have more to learn. These questions go beyond the textbook material. They are the sort of questions that distinguish A+ or A work from A-work. Some of them may even serve as starting points for junior or senior year research papers.

1. The real interest rate, r, is the difference between the nominal interest rate and the expected future inflation rate. But when economists calculate the real interest rate, they generally take the difference between the nominal interest rate and the *actual* inflation rate. For this approach to be valid, what assumption must be made regarding expectations? Is that assumption valid? If the assumption is invalid, how does the investment model change?

2. Were investors in the stock market behaving rationally in 1999 and 2000?

3. When government spending increases, is it sensible to assume that the parameters of the equations describing aggregate demand remain constant? How is the model of Chapter 10 affected if, for instance, the marginal propensity to consume depends in part on government fiscal policy?

SOLUTIONS   SOLUTIONS   SOLUTIONS   SOLUTIONS

A. BASIC DEFINITIONS
1. opportunity cost
2. investment spending; gross exports
3. equilibrium income

4. investment

5. decreases

6. long

7. movement along

8. flexible-price

9. movement along

10. risky

11. fewer

12. shift of

13. buys

14. right; more than

15. decrease

16. shift of

17. higher

18. C.

19. E.

B. MANIPULATION OF CONCEPTS AND MODELS

1. A.

r	I
6	200
4	800
2	1,400
0	2,000
−2	2,600

B. Yes, the real interest rate, r, can be negative. The real interest rate is the nominal interest rate minus expected inflation. If the expected inflation rate is greater than the nominal interest rate, then the real interest rate is negative.

C. The investment function is depicted at the right.

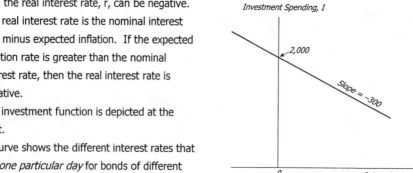

Investment Spending, I

2,000

Slope = −300

0   Interest rate, r

2. A yield curve shows the different interest rates that exist *on one particular day* for bonds of different terms. For instance, a yield curve for 2 April 2000 will show what the 3-month rate, 6-month rate, 12-month rate, 2-year rate, 5-year rate, 10-year rate, and 30-year rate were on 2 April 2000.

3. When the long-term rate is greater than the short-term rate, borrowers and lenders expect that short-term rates will increase in the future.

4. A. Increasing pessimism lowers baseline investment, I_0, and therefore also lowers investment spending, I. Graphically, increasing pessimism shifts the investment function down.

   B. Increasing uncertainty lowers baseline investment, I_0, and therefore also lowers investment spending, I. Graphically, increasing uncertainty shifts the investment function down.

5. A. A higher real interest rate makes some previously profitable investment projects now unprofitable. Those projects will not be undertaken. The total number of investment projects and the total amount of money spent on investment goods will thus fall.

   B. When the real interest rate rises in the United States, U.S. assets become more attractive relative to foreign assets. Investors around the world will increase their demand for dollar-denominated assets, increasing the supply of foreign currency offered in exchange for dollars. The nominal exchange rate – the dollar price of one unit of foreign currency – will decline. The real exchange rate will decline as well, decreasing the price of foreign goods and services relative to domestic goods and services. People and firms in other countries will thus find their own goods and services are more favorably priced, and so foreign demand for U.S.-produced goods and services will decrease. That is, U.S. exports of goods and services will decline.

6. A. It is easiest to answer the questions in reverse order.

$AD = C + I + G + NX$

$AD = 600 + 0.8(1 - 0.2)Y + 1{,}000 - 40r + 2{,}000 + 40(95) + 300[40 - 10(r - 2)] - 0.15Y$

$AD = 600 + 0.64Y + 1{,}000 - 40r + 2{,}000 + 3{,}800 + 12{,}000 - 3{,}000r + 6{,}000 - 0.15Y$

$AD = 25{,}400 - 3{,}040r + 0.49Y$

Autonomous spending, $A = 25{,}400 - 3{,}040r$

Baseline spending, $A_0 = 25{,}400$

Interest-rate-dependent spending $= 3{,}040r$

B. $AD = 10{,}200 + 0.49Y$

Equilibrium $Y = 20{,}000$

$Y = AD = 25{,}400 - 3{,}040(5) + 0.49Y = 25{,}400 - 15{,}200 + 0.49Y$

$Y = 10{,}200 / (1 - 0.49) = 10{,}200 / 0.51 = 20{,}000$

C. $AD = 7{,}160 + 0.49Y$

Equilibrium $Y = 14{,}039.22$

$Y = AD = 25{,}400 - 3{,}040(6) + 0.49Y = 25{,}400 - 18{,}240 + 0.49Y$

$Y = 7{,}160 / (1 - 0.49) = 7{,}160 / 0.51 = 14{,}039.22$

D. $\Delta AD = 7{,}160 + 0.49Y - (10{,}200 + 0.49Y) = -3{,}040$

$\Delta Y = 14{,}039.22 - 20{,}000 = -5{,}960.78$

E. The size of the change in aggregate demand depends upon the responsiveness of investment spending to a change in the real interest rate, and upon the responsiveness of the real exchange rate to a change in the real interest rate. The size of the change in equilibrium income, given the size of the change in aggregate demand, depends upon the responsiveness of aggregate demand to changes in income (that is, upon the size of the multiplier). In this case, aggregate demand changes when income changes because consumption and imports both change.

F.

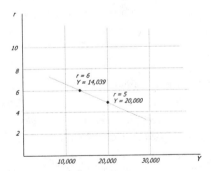

7. A. An increase in the marginal propensity to consume, C_y, increases the negative slope of the IS curve, making the IS curve flatter. For example, when interest rates fall and autonomous spending therefore rises, the changes in consumer spending that are part of the multiplier process are larger than they would have been with a smaller mpc. The total change in equilibrium output and income in response to a change in real interest rates is therefore larger than it would have been with a smaller mpc.

B. An increase in the marginal tax rate, t, decreases the negative slope of the IS curve, making the IS curve steeper. For example, when interest rates fall and autonomous spending therefore rises, the multiplier process begins as usual. But with a higher tax rate, the changes in disposable income that result from each change in national income and output are smaller than they would have been with a smaller tax rate. The subsequent change in consumption spending that is part of the multiplier process will therefore be smaller than they would have been with a smaller tax rate. The total change in equilibrium output and income in response to a change in real interest rates is therefore smaller than it would have been with a smaller marginal tax rate.

C. An increase in the marginal propensity to import, IM_y, decreases the negative slope of the IS curve, making the IS curve steeper. For example, when interest rates fall and autonomous spending therefore rises, the changes in imports that are part of the multiplier process are larger than they would have been with a smaller marginal propensity to import. The changes in spending for domestically produced goods and services are therefore smaller than they would have been with a smaller marginal propensity to import. The total change in equilibrium output and income in response to a change in real interest rates is therefore smaller than it would have been with a smaller marginal propensity to import.

D. An increase in the responsiveness of investment spending to changes in the real interest rate, I_r, increases the negative slope of the IS curve, making the IS curve flatter. For example, when interest rates fall, the resulting increase in investment spending is larger than it would have been with a smaller responsiveness of investment spending to changes in the real interest rate. The multiplier process then continues as usual. The total change in equilibrium output and income in response to a change in real interest rates is therefore larger than it would have been with a smaller responsiveness of investment spending to changes in the real interest rate.

E. An increase in the responsiveness of gross exports to changes in the real exchange rate, X_ε, increases the negative slope of the IS curve, making the IS curve flatter. For example, when the real interest rate falls, the real exchange rate rises, making foreign goods and services relatively more expensive. Foreign demand for domestically-produced goods and services (that is, gross exports) will increase more than they would have with a smaller responsiveness of gross exports to changes in the real exchange rate. The multiplier process then continues as usual. The total change in equilibrium output and income in response to a change in real interest rates is therefore larger than it would have been with a smaller responsiveness of gross exports to changes in the real exchange rate.

F. An increase in the responsiveness of the real exchange rate to changes in the real interest rate, ε_r, increases the negative slope of the IS curve, making the IS curve flatter. For example, when the real interest rate falls, the resulting increase in the real exchange rate is larger than it would have been with a smaller responsiveness of the real exchange rate to changes in the real interest rate. A higher real exchange rate makes foreign goods and services relatively more expensive, increasing foreign demand for domestically-produced goods and services. That is, gross exports increase more than they would have with a smaller responsiveness of the real exchange rate to changes in the real interest rate. The multiplier process then continues as usual. The total change in equilibrium output and income in response to a change in real interest rates is therefore larger than it would have been with a smaller responsiveness of the real exchange rate to changes in the real interest rate.

8. A. AD = C + I + G + NX

   = 25,400 - 3,040·r + 0.49·Y

   Y = (25,400 - 3,040·r) / (1 - 0.49)

   = 49,803.9 - 5,960.8·r

   B. $\Delta Y / \Delta r = -5,960.8$

   C. When r = 4, Y = 13,240 / 0.51 = 25,960.8.

   When r = 6, Y = 7,160 / 0.51 = 14,039.2.

   The IS curve is shown at the right.

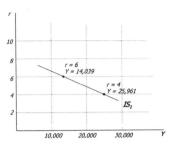

9. A. AD = C + I + G + NX

   = 25,400 - 3,040·r + 0.57·Y

   Y = (25,400 - 3,040·r) / (1 - 0.57)

   = 59,069.8 - 7,069.8·r

   B. $\Delta Y / \Delta r = -7,069.8$

   C. When r = 4, Y = 13,240 / 0.43 = 30,790.7.

   When r = 6, Y = 7,160 / 0.43 = 16,651.2.

   The second IS curve is shown at the right. It is indeed flatter

   than the original IS curve.

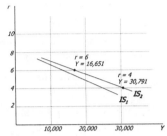

10. A. AD = C + I + G + NX

   = 25,400 - 3,040·r + 0.41·Y

   Y = (25,400 - 3,040·r) / (1 - 0.41)

   = 43,050.8 - 5,152.5·r

   B. $\Delta Y / \Delta r = -5,152.5$

   C. When r = 4, Y = 13,240 / 0.59 = 22,440.7.

   When r = 6, Y = 7,160 / 0.59 = 12,135.6.

   The second IS curve is shown at the right. It is indeed

   steeper than the original IS curve.

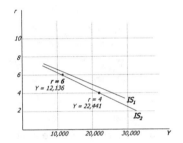

11. A. AD = C + I + G + NX

   = 25,400 - 3,040·r + 0.44·Y

   Y = (25,400 - 3,040·r) / (1 - 0.44)

   = 45,357.1 - 5,428.6·r

   B. $\Delta Y / \Delta r = -5,428.6$

   C. When r = 4, Y = 13,240 / 0.56 = 23,642.9.

   When r = 6, Y = 7,160 / 0.56 = 12,785.7.

   The second IS curve is shown at the right. It is indeed

   steeper than the original IS curve.

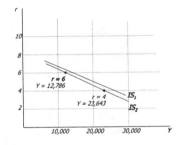

12. A. AD = C + I + G + NX

   = 25,400 - 3,050·r + 0.49·Y

   Y = (25,400 - 3,050·r) / (1 - 0.49)

   = 49,803.9 - 5,980.4·r

   B. $\Delta Y / \Delta r = -5,980.4$

   C. When r = 4, Y = 13,200 / 0.51 = 25,882.4.

   When r = 6, Y = 7,100 / 0.51 = 13,921.6.

   The second IS curve is shown at the right. It is indeed flatter

   than the original IS curve.

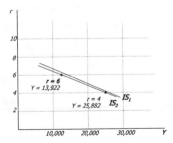

13. A. AD = C + I + G + NX
   = 26,000 - 3,140·r + 0.49·Y
   Y = (26,000 - 3,140·r) / (1 - 0.49)
   = 50,980.4 - 6,156.9·r
   B. $\Delta Y / \Delta r = -6,156.9$
   C. When r = 4, Y = 13,440 / 0.51 = 26,352.9.
   When r = 6, Y = 7,160 / 0.51 = 14,039.2.
   The second IS curve is shown at the right. It is indeed flatter
   than the original IS curve.

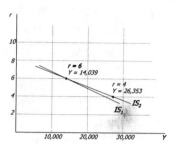

14. A. AD = C + I + G + NX
   = 25,520 - 3,100·r + 0.49·Y
   Y = (25,520 - 3,100·r) / (1 - 0.49)
   = 50,039.2 - 6,078.4·r
   B. $\Delta Y / \Delta r = -6,078.4$
   C. When r = 4, Y = 13,120 / 0.51 = 25,725.5.
   When r = 6, Y = 6,920 / 0.51 = 13,568.6.
   The second IS curve is shown at the right. It is indeed flatter
   than the original IS curve.

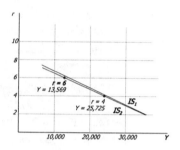

15. A. AD = C + I + G + NX
   = 26,930 - 3,040·r + 0.49·Y
   Y = (26,930 - 3,040·r) / (1 - 0.49)
   = 52,803.9 - 5,960.8·r
   B. When r = 4, Y = 14,770 / 0.51 = 28,960.8.
   When r = 6, Y = 8,690 / 0.51 = 17,039.2.
   The second IS curve is shown at the right. It is to the right
   of the original IS curve.

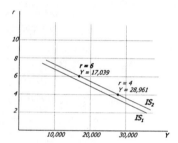

16. A. AD = C + I + G + NX
   = 29,480 - 3,040·r + 0.49·Y
   Y = (29,480 - 3,040·r) / (1 - 0.49)
   = 57,803.9 - 5,960.8·r
   B. When r = 4, Y = 17,320 / 0.51 = 33,960.8.
   When r = 6, Y = 11,240 / 0.51 = 22,039.2.
   The second IS curve is shown at the right. It is to the right
   of the original IS curve.

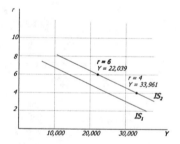

17. A. AD = C + I + G + NX
   = 21,320 - 3,040·r + 0.49·Y
   Y = (21,320 - 3,040·r) / (1 - 0.49)
   = 41,803.9 - 5,960.8·r
   B. When r = 4, Y = 9,160 / 0.51 = 17,960.8.
   When r = 6, Y = 3,080 / 0.51 = 6,039.2.
   The second IS curve is shown at the right. It is to the left of
   the original IS curve.

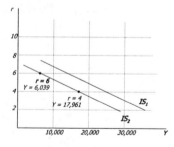

18. In Question 8, we found that when r = 4, equilibrium Y = 25,960.8.
    A. If real GDP = 25,000 when r = 4, then actual output (real GDP) is less than aggregate demand (equilibrium output), so inventories will be depleted.
    B. If real GDP = 27,000 when r = 4, then actual output is more than aggregate demand, so inventories will accumulate.
    C. Point A is to the left of the IS curve; Point B is to the right of the IS curve. Any point to the left of the IS curve is a combination of interest rates and output that will cause inventories to be depleted because actual output is less than aggregate demand. Any point to the right of the IS curve is a combination of interest rates and output that will cause inventories to accumulate because actual output is more than aggregate demand.

19. The size of the shift depends upon the spending multiplier, which in turn depends upon the size of the marginal propensity to consume, the tax rate, and the marginal propensity to import.

20. The textbook mentions several difficulties faced by the Fed.
    - Policy makers do not have perfect knowledge of the structure of the economy. They have to guess at the slope of the IS curve, for instance.
    - Policies affect the economy only over time. The time lag between implementation of a policy and economic effect of that policy is long and variable.
    - The Fed can manipulate short-term, nominal, safe interest rates, but the interest rates that matter to investment spending are long-term, real, risky interest rates. The term premium, inflation rate, and risk premium can change over time and are therefore difficult for the Fed to predict.

C. APPLYING CONCEPTS AND MODELS

1. No. The IS curve shifted several times in the past forty years of the twentieth century. See the textbook for a great discussion of late-twentieth-century economic history.

2. A. Carmen should consider a three-year risky interest rate. She should consider a three-year rate because that is the expected life length of her investment. She should consider a risky rate because she can not be completely confident in her estimates of the future revenues that will be generated with the new machine.
   B. Carmen should not consider the same interest rate for both decisions. The investment project in Part B has a thirty-year life length, so for this decision she should consider a thirty-year risky interest rate. She needs to match the term of the interest rate with the expected life length of the investment.

3. Investment spending fell because I_0, baseline investment, declined. Business people became both uncertain and pessimistic about the economy's future. The stock market reflected these changes; stock market prices fell markedly in the weeks following the attack.

4. Decreased tax rates increase the size of the spending multiplier, increasing the responsiveness of equilibrium income to changes in the interest rate.

D. EXPLAINING THE REAL WORLD

1. Long-term interest rates reflect current and future expected short-term rates. If long-term rates fluctuate less than short-term rates, then it must be the case that expected short-term rates fluctuate less than current short-term rates.

2. Investors largely believed that the Fed's reductions in interest rates were a temporary measure meant to stimulate a slowing economy. They did not expect interest rates to remain low in future years. Therefore long-term rates did not decline by as much as short-term rates.

3. Lower marginal tax rates should boost the economy in two ways. First, the lower tax rate creates a larger spending multiplier, so any initial change in spending has a larger effect on real GDP and income. Second, lower tax rates immediately increase disposable income, leading to increased consumption spending so long as the marginal propensity to consume is not zero. Lower interest rates should also boost the economy, both by increasing investment spending and also by increasing export spending. The combination of tax cuts and interest rate cuts is therefore supposed to increase real GDP and income substantially.

E. POSSIBILITIES TO PONDER

No solutions are given to these questions. The questions are designed to be somewhat open ended. Each question draws on your understanding of the concepts covered in this chapter.

Chapter 11

Extending the Sticky-Price Model: More Analytical Tools

- Equilibrium in the money market depends upon real output, velocity, nominal money supply, and the price level. The LM curve is a graphical way of showing the combinations of real income and interest rates that produce money-market equilibrium.

- The short-run determination of real GDP depends upon aggregate demand and the central bank's choice of target: money, interest rate, or inflation rate. The short-run determination of the inflation rate depends upon these factors plus the aggregate supply function.

LEARNING GUIDE

This chapter is very long and contains a great amount of material. It is difficult. Expect to spend many hours studying Chapter 11. There are several concepts and models introduced in Chapter 11: short-run equilibrium in the money market; the LM curve, which completes the IS-LM model; the Aggregate Demand curve; the Taylor Rule; and the Aggregate Supply curve. The international side of the economy is emphasized in Chapter 11, but none of the material in that section is new to this chapter.

When you get bogged down with the equations, go back to the graphs. Much of the material is relatively intuitive when approached graphically. Go slowly. Be sure you are clear on each new concept before you go on to the next one. If you need to review concepts that were introduced previously, go back to earlier chapters. If you get stuck on the new material, it sometimes helps to back up a few sections – or chapters – to the material you know you understand. Be patient. The material will eventually make sense.

Short on time?

If you are short on time, you are in big trouble. This chapter is long, packed with new information and is challenging. Your only possible hope is that your instructor skips some of the material in this chapter. Check your syllabus before you begin.

You need to understand the LM curve: what it is, why it is upward sloped, what determines its slope, what makes it shift, what it means to be off of the LM curve, and how a change in the price level affects it. The impact of the central bank's choice of a money, interest rate, or inflation rate target is important. You need to understand the determinants of the AD curve and why the AS curve slopes up.

A. BASIC DEFINITIONS

Before you apply knowledge, you need a basic grasp of the fundamentals. In other words, there are some things you just have to know. Knowing the material in this section won't guarantee a good grade in the course, but not knowing it will guarantee a poor or failing grade.

USE THE WORDS OR PHRASES FROM THE LIST BELOW TO COMPLETE THE SENTENCES. SOME ARE USED MORE THAN ONCE; SOME ARE NOT USED AT ALL.

actual inflation rate	money
AD Curve	nominal interest rate
aggregate demand	nominal money stock
aggregate supply	nominal output
AS Curve	opportunity cost
expected inflation rate	real interest rate
goods and services	real money stock
IS Curve	real output
LM Curve	Taylor Rule

1. The nominal interest rate is the sum of the real interest rate and the _____.

2. The LM curve gives the set of combinations of interest rates and output that produce equilibrium in the _____ market(s).

3. If the Fed targets the real interest rate, the _____ should be drawn as a horizontal line.

4. The AD curve gives the set of combinations of price level and _____ that produce equilibrium in both the _____ market(s) and the money market.

5. The nominal interest rate is the _____ of holding money.

6. If the Fed sets the real interest rate based on the gap between the actual inflation rate and the Fed's target inflation rate, it is following the _____.

7. The _____ curve slopes upward because a higher inflation rate calls forth a higher level of production.

8. The AD curve can be drawn with the price level on the vertical axis and _____ on the horizontal axis.

9. The IS curve gives the set of combinations of interest rates and output that produce equilibrium in the _____ market(s).

10. The graph depicting the money market is drawn with the _____ on the vertical axis and the _____ on the horizontal axis.

11. If the Fed follows the Taylor Rule, it sets the _____ in reaction to the inflation rate.

12. The IS-LM graph is drawn with _____ on the vertical axis and _____ on the horizontal axis.

> **HINT**: Here is a very quick synopsis of the IS-LM curves.
>
> The **IS curve** is the set of combinations (r, Y) such that Y = AD.
>
> The **LM curve** is the set of combinations (r, Y) such the $M^S/P = M^d/P$.
>
> The **intersection** of the IS and LM curves is the one combination (r, Y) such that Y = AD **and** $M^S/P = M^d/P$.

CIRCLE THE CORRECT WORD OR PHRASE IN EACH OF THE FOLLOWING SENTENCES.

13. A change in the price level shifts the IS / LM curve.

14. Over time, nominal money demand increases / stays the same / decreases because of changes in financial technology.

15. The aggregate demand curve typically slopes upward / downward.

16. Real money demand increases / decreases when total real spending increases.

17. An increase in autonomous spending causes the equilibrium real interest rate to increase / decrease and the equilibrium real output to increase / decrease.

18. If the Fed targets the money supply, the LM curve slopes upward / downward.

19. When real GDP is greater than potential output, inflation is likely to be higher / lower than had previously been anticipated.

20. An increase in real money demand causes nominal interest rates to increase / decrease.

21. An increase in the real money supply causes the equilibrium real interest rate to increase / decrease and the equilibrium real output to increase / decrease.

22. Nominal money demand increases / decreases when nominal interest rates increase.

23. The aggregate supply curve typically slopes upward / downward.

24. An increase in government purchases shifts the IS curve to the left / right.

25. An increase in the money stock shifts the <u>IS / LM</u> curve to the <u>left / right</u>.

26. A change in autonomous spending shifts the <u>IS / LM</u> curve.

27. If the central bank targets the interest rate, the LM curve is <u>horizontal / vertical</u>.

28. An increase in real money supply causes nominal interest rates to <u>increase / decrease</u>.

B. MANIPULATION OF CONCEPTS AND MODELS

Most instructors expect you to be able to do basic manipulation of the concepts. Being able to do so often means you can earn a C in a course. But if you want a better grade, you'll need to be able to complete this next section easily and move on to Sections C and D.

NOTE: Do not start working on this chapter until you fully understand Chapter 10. The material in this chapter builds on the material in that chapter. If you did not understand Chapter 10, you will not understand Chapter 11.

TO THE CHALKBOARD:
Deriving the Money Demand Equation

We first derived the money demand equation in Chapter 8. You may want to review Chapter 8 before working with money demand in this chapter. Here is a step-by-step derivation of the expression for real money demand used in Chapter 11.

Recall from Chapter 8, nominal money demand, M^d, is described by the equation $M^d = \dfrac{L(r + \pi^e)}{V^L} \cdot (P \cdot Y)$

where $L(r + \pi^e)$ is "relative money demand." We can then derive real money demand:

$$\frac{M^d}{P} = \frac{L(r + \pi^e) \cdot Y}{V^L} \qquad \textit{dividing both sides by P}$$

$$\frac{M^d}{P} = L(r + \pi^e) \cdot Y \qquad \textit{assuming time trend, } V^L, \textit{ equals 1}$$

$$\frac{M^d}{P} = \frac{Y}{V_0 + V_i \cdot i} \qquad \textit{substituting definition of } L(r + \pi^e)$$

A little dot shouldn't be so important, but in this case it is. $L(r + \pi^e)$ is a statement of a functional form; it means that the function L depends upon $(r + \pi^e)$. On the other hand, $V_i \cdot (r + \pi^e)$ is a product; it says V_i times $(r + \pi^e)$. Remember that the nominal interest rate, i, equals the sum of the real interest rate, r, and the expected inflation rate, π^e. Real money demand is therefore equal to

$$\frac{M^d}{P} = \frac{Y}{V_0 + V_i \cdot (r + \pi^e)}$$

1. Suppose real money demand can be described as $\dfrac{M^d}{P} = \dfrac{Y}{7 + 20 \cdot (r + \pi^e)}$. Suppose the inflation rate is 3 percent and is expected to remain 3 percent.

    A. Complete the table below.

Y	r	$\dfrac{M^d}{P}$
1,000	2	
1,000	7	
2,000	7	

    CAUTION: In Chapter 11, when the interest rate is 5 percent, you should express it as r = 0.05. This is different than how you expressed the interest rate in Chapter 10. Check with your instructor to find out how you should express interest rates for problem sets and exams.

    B. Explain why real money demand falls when the real interest rate rises.

    C. Explain why real money demand rises when income rises.

2. If real income doubles, all else being constant, what happens to real money demand?

3. If prices double, all else being constant, what happens to nominal money demand?

TO THE CHALKBOARD:
Explaining Money Market Equilibrium and Figure 11.1

Money market equilibrium occurs when real money demand equals real money supply. We can find the equilibrium algebraically or graphically. Regardless of how you find money market equilibrium, you need to understand how the equilibrium nominal interest rate changes with a change in any of the determining factors. If the algebra looks too messy, use the graph.

The real supply of money, $\frac{M^s}{P}$, is straightforward. We assume the central bank sets the nominal money supply, M^S. The price level, P, is fixed in the short run. So the real money supply is the same no matter what the nominal interest rate is.

The real demand for money, $\frac{M^d}{P}$, depends upon real GDP (Y), and upon the determinants of velocity: V^L, V_0, V_i, i. If we assume the time trend of velocity (V^L) is constant and equal to 1, then $\frac{M^d}{P} = \frac{Y}{V_0 + V_i i}$. Real money demand is inversely related to the nominal interest rate.

Graphically, equilibrium is the intersection of the real money supply and real money demand curves. Real money supply does not change when the interest rate changes. So we draw the real money supply curve as a vertical line at $\frac{M^s}{P}$. Real money demand increases nonlinearly as nominal interest rates decline, as shown at the right. The money market is in equilibrium when the nominal interest rate equals i_1.

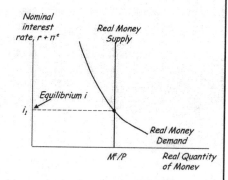

We can also find money market equilibrium algebraically. Money market equilibrium occurs when real money supply equals real money demand.

$$\frac{M^s}{P} = \frac{M^d}{P} \qquad \text{money market equilibrium}$$

$$\frac{M^s}{P} = \frac{Y}{V_0 + V_i i} \qquad \text{substituting definition of real money demand}$$

$$M^s \cdot \left(V_0 + V_i i\right) = P \cdot Y \qquad \text{multiplying both sides by } P \cdot \left(V_0 + V_i i\right)$$

$$V_0 + V_i i = \frac{P \cdot Y}{M^s} \qquad \text{dividing both sides by } M^s$$

$$V_i i = \frac{P \cdot Y}{M^s} - V_0 \qquad \text{subtracting } V_0 \text{ from both sides}$$

$$i = \frac{\left(\frac{P \cdot Y}{M^s}\right) - V_0}{V_i} \qquad \text{dividing both sides by } V_i$$

When the money market is in equilibrium, $i = \dfrac{\left(\frac{P \cdot Y}{M^s}\right) - V_0}{V_i}$. Algebraically, you should be able to see that an increase in M^S, a decrease in P, a decrease in Y, an increase in V_0, and an increase in V_i will decrease nominal interest rates.

NOTE: In the textbook, money demand is usually drawn as a straight line. But the relationship between the nominal interest rate and money demand is nonlinear. Drawing a straight line is acceptable, however, because none of our conclusions depend on the slope of the money demand curve.

4. Consider the money market illustrated in the graph at the right.

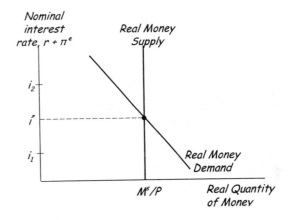

A. When the nominal interest rate is i_1, is the money market in equilibrium? Describe the process by which the money market moves to equilibrium.

B. When the nominal interest rate is i_2, is the money market in equilibrium? Describe the process by which the money market moves to equilibrium.

TO THE CHALKBOARD:
Explaining Figure 11.2

Figure 11.2 shows what happens to the demand for money when income increases. The figure is repeated at the right, with a slight change. An increase in income shifts the real money demand curve to the right as shown at the right, increasing the equilibrium value of the nominal interest rate.

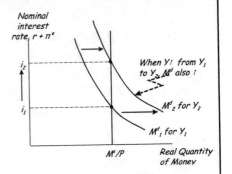

In the textbook, the money demand curves are drawn as straight lines that share a common point on the vertical axis. But because the nominal interest rate is in the denominator of the money demand expression, money demand should be drawn as a nonlinear curve as shown above. And while it is technically correct that all of the money demand curves will share a common point on the vertical axis where the real demand for money equals zero, that point is when the nominal interest rate equals infinity; $\dfrac{Y}{V_0 + V_i \cdot i}$ approaches zero only as $V_0 + V_i \cdot i$ approaches infinity.

5. A. Suppose the money market is initially in equilibrium. If income **increases**, will the money market still be in equilibrium? Describe the process by which the money market moves to equilibrium.

   B. Suppose the money market is initially in equilibrium. If income **decreases**, will the money market still be in equilibrium? Describe the process by which the money market moves to equilibrium.

 NOTE: Remember: when the nominal interest rate is 2 percent, in Chapter 11 you should use i = 0.02.

6. Suppose $V_0 + V_i \cdot i = 7 + 20i$. Suppose the nominal money supply is $8,000 billion. Suppose the price level is 20. Suppose the current and future expected inflation rate is 1 percent.

   A. For each value of the real interest rate given in the table at the right, compute the value of income that will produce equilibrium in the money market.

r	Y
2	
4	
6	
8	

   B. Using the graph at the right, plot the combinations of income and interest rate that yielded equilibrium in the money market. Draw a line that connects the points.

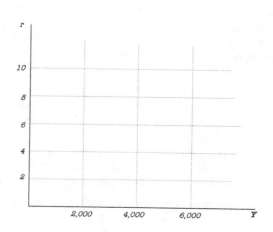

7. Suppose $V_0 + V_i \cdot i = 7 + 20i$. Suppose the nominal money supply is $8,000 billion. Suppose the price level is 20. Suppose the current and future expected inflation rate is 1 percent.

A. For each value of income given in the table at the right, compute the value of the real interest rate that will produce equilibrium in the money market.

r	Y
	$3,000 billion
	$3,300 billion
	$3,700 billion
	$4,000 billion

B. Using the graph at the right, plot the combinations of income and interest rate that yielded equilibrium in the money market. Draw a line that connects the points.

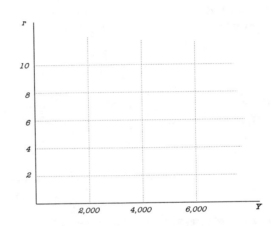

8. A. Explain why an increase in interest rates leads to a decrease in money demand.

B. When income increases, what happens to the nominal interest rate that produces equilibrium in the money market?

C. Using the graph at the right and drawing on your answer to Part B, sketch in a curve or line that show the combinations of income and nominal interest rate that would produce equilibrium in the money market.

9. Suppose nominal money supply is $2,500 billion. Suppose the price level is 10. Suppose velocity is given by $V = 10 + 10 \cdot i$. Complete the table at the right as you answer the questions below and on the next page.

	i	Y	M^d/P	Is $M^d/P = M^S/P$?
A.	4	2,600		
B.	4	2,700		

A. When nominal interest rates are 4 percent and real income is $2,600 billion, is the money market in equilibrium? If not, is real money demand greater than or less than real money supply?

B. When nominal interest rates are 4 percent and real income is $2,700 billion, is the money market in equilibrium? If not, is real money demand greater than or less than real money supply?

C. When real income is $2,700 billion, what nominal interest rate puts the money market in equilibrium?

TO THE CHALKBOARD:
The Algebra of the LM Curve

The equation for the LM curve is based on the money-market equilibrium equation. In the "To the Chalkboard" box on page 286, we derived the expression for the equilibrium interest rate. Here, we use the same process but instead derive an expression for income.

$$\frac{M^s}{P} = \frac{M^d}{P} \qquad \text{money market equilibrium}$$

$$\frac{M^s}{P} = \frac{Y}{V_0 + V_i \cdot i} \qquad \text{substituting definition of real money demand}$$

$$M^s \cdot (V_0 + V_i \cdot i) = P \cdot Y \qquad \text{multiplying both sides by } P \cdot (V_0 + V_i \cdot i)$$

$$\frac{M^s}{P} \cdot (V_0 + V_i \cdot i) = Y \qquad \text{dividing both sides by } P$$

$$\frac{M^s}{P} \cdot [V_0 + V_i \cdot (r + \pi^e)] = Y \qquad \text{substituting definition of } i$$

$$\left(\frac{M^s}{P} \cdot V_0 + \frac{M^s}{P} \cdot V_i \cdot \pi^e \right) + \left(\frac{M^s}{P} \cdot V_i \right) \cdot r = Y \qquad \text{rearranging terms}$$

In the LM equation in your textbook, the money supply is labeled M rather than M^S. That is not a problem nor an error. We are assuming that once the central bank determines the monetary base, the money supply does not vary with a change in nominal interest rates. The assumption is not a good reflection of the real world. But because we are not focusing on bank behavior in this class, none of our conclusions rest on the assumption. So equating M and M^S is an acceptable assumption for our purposes.

10. The equation for the LM curve is $Y = \dfrac{M^s}{P} \cdot \left(V_0 + V_i \cdot i\right)$. Suppose

$$M^S = \$9,000 \text{ billion}$$
$$P = 30$$
$$V_0 = 40$$
$$V_i = 1,000$$

A. What is the equation for the LM curve that expresses Y as a function of the nominal interest rate?

B. Using the LM equation, complete the table at the right. Remember: when the interest rate is 4 percent, i = 0.04.

i	Y
4	
8	
12	

C. Using the values in Part B, plot the combinations of nominal interest rate and real GDP that yield equilibrium in the money market in the axes at the right. Label your axes and curve.

11. A. What is the LM curve? Why does it slope upward?

B. Suppose the economy is initially at a combination of the nominal interest rate, i, and real income, Y, such that the money market is in equilibrium. Now suppose that the central bank increases the nominal money supply. If there is no change in income, what effect does the increase in M^S have on the level of nominal interest rate that yields money market equilibrium? Describe the process by which the

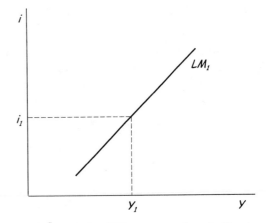

interest rate changes. Does the increase in M^S shift the LM curve or change the slope of the LM curve or both? Sketch in the new LM curve in the graph at the right.

C. Suppose the economy is initially at a combination of the nominal interest rate, i, and real income, Y, such that the money market is in equilibrium. Now suppose that the price level, P, increases. If there is no change in income, what effect does the increase in P have on the level of nominal interest rate that yields money market equilibrium? Describe the process by which the interest rate changes. Does the increase in P shift the LM curve or change the slope of the LM curve or both? Sketch in the new LM curve in the graph at the right.

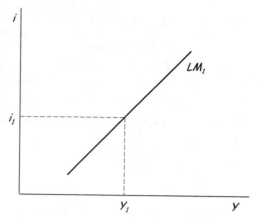

D. Suppose the economy is initially at a combination of the nominal interest rate, i, and real income, Y, such that the money market is in equilibrium. Now suppose that baseline velocity, V_0, increases. If there is no change in income, what effect does the increase in V_0 have on the level of nominal interest rate that yields money market equilibrium? Describe the process by which the interest rate changes. Does the increase in V_0 shift the LM curve or change the slope of the LM curve or both? Sketch in the new LM curve in the graph at the right.

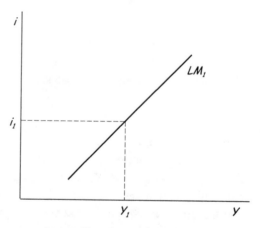

E. Suppose the economy is initially at a combination of the nominal interest rate, i, and real income, Y, such that the money market is in equilibrium. Now suppose that interest sensitivity of velocity, V_i, increases. If there is no change in income, what effect does the increase in V_i have on the level of nominal interest rate that yields money market equilibrium? Describe the process by which the interest rate changes. Does the increase in V_i shift the LM curve or change the slope of the LM curve or both? Sketch in the new LM curve in the graph at the right.

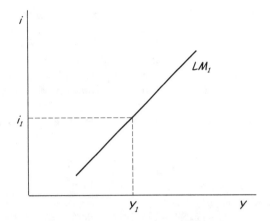

TO THE CHALKBOARD:

The LM Curve and the Interest Rate: Real or Nominal?

The money market graphs are drawn with the nominal interest rate on the vertical axis. Except in Figure 11.3, the IS and LM curves are drawn with the real interest rate on the vertical axis. Are the nominal interest rate and the real interest rate the same? NO! But there is a relationship between the nominal and real interest rates: $i = r + \pi^e$. If inflation, Π, and inflationary expectations, Πe are constant and equal, then any change in the nominal interest rate corresponds directly to a change in the real interest rate.

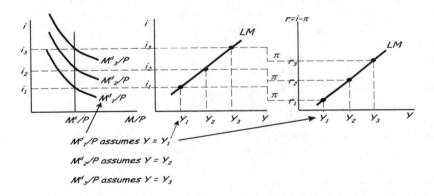

The connection between the graphs depicting money market equilibrium and the LM curve are shown at left. Suppose each money demand curve shown in the far left graph corresponds to an income level depicted along the horizontal axis in the middle and far right graphs. Suppose the inflation rate and expected inflation rate are constant and equal to π. Then each level of the nominal interest rate corresponds to a real interest rate that equals $i - \pi$.

The far left graph depicts the money market, with nominal interest rates on the vertical axis. The middle graph shows the equilibrium nominal interest rate that clears the money market in combination with the income level that determines money demand, producing three points (i_1, Y_1), (i_2, Y_2), and (i_3, Y_3). Connecting those points gives us an LM curve that is the set of combinations of **nominal** interest rate and real income that produce equilibrium in the money market. The far right graph redraws the LM curve with the real interest rate on the vertical axis. Doing so shifts the curve down by the inflation rate, π. The LM curve in the far right graph is the set of combinations of **real** interest rate and real income that produce equilibrium in the money market.

12. The graph at the right depicts the IS-LM model. Label the axes, curves, and equilibrium.

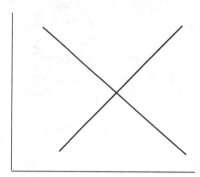

TO THE CHALKBOARD:

The LM Curve

It is important to understand three things about the LM curve:
- why it is upward sloped
- what makes it shift and by how much it shifts
- what it means to be "off of" the LM curve.

Why the LM curve is upward sloped

Suppose that (r_1, Y_1) is a combination of interest rates and income that yields equilibrium in the money market; that is, money supply equals money demand when income equals Y_1 and the real interest rate equals r_1. If instead the income level is higher, then what can we conclude about the corresponding equilibrium value of interest rates? At a higher income, Y_2, real money demand is also higher. Because money supply is unchanged, people and businesses try to satisfy their increased demand for money by selling some of their nonmoney assets in exchange for money. The prices of nonmoney assets decline, increasing the rates of return and nominal interest rates associated with those assets. So (r_2, Y_2) will be a second combination of interest rates and income at which $M^S/P = M^d/P$. At a higher income level, the interest rate that yields equilibrium in the money market will be higher. The curve that connects all of the combinations of interest rates and income that yield equilibrium in the money market will thus slope upward.

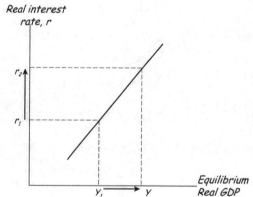

What makes the LM Curve shift and by how much

The position of the LM curve depends upon nominal money supply, the price level, and the determinants of velocity. If there is a change in nominal money supply, or price level, then at every income level there will be a different interest rate that yields equilibrium in the money market. Because the LM curve shows the equilibrium level of the real interest rate that corresponds to each level of income, a change in nominal money supply or the price level will therefore shift the LM curve. If real money supply increases, the LM curve will shift down (see graph at the right). If real money supply decreases, the LM curve will shift up.

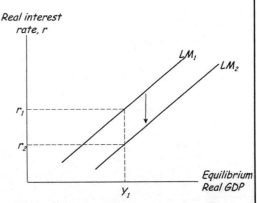

Similarly, if velocity changes, then again at every income level there will be a different interest rate that yields equilibrium in the money market, and the LM curve will shift. If velocity increases due to an increase in V_0 or V_i, then at every income level, a lower interest rate will clear the money market, shifting the LM curve down.

The size of the shift of the LM curve depends upon the interest sensitivity of velocity. If velocity changes very little when interest rates change, then for any initial change in real money supply or velocity, it will take a large change in interest rates to bring money demand into equilibrium with money supply, so the shift in the LM curve will be relatively large.

What it means to be "off of" the LM Curve

The LM curve does not depict all possible combinations of interest rates and income. It depicts all possible **equilibrium** combinations of interest rates and income. So if the money market is not at equilibrium, the economy will be depicted by a point that is off of the LM curve.

Suppose the economy is operating at point A depicted in the graph at the right. That is, the interest rate is r_A and real income is Y_A. Is the money market in equilibrium? No. How do we know? Because (r_A, Y_A) is not on the LM curve and if (r_A, Y_A) was an equilibrium combination of interest rates and income, it would be on the LM curve. Is money demand greater or less than money supply when the economy is at (r_A, Y_A)? Less. How do we know? Because we know from the graph that when income is Y_A, the equilibrium interest rate will equal r_1. The equilibrium interest rate produces money demand equal to money supply (because that is the definition of

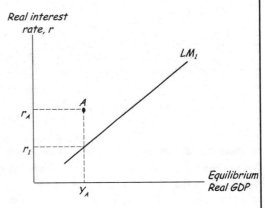

equilibrium). Money demand falls as interest rates rise, so actual money demand at r_A is less than money demand at r_1. Actual money demand is therefore less than money supply.

13. Consider the diagram at the right.

A. Suppose the economy is at point A. What markets are in equilibrium? What markets are out of equilibrium? In the markets that are out of equilibrium, is there excess demand or excess supply?

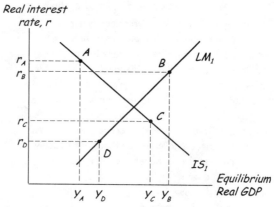

B. Suppose the economy is at point B. What markets are in equilibrium? What markets are out of equilibrium? In the markets that are out of equilibrium, is there excess demand or excess supply?

C. Suppose the economy is at point C. What markets are in equilibrium? What markets are out of equilibrium? In the markets that are out of equilibrium, is there excess demand or excess supply?

D. Suppose the economy is at point D. What markets are in equilibrium? What markets are out of equilibrium? In the markets that are out of equilibrium, is there excess demand or excess supply?

TO THE CHALKBOARD:
Deriving the Equation for IS-LM Equilibrium

Please don't panic. You should not memorize what you are about to see. All you should know are the definitions of the IS and LM relationships, and the process to use to find equilibrium. But on the off chance you want to see how the equations for the equilibrium of IS and LM are determined, here we go.

The IS curve is the set of combinations of real interest rate, r, and real income, Y, that yield equilibrium in the goods and services markets: (r, Y) such that Y = AD. In the Chapter 10 box, "To The Chalkboard: The Algebra of the IS Curve," we found the equation for the IS curve:

$$y = \frac{\left(C_0 + I_0 + G + X_f \cdot Y^f + X_\varepsilon \cdot \varepsilon_0 + X_\varepsilon \cdot \varepsilon_r \cdot r^f\right) - \left(I_r + X_\varepsilon \cdot \varepsilon_r\right) \cdot r}{1 - \left(C_y \cdot (1 - t) - IM_y\right)}$$

We can use two shortcuts and simplify the IS equation somewhat:

$$\textit{define} \left(C_0 + I_0 + G + X_f \cdot Y^f + X_\varepsilon \cdot \varepsilon_0 + X_\varepsilon \cdot \varepsilon_r \cdot r^f \right) = A_0$$

$$\textit{define } 1 - \left(C_y \cdot (1 - t) - IM_y \right) = 1 - MPE$$

$$\textit{thus, } Y = \frac{A_0}{1 - MPE} - \frac{\left(I_r + X_\varepsilon \cdot \varepsilon_r \right)}{1 - MPE} \cdot r$$

The LM curve is the set of combinations of real interest rate, r, and real income, Y, that yield equilibrium in the money market: (r, Y) such that $M^S/P = M^d/P$. In the "To The Chalkboard" box on page 291, we found the equation for the LM curve:

$$\left(\frac{M^s}{P} \cdot V_0 + \frac{M^s}{P} \cdot V_i \cdot \pi^e \right) + \left(\frac{M^s}{P} \cdot V_i \right) \cdot r = Y$$

When the goods and services markets are in equilibrium (Y = AD) and the money market is in equilibrium ($M^S/P = M^d/P$), then both the IS and LM equations are satisfied. So we can solve for the equilibrium value of the real interest rate as follows.

$$\left(\frac{M^s}{P} \cdot V_0 + \frac{M^s}{P} \cdot V_i \cdot \pi^e \right) + \left(\frac{M^s}{P} \cdot V_i \right) \cdot r = Y \ \ and \ \ Y = \frac{A_0}{1 - MPE} - \frac{\left(I_r + X_\varepsilon \cdot \varepsilon_r \right)}{1 - MPE} \cdot r$$

$$\textit{thus, } \left(\frac{M^s}{P} \cdot V_0 + \frac{M^s}{P} \cdot V_i \cdot \pi^e \right) + \left(\frac{M^s}{P} \cdot V_i \right) \cdot r = \frac{A_0}{1 - MPE} - \frac{\left(I_r + X_\varepsilon \cdot \varepsilon_r \right)}{1 - MPE} \cdot r$$

Collecting all terms with the real interest rate on the left and all constant terms on the right yields

$$\left[\frac{\left(I_r + X_\varepsilon \cdot \varepsilon_r \right)}{1 - MPE} + \left(\frac{M^s}{P} \cdot V_i \right) \right] \cdot r = \frac{A_0}{1 - MPE} - \left(\frac{M^s}{P} \cdot V_0 + \frac{M^s}{P} \cdot V_i \cdot \pi^e \right)$$

Solving for the equilibrium real interest rate yields

$$r = \frac{\dfrac{A_0}{1 - MPE} - \left(\dfrac{M^s}{P} \cdot V_0 + \dfrac{M^s}{P} \cdot V_i \cdot \pi^e \right)}{\left[\dfrac{\left(I_r + X_\varepsilon \cdot \varepsilon_r \right)}{1 - MPE} + \left(\dfrac{M^s}{P} \cdot V_i \right) \right]}$$

To find the equilibrium value of real income, substitute this expression into either the equation for the IS curve or the equation for the LM curve, and simplify.

$$Y = \frac{A_0}{1 - MPE} - \frac{\left(I_r + X_\varepsilon \varepsilon_r \right)}{1 - MPE} \cdot \frac{\dfrac{A_0}{1 - MPE} - \left(\dfrac{M^s}{P} \cdot V_0 + \dfrac{M^s}{P} \cdot V_i \cdot \pi^e \right)}{\left[\dfrac{\left(I_r + X_\varepsilon \cdot \varepsilon_r \right)}{1 - MPE} + \left(\dfrac{M^s}{P} \cdot V_i \right) \right]}$$

Is that scary, or what? Will you be expected to use these equations? Unlikely. You can tell the stories you need to tell with the graphs. Do you need to memorize these equations? I hope not! But you do need to know how to derive them and why the equilibrium real interest rate and real income levels depend upon the conditions that determine equilibrium in the goods market (A_0, MPE, and so on) and upon the conditions that determine equilibrium in the money market (M^S, velocity, expected inflation rates, and so on).

14. Suppose

   autonomous spending, $A_0 = 60$
   interest sensitivity of investment, $I_r = 300$
   sensitivity of exports to changes in the exchange rate, $X_\varepsilon = 50$
   interest sensitivity of the exchange rate, $\varepsilon_r = 12$
   marginal propensity to spend, MPE $= 0.70$
   nominal money supply, $M^S = 150$
   price level, $P = 30$
   expected inflation rate, $\pi^e = 0.01$
   baseline velocity, $V_0 = 4$
   interest sensitivity of velocity, $V_i = 800$

A. What is the AD equation? What is the IS equation?

B. What is the real money demand equation? What is the LM equation?

C. What is the equilibrium combination of the real interest rate and income?

D. Graph the IS equation and the LM equation using the axes at the right. Show the equilibrium combination of real interest rate and real GDP. Also draw these IS and LM curves on the graph in Questions 16 and 17, labeling the curves IS_1 and LM_1 each time.

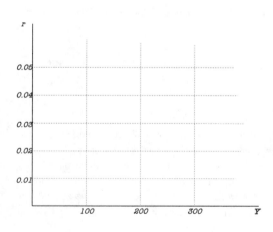

15. Compare the two IS-LM graphs below. Suppose the difference between the two LM curves is due to differences in the interest sensitivity of velocity. In which case is the interest sensitivity of velocity greater? In which case would a decrease in government spending have a larger effect on real income? Explain.

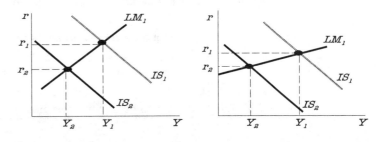

16. Suppose that the parameter values in Question 14 describe the economy, with the following exception: government purchases are increased by 21.

A. In general, what effect will this change have on the IS curve? On the LM curve?

B. What are the new equilibrium values of the real interest rate and real income?

C. Draw the new IS curve in the graph at right. Show the new equilibrium combination of the interest rate and income.

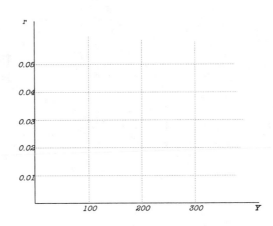

NOTE: When workers are laid off and income declines and real money demand therefore falls, people and firms find they have more money in their wealth portfolios than they wish to have. They respond by buying nonmoney assets. Whoa, you say, that doesn't make any sense. Why would someone who was just laid off put their money into stocks or bonds? They probably wouldn't. But the businesses which just trimmed their work forces by laying off workers probably now have higher balances in their checking accounts than they need. That is, *the businesses have found their new lower money demand is below their current money holdings.* They will transfer some of their low-interest checking account balances to higher-interest nonmoney assets.

17. Suppose that the parameter values in Question 14 describe the economy, with the following exception: nominal money supply is increased by 105.

   A. In general, what effect will this change have on the IS curve? On the LM curve?

   B. What are the new equilibrium values of the real interest rate and real income?

   C. Draw in the new LM curve in the graph at right. Show the new equilibrium combination of the interest rate and income.

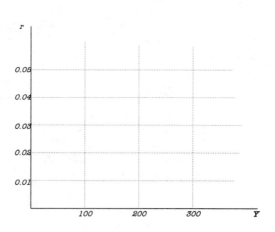

18. Suppose the expected inflation rate increases. What effect does this change have on the LM curve? Explain.

TO THE CHALKBOARD:
Explaining Figure 11.16

Figure 11.16 shows the effect of a change in the price level on the LM curve. Here we use three graphs to depict the effect.

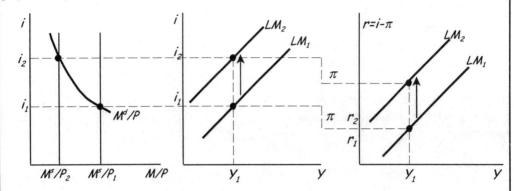

When the price level increases, the real value of the money supply declines. People and businesses sell nonmoney assets, raising the nominal interest rate. A higher nominal interest rate, given expected inflation, corresponds to a higher real interest rate. The LM curve shifts up.

19. Suppose the economy is initially at equilibrium at real interest rate, r_1, and real GDP, Y_1. Draw the relevant IS-LM graph using the axes at the right.

Now suppose that the price level, P, increases. What effect does this change have on the LM curve? What effect does it have on the equilibrium levels of the real interest rate and real GDP? Draw the new LM curve, and label the new equilibrium point as r_2 and Y_2.

Explain why the real interest rate and real GDP change after the price level rises.

20. Suppose the economy is initially at equilibrium at real interest rate, r_1, and real GDP, Y_1. Draw the relevant IS-LM graph using the axes at the right.

Now suppose that the expected inflation rate, π^e, increases. What effect does this change have on the LM curve? What effect does it have on the equilibrium levels of the real interest rate and real GDP? Draw the new LM curve, and label the new equilibrium point as r_2 and Y_2.

Explain why the real interest rate and real GDP change after the expected inflation rate rises.

21. Suppose the economy is initially at equilibrium at real interest rate, r_1, and real GDP, Y_1. Draw the relevant IS-LM graph using the axes at the right.

Now suppose that the baseline velocity, V_0, increases. What effect does this change have on the LM curve? What effect does it have on the equilibrium levels of the real interest rate and real GDP? Draw the new LM curve, and label the new equilibrium point as r_2 and Y_2.

Explain why the real interest rate and real GDP change after baseline velocity rises.

TO THE CHALKBOARD:
Explaining Figure 11.12

Figure 11.12 reminds us of a relationship we first examined in Chapter 6: gross exports depend upon the real exchange rate, which in turn depends upon the real interest rate. When the real interest rate falls, as shown at the right, the real exchange rate rises from ε_1 to ε_2. The decrease in the domestic real interest rate from r_1 to r_2 leads to a decrease in demand for dollar-denominated assets and an increase in demand for assets denominated in other currencies. The resulting decrease in the supply of foreign currency offered in exchange for dollars and increase in demand for foreign currency by those currently holding dollars leads to an increase in the dollar-price of foreign currency (that is, an increase in the nominal exchange rate) and thus to an increase in the real exchange rate. The relationship

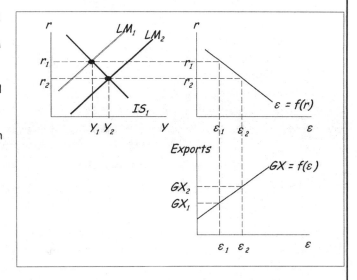

is captured by the equation $\varepsilon = \varepsilon_0 - \varepsilon_r(r - r^f)$ and by the graph in the upper-right corner that shows the inverse relationship between ε and r. The rise in the real exchange rate (the relative price of foreign-produced products) leads to an increase in gross exports because domestically-produced goods and services are now relatively less expensive than foreign-produced goods and services. The relationship is captured by the equation $GX = X_f y^f + X_\varepsilon \varepsilon$ and by the graph in the lower-right corner that shows the direct relationship between gross exports and the real exchange rate, ε. The increase in gross exports from GX_1 to GX_2 is part of the reason the IS curve slopes downward, with equilibrium output increasing from Y_1 to Y_2 when real interest rates decrease from r_1 to r_2.

22. As the central bank decreases interest rates, what happens to gross exports? Does the IS curve shift?

23. Suppose the economy is described by the parameters given in Question 14 (and repeated here):

   autonomous spending, $A_0 = 60$
   interest sensitivity of investment, $I_r = 300$
   sensitivity of exports to changes in the exchange rate, $X_\varepsilon = 50$
   interest sensitivity of the exchange rate, $\varepsilon_r = 12$
   marginal propensity to spend, $MPE = 0.70$
   nominal money supply, $M^S = 150$
   price level, $P = 30$
   expected inflation rate, $\pi^e = 0.01$
   baseline velocity, $V_0 = 4$
   interest sensitivity of velocity, $V_i = 800$

   A. Referring to your answer to Question 14, what are the real interest rate and real GDP values that produce equilibrium in the money market and the goods and services markets?

   B. Suppose that government purchases increase by 21. Referring to your answer to Question 16, what are the new equilibrium values of the real interest rate and real GDP?

   C. Suppose that gross exports and imports are described by the equations
   $$GX = X_f Y^f + X_\varepsilon \varepsilon_0 - X_\varepsilon \varepsilon_r r + X_\varepsilon \varepsilon_r r^f = 25 - 50(12)r$$
   $$IM = IM_y Y = 0.1Y$$
   When government purchases increase by 21, what is the effect on gross exports? On imports? On net exports? Does the trade deficit increase or decrease?

   D. In general, how do we show these changes in gross exports and imports in the IS-LM graph?

24. Suppose the economy is described by the parameters given in Questions 14 and 23.

   A. What are the equilibrium values of the real interest rate and real GDP for the economy?

   B. Now suppose nominal money supply is increased by 105. Referring to your answer to Question 17, what are the new equilibrium values of the real interest rate and real GDP?

C. Suppose that gross exports and imports are described by the equations

$$GX = X_f Y^f + X_\varepsilon \varepsilon_0 - X_\varepsilon \varepsilon_r r + X_\varepsilon \varepsilon_r r^f = 25 - 50(12)r$$

$$IM = IM_y Y = 0.1Y$$

When nominal money supply is increased by 105, what is the effect on gross exports? On imports? On net exports? Does the trade deficit increase or decrease?

D. In general, how do we show these changes in gross exports and imports in the IS-LM graph?

TO THE CHALKBOARD:
Explaining Figure 11.17

Figure 11.17 shows how the Aggregate Demand (AD) curve is derived from the IS-LM graph. It is repeated here.

The AD curve shows the set of combinations of price level, P, and real GDP, Y, that yield equilibrium in both the goods and services and the money markets. The IS-LM graph shows how a change in price level affects the equilibrium level of real GDP. Notice that the change in price level also changes the real interest rate. But the AD curve only shows the relationship between P and equilibrium Y. We must use the IS-LM graph to remind ourselves of the relationship between P and equilibrium r.

For each price level along the vertical axis of the bottom graph, there is a corresponding LM curve depicted in the top graph. (Recall from the previous "To the Chalkboard" box: when the price level increases, the LM curve shifts up.) When P = P_1, the real interest rate and real GDP levels that will produce equilibrium in the money market

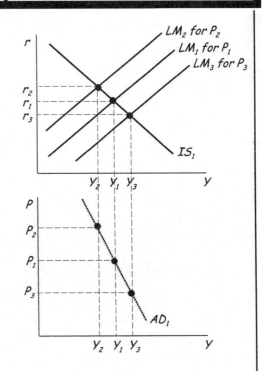

and in the goods and services markets are r_1 and Y_1. So in the bottom graph, we now have one equilibrium combination of P and Y: (P_1, Y_1). At a higher price level, P_2, the equilibrium real interest rate, r_2, is higher and the equilibrium real output level, Y_2, is lower. Now we have a second equilibrium combination of P and Y: (P_2, Y_2). At a lower price level, P_3, the equilibrium real interest rate, r_3, is lower and the equilibrium real output level, Y_3, is higher. Now we have a third equilibrium combination of P and Y: (P_3, Y_3). Connecting these three combinations yields the aggregate demand curve, AD_1, which is the set of combinations of price level, P, and output level, Y, that yield equilibrium in the goods and services markets and the money market.

25. Why does the aggregate demand curve slope down? Using the axes at the right, sketch in an AD curve. Label your axes as well as your curve.

26. Suppose the central bank pegs the real interest rate. Draw the relevant IS-LM graph using the axes at the right. As price level increases, what happens to the LM curve? In this case, what does the AD curve look like?

27. The Taylor rule states that the central bank has neither a money target nor an interest rate target, but instead has an inflation rate target. The central bank adjusts the real interest rate in reaction to changes in the inflation rate:
$$r = r^* + \phi'' \cdot (\pi - \pi')$$
If the Fed increases interest rates by one-quarter percentage point for every one percentage point increase in inflation above its target level, what is the value of ϕ'' in the Taylor rule? Do you have enough information to determine the Fed's target level of the real interest rate?

28. Suppose the Taylor rule is $r = r^* + 0.5(\pi - 0.02)$. What is the target inflation rate? For every one percentage point by which actual inflation exceeds the target inflation rate, by how much does the Fed increase interest rates?

29. Suppose the Taylor rule is $r = r^* + 0.25 (\pi - 0.03)$. Suppose the Fed believes the "normal" real interest rate is 2 percent. If the inflation rate is 6 percent, what will the real interest rate be? If instead prices are falling by 1 percent annually, what will the real interest rate be?

30. Using the axes at right, draw a standard IS graph.

   A. Suppose the Fed follows the Taylor rule. Suppose the inflation rate equals the Fed's target inflation rate. Draw in the LM curve. Show the equilibrium combination of real interest rates and real GDP that produces equilibrium in the goods and services markets and the money market.

   B. If the Fed is following the Taylor rule and the inflation rate equals the Fed's target inflation rate, then what can cause equilibrium real GDP to change?

31. Suppose the economy can be described by the equations given in Problem 14 (repeated here):

   autonomous spending, $A_0 = 60$
   interest sensitivity of investment, $I_r = 300$
   sensitivity of exports to changes in the exchange rate, $X_\varepsilon = 50$
   interest sensitivity of the exchange rate, $\varepsilon_r = 12$
   marginal propensity to spend, MPE = 0.70

   Suppose the Fed follows the Taylor rule, setting the real interest rate so as to target an inflation rate. Suppose that their target inflation rate is 2 percent and they believe the "normal" real interest rate is 3 percent. Suppose that they increase the real interest rate by one-quarter percentage point for every one-half point increase in the inflation rate above 2 percent.

   A. Suppose the inflation rate is currently 3 percent. What is the real interest rate targeted by the Fed?

   B. If the inflation rate is 3 percent, what is the equilibrium level of real output?

   C. Suppose the inflation rate increases to 5 percent. What is the new value of the real interest rate? What is the new equilibrium level of output?

32. Consider again the economy described in Question 31.

A. If the Fed sets the real interest rate so it equals the long-run "normal" level of 3 percent, what is the inflation rate?

B. For the economy described in Problem 31, what is Y_0, the equilibrium level of real GDP when the real interest rate is at its long-run "normal" level of 3 percent?

C. On the graph at the right, plot the point that is the combination of the inflation rate from Part A and equilibrium output from Part B.

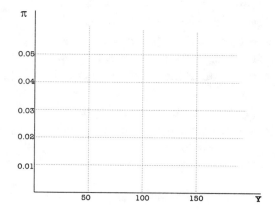

D. Now plot the combination of the inflation rate and equilibrium output that you found in Question 31, Part B. Plot a third combination: the inflation rate and equilibrium output that you found in Question 31, Part C. Connect the three points you have plotted with a line. Label it AD.

E. Is the AD curve you drew the "Monetary Policy Reaction Function"?

NOTE: The aggregate supply equation is $\frac{Y - Y^*}{Y^*} = \theta \cdot \left(\frac{P - P^e}{P^e} \right)$. The anticipated price level, P^e, is not what we expect the price level to be **in the future**. Instead P^e is what we **had** expected prices to be in the current period. For instance, suppose that in 2000 we had looked ahead to 2001 and anticipated the price level as measured by the GDP deflator would be 102 in 2001. Suppose that instead the price level for 2001 turned out to be 105. In this case, $\left(\frac{P - P^e}{P^e} \right)$ is 0.029 or 2.9 percent; that is, the price level was 2.9 percent greater than we had expected it to be.

33. Suppose potential output is 500. Suppose the inflation rate had been expected to be 2 percent. Suppose the parameter that measures how strongly inflation responds to the difference between actual and potential output, θ, is 0.25. The short-run aggregate supply curve is then $\dfrac{Y-500}{500} = 0.25\cdot(\pi - 2)$.

A. Suppose actual output is 600. What will the inflation rate be?

B. Suppose actual output is 500. What will the inflation rate be?

C. Suppose actual output is 400. What will the inflation rate be?

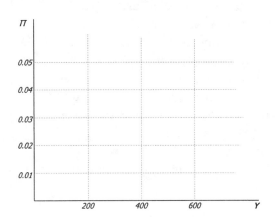

D. Using the graph at the right, plot the relationship between inflation and output. Clearly mark potential output and the anticipated inflation rate.

34. The Aggregate Supply curve depicts the short-run relationship between real GDP and the rate of inflation. The AS curve slopes upward; at higher levels of real GDP, the inflation rate is higher. Give two explanations why the AS curve slopes upward.

$\mathcal{C}$. APPLYING CONCEPTS AND MODELS

Now we're getting to the good stuff. Being able to apply a specific concept or model to a real-world situation — where you are told which model to apply but you have to figure out how to apply it — is often what you need to earn a B in a course. This is where macroeconomics starts to become interesting and the world starts to make more sense.

1. During the 1930s, the federal government created the Works Progress Administration (W.P.A.) to hire artists, writers, and others in similar fields. The government paid them to create art, literature, and music. Using the IS-LM model, explain what effect the increase in government spending had on the short-run equilibrium levels of the real interest rate and real income. Describe the process by which the economy adjusted to the new equilibrium. Supplement your answer with a graph using the axes above.

2. Fears of rising oil prices in the mid-1970s led many companies to cancel fuel-intensive investment projects. Using the IS-LM model, explain what effect the decrease in investment spending had on the short-run equilibrium levels of the real interest rate and real income. Describe the process by which the economy adjusted to the new equilibrium. Supplement your answer with a graph using the axes above.

3. Suppose the interest sensitivity of investment is very high. If the government increases its purchases by $75 billion, will the government's fiscal policy action be strongly or weakly expansionary? Explain.

4. Suppose the interest sensitivity of investment is very high. If the central bank increases the money supply, will its monetary policy action be strongly or weakly expansionary? Explain.

5. Following the September 11 attack on America, consumers reduced their spending. Use the IS-LM model to predict the short-run effect on real interest rates and real output. Does your answer depend upon whether the Fed targeted the money supply or the real interest rate? Explain.

6. If the central bank targets interest rates, do changes in government purchases affect gross exports? If the central bank targets the money supply, do changes in government purchases affect gross exports? Explain, supplementing your explanation with a graph.

7. Prices are falling. Can the Fed follow the Taylor rule as they set the real interest rate? Explain.

D. EXPLAINING THE REAL WORLD

Most instructors are delighted when you are able to figure out which concept or model to apply to a real-world situation. Being able to do so means you thoroughly understand the material and is often what you need to do to earn an A in a course. This is where you experience the power of macroeconomic theory.

1. Why would economists be concerned that increased government spending for airline bailouts, airport security, and a War on Terrorism could be harmful to the economy?

2. Online stock trading companies such as E-Trade allow customers to buy and sell stock with the click of a mouse. Customers can electronically transfer funds from their checking accounts to their E-Trade account, again with the click of a mouse. Does the development of such online trading increase or decrease the ability of the federal government to use fiscal policy to change real GDP?

3. Business analysts today have a full array of computer-based analysis tools at their disposal. At relatively low cost, a business analyst can evaluate the expected rates of return on a large number of investment projects. As a result, the company can have a business plan that sets out an array of investment projects that can be profitably undertaken if the central bank lowers interest rates. Forty or fifty years ago, the cost of preparing a similar business plan would have been prohibitive. Does the development of computer-based business analysis tools increase or decrease the ability of a central bank to change real GDP? (Assume the central bank targets the money supply.)

4. Consumer confidence dropped precipitously in September 2001. Investor confidence followed suit. Twice during September 2001, the Fed reduced interest rates by one-half percentage point. What economic effect was the Fed hoping would result from their action? Draw a graph to supplement your explanation.

5. As the Fed lowered interest rates in the wake of the economic repercussions of the September 11 attack on America, would gross exports be expected to rise?

E. POSSIBILITIES TO PONDER

The more you learn, the more you realize you have more to learn. These questions go beyond the textbook material. They are the sort of questions that distinguish A+ or A work from A- work. Some of them may even serve as starting points for junior or senior year research papers.

1. There are three possible targets for monetary policy described in the chapter: a money supply target, an interest rate target, and an inflation rate target. What factors – economic, political, or other – determine which target a central bank will follow?

2. Most economic models assume that economic behavior is independent of the direction of change. For instance, the size of the marginal propensity to consume does not depend upon whether disposable income is increasing or decreasing. The interest sensitivity of velocity does not depend upon whether interest rates are rising or falling. Is this assumption realistic? If we drop the assumption of symmetric behavior, how do the IS-LM and AS-AD models change?

3. Can we use the IS-LM and AS-AD models to explain the United States economy of the late 1800s? Can we use them to explain the Soviet economy of the 1970s? Can we use them to explain the Afghan economy of the 1990s?

SOLUTIONS   SOLUTIONS   SOLUTIONS   SOLUTIONS

A. BASIC DEFINITIONS

1. expected inflation rate
2. money
3. LM Curve
4. real output; goods and services
5. opportunity cost
6. Taylor Rule
7. aggregate supply
8. real output
9. goods and services
10. nominal interest rate; real money stock
11. real interest rate
12. real interest rate; real output

13. LM
14. decreases
15. downward
16. increases
17. increase; increase
18. upward
19. higher
20. increase
21. decrease; increase
22. decreases
23. upward
24. right
25. LM; right
26. IS
27. horizontal
28. decrease

B. MANIPULATION OF CONCEPTS AND MODELS

1. A. Remember that the nominal interest rate, i, is the sum of the real interest rate shown in the table and the expected inflation rate. Assume the expected inflation rate is 3 percent.

Y	r	$\frac{M^d}{P}$
1,000	2	125.0
1,000	7	111.1
2,000	7	222.2

   B. Real money demand falls when interest rates rises. A higher interest rate corresponds to a higher opportunity cost of holding money. When interest rates rise, people and businesses are more likely to hold their wealth as nonmoney assets than as money, decreasing the demand for money.

   C. Real money demand rises when income rises because more income corresponds to more spending. When there is more spending, people and businesses need larger money balances because money is the asset we use to pay for goods and services. Money demand increases.

2. When real income, Y, doubles, real money demand also doubles. This result is simply an implication of the form of the money demand equation used in this textbook.

3. When prices, P, double, nominal money demand also doubles. Again, this result is simply an implication of the form of the money demand equation used in this textbook.

4. A. At interest rate i_1, where $i_1 < i^*$, the money market is not in equilibrium. Real money demand is greater than real money supply. People and firms will try to increase their money balances because the amount of money they are currently holding is less than they wish to hold. To increase their money holdings, people and firms could borrow funds, increasing the demand for loans and thus increasing interest rates. Alternatively, for an explanation not based on the textbook, when people and firms try 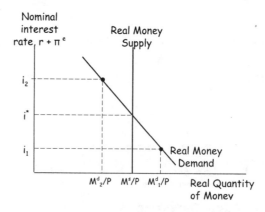 to increase their money holdings they do so by exchanging some of their nonmoney assets for money. For instance, if they sell bonds and put the proceeds into their checking accounts, the increase in the supply of bonds for sale will decrease prices of bonds and increase nominal interest rates. As interest rates increase, the opportunity cost of holding wealth in the form of money increases, so the demand for money will decline. Interest rates will continue to increase until money demand declines to the level of money supply.

   B. At interest rate i_2, where $i_2 > i^*$, the money market is not in equilibrium. Real money demand is less than real money supply. People and firms will try to decrease their money balances because the amount of money they are currently holding is more than they wish to hold. To decrease their money holdings, people and firms will buy nonmoney assets such as stocks and bonds with their money. Doing so increases the demand for stocks and bonds, increasing the prices of nonmoney assets, and thus decreasing nominal returns and interest rates. As interest rates decrease, the opportunity cost of holding wealth in the form of money decreases, so the demand for money will rise. Interest rates will continue to fall until money demand rises to the level of money supply.

5. A. When income increases, spending increases, which increases the transactions demand for money. The demand for money will then be greater than the supply of money. People and firms will try to increase their money balances because the amount of money they are currently holding is less than they wish to hold. They will sell some of their nonmoney assets such as stock and bonds, lowering the prices of those assets, and thus increasing nominal rates of return and interest rates. At higher interest rates, the opportunity cost of holding money is higher, decreasing the demand for money. Interest rates will continue to rise until money demand decreases to its original level.

   B. When income decreases, spending decreases, which decreases the transactions demand for money. The demand for money will then be more than the supply of money. People and firms will try to decrease their money balances because the amount of money they are currently holding is more than they wish to hold. They will exchange some of their money for nonmoney assets such as stock and bonds, raising the prices of those assets, and thus decreasing nominal rates of return and interest rates. At lower interest rates, the opportunity cost of holding money is lower, increasing the demand for money. Interest rates will continue to fall until money demand increases to its original level.

6. A. Money market equilibrium occurs when $M^s/P = M^d/P$. Starting from that point, solve algebraically for Y. Remember that interest rates are expressed in decimal form: 1 percent = 0.01.

$$\frac{M^s}{P} = \frac{Y}{V_0 + V_i \cdot (r + \pi^e)} \qquad \text{\textit{definition of real money demand}}$$

$$\frac{8000}{20} = \frac{Y}{7 + 20 \cdot (r + 0.01)} \qquad \text{\textit{substituting values given in problem}}$$

$$400 \cdot (7 + 20 \cdot r + 0.2) = Y \qquad \text{\textit{simplifying and solving for Y}}$$

$$2{,}880 + 8{,}000 \cdot r = Y \qquad \text{\textit{simplifying}}$$

r	Y
2	$3,040 billion
4	$3,200 billion
6	$3,360 billion
8	$3,520 billion

   B.

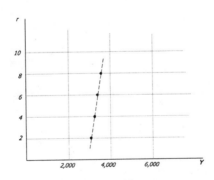

Notice that the combinations of real interest rate and income that generate equilibrium in the money market are positively related. At a higher interest rate, a higher income level produces money market equilibrium. Equivalently, at a higher income level, a higher interest rate produces money market equilibrium.

7. A.

$$\frac{M^s}{P} = \frac{Y}{V_0 + V_i \cdot (r + \pi^e)} \qquad \text{\textit{definition of real money demand}}$$

$$\frac{8000}{20} = \frac{Y}{7 + 20 \cdot (r + 0.01)} \qquad \text{\textit{substituting values given in problem}}$$

$$2{,}880 + 8{,}000 \cdot r = Y \qquad \text{\textit{simplifying}}$$

$$r = \frac{Y - 2{,}880}{8{,}000} \qquad \text{\textit{solving for r}}$$

r	Y
1.5 %	$3,000 billion
5.25 %	$3,300 billion
10.25 %	$3,700 billion
14.0 %	$4,000 billion

B.

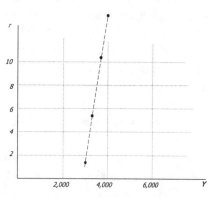

Notice what we have drawn: an LM curve! It is the set of combinations of real interest rate, r, and real income, Y, that produce equilibrium in the money market.

8. A. When interest rates increase, the opportunity cost of holding wealth in the form of money also increases. People and businesses therefore wish to hold less money and more nonmoney assets in their wealth portfolios.

    B. When income increases, the transactions demand for money increases. If the money market was initially in equilibrium, now money demand will exceed money supply. People and businesses will want to exchange some of their nonmoney assets such as stocks and bonds for money. As they sell some of their stocks and bonds, their actions increase the supply of nonmoney assets for sale, decreasing the price of those assets, and thus increasing the nominal return and interest rates. But at higher nominal interest rates, money demand decreases. Interest rates will continue to rise until money demand falls to its initial level.

    C.

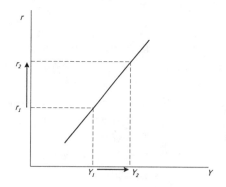

9.

	i	Y	M^d/P	Is $M^d/P = M^s/P$?
A.	4	2,600	250	yes
B.	4	2,700	259.6	No. $M^d/P > M^s/P$?
C.	8	2,700	250	yes

10. A. $Y = 12,000 + 3,000 \cdot i$

B.

i	Y
4	13,200
8	14,400
12	15,600

C.

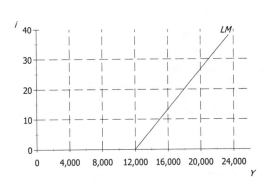

11. A. The LM curve gives the combinations of interest rates (measured on the vertical axis) and real income (measured on the horizontal axis) that produce equilibrium in the money market. It can be expressed as a relationship between the nominal interest rate, i, and real income, Y; or as a relationship between the real interest rate, r, and real income, Y. It slopes up because when real income increases, the resulting increase in the demand for money leads people and businesses to sell nonmoney assets, decreasing the price of those assets and thus increasing the nominal rates of return and nominal interest rates. Assuming the expected inflation rate is unchanged, an increase in the nominal interest rate also increases the real interest rate.

B. The nominal interest rate will fall. If the nominal money supply increases, then $M^S > M^d$. To increase the nominal money supply, the Fed bought bonds from the public. People and businesses therefore find themselves holding larger money balances than they wish to hold. As a result, they will purchase nonmoney assets, increasing the price of those assets and thus decreasing the rates of return and interest rates on nonmoney assets. The nominal interest rate will decline. The LM curve will shift

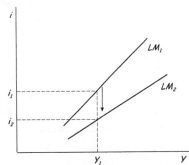

down. (Equivalently, we could say the LM curve shifts to the right, but the logic of the story is consistent with shifting the LM curve down). To see the effect on the slope of the LM curve, use the equation for the LM curve: $i = -\dfrac{V_0}{V_i} + \dfrac{1}{\left(\left(\dfrac{M^s}{P}\right) \cdot V_i\right)} \cdot Y$. When M^S increases, the slope of the LM curve will decline. The equation for the LM curve also makes clear that the new and old LM curves will have the same intercept, $-\dfrac{V_0}{V_i}$. The old and new LM curves are shown at the right.

C. The nominal interest rate will rise. If the price level increases, then the real value of the money supply declines, so $M^s/P < M^d/P$. People and businesses therefore find themselves holding smaller real money balances than they wish to hold. As a result, they will sell nonmoney assets, decreasing the price of those assets and thus increasing the rates of return and interest rates on nonmoney assets. The nominal interest rate will rise. The LM curve will shift up. (Equivalently, we could say the LM curve shifts to the

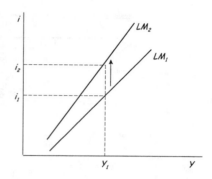

left, but the logic of the story is consistent with shifting the LM curve down). The slope of the LM curve will increase. The new and old LM curves will have the same intercept, $-\dfrac{V_0}{V_i}$. The old and new LM curves are shown at the right.

D. The nominal interest rate will fall. If baseline velocity increases, then relative money demand declines, as does real money demand. So $M^s/P > M^d/P$. People and businesses therefore find themselves holding larger real money balances than they wish to hold. As a result, they will buy nonmoney assets, increasing the price of those assets and thus decreasing the rates of return and interest rates on nonmoney assets. The nominal interest rate will fall. The LM curve will shift down

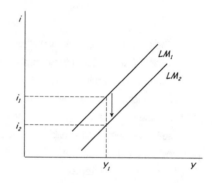

but its slope does not change. The old and new LM curves are shown at the right.

E. The nominal interest rate will fall. If the interest sensitivity of velocity, V_i, increases, then relative money demand declines, as does real money demand. So $M^s/P > M^d/P$. People and businesses therefore find themselves holding larger real money balances than they wish to hold. As a result, they will buy nonmoney assets, increasing the price of those assets and thus decreasing the rates of return and interest rates on nonmoney assets. The nominal interest rate will fall. The LM curve will shift down.

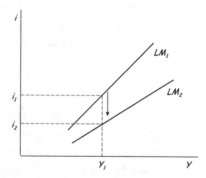

The equation for the LM curve indicates that the slope of the LM curve will decrease. The old and new LM curves are shown at the right.

12.

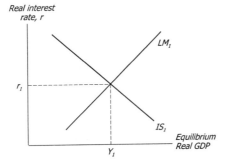

13. A. When the economy is at A, on the IS curve, the goods and services markets are in equilibrium. The money market is out of equilibrium. At A, the actual interest rate, r_A, is greater than the interest rate that would produce equilibrium in the money market when income is Y_A. Therefore $M^d < M^s$; there is excess supply of money.

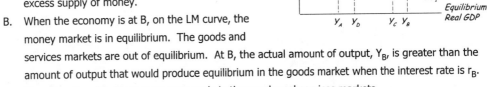

   B. When the economy is at B, on the LM curve, the money market is in equilibrium. The goods and services markets are out of equilibrium. At B, the actual amount of output, Y_B, is greater than the amount of output that would produce equilibrium in the goods market when the interest rate is r_B. Therefore Y > AD; there is excess supply in the goods and services markets.

   C. When the economy is at C, on the IS curve, the goods and services markets are in equilibrium. The money market is out of equilibrium. At C, the actual interest rate, r_C, is less than the interest rate that would produce equilibrium in the money market when income is Y_C. Therefore $M^d > M^s$; there is excess demand for money.

   D. When the economy is at D, on the LM curve, the money market is in equilibrium. The goods and services markets are out of equilibrium. At D, the actual amount of output, Y_D, is less than the amount of output that would produce equilibrium in the goods market when the interest rate is r_D. Therefore Y < AD; there is excess demand in the goods and services markets.

14. A. $AD = A_0 - (I_r + X_\varepsilon \varepsilon_r) \cdot r + MPE \cdot Y = 60 - 900 \cdot r + 0.7 \cdot Y$
      IS: When Y = AD, Y = 200 - 3,000·r

   B. $M^d/P = Y / [V_0 + V_i \cdot (r + \pi^e)] = Y / (12 + 800 \cdot r)$
      LM: When $M^s/P = M^d/P$, Y = 60 + 4,000·r

   C. When Y = 200 - 3,000·r and Y = 60 + 4,000·r, r = 0.02, Y = 140

   D.

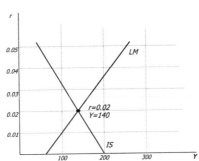

15. A flatter LM curve has a greater interest sensitivity of velocity, so the interest sensitivity of velocity is greater in the right hand graph. A decrease in government spending has a larger effect on income when the interest sensitivity of velocity is greater. When government spending and, through the multiplier, consumption spending decrease, money demand decreases. People and businesses respond by buying nonmoney assets to decrease their money holdings. Interest rates fall. If money demand responds quickly to a change in interest rates, then it will take only a relatively small decrease in interest rates to restore money market equilibrium. A relatively small decrease in real interest rates results in a relatively small offsetting increase in investment and gross export spending. Therefore the greater the sensitivity of velocity and money demand to changes in the interest rate, the larger is the change in income for any change in government spending.

16. A. When government purchases increase, the IS curve shifts to the right. The LM curve is unaffected.

    B. The new IS curve is $Y = 270 - 3{,}000 \cdot r$. The LM curve is still $Y = 60 + 4{,}000 \cdot r$. The new equilibrium is therefore $r = 0.03$, $Y = 180$.

    C.

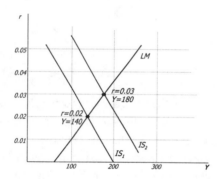

17. A. When the nominal money supply increases, the LM curve shifts to the right. The IS curve is unaffected.

    B. The new LM curve is $Y = 102 + 6{,}800 \cdot r$. The IS curve is still $Y = 200 - 3{,}000 \cdot r$. The new equilibrium is therefore $r = 0.01$, $Y = 170$.

    C.

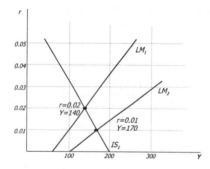

18. If the expected inflation rate rises, then the gap between nominal and real interest rates also rises. The LM relationship is found by finding the nominal interest rate that clears the money market. An increase in the expected inflation rate does not affect the relationship between the **nominal** interest rates and real income levels that produce equilibrium in the money market, depicted in the graph on the left. But the increased gap between the nominal and real interest rate means that the relationship between the **real** interest rates and real income levels that produce equilibrium in the money market is affected. The LM curve in the graph on the right shifts down.

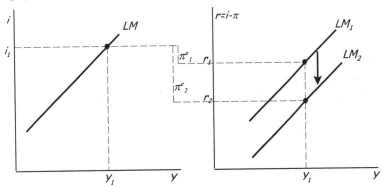

19. When the price level, P, increases, the real value of the money supply decreases, shifting the LM curve up and increasing its slope. (See Question 11, Part B.) The equilibrium real interest rate will increase and equilibrium real GDP will decrease. These changes in real interest rate and real GDP occur because of the reactions that businesses and people have to the decrease in the value of the money supply. At higher prices, existing money holdings are insufficient and so people and businesses sell nonmoney assets in exchange for money, increasing

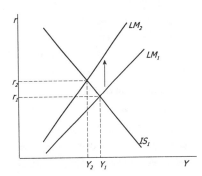

the supply of nonmoney assets, decreasing their price, and increasing their rates of return and nominal interest rates. At higher nominal interest rates, assuming no change in expected inflation, the real interest rate will also be higher. Two effects follow: real money demand declines at higher nominal interest rates, making people and businesses more content with their existing real money holdings; and investment and gross export spending decline, lowering consumption spending through the multiplier, and thus decreasing real GDP. The decline in real GDP also lowers real money demand, ultimately bringing real money demand into equilibrium with the new, lower level of real money supply. The money market and the goods and services markets will return to equilibrium once the real interest rate has increased to r_2 and real GDP has fallen to Y_2.

20. When the expected inflation rate, π^e, increases, the real interest rate associated with each level of the nominal interest rate declines, shifting the LM curve down. (See Question 18.) The equilibrium real interest rate will decrease and equilibrium real GDP will increase. These changes in real interest rate and real GDP occur because of the reactions that businesses and people have to the decrease in the real interest rate associated with the existing value of the nominal interest rate. At a lower real interest rate, investment and gross export spending

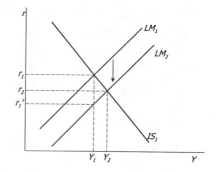

increases, increasing consumption spending through the multiplier effect, and thus increasing real GDP. The increase in income and spending causes the transactions demand for money to increase. People and businesses will sell nonmoney assets in exchange for money, increasing the supply of nonmoney assets, decreasing their price, and thus increasing their rates of return and nominal interest rates. The real interest rate does not fall all the way to r_1' as shown on the graph above, but instead falls only to r_2. The money market and the goods and services markets will return to equilibrium once the real interest rate has decreased to r_2 and real GDP has risen to Y_2. (Note that this scenario is a bit unrealistic. The central bank is likely to react to a change in inflationary expectations by changing the money stock and real interest rates.)

21. When baseline velocity increases, then the level of money demand associated with each level of the nominal and real interest rate declines, shifting the LM curve down. The equilibrium real interest rate will decrease and equilibrium real GDP will increase. These changes in real interest rate and real GDP occur because of the reactions that businesses and people have to the decrease in velocity and money demand. People and businesses find themselves holding larger real money balances than they wish to hold. As a result, they will buy nonmoney assets,

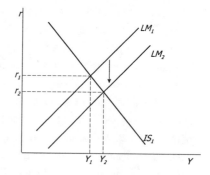

increasing the price of those assets and thus decreasing the rates of return and interest rates on nonmoney assets. At lower nominal interest rates, assuming no change in expected inflation, the real interest rate will also be lower. Two effects follow: real money demand rises at lower nominal interest rates, making people and businesses more content with their existing real money holdings; and investment and gross export spending rise, raising consumption spending through the multiplier, and thus increasing real GDP. The increase in real GDP also raises real money demand, ultimately bringing real money demand into equilibrium with the existing level of real money supply. The money market and the goods and services markets will return to equilibrium once the real interest rate has decreased to r_2 and real GDP has risen to Y_2.

22. When the real interest rate falls, gross exports rise. A decrease in the real interest rate leads to a decrease in the supply of foreign currency offered in exchange for dollars and increase in demand for foreign currency by those currently holding dollars. As a result, the dollar-price of foreign currency (that is, the nominal exchange rate) increases and thus the real exchange rate also increases. The rise in the real exchange rate leads to an increase in gross exports because domestically-produced goods and services are now relatively less expensive than foreign-produced goods and services. No, the IS curve does not shift when gross exports change in response to a change in the real interest rate. The

responsiveness of gross exports to a change in the real interest rate, $X_\varepsilon \varepsilon_r$, is one of the determinants of the slope of the IS curve.

23. A. $r = 2$ % and $Y = 140$.

    B. $r = 3$ % and $Y = 180$.

    C. $\Delta r = +0.01$; $\Delta Y = +40$. Therefore $\Delta GX = -600(\Delta r) = -600(0.01) = -6$. $\Delta IM = 0.1(\Delta Y) = 0.1(40) = +4$. $\Delta NX = \Delta GX - \Delta IM = -6 - 4 = -10$. The trade deficit increases.

    D. The changes in gross exports and imports are already incorporated into the IS-LM graph. The slope of the IS curve takes into account the interest sensitivity of gross exports and the marginal propensity to import. These changes are therefore simply a movement along the IS curve.

24. A. $r = 2$ % and $Y = 140$.

    B. $r = 1$ % and $Y = 170$.

    C. $\Delta r = -0.01$; $\Delta Y = +30$.

    Therefore $\Delta GX = -600(\Delta r) = -600(-0.01) = +6$. $\Delta IM = 0.1(\Delta Y) = 0.1(30) = +3$. $\Delta NX = \Delta GX - \Delta IM = +6 - 3 = +3$. The trade deficit decreases.

    D. The changes in gross exports and imports are already incorporated into the IS-LM graph. The slope of the IS curve takes into account the interest sensitivity of gross exports and the marginal propensity to import. These changes are therefore simply a movement along the IS curve.

25. The aggregate demand curve shows the set of combinations of price level, P, and output level, Y, that produce equilibrium in both the goods and services markets and the money market. It is drawn with the price level on the vertical axis and real GDP on the horizontal axis. It slopes downward because at a higher price level, the real value of the money supply is lower, leading people and businesses to sell nonmoney assets in an attempt to increase their real money holdings, which decreases the prices on nonmoney assets and increases their rates of return and interest rates. But at higher interest rates, investment spending and gross exports decline, leading through the multiplier to decreases in consumption spending as well. The amount of output that will produce equilibrium in the markets for goods and services will therefore be lower as price level rises.

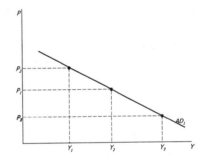

26. If the Fed targets the interest rate, then regardless of the price level, the LM curve will be horizontal at real interest rate r_1. When the price level increases, the Fed responds by increasing the nominal money supply so that real interest rates remain unchanged. If the real interest rate is unchanged then the equilibrium real output level will also be unchanged. Therefore when the Fed targets interest rates, the AD curve will be vertical at the existing level of real GDP. That level of GDP will be determined entirely by the position of the IS curve; that is, the equilibrium real GDP will depend upon autonomous spending.

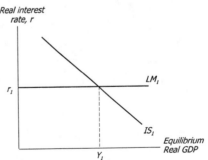

27. If the Fed increases interest rates by one-quarter percentage point for every one point increase in inflation above the expected level, the Taylor rule is $r = r^* + 0.25 \cdot (\pi - \pi')$, where an inflation rate of 3 percent is expressed as either $\pi = 3$ or $\pi = 0.03$. We do not have enough information to determine the

Fed's target level of the real interest rate. We still need to know their estimate of a "normal" real interest rate, r*, their target inflation rate, π', and the actual inflation rate, π.

28. The target inflation rate is 0.02 = 2 percent. For every one percentage point that the actual inflation rate is above 2 percent, the Fed increases the real interest rate by 0.5 percentage points.

29. If $\pi = 0.06$, then $r = 0.02 + 0.25(0.06 - 0.03) = 0.0275 = 2.75$ %.
    If $\pi = -0.01$, then $r = 0.02 + 0.25(-0.01 - 0.03) = 0.01 = 1.0$ %.

30. A. If the Fed follows the Taylor rule and the inflation rate equals the target inflation rate, then the Fed will adjust the money supply so that the real interest rate equals its "normal" real interest rate, r*. The LM curve will therefore be horizontal at r*.

    B. Equilibrium output depends entirely on the position of the IS curve. That is, equilibrium output depends upon the levels of autonomous spending and the marginal propensity to spend.

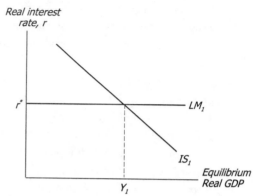

31. A. Note that the quarter-point increases in the real interest rate are triggered by just a half-point jump in the inflation rate, so for a full one-point jump in the inflation rate the real interest rate would increase by 0.5 percentage points. Therefore the Taylor rule is $r = 0.03 + 0.5(\pi - 0.02)$. If the inflation rate is 3 percent, $r = 0.035 = 3.5$ %.

    B. $AD = 60 - (300 + 50(12)) \cdot r + 0.7Y = 60 - 31.5 + 0.7Y = 28.5 + 0.7Y$
       Equilibrium output is therefore $Y = 28.5/(0.3) = 95$.

    C. If the inflation rate increases to 5 percent, the Fed increases r to 4.5 percent. Aggregate demand decreases to $AD = 60 - 900(0.045) + 0.7Y = 19.5 + 0.7Y$. Equilibrium output is therefore $Y = 19.5/(0.3) = 65$. To decrease the inflation rate, the Fed increases interest rates and puts the economy into recession.

32. A. If $r = r^*$, then the actual inflation rate must equal the target inflation rate. In this case, $\pi = 0.02$.

    B. When $r = 0.03$, $AD = 60 - 900(0.03) + 0.7Y = 33 + 0.7Y$. Therefore equilibrium output, Y_0, equals $33/(0.3) = 110$.

    C. See graph.

    D. See graph.

    E. Yes! This is the AD Curve for the Monetary Policy Reaction Function that is presented in the textbook in Figure 11.18.

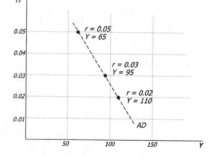

33. A. $\pi = 2.8$ %

    B. $\pi = 2.0$ %

    C. $\pi = 1.2$ %

    D. See graph.

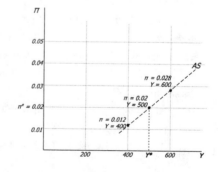

34. The AS curve slopes upward because

- When demand for output is greater than anticipated, firms raise their prices higher than had been anticipated.
- When demand for output is higher than potential output, businesses encounter bottlenecks in production, and bid up costs of production. The prices they charge for their output are then increased.

C. APPLYING CONCEPTS AND MODELS

1. When government spending increases, real income, Y, and the real interest rate, r, increase in the short run.

    Suppose the economy is initially in equilibrium at (r_1, Y_1). The increase in government spending creates unintended inventory depletion, leading to an increase in output for the government. A multiplier process ensues: The increased income for the workers and owners of the firms producing government output causes them to increase their consumption spending. At the existing interest rate, r_1, the amount of output that produces equilibrium in the markets for goods and services increases by the change in government spending times the spending multiplier, to Y_1', depicted as a shift to the right of the IS curve to IS_2.

    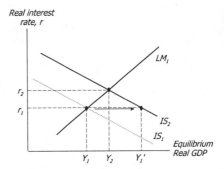

    As income and spending increase toward Y_1', the transactions demand for money rises. But the central bank has not changed the money supply. People and businesses try to satisfy their increased demand for money by selling nonmoney assets in exchange for money, increasing the supply of nonmoney assets, decreasing the price of nonmoney assets, and thus increasing the rates of return and nominal interest rates associated with those nonmoney assets. As the nominal interest rate rises, the opportunity cost of holding money increases, lowering the real demand for money and thus closing some of the gap between the money supply and money demand that was created when income rose following the increase in government spending. So long as expected inflation is unchanged (and in this sticky-price model, we can safely make this assumption), the increase in nominal interest rates corresponds to an increase in real interest rates. When the real interest rate increases, investment spending and net export spending both decrease, offsetting some of the stimulative effect of the initial increase in government spending. At the conclusion of the adjustment process, income has increased from Y_1 to Y_2 (less than it would have increased had interest rates remained at r_1), and the real interest rate has increased from r_1 to r_2 as depicted in the graph above.

    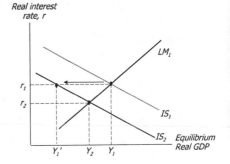

2. When autonomous investment spending, I_0, decreases, real income, Y, and the real interest rate, r, both decrease in the short run.

    Suppose the economy is initially in equilibrium at (r_1, Y_1). The decrease in autonomous investment spending creates unintended inventory accumulation, leading to a decrease in output of investment goods. A multiplier process ensues: The decreased income for the workers and owners of the firms producing investment goods causes them to decrease their consumption spending. At the existing interest rate, r_1, the amount of output that produces equilibrium in the markets for goods and services decreases by the autonomous change in investment spending times the spending multiplier, to Y_1', depicted as a shift to the left of the IS curve to IS_2.

As income and spending decrease toward Y_1', the transactions demand for money falls. But the central bank has not changed the money supply. People and businesses try to rid themselves of excess money by buying nonmoney assets in exchange for money, increasing the demand for nonmoney assets, increasing the price of nonmoney assets, and thus decreasing the rates of return and nominal interest rates associated with those nonmoney assets. As the nominal interest rate falls, the opportunity cost of holding money decreases, raising the real demand for money and thus closing some of the gap between the money supply and money demand that was created when income fell following the autonomous decrease in investment spending. So long as expected inflation is unchanged (and in this sticky-price model, we can safely make this assumption), the decrease in nominal interest rates corresponds to a decrease in real interest rates. When the real interest rate decreases, investment spending and net export spending both increase, offsetting some of the contractionary effect of the initial autonomous decrease in investment spending. At the conclusion of the adjustment process, income has decreased from Y_1 to Y_2 (a smaller decrease than would have resulted had interest rates remained at r_1), and the real interest rate has decreased from r_1 to r_2 as depicted in the graph above.

3. If the interest sensitivity of investment is high, then when the government increases its purchases by $75 billion, which increases income by $75 billion times the multiplier, causing money demand to increase, and thus causing real interest rates to increase, investment will decline sharply in response to the increase in real interest rates. Much of the beneficial effect of the increase in government purchases will be offset by a decrease in investment spending. The government's fiscal policy will therefore be only weakly expansionary.

4. If the interest sensitivity of investment is high, then when the central bank increases the money supply, which lowers the real interest rate, investment will rise sharply in response to the decline in the real interest rate. The central bank's monetary policy will therefore be strongly expansionary.

5. A reduction in autonomous consumption is depicted by a shift to the left of the IS curve. If the Fed targets the money supply, then the LM curve is upward sloping as shown in the graph at the right. Real interest rates decline and real GDP drops in reaction to the drop in consumer spending. If instead the Fed targets the real interest rate, then the LM curve would be horizontal at the existing real interest rate. The real interest rate would have remained at r_1 and real GDP would have declined all the way to Y_2'.

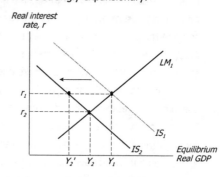

6. If the Fed targets interest rates, the LM curve is horizontal as shown with LM_r at the right. When the Fed targets interest rates and government purchases decrease as shown, the real interest rate does not change. As a result, there will be no change in gross exports.

On the other hand, if the Fed targets the money supply, the LM curve is upward sloping as shown with LM_{MS} at the right. In this case, when government purchases decrease, the real interest rate falls. A decline in the real interest rate increases the real exchange rate according to the equation $\varepsilon = \varepsilon_0 - \varepsilon_r(r - r^f)$, and gross exports increase with an increase in the real exchange rate. Therefore when the Fed targets the money supply, a drop in government purchases leads to an increase in gross exports. (The change in gross exports does not shift the IS curve. It is part of the reason the IS curve is downward sloping.)

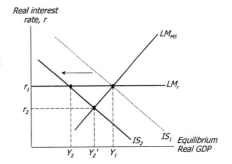

7. The Fed will run into trouble. If price deflation is minor, the Fed can lower real interest rates in an attempt to stimulate the economy and increase inflation. But the Fed cannot push the nominal interest rate below zero. When prices are falling, the real interest rate is greater than the nominal interest rate. The real interest rate cannot be pushed lower than the deflation rate. If prices are falling by 2 percent per year and are expected to continue falling at this rate, a nominal interest rate of zero corresponds to a real interest rate of 2 percent. The Fed can not push the real interest rate any lower than this.

D. EXPLAINING THE REAL WORLD

1. The increase in government spending – regardless of what the spending is for – has the positive effect of increasing real GDP and employment. But at the same time, an increase in government spending leads to an increase in real interest rates. Higher real interest rates "crowd out" investment spending. In the short run, the positive effect of increased government spending typically outweighs the negative effect of decreased investment spending. But in the long run, decreased investment spending can harm the economy's prospects for growth.

2. The development of online trading increases the ability of the federal government to use fiscal policy to change real GDP. The development of online trading decreases the costs of responding to changes in interest rates, and thus increases the interest sensitivity of velocity and money demand. Small changes in interest rates will result in relatively large changes in money demand. When the government conducts expansionary fiscal policy, income rises. The increase in income causes money demand to increase, which in turn leads to increased supply of nonmoney assets, decreased prices of nonmoney assets, and increases in the rates of return and nominal interest rates of nonmoney assets such as stocks and bonds. With online trading, a small increase in the rate of return on nonmoney assets can lead to a rapid reduction in money demand. A relatively small increase in real interest rates therefore brings the money market quickly back to equilibrium. Because the increase in interest rates is small, the offsetting decrease in investment and gross export spending will be relatively small. The effectiveness of expansionary fiscal policy in changing real GDP is increased.

3. The development of computer-based business analysis tools increases the ability of a central bank to change real GDP. The development of computer-based business analysis tools allows firms to respond more quickly to a change in interest rates, increasing the interest sensitivity of investment spending. Therefore when the central bank lowers the interest rate, business spending on investment increases more than it would have previously.

4. The Fed was struggling to prevent the economy from falling into a deep recession. If the Fed had not lowered interest rates, real GDP would have certainly declined markedly. By lowering interest rates the Fed was hoping to restore some investment and gross export spending, preventing or at least softening a recession.

    The Fed, which announces changes in the interest rate, targets interest rates. The LM curve should therefore be drawn as a horizontal line. Lowering the target interest rate shifts the LM curve down to LM_2. The drops in consumption and investment spending are depicted as a shift to the left of the IS curve to IS_2. If the Fed has successfully targeted the real interest rate, real GDP will remain at Y_1.

    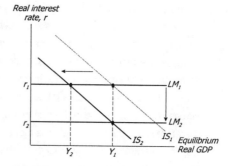

5. In general, a decrease in real interest rates leads to an increase in gross exports. This is one of the reasons the IS curve slopes downward; that is, one of the reasons that equilibrium output rises in responses to a decrease in real interest rates. But the responsiveness of gross exports to a change in real interest rates depends upon how long the drop in real interest rates is expected to remain in place. If speculators who buy and sell foreign currency think that the Fed's action is a short-term action that is likely to be reversed in a few months as economic activity in the United States rises, then the interest sensitivity of the exchange rate will be low. In this case, there will be little trading of currency in response to the Fed's changes in the interest rate, and thus little change in exchange rates, and thus little change in gross exports.

E. POSSIBILITIES TO PONDER

No solutions are given to these questions. The questions are designed to be somewhat open ended. Each question draws on your understanding of the concepts covered in this chapter.

Chapter 12

The Phillips Curve and Expectations

- The Phillips curve describes the supply-side relationship between the inflation rate and the unemployment rate. We can combine it with the monetary policy reaction function (MPRF), which describes the demand-side relationship between inflation and unemployment. In combination, the Phillips curve and the MPRF determine the equilibrium values of the inflation and unemployment rates.

- Expectations are an important determinant of the inflation rate. Expectations link the long-run view of the economy of Chapters 6, 7, and 8 with the short-run view of the economy of Chapters 9, 10, 11, and 12.

LEARNING GUIDE

This chapter is the payoff. If you have gotten this far, pat yourself on the back and get ready for a treat: we are about to pull everything in the previous eleven chapters together into one simple story about the short-run determinants of the unemployment and inflation rates. There is only one new model in Chapter 12: the Phillips curve. But everything we did in Chapters 9, 10, and 11 is folded into the new material presented in Chapter 12.

Because the material in Chapter 12 draws on the material in the previous chapter, you might find it useful to review parts of Chapter 11 as you work through Chapter 12. The key idea that you need from Chapter 11 is that the central bank targets the inflation rate, and it sets the real interest rate in reaction to the actual inflation rate.

Short on time?

 Check with your instructor to find out how much of the algebra you really need to know. It is unlikely that you will need to know how to derive the equations in Box 12.4.

Be sure you have an intuitive understanding of the material and can manipulate the graphs. You need to understand why the MPRF captures the demand-side of the economy. You need to be able to explain why and how the Phillips curve and the MPRF shift. And you need to understand the role of expectations in determining the responsiveness of the economy to a change in policy.

A. BASIC DEFINITIONS

Before you apply knowledge, you need a basic grasp of the fundamentals. In other words, there are some things you just have to know. Knowing the material in this section won't guarantee a good grade in the course, but not knowing it will guarantee a poor or failing grade.

USE THE WORDS OR PHRASES FROM THE LIST BELOW TO COMPLETE THE SENTENCES. SOME ARE USED MORE THAN ONCE; SOME ARE NOT USED AT ALL.

adaptive	*rational*
Okun's law	*real GDP*
Phillips curve	*static*
price inertia	*unemployment rate*

1. _____ expectations of inflation prevail when people think the inflation rate will be the same as it was last year.

2. Okun's law describes the relationship between the _____ and _____ .

> **NOTE:** You may want to review Chapter 2, where Okun's law was first presented. In the study guide, review Chapter 2, Section C, Question 9, and the "To The Chalkboard" box just before that question.

3. _____ presents the relationship between the unemployment rate and real GDP.

4. _____ expectations of inflation prevail when people think the inflation rate will be the same every year.

5. When the inflation rate is hardly changing from year to year, businesses are likely to hold _____ expectations.

6. When the lags in decision making make the economy behaves as if inflationary expectations are adaptive when in fact they are "rational," we say the economy displays _____ .

7. _____ expectations of inflation prevail when people think about how the inflation rate will depend upon fiscal and monetary policies and supply shocks.

8. The Aggregate Supply curve shows the relationship between the inflation rate and _____ .

9. The Phillips curve shows the relationship between the inflation rate and the

    _____ .

10. When the inflation rate is changing a great deal from year to year with no apparent time trend, businesses are likely to hold _____ expectations.

CIRCLE THE CORRECT WORD OR PHRASE IN EACH OF THE FOLLOWING SENTENCES.

11. If expectations are static / adaptive / rational, the economy is always in the long run.

12. When the Phillips curve is nearly vertical, even small movements in the unemployment rate can cause small / large changes in prices.

13. Under rational expectations, anticipated changes in economic policy have no / small / large effects on real GDP.

14. Under rational expectations, people form their forecasts of future inflation by looking backward / forward.

> **NOTE:** Saying expectations are "rational" does not necessarily mean the expectations are rational in the sense defined in the dictionary on your bookshelf. Nor does it mean that people have perfect understanding of how the economy functions. Nor does it mean that they have perfect foresight. It simply means that they form guesses about the future using all information that is readily available to them. Listen to the people around you. They are probably forming "rational" expectations all the time. When you hear someone say, "I'm worried about getting a job after graduation; I think the drop in consumer confidence means that the unemployment rate will stay high," and someone else responds, "I wouldn't worry too much; I heard that the Fed is supposed to be lowering interest rates again," you've just heard two expressions of "rational" expectations,

15. The stickier are wages and prices, the smaller / larger is the parameter β, and the flatter / steeper is the Phillips curve.

16. When the natural rate of unemployment is high, fiscal and monetary policy tools are relatively effective / ineffective in decreasing the unemployment rate.

SELECT THE ONE BEST ANSWER FOR EACH MULTIPLE-CHOICE QUESTION.

17. The Phillips curve
    A. shifts around as expected inflation changes.
    B. shifts around as the natural rate of unemployment changes.
    C. shifts around as both expected inflation and the natural rate of unemployment changes.
    D. is stable.

$\mathcal{B}$. Manipulation of Concepts and Models

Most instructors expect you to be able to do basic manipulation of the concepts. Being able to do so often means you can earn a C in a course. But if you want a better grade, you'll need to be able to complete this next section easily and move on to Sections C and D.

> **HINT**: Here is a quick guide to the three most important equations in Chapter 12.
>
> - Aggregate Supply Curve: $\dfrac{Y-Y^*}{Y^*} = \theta \cdot (\pi - \pi^e)$
>
> - Okun's law: $u = u^* - 0.4 \cdot \left(\dfrac{Y-Y^*}{Y^*}\right)$
>
> - Phillips curve: $\pi = \pi^e - \beta \cdot (u - u^*) + \varepsilon^s$

1. Suppose Okun's law can be expressed as $u - u^* = -0.4 \cdot \left(\dfrac{Y-Y^*}{Y^*}\right)$. Suppose the natural rate of unemployment, u^*, is 4 percent. Suppose potential output, Y^*, is \$10,000 billion.

> **HINT**: Remember to express an unemployment rate of 4 percent as $u = 0.04$.

A. If actual output is \$9,800 billion, what is the unemployment rate?

B. If actual output is \$9,600 billion, what is the unemployment rate?

2. Suppose the unemployment rate is 3 percentage points above the natural rate of unemployment. How large is the output gap, the gap between actual and potential output?

3. Suppose Okun's law can be expressed as $u - u^* = -0.4 \cdot \left(\dfrac{Y - Y^*}{Y^*} \right)$. Suppose autonomous consumption drops by $100 billion. Suppose the spending multiplier, $\dfrac{1}{1 - \left(C_y \cdot (1 - t) - IM_y \right)}$, equals 3. Suppose the Fed targets the real interest rate and does not change the interest rate despite the change in autonomous consumption spending.

    A. Suppose potential output equals $10,000. What effect does the drop in consumption spending have on the unemployment rate?

    B. Suppose instead that potential output equals $8,000. In this case, what effect does the drop in consumption spending have on the unemployment rate?

MATH: To follow part of the derivation in the next "To The Chalkboard" box, you must understand the concept of total differential. This math skill is covered in Chapter B.

TO THE CHALKBOARD:
Explaining Box 12.1: Okun's Law

Box 12.1 shows various ways to depict the relationship between output and unemployment. In general it makes sense that there is such a relationship: the more output that is produced, the more workers who are needed to produce output. And, in turn, the more workers who are employed, the lower is unemployment. Okun's law takes this very intuitive relationship and simply specifies how **much** unemployment falls when output rises.

Late twentieth-century data indicate that for every 1 percentage point increase in the gap between actual output (real GDP) and potential output, the unemployment rate falls by 0.4 percentage points.

$$u - u^* = -0.4 \cdot \left(\frac{Y - Y^*}{Y^*} \right)$$

In Box 12.1, Prof. DeLong manipulates this basic Okun's law equation. The first change is a quick bit of algebra that changes the focus of the equation from "What happens to the unemployment rate when output changes?" to "How much of a change in output must policy-makers generate if they want to alter the unemployment rate?"

$$u - u^* = -0.4 \cdot \left(\frac{Y - Y^*}{Y^*} \right) \qquad \textit{Okun's Law}$$

$$-2.5 \cdot (u - u^*) = \left(\frac{Y - Y^*}{Y^*} \right) \qquad \textit{dividing both sides by } -0.4$$

The second equation above indicates that lowering the unemployment rate by 1 percentage point requires a 2.5 percentage point increase in real GDP relative to potential output.

The next manipulation in Box 12.1 allows us to look at the relationship between changes in the unemployment rate and in real GDP. The best way to derive the relationship uses the calculus concept of total differential. If you haven't had calculus, you can just skip the derivation. Again, start from the usual expression of Okun's law.

$$u - u^* = -0.4 \cdot \left(\frac{Y - Y^*}{Y^*} \right) \qquad \textit{Okun's Law}$$

$$u - u^* = -0.4 \cdot \left(\frac{Y}{Y^*} - 1 \right) \qquad \textit{simplifying}$$

$$d\left[u - u^* \right] = d\left[-0.4 \cdot \left(\frac{Y}{Y^*} - 1 \right) \right] \qquad \textit{take the total differential of both sides}$$

$$du - du^* = -0.4 \cdot d\left(\frac{Y}{Y^*} - 1 \right) \qquad \textit{applying calculus rules}$$

$$du - du^* = -0.4 \cdot \left[d\left(\frac{Y}{Y^*} \right) - d(1) \right] \qquad \textit{applying calculus rules}$$

$$du - du^* = -0.4 \cdot \left[\frac{\partial}{\partial Y}\left(\frac{Y}{Y^*} \right) dY + \frac{\partial}{\partial Y^*}\left(\frac{Y}{Y^*} \right) dY^* - 0 \right] \qquad \textit{applying total differential rule}$$

$$du - du^* = -0.4 \cdot \left[\left(\frac{1}{Y^*} \right) dY - \left(\frac{Y}{Y^* \cdot Y^*} \right) dY^* \right] \qquad \textit{taking partial derivatives}$$

$$du - du^* = -0.4 \cdot \left[\frac{dY}{Y^*} - \left(\frac{Y}{Y^*} \cdot \frac{dY^*}{Y^*} \right) \right] \qquad \textit{simplifying}$$

At this point, we need to introduce an assumption. **Assume that Y/Y* is approximately 1.** The assumption is a bit of a problem in the short run; it says that there is never any unemployment above the natural rate. But we can invoke the assumption and come up with some interesting observations.

$$du - du^* = -0.4 \cdot \left[\frac{dY}{Y^*} - \left(1 \cdot \frac{dY^*}{Y^*} \right) \right] \qquad \textit{assume } \frac{Y}{Y^*} \approx 1$$

$$\Delta u - \Delta u^* = -0.4 \cdot \left(\frac{\Delta Y}{Y^*} - \frac{\Delta Y^*}{Y^*} \right) \qquad \textit{differentials are equivalent to changes } (\Delta)$$

$$\Delta u - 0 = -0.4 \cdot \left(\frac{\Delta Y}{Y^*} - \frac{\Delta Y^*}{Y^*} \right) \qquad \Delta u^* = 0 \textit{ because NRU is constant}$$

$$\Delta u = -0.4 \cdot \left(\frac{\Delta Y}{Y^*} - (n + g) \right) \qquad \textit{assume potential output, } Y^*, \textit{ grows at rate } (n + g)$$

You might want to flip to the textbook, Chapter 4, pp. 94 - 95 at this point. We've assumed that potential output grows at the rate n + g, where n is the rate of growth of the labor force and g is the rate of growth of labor efficiency.

The equation makes an important point: If actual output is growing, but does not grow fast enough to keep up with growth in the labor force (n) and in labor efficiency (g), then unemployment will rise. The U.S. economy experienced such a "**growth recession**" in the early 1990s; both unemployment and real GDP were increasing.

4. If potential output grows at the rate n + g, and assuming Y/Y* is approximately 1, we can derive the equation $\frac{\Delta Y}{Y^*} = (n + g) - 2.5 \cdot \Delta u$.

A. Suppose that this year's unemployment rate is 4 percent, the labor force is growing by 2 percent per year, labor efficiency is constant from year to year, potential output is initially $10,000 billion, and output is increasing by $200 billion per year. What will the unemployment rate be next year?

B. Assume the above, but suppose instead that labor efficiency is increasing by 2 percent annually. In this case, what will the unemployment rate be next year?

C. Why does the unemployment rate increase if real GDP is growing, but at a slower rate than the rate of growth of potential output?

NOTE: Do you remember why prices rise when output increases? If not, review the last section of Chapter 11 in the textbook. You might also want to review Study Guide Chapter 11, Section B, Questions 33 and 34, where the Aggregate Supply equation was first presented

5. The Aggregate Supply equation can be expressed as a relationship between the inflation rate and the level of real GDP: $\frac{Y - Y^*}{Y^*} = \theta \cdot (\pi - \pi^e)$. Suppose potential output is $10,000 billion, actual output is $9,600 billion, the expected inflation rate is 2 percent, and $\theta = 5$.

A. What is the actual inflation rate?

B. Why is the inflation rate below the expected inflation rate when output is below potential output?

TO THE CHALKBOARD:
Deriving the Phillips Curve

On pages 332-333 of the textbook, the equation for the Phillips curve is derived. Here we go through the derivation step-by-step.

Start with two relationships that were previously introduced:

- The AS Curve: $\dfrac{y - y^*}{y^*} = \theta \cdot (\pi - \pi^e)$

- Okun's law: $-2.5 \cdot (u - u^*) = \dfrac{y - y^*}{y^*}$

Now equate the two expressions for the output gap and then simplify.

$$\theta \cdot \left(\pi - \pi^e\right) = \frac{y - y^*}{y^*} = -2.5 \cdot (u - u^*) \qquad \textit{AS curve and Okun's Law both define output gap}$$

$$\pi - \pi^e = \frac{-2.5}{\theta} \cdot (u - u^*) \qquad \textit{dividing both sides by } \theta$$

$$\pi = \pi^e - \frac{2.5}{\theta} \cdot (u - u^*) \qquad \textit{adding } \pi^e \textit{ to both sides}$$

Remembering $\dfrac{2.5}{\theta}$ is a bit cumbersome, so define $\beta = \dfrac{2.5}{\theta}$. We then have

$$\pi = \pi^e - \beta \cdot (u - u^*)$$

The inflation rate equals the expected inflation rate minus some proportion of the gap between the actual unemployment rate and the natural rate of unemployment. The higher is unemployment, the lower is inflation.

And then add one more thing, not based on any equation we have seen so far, but rather on logic, intuition, (and research by economists): sometimes the inflation rate changes because there are "supply shocks" to the economy that alter the inflation rate. The most famous such supply shock is the oil price shock of the mid-1970s when the price of a barrel of oil tripled in a very short period of time.

The symbol is a bit of a problem. The textbook uses ε^s to stand for the supply shock. You have to forget that you've seen ε before. ε^s has nothing to do with the exchange rate. ε^s is the change in the inflation rate due to a supply shock. (Because we already used ε to stand for the real exchange rate, the symbol will no doubt be changed in future editions of the textbook.)

$$\pi = \pi^e - \beta \cdot (u - u^*) + \varepsilon^s$$

The inflation rate depends upon the expected rate of inflation, the actual rate of unemployment (and thus on actual real GDP), the natural rate of unemployment, and supply shocks.

NOTE: The factor θ measures the extent to which prices change in response to changes in real GDP.

6.   The Phillips curve equation is $\pi = \pi^e - \dfrac{2.5}{\theta}\cdot(u - u^*) + \varepsilon^s$.

   A. Suppose there are no supply shocks, the natural rate of unemployment is 4 percent, the actual unemployment rate is 5.6 percent, the value of θ is 5, and the expected inflation rate is 2 percent. What is the inflation rate? Plot this combination of unemployment rate and inflation rate on the graph below. Label it "A."

   B. Assuming the above, suppose instead the actual unemployment rate is 4.0 percent. In that case, what is the inflation rate? Plot this combination of unemployment rate and inflation rate on the graph below. Label it "B."

   C. Assuming the above, suppose instead the unemployment rate is 3 percent. In that case, what is the inflation rate? Plot this combination of unemployment rate and inflation rate on the graph at the right. Label it "C."

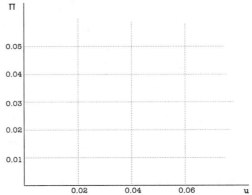

   D. Connect the three points in the graph with a smooth curve. What is the name of the curve you have drawn?

7.   The Phillips curve equation is $\pi = \pi^e - \beta\cdot(u - u^*) + \varepsilon^s$. Suppose the natural rate of unemployment is 4 percent, the actual unemployment rate is 6 percent, the value of β is 0.5, and the expected inflation rate is 2 percent.

   A. Suppose there are no supply shocks. What is the inflation rate?

   B. Suppose instead that there is a supply shock that increases the inflation rate by 3 percent. In this case, what is the inflation rate?

8. The aggregate supply equation is $\dfrac{Y-Y^*}{Y^*} = \theta \cdot (\pi - \pi^e)$. The Okun's law equation is

$u = u^* - 0.4\left(\dfrac{Y-Y^*}{Y^*}\right)$. The Phillips curve equation is derived by combining the AS

equation and Okun's law. The Phillips curve equation is $\pi = \pi^e - \beta \cdot (u - u^*) + \varepsilon^s$.
Suppose $\theta = 5$ and therefore $\beta = 2.5 / \theta = 0.5$. Suppose potential output is \$10,000
billion, the natural rate of unemployment is 4 percent, the expected inflation rate is 2
percent, and there are no supply shocks.

A. Using the aggregate supply equation, express inflation, π, as a function of the other
variables.

B. For each value of income given in the table, use the aggregate supply equation you derived in Part A to calculate the inflation rate. Write your answers in the table at the right.

Y	AS		PC	
	π	u		π
9,000				
9,500				
10,000				
10,500				
11,000				

C. For each value of income given in the table, use Okun's law to calculate the
unemployment rate. Then use the Phillips curve equation to calculate the inflation
rate. Write your answers in the table at the right.

D. Using the left-hand set of axes below, plot the combinations of income and inflation
rate you found using the aggregate supply equation. Connect the points with a
smooth line. Label the line "AS."

E. Using the right-hand set of axes below, plot the combinations of unemployment rate
and inflation rate you found using the Phillips curve equation. Connect the points
with a smooth line. Label the line "PC."

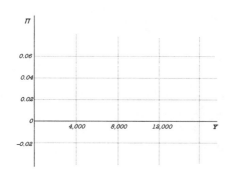
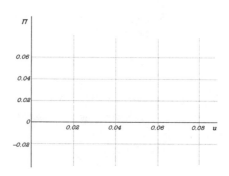

F. Congratulations! You have just replicated textbook Figure 12.2. Explain why the aggregate supply relationship between inflation and output can be expressed instead as the Phillips curve relationship between inflation and unemployment.

9. The Phillips curve equation is $\pi = \pi^e - \beta \cdot (u - u^*) + \varepsilon^s$. Suppose the expected inflation rate is 2 percent, the natural rate of unemployment is 4 percent, and there are no supply shocks to inflation.

A. Complete the table below.

	$\beta = 0.1$	$\beta = 0.5$	$\beta = 1.0$	$\beta = 5.0$
	π	π	π	π
$u = 1\%$				
$u = 3\%$				
$u = 4\%$				
$u = 5\%$				
$u = 8\%$				

B. Using the axes at the right, plot the Phillips curve for $\beta = 0.1$. Label it "PC_1."

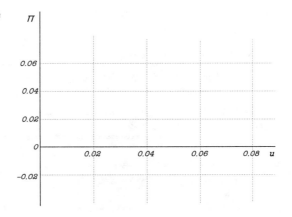

C. Using the same axes, plot the Phillips curve for $\beta = 1$. Label it "PC_2."

D. Does a higher value of β correspond to more or less price flexibility? When prices are very flexible, does a 1 percentage point increase in the unemployment rate cause a large or small change in the inflation rate? Explain.

10. Compare the two Phillips curves in the graph at the right.

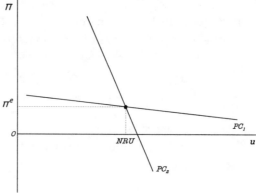

A. When is β larger: PC_1 or PC_2?

B. When are prices more flexible: PC_1 or PC_2?

C. When government purchases increase, in which case will the increase in government purchases have the larger effect on inflation: PC_1 or PC_2?

11. The Phillips curve equation is $\pi = \pi^e - \beta \cdot (u - u^*) + \varepsilon^s$. Suppose the expected inflation rate is 2 percent, the natural rate of unemployment is 4 percent, and $\beta = 0.5$.

A. Complete the table below.

	$\varepsilon^s = 0$ π	$\varepsilon^s = 0.04$ π	$\varepsilon^s = -0.03$ π
u = 1 %			
u = 3 %			
u = 4 %			
u = 5 %			
u = 8 %			

B. Using the axes at the right, plot the Phillips curve for $\varepsilon^s = 0$. Label it "PC_1."

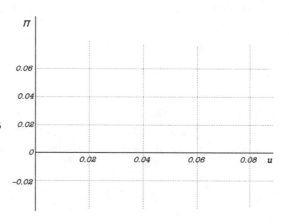

C. Using the same axes, plot the Phillips curve for $\varepsilon^s = 0.04$. Label it "PC_2."

D. Using the same axes, plot the Phillips curve for $\varepsilon^s = -0.03$. Label it "PC_3."

12. The Phillips curve equation is $\pi = \pi^e - \beta \cdot (u - u^*) + \varepsilon^s$. Suppose there are no supply shocks, the natural rate of unemployment is 4 percent, and $\beta = 0.5$.

   A. Complete the table below.

	$\pi^e = 0.02$ π	$\pi^e = 0.04$ π	$\pi^e = 0.06$ π
u = 1 %			
u = 3 %			
u = 4 %			
u = 5 %			
u = 8 %			

   B. Using the axes at the right, plot the Phillips curve for $\pi^e = 0.02$. Label it "PC$_1$."

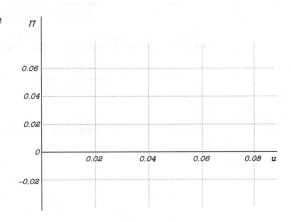

   C. Using the same axes, plot the Phillips curve for $\pi^e = 0.04$. Label it "PC$_2$."

   D. Using the same axes, plot the Phillips curve for $\pi^e = 0.06$. Label it "PC$_3$."

13. The Phillips curve equation is $\pi = \pi^e - \beta \cdot (u - u^*) + \varepsilon^s$. Suppose the expected inflation rate is 2 percent, there are no supply shocks, and $\beta = 0.5$.

   A. Complete the table below.

	$u^* = 0.04$ π	$u^* = 0.05$ π	$u^* = 0.08$ π
u = 1 %			
u = 3 %			
u = 4 %			
u = 5 %			
u = 8 %			

B. Using the axes at the right, plot the Phillips curve for u* = 0.04. Label it "PC$_1$."

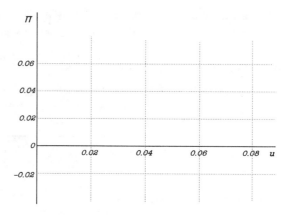

C. Using the same axes, plot the Phillips curve for u* = 0.05. Label it "PC$_2$."

D. Using the same axes, plot the Phillips curve for u* = 0.08. Label it "PC$_3$."

TO THE CHALKBOARD:
Reviewing Chapter 11's Monetary Policy Reaction Function

The "monetary policy reaction function" (MPRF) was first presented in Chapter 11. You may want to review pp. 322 - 324 of the textbook and Questions 27 - 32 of Section B of study guide Chapter 11.

The MPRF, based on work by John Taylor, asserts that the central bank's monetary policy reacts to changes in the inflation rate. In particular, the central bank adjusts the real interest rate if the inflation rate is not equal to the bank's target inflation rate. The "Taylor rule" expresses this relationship as

$$r = r^* + \phi'' \cdot (\pi - \pi')$$

where r^* is the central bank's notion of the "normal" value of the real interest rate, π' is their target inflation rate, and ϕ'' is the responsiveness of the central bank's real interest rate target, r, to differences between the actual inflation rate, π, and the target inflation rate. The larger is ϕ'', the more contractionary is monetary policy in reaction to a rise in the inflation rate.

If the inflation rate equals the central bank's target inflation rate, then the real interest rate equals its normal value, $r = r^*$. The aggregate demand relationship presented in the previous chapters then determines how much output is produced in equilibrium. Let Y_0 represent this level of "output at 'normal' real interest rates."

$$Y_0 = \frac{A_0}{1 - MPE} - \frac{(I_r + X_\varepsilon \varepsilon_r)}{1 - MPE} \cdot r^*$$

If the inflation rate is different than the central bank's target, the central bank will change the interest rate using the "Taylor rule." For any value of inflation, π, the equilibrium level of output is

$$y = \frac{A_0}{1 - MPE} - \frac{(I_r + X_\varepsilon \varepsilon_r)}{1 - MPE} \cdot \left[r^* + \phi'' \cdot (\pi - \pi') \right]$$

This expression for equilibrium output can be simplified.

$$y = \frac{A_0}{1 - MPE} - \frac{(I_r + X_\varepsilon \varepsilon_r)}{1 - MPE} \cdot r^* - \frac{(I_r + X_\varepsilon \varepsilon_r)}{1 - MPE} \cdot \left[\phi'' \cdot (\pi - \pi') \right] \qquad \textit{distributing}$$

$$y = Y_0 - \frac{(I_r + X_\varepsilon \varepsilon_r)}{1 - MPE} \cdot \left[\phi'' \cdot (\pi - \pi') \right] \qquad \textit{substituting } Y_0$$

$$y = Y_0 - \phi' \cdot (\pi - \pi') \qquad \textit{defining } \phi' = \frac{(I_r + X_\varepsilon \varepsilon_r)}{1 - MPE} \cdot \phi''$$

When the inflation rate is above the target inflation rate, $\pi > \pi'$, the central bank raises the real interest rate above its normal level. The extent to which the central bank raises the real interest rate depends upon the size of ϕ''. But at a higher real interest rate, investment and gross export spending are lower. The extent to which investment and gross export spending decline depends upon the size of $I_r + X_\varepsilon \varepsilon_r$. And when investment and gross exports spending decline, the spending multiplier leads to round after round of declines in consumer spending for domestically produced goods, so that the total drop in income is greater than just the drop in investment and gross export spending. The extent to which consumer spending for domestically produced goods declines depends upon the size of MPE. All of these factors that reduce real income are summarized with one symbol, ϕ'. When the inflation rate rises above the target inflation rate, then, real income declines by an amount equal to $\phi' \cdot (\pi - \pi')$.

TO THE CHALKBOARD:
Deriving Chapter 12's Monetary Policy Reaction Function

In Chapter 11, the monetary policy reaction function (MPRF) was expressed as a relationship between output and inflation:

$$Y = Y_0 - \phi' \cdot (\pi - \pi')$$

But it would be more helpful if we could express it as a relationship between unemployment and inflation. That is straightforward, because Okun's law tells us that actual output relative to potential output determines the unemployment rate. The unemployment rate for any level of output, Y, is

$$u = u^* - 0.4\left(\frac{Y - Y^*}{Y^*}\right)$$

So the unemployment rate for output level Y_0, the equilibrium level of output when interest rates are at their "normal" level, is

$$u_0 = u^* - 0.4\left(\frac{Y_0 - Y^*}{Y^*}\right)$$

Now we can derive the MPRF as a relationship between unemployment and inflation.

$$u = u^* - 0.4\left(\frac{Y - Y^*}{Y^*}\right) \qquad \textit{Okun's Law}$$

$$u = u^* - 0.4\left(\frac{Y_0 - \phi' \cdot (\pi - \pi') - Y^*}{Y^*}\right) \qquad \textit{substituting } Y_0 - \phi'(\pi - \pi')$$

$$u = u^* - 0.4\left(\frac{Y_0 - Y^*}{Y^*}\right) + \frac{0.4 \cdot \phi' \cdot (\pi - \pi')}{Y^*} \qquad \textit{distributing 0.4 and rearranging terms}$$

$$u = u_0 + \frac{0.4 \cdot \phi' \cdot (\pi - \pi')}{Y^*} \qquad \textit{substituting } u_0$$

$$u = u_0 + \phi \cdot (\pi - \pi') \qquad \textit{defining } \phi \textit{ as } \frac{0.4 \cdot \phi'}{Y^*}$$

The higher is the inflation rate, the higher the central bank pushes interest rates. But higher interest rates lower equilibrium output and thus raise the unemployment rate.

14. A. Using the axes at the right, graph the monetary policy reaction function, MPRF. Label your axes and your curve.

   B. In the same graph, graph the Phillips curve.

   C. Label the equilibrium point.

15. Suppose the graph at the right depicts the original positions of the Fed's monetary policy reaction function (MPRF) and the economy's Phillips curve (PC).

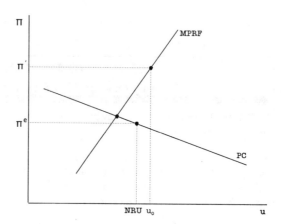

   A. If the natural rate of unemployment, u^*, increases, what effect does this have on the MPRF? On the PC? On the equilibrium level of inflation and unemployment in the economy?

   B. If the expected rate of inflation, π^e, increases, what effect does this have on the MPRF? On the PC? On the equilibrium level of inflation and unemployment in the economy?

   C. If an adverse supply shock, ε^S, affects the economy, what effect does this have on the MPRF? On the PC? On the equilibrium level of inflation and unemployment in the economy?

   D. If the level of unemployment, u_0, generated when the central bank sets the real interest rate at its target rate increases, what effect does this have on the MPRF? On the PC? On the equilibrium level of inflation and unemployment in the economy?

   E. If the central bank's target inflation rate, π', increases, what effect does this have on the MPRF? On the PC? On the equilibrium level of inflation and unemployment in the economy?

TO THE CHALKBOARD:
Explaining Box 12.3

The monetary policy reaction function, MPRF, is $u = u_0 + \phi \cdot (\pi - \pi')$. Box 12.3 sets out the determinants of ϕ.

Remember that

$$\phi = \frac{0.4 \cdot \phi'}{y^*} \quad \text{and} \quad \phi' = \frac{\left(I_r + X_\varepsilon \varepsilon_r\right)}{1 - MPE} \cdot \phi''$$

where ϕ'' is the extent to which the central bank monetary policy reacts to a change in the inflation rate. Combining these two expressions yields

$$\phi = \frac{0.4 \cdot \dfrac{\left(I_r + X_\varepsilon \varepsilon_r\right)}{1 - MPE} \cdot \phi''}{y^*} = \frac{1}{2.5} \cdot \dfrac{\dfrac{\left(I_r + X_\varepsilon \varepsilon_r\right)}{1 - MPE} \cdot \phi''}{y^*}$$

In previous chapters we defined MPE:

$$MPE = C_y \cdot (1 - t) - IM_y$$

So we have

$$\phi = \frac{1}{2.5} \cdot \left(I_r + X_\varepsilon \varepsilon_r\right) \cdot \frac{1}{1 - \left[C_y \cdot (1 - t) - IM_y\right]} \cdot \phi'' \cdot \frac{1}{y^*}$$

The determinants of the first four of the five factors that comprise ϕ are discussed in Box 12.3.

TO THE CHALKBOARD:
Explaining Box 12.4

In Box 12.4, Prof. DeLong derives the algebraic expressions for the equilibrium values of the unemployment rate and the inflation rate. Here is a step-by-step explanation of the derivation.

Start with the expressions for the aggregate demand and aggregate supply relationships. Aggregate demand is captured with the monetary policy reaction function (MPRF):

$$u = u_0 + \phi \cdot (\pi - \pi')$$

Aggregate supply is captured with the Phillips curve:

$$\pi = \pi^e - \beta \cdot (u - u^*) + \varepsilon^s$$

Now manipulate the MPRF equation until you have inflation isolated on the left-hand side,

$u = u_0 + \phi(\pi - \pi')$	*MPRF*
$u - u_0 = \phi(\pi - \pi')$	*subtracting u_0 from both sides*
$\dfrac{u - u_0}{\phi} = \pi - \pi'$	*dividing both sides by ϕ*
$\dfrac{u - u_0}{\phi} + \pi' = \pi$	*adding π' to both sides*
$\dfrac{u - u_0 + \phi \cdot \pi'}{\phi} = \pi$	*making ϕ the common denominator*

Now equate the MPRF and the Phillips curve and simplify. The result is a mess, but it tells you something.

$$\frac{u - u_0 + \phi \cdot \pi'}{\phi} = \pi = \pi^e - \beta \cdot (u - u^*) + \varepsilon^s \qquad \textit{equating MPRF and PC expressions}$$

$$u - u_0 + \phi \cdot \pi' = \phi \cdot \pi^e - \phi \cdot \beta \cdot (u - u^*) + \phi \cdot \varepsilon^s \qquad \textit{multiplying both sides by } \phi$$

$$u - u_0 + \phi \cdot \pi' = \phi \cdot \pi^e - \phi \cdot \beta \cdot u + \phi \cdot \beta \cdot u^* + \phi \cdot \varepsilon^s \qquad \textit{distributing } \phi \cdot \beta$$

$$u + \phi \cdot \beta \cdot u = u_0 + \phi \cdot \pi^e + \phi \cdot \beta \cdot u^* - \phi \cdot \pi' + \phi \cdot \varepsilon^s \qquad \textit{adding } u_0 + \phi \cdot \beta \cdot u, \textit{ subtracting } \phi \cdot \pi'$$

$$(1 + \phi \cdot \beta) \cdot u = u_0 + \phi \cdot \pi^e + \phi \cdot \beta \cdot u^* - \phi \cdot \pi' + \phi \cdot \varepsilon^s \qquad \textit{factoring out } u$$

$$(1 + \phi \cdot \beta) \cdot u = u_0 + \phi \cdot \beta \cdot u^* + \phi \cdot \pi^e - \phi \cdot \pi' + \phi \cdot \varepsilon^s \qquad \textit{rearranging terms}$$

$$u = \frac{u_0 + \phi \cdot \beta \cdot u^* + \phi \cdot \pi^e - \phi \cdot \pi' + \phi \cdot \varepsilon^s}{1 + \phi \cdot \beta} \qquad \textit{dividing by } (1 + \phi \cdot \beta)$$

And then just break up that fraction and group terms to get the expression in the text:

$$u = \left(\frac{1}{1 + \phi \cdot \beta} \cdot u_0 + \frac{\phi \cdot \beta}{1 + \phi \cdot \beta} \cdot u^* \right) + \frac{\phi}{1 + \phi \cdot \beta} \cdot (\pi^e - \pi') + \frac{\phi}{1 + \phi \cdot \beta} \cdot \varepsilon^s$$

The equation tells you that the actual unemployment rate depends upon

- u_0, the unemployment rate when the central bank sets the real interest rate to its "normal" level
- u^*, the natural rate of unemployment
- π^e, the expected rate of inflation
- π', the central bank's target rate of inflation
- ε^s, supply shocks
- ϕ and β, the parameters of the MPRF and the Phillips curve

To obtain an expression for the equilibrium value of the inflation rate, we substitute the MPRF,

$$u = u_0 + \phi \cdot (\pi - \pi')$$

into the expression for the Phillips curve

$$\pi = \pi^e - \beta \cdot (u - u^*) + \varepsilon^s$$

and simplify.

$$\pi = \pi^e - \beta \cdot (u - u^*) + \varepsilon^s \qquad \textit{Phillips curve}$$

$$\pi = \pi^e - \beta \cdot [u_0 + \phi \cdot (\pi - \pi') - u^*] + \varepsilon^s \qquad \textit{substituting MPRF's expression of } u$$

$$\pi = \pi^e - \beta \cdot u_0 - \beta \cdot \phi \cdot (\pi - \pi') + \beta \cdot u^* + \varepsilon^s \qquad \textit{distributing } -\beta$$

$$\pi = \pi^e - \beta \cdot u_0 - \beta \cdot \phi \cdot \pi + \beta \cdot \phi \cdot \pi' + \beta \cdot u^* + \varepsilon^s \qquad \textit{distributing } -\beta \cdot \phi$$

$$\pi + \beta \cdot \phi \cdot \pi = \pi^e - \beta \cdot u_0 + \beta \cdot \phi \cdot \pi' + \beta \cdot u^* + \varepsilon^s \qquad \textit{adding } \beta \cdot \phi \cdot \pi$$

$$(1 + \beta \cdot \phi) \cdot \pi = \pi^e + \beta \cdot \phi \cdot \pi' + \beta \cdot u^* - \beta \cdot u_0 + \varepsilon^s \qquad \textit{rearranging terms}$$

$$(1 + \beta \cdot \phi) \cdot \pi = \pi^e + \beta \cdot \phi \cdot \pi' + \beta \cdot u^* - \beta \cdot u_0 + \varepsilon^s \qquad \textit{factoring out } \pi$$

$$\pi = \frac{\pi^e + \beta \cdot \phi \cdot \pi' + \beta \cdot u^* - \beta \cdot u_0 + \varepsilon^s}{1 + \beta \cdot \phi} \qquad \textit{dividing by } (1 + \beta \cdot \phi)$$

And then just break up that fraction and group terms to get the expression in the text:

$$\pi = \left(\frac{1}{1 + \phi \cdot \beta} \cdot \pi^e + \frac{\phi \cdot \beta}{1 + \phi \cdot \beta} \cdot \pi' \right) + \frac{\beta}{1 + \phi \cdot \beta} \cdot (u^* - u_0) + \frac{1}{1 + \phi \cdot \beta} \cdot \varepsilon^s$$

The equation tells you that the actual inflation rate depends upon the same six factors that determine the actual unemployment rate.

16. Suppose the graph at the right depicts the original positions of the Fed's monetary policy reaction function (MPRF) and the economy's Phillips curve (PC). Now suppose there is an increase in government purchases, G_0. What effect does the increase in government purchases have on the MPRF? On the PC? On the equilibrium level of inflation and unemployment in the economy?

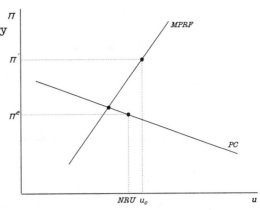

17. The definition of the natural rate of unemployment (NRU) is the rate of unemployment such that the actual and expected inflation rates are equal, and there is no change in the inflation rate over time. Give three factors that can cause the NRU to change.

18. Do economists know with certainty what determines the natural rate of unemployment?

19. The inflation rate in the United States averaged about 1.5 percent in the 1950s. If people had static expectations, what inflation rate did they expect for 1960? For 1965? For 1969? For 1975? Look at the inflation rate data that is at the back of the textbook. Do you think people had static expectations in 1960? 1965? 1969? 1975?

20. When individuals hold adaptive expectations, they think that this year's inflation rate will be the same as last year's inflation rate: $\pi^e_t = \pi_{t-1}$. Using the inflation data at the back of your textbook and assuming adaptive expectations, complete the table at the right.

	π^e_t
t = 1968	
t = 1969	
t = 1991	
t = 1992	

21. The Phillips curve relates inflation and unemployment: $\pi = \pi^e - \beta \cdot (u - u^*) + \epsilon^s$. Suppose there are no supply shocks. Suppose $\beta = 0.5$. Suppose last year's inflation rate was 3 percent. Suppose individuals hold adaptive expectations, $\pi^e_t = \pi_{t-1}$.

   A. Suppose the Fed adjusts the real interest rate from year to year so that the unemployment rate always equals the natural rate of unemployment. Describe what will happen to the inflation rate over time.

B. Suppose instead that the Fed adjusts the real interest rate from year to year in order to keep the unemployment rate, u, 1 percentage point below the NRU. Describe what will happen to the inflation rate over time.

C. Suppose instead that the Fed adjusts the real interest rate from year to year in order to keep the unemployment rate, u, 2 percentage points above the NRU. Describe what will happen to the inflation rate over time.

D. Is the course of action described in Part B or in Part C likely to happen in the real world? Explain.

22. Suppose the graph at the right depicts the original positions of the Fed's monetary policy reaction function (MPRF) and the economy's Phillips curve (PC). Suppose expectations are "rational."

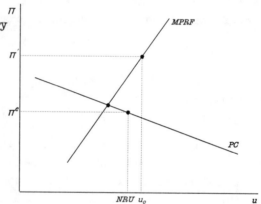

A. Suppose there is an increase in government purchases that comes as a surprise. What effect will the policy have on the MPRF? On the PC? On the equilibrium levels of the inflation rate and the unemployment rate?

B. Suppose there is an increase in government purchases that has been fully anticipated. What effect will the policy have on the MPRF? On the PC? On the equilibrium levels of the inflation rate and the unemployment rate?

C. Suppose there is a decrease in real interest rates that comes as a surprise. What effect will the policy have on the MPRF? On the PC? On the equilibrium levels of the inflation rate and the unemployment rate?

D. Suppose there is a decrease in real interest rates that has been fully anticipated. What effect will the policy have on the MPRF? On the PC? On the equilibrium levels of the inflation rate and the unemployment rate?

23. Suppose the graph at the right depicts the original positions of the Fed's monetary policy reaction function (MPRF) and the economy's Phillips curve (PC). Suppose the government then undertakes expansionary fiscal policy.

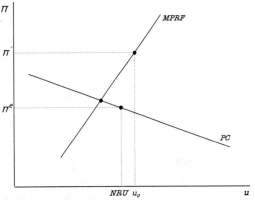

A. Suppose expectations are "rational" and the policy is fully anticipated. What effect does the expansionary fiscal policy have on unemployment and inflation?

B. Suppose instead that expectations are adaptive. In this case, what effect does the expansionary fiscal policy have on unemployment and inflation?

C. Suppose instead that expectations are static. In this case, what effect does the expansionary fiscal policy have on unemployment and inflation?

$\boldsymbol{C}$. APPLYING CONCEPTS AND MODELS

Now we're getting to the good stuff. Being able to apply a specific concept or model to a real world situation — where you are told which model to apply but you have to figure out how to apply it — is often what you need to earn a B in a course. This is where macroeconomics starts to become interesting and the world starts to make more sense.

1. When the economy goes into recession, unemployment rises and income falls. When they economy experiences a boom, unemployment falls and income rises. In general, what can you say about the distribution of unemployment in a recession? Who experiences unemployment? Who fears or expects it? Is the distribution of unemployment the same as the distribution of gains that workers receive during a boom? Is the distribution of the fear of recession the same as the distribution of the expectation of gains during a boom?

2. Pages 524 - 525 of your textbook present economic data for the last four decades of the twentieth century.

   A. Use the AS equation to explain why inflation was increasing from 1965 to 1969.

   B. Use the Phillips curve equation to explain why inflation was increasing from 1965 to 1969.

3. Suppose firms experience an unexpected change in their inventory holdings. Businesses will respond to this signal that they are not producing an equilibrium amount of output. When prices are relatively flexible, do businesses rely more on changes in output or on changes in prices? When prices are relatively flexible, is the Phillips curve relatively flat or relatively steep? What unemployment rate "anchors" the Phillips curve?

4. Look at the inflation data at the back of the textbook. During what period do you suppose people had static expectations? When do you suppose they had adaptive expectations? Rational expectations? Does it surprise you to learn that the idea of "rational expectations" did not exist in 1966? Explain.

5. The Kennedy-Johnson tax cuts were implemented in the early 1960s by the Kennedy and Johnson administrations in an effort to decrease unemployment without spurring a higher inflation rate. The tax cuts were phased in slowly over a period of years. What effect did the slow pace of implementation probably have on the Phillips curve?

D. EXPLAINING THE REAL WORLD

Most instructors are delighted when you are able to figure out which concept or model to apply to a real world situation. Being able to do so means you thoroughly understand the material and is often what you need to do to earn an A in a course. This is where you experience the power of macroeconomic theory.

1. A policy activist argues that the government should devote resources to ending labor market discrimination. Policies that decrease labor market discrimination, she argues, can decrease the inflation rate. Explain.

2. In many inner-cities, school boards have introduced "academies" into the high school. A student who enrolls in an "academy" within a high school receives job-specific training and internships while earning a high school diploma. For instance, students in a "health academy" would take classes that focused on biology and physiology and would be placed in internships at local doctor's offices and hospitals. What effect would successful academies have on the NRU? On the inflation rate?

3. Government purchases were increased and taxes were decreased following the September 11 attack. Prior to September 11, the inflation rate had been in the range of 1.5 to 2.0 percent. After September 11, what do you suppose happened to people's expectations of the inflation rate? Explain.

4. To increase economic literacy, many high schools now require all graduates to complete one semester of economics prior to graduation. In a time of economic uncertainty, why would we want the population to be economically literate?

5. Tax "rebates" of $300 to $600 that were actually just advances on April 2002 tax refunds were mailed to American taxpayers during Summer 2001. The government expected the checks would trigger a substantial increase in consumption spending. But apparently consumers did not spend much of their tax "rebate" checks. Use the concept of rational expectations to explain why the increase in consumption spending was so small.

6. Can a skilled rhetorician – or actor – convince people and businesses to decrease their inflationary expectations? If so, what effect would the change in inflationary expectations have on the unemployment rate and the actual level of inflation?

7. If expectations are "rational," then the unemployment rate will equal the natural rate of unemployment. Do you think expectations are "rational" in the United States?

E. POSSIBILITIES TO PONDER

The more you learn, the more you realize you have more to learn. These questions go beyond the textbook material. They are the sort of questions that distinguish A+ or A work from A-work. Some of them may even serve as starting points for junior or senior year research papers.

1. If it is indeed true (and this is debatable) that the Natural Rate of Unemployment rises as the number of immigrants in the labor force increases, should the United States pass restrictive immigration legislation?

2. Suppose the government did not fully disclose the inflation rate data. Or suppose the government published inflation data that had been falsified. What effect would the government's action have on the economy?

3. The textbook refers simply to **businesses'** expectations of inflation, with no mention of the inflation rate expected by consumers. Yet consumption spending is two-thirds of total spending. Should we be concerned with how consumers form their inflationary expectations?

4. If expectations are "rational," then the unemployment rate will equal the natural rate of unemployment. Do we want everyone to have rational expectations? If so, how should we go about achieving that goal?

SOLUTIONS   SOLUTIONS   SOLUTIONS   SOLUTIONS

A. BASIC DEFINITIONS

1. adaptive
2. unemployment rate; real GDP
3. Okun's law
4. static
5. static
6. price inertia
7. rational
8. real GDP
9. unemployment rate
10. rational

---

11. rational
12. large
13. no
14. forward
15. smaller; flatter
16. ineffective

17. C.

B. MANIPULATION OF CONCEPTS AND MODELS

1. A. $u = 0.04 - 0.4 \cdot (9{,}800 - 10{,}000)/10{,}000 = 0.048 = 4.8$ percent.

   B. $u = 0.04 - 0.4 \cdot (9{,}600 - 10{,}000)/10{,}000 = 0.056 = 5.6$ percent.

2. $(-2.5) \cdot (u - u^*) =$ output gap $= (-2.5) \cdot (0.03) = -0.075$. The output gap is 7.5 percent.

3. The total drop in income will equal the initial change in consumption spending times the multiplier:

$$\Delta Y = \Delta C_0 \cdot \frac{1}{1 - \left(C_y \cdot (1 - t) - IM_y\right)} = (-100) \cdot (3) = -300.$$

   A. $\Delta u = -0.4 \cdot (\Delta Y) = -0.4 \cdot (-300)/10{,}000 = +0.012$

   The unemployment rate rises by 1.2 percentage points.

   B. $\Delta u = -0.4 \cdot (\Delta Y) = -0.4 \cdot (-300)/8{,}000 = +0.015$

   The unemployment rate rises by 1.5 percentage points.

4. First, transform the equation to $\Delta u = -\left(\frac{1}{2.5}\right) \cdot \left(\frac{\Delta Y}{Y^*} - (n+g)\right)$.

   A. $\Delta u = -(0.4) \cdot [200/10{,}000 - (0.02 + 0)] = -0.4 \cdot (0.02 - 0.02) = 0$.

   The unemployment rate next year will remain at 4 percent.

   B. $\Delta u = -(0.4) \cdot [200/10{,}000 - (0.02 + 0.02)] = -0.4 \cdot (0.02 - 0.04) = +0.08$

   The unemployment rate next year will rise to 4.8 percent.

   C. As real GDP increases, labor demand increases. If the labor force were constant, the increase in real GDP would lower the unemployment rate. But if the labor force is increasing, then if the unemployment rate is to remain constant, real GDP has to grow fast enough to provide jobs for the workers entering the labor force. Moreover, if labor efficiency is increasing (g > 0), then the good long-run news of increases in worker productivity is offset by the bad short-run news of lay offs for workers whose labor is no longer needed because fewer workers can now produce the existing quantity of output. So if unemployment is to remain constant, then real GDP must increase fast enough not only to create jobs for the new entrants to the labor force (determined by n) but also to create jobs for workers who are laid off because of productivity increases (determined by g).

5. A. $\pi = (-400/10{,}000) \cdot (0.2) + 0.02 = 1.2\%$.

   B. The answer draws on material originally presented in Chapter 11. When output is below potential output, firms can not raise their prices as high as they had previously planned. Moreover, when output is below potential output, firms have additional bargaining power in negotiations with workers, and use this power to bargain for slower growth in wages.

6. A. $\pi = 0.02 - (2.5 / 5) \cdot (0.056 - 0.04) = 0.012 = 1.2\%$

   B. $\pi = 0.02 - (2.5 / 5) \cdot (0.040 - 0.04) = 0.020 = 2.0\%$

   C. $\pi = 0.02 - (2.5 / 5) \cdot (0.030 - 0.04) = 0.025 = 2.5\%$

   D. Phillips curve.

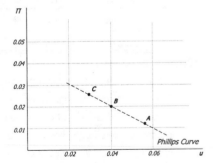

7. A. $\pi = 0.02 - (2.5 / 5) \cdot (0.06 - 0.04) + 0 = 0.01$

   $= 1.0\%$

   B. $\pi = 0.02 - (2.5 / 5) \cdot (0.06 - 0.04) + 0.03 = 0.04$

   $= 4.0\%$

8. A. $\pi = \pi^e + \frac{1}{\theta}\left(\frac{Y - Y^*}{Y^*}\right).$

    B. See table.

    C. See table.

Y	AS	PC	
	π	u	π
9,000	0.0	0.08	0.0
9,500	0.01	0.06	0.01
10,000	0.02	0.04	0.02
10,500	0.03	0.02	0.03
11,000	0.04	0.0	0.04

    D. and E.

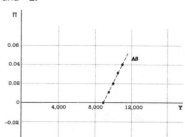 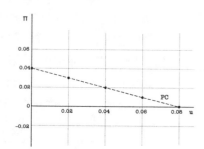

    F. The aggregate supply relationship can be expressed as the Phillips curve relationship because for any level of output, given potential output, there is a corresponding unemployment rate. The unemployment rate that corresponds to any output level is determined using Okun's law. Potential output must be specified in order to determine the unemployment rate. ($9 trillion worth of output would generate a much higher unemployment rate if the economy was capable of producing $20 trillion worth of output than it would if the economy was capable of producing $10 trillion worth of output.)

9. A.

	$\beta = 0.1$	$\beta = 0.5$	$\beta = 1.0$	$\beta = 5.0$
	π	π	π	π
u = 1 %	2.3 %	3.5 %	5.0 %	17.0 %
u = 3 %	2.1	2.5	3.0	7.0
u = 4 %	2.0	2.0	2.0	2.0
u = 5 %	1.9	1.5	1.0	-3.0
u = 8 %	1.6	0.0	-2.0	-18.0

    B. and C. graph

    D. A higher value of β corresponds to more price flexibility. A small change in the unemployment rate (that is, in the amount of output being produced), produces a very large change in the inflation rate when β is high. When prices are very flexible, changes in output (and thus in unemployment) will cause producers to change their prices. Even small

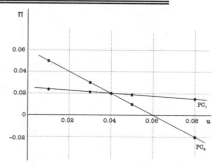

swings in unemployment (and thus in output) will lead producers to change their prices. The higher the value of β, the more vertical is the Phillips curve.

10. A. β measures the responsiveness of inflation to changes in the unemployment rate. β is larger for the steep Phillips curve, PC_2.

    B. Prices are more flexible in PC_2. A relatively small change in the amount of output produced (and thus in unemployment), causes a relatively large change in the inflation rate for PC_2.

    C. An increase in government purchases will have the larger effect on inflation in PC_2, when prices are relatively flexible and β is relatively large.

11. A.

	$\varepsilon^s = 0$ π	$\varepsilon^s = 0.04$ π	$\varepsilon^s = -0.03$ π
$u = 1\%$	0.035	0.075	0.005
$u = 3\%$	0.025	0.065	-0.005
$u = 4\%$	0.02	0.06	-0.01
$u = 5\%$	0.015	0.055	-0.015
$u = 8\%$	0.0	0.04	-0.03

    B.

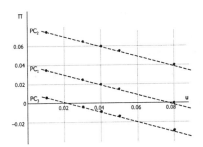

12. A.

	$\pi^e = 0.02$ π	$\pi^e = 0.04$ π	$\pi^e = 0.06$ π
$u = 1\%$	0.035	0.055	0.075
$u = 3\%$	0.025	0.045	0.065
$u = 4\%$	0.02	0.04	0.06
$u = 5\%$	0.015	0.035	0.055
$u = 8\%$	0.0	0.02	0.04

    B.

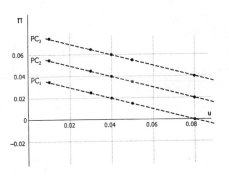

13. A.

	u* = 0.04 π	u* = 0.05 π	u* = 0.08 π
u = 1 %	0.035	0.04	0.055
u = 3 %	0.025	0.03	0.045
u = 4 %	0.02	0.025	0.04
u = 5 %	0.015	0.02	0.035
u = 8 %	0.0	0.005	0.02

B.

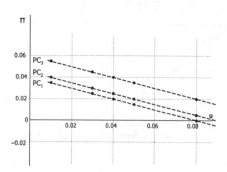

14.

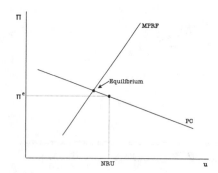

15. A. An increase in the NRU does not affect the MPRF; it only affects the Phillips curve. An increase in the NRU shifts the PC to the right. The logic of the shift, however, is clearer if you envision the curve shifting up. With a higher NRU, there is a higher rate of inflation consistent with every unemployment rate. Workers will have greater bargaining power at any unemployment rate after the NRU rises, allowing them to push for greater wage increases which then produce faster price increases. As prices rise more quickly,

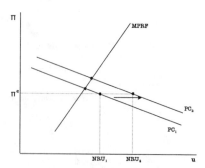

however, the central bank responds by increasing the real interest rate, which generates additional unemployment. In equilibrium, the unemployment rate will rise, as will the inflation rate.

B. An increase in the expected inflation rate does not affect the MPRF; it only affects the Phillips curve. An increase in the expected inflation rate shifts the PC up. With a higher expected inflation rate, there is a higher rate of inflation consistent with every unemployment rate. As workers and firms bargain over wages, they begin their negotiations with a higher base rate of inflation that workers hope to have covered with increased wages. Firms are willing to make an initial offer of higher wage increases because they anticipate being able to pass on the increased wages in increased prices at the expected inflation rate. Wages and prices therefore rise faster at every unemployment rate. As prices rise more quickly, however, the central bank responds by increasing the real interest rate, which generates additional unemployment. In equilibrium, the unemployment rate will rise, as will the inflation rate.

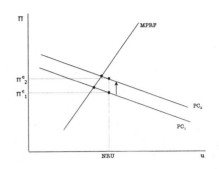

C. An adverse supply shock does not affect the MPRF; it only affects the Phillips curve. An adverse supply shock shifts the PC up. There is a higher rate of inflation consistent with every unemployment rate. The costs of production have risen relatively quickly, independent of changes in output, leading firms to increase their prices. Prices therefore rise faster at every unemployment rate. As prices rise more quickly, however, the central bank responds by increasing the real interest rate, which generates additional unemployment. In equilibrium, the unemployment rate will rise, as will the inflation rate.

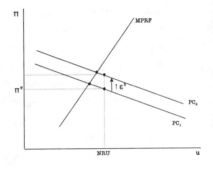

D. An increase in the level of unemployment, u_0, generated when the central bank sets the real interest rate at its target rate affects only the MPRF; it does not affect the Phillips curve. An increase in u_0 shifts the MPRF to the right. A higher u_0 increases the baseline level of unemployment that occurs when inflation is at the central bank's target rate. For any inflation rate, then, there is a higher rate of unemployment generated by the Fed's interest rate policy. But as the unemployment rate rises, workers will have less bargaining power in wage negotiations, and wages will therefore rise less rapidly. In equilibrium, the unemployment rate will rise, but the inflation rate will fall.

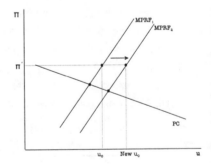

E. An increase in central bank's target inflation rate, π', affects only the MPRF; it does not affect the Phillips curve. An increase in π' shifts the MPRF up. The logic of the shift, however, is clearer if you envision the curve shifting left. A higher target inflation rate allows the central bank to lower the real interest rate, which increases real output and decreases unemployment at the existing inflation rate. For any inflation rate, then, there is a lower rate of unemployment generated by the Fed's interest rate

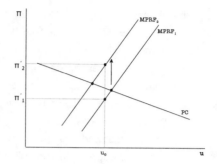

policy. But as the unemployment rate falls, workers will have more bargaining power in wage negotiations, and wages will therefore rise more rapidly. In equilibrium, the unemployment rate will fall, but the inflation rate will rise.

16. When government purchases increase, consumption spending for domestically-produced goods and services also rises through the multiplier effect, and therefore equilibrium output increases. If the Fed does not change its estimate of the "normal" level of the real interest rate, r^*, then there is a decrease in u_0, the unemployment rate associated with r^*. At any inflation rate, there is a lower unemployment rate. The MPRF shifts to the left. But as unemployment decreases, workers' bargaining power rises and they are able to negotiate successfully for larger

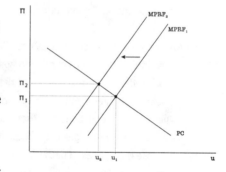

wage increases. Firms increase their prices. In equilibrium, there is a higher inflation rate and a lower unemployment rate.

17. The textbook gives four reasons why the NRU can change.
   * The relative age and educational distribution of the labor force changes.
   * Economic institutions that affect employment opportunities can change.
   * The rate of growth of labor productivity can change.
   * Recent levels of the unemployment rate have been well above or well below the NRU.

18. No.

19. With static expectations, the expected inflation rate never changes. So the expected inflation rate for 1960, 1965, 1969, and 1975 would have been 1.5 percent.

20.

	π^e_t
t = 1968	3.1 %
t = 1969	4.3 %
t = 1991	3.8 %
t = 1992	3.9 %

21. A. If the Fed adjusts the real interest rate from year to year so the $u = u^*$, then the inflation rate will remain at 3 percent year after year.

   B. If the Fed adjusts the real interest rate from year to year so that $u = u^* - 1$, then the inflation rate will rise by ½ percentage point per year.

$$\pi = \pi^e - 0.5 \cdot (u^* - 1 - u^*) + 0 = \pi^e + 0.5$$

C. If the Fed adjusts the real interest rate from year to year so that u = u* + 2, then the inflation rate will fall by 1 percentage point per year.

$$\pi = \pi^e - 0.5 \cdot (u^* + 2 - u^*) + 0 = \pi^e - 1.0$$

D. It is unlikely that the Fed would follow the course of action described in Part B or Part C. Political pressure, and just flat-out concern for the economic lives of Americans, would lead them to adjust their course of action.

22. A. If the increase in G is a surprise, people's expectations of inflation have not changed to take account of the policy's effects on the economy. The expansionary fiscal policy therefore leads to a shift to the left in the MPRF but no change in the PC. (See the graph at the right.) The inflation rate will rise and the unemployment rate will fall.

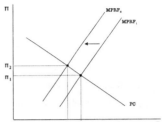

B. On the other hand, if the increase in G is anticipated, people's expectations of inflation have already been increased to reflect the policy's expected effects on the economy. The expansionary fiscal policy therefore leads to a shift to the left in the MPRF and also a shift up of the PC. (See the graph below.) The inflation rate will rise substantially.

C. If the decrease in r is a surprise, people's expectations of inflation have not changed to take account of the policy's effects on the economy. The expansionary monetary policy therefore leads to a shift to the left in the MPRF but no change in the PC. The inflation rate will rise and the unemployment rate will fall.

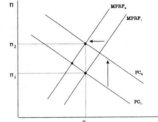

D. On the other hand, if the decrease in r is anticipated, people's expectations of inflation have already been increased to reflect the policy's expected effects on the economy. The expansionary monetary policy therefore leads to a shift to the left in the MPRF and also a shift up of the PC. The inflation rate will rise substantially.

23. A. If expectations are rational and the policy is fully anticipated, then inflationary expectations rise because the policy is expected to increase the inflation rate. The policy then has no effect on the unemployment rate. The anticipated fiscal policy changes only the inflation rate. (See the graph at the right.) Unless there are surprising shocks to the economy, the unemployment rate will always equal the natural rate of unemployment.

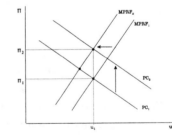

B. If expectations are adaptive, then inflationary expectations will shift up slowly. The expansionary fiscal policy will be able to affect the unemployment rate at least initially. (See the graph at the right.) Over time, inflationary expectations will adjust, eliminating the policy's expansionary effects on output.

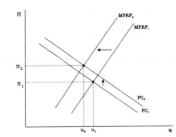

C.   If expectations are static, then inflationary expectations never change. The expansionary fiscal policy will lower the unemployment rate and increase the inflation rate.

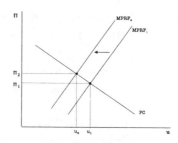

C. APPLYING CONCEPTS AND MODELS

1.   See Box 12.2 of the textbook. Unemployment is not evenly distributed during a recession. Workers in consumer goods industries, and in particular in industries producing goods that have relatively high levels of income-elasticity of demand, are most likely to experience unemployment. There are also important differences in the likelihood of experiencing unemployment by race, gender, and marital status. But when economic times are good, almost all workers expect they will experience raises and other benefits of the boom. Nevertheless, based on voting patterns and responses to polls, workers' fear of recession seems to be greater than their anticipation of gains during booms.

2.   A.   The AS equation relates real GDP and inflation. As real output increases relative to potential output, inflation also increases. From 1965 to 1969, real GDP increased from $3.0 trillion to $3.6 trillion (in chained 1996 dollars), an increase of 4.2 percent annually. As real GDP increased at this relatively rapid rate, the inflation rate increased from 1.9 percent in 1965 to 4.9 percent in 1969.

   B.   The Phillips curve equation relates the unemployment rate and inflation. As the unemployment rate falls, the inflation rate rises. From 1965 to 1969, the unemployment rate fell from 4.5 to 3.5 percent. Not surprisingly, inflation increased over the same period, rising from 1.9 percent in 1965 to 4.9 percent in 1969.

3.   When prices are relatively flexible, firms rely more on changes in prices than on changes in output when they experience unexpected changes in their inventory holdings. In this case, the Phillips curve will be relatively steep; unemployment will not vary much but prices will vary a great deal even for a small change in the unemployment rate. The Phillips curve is "anchored" by the natural rate of unemployment, so a steep Phillips curve will be located in the vicinity of the NRU.

4.   Based on the inflation data at the back of the textbook, it seems reasonable to conclude that people had static expectations for the first half of the 1960s, and possibly again in the late 1990s. By the late 1960s, though, the inflation rate was rising. Adaptive expectations probably were held in the late 1960s and early 1970s. In the late 1970s and 1980s, the inflation rate increased some years and decreased other years. People probably tried to form rational expectations in these years. The inflation rate came down by the mid-1980s and remained relatively low through the end of the century. By the early 1990s, people probably had adaptive expectations again.

   It is not surprising that the idea of "rational expectations" did not yet exist in 1966. Nothing about the experience of inflation would have led anyone to believe that the inflation rate could jump up and down as wildly as it did from the mid-1970s through the end of the 1980s.

5.   On the one hand, the slow pace of implementation meant that the fiscal policy was fully anticipated. If expectations were "rational," then individuals would have increased their inflationary expectations before the tax cuts were received. The tax cuts would therefore have affected inflation without altering unemployment. But in the early 1960s, the inflation rate had been low and stable for over a decade. Inflationary expectations were more likely static or adaptive than "rational." By phasing the tax cut in slowly, the policy avoided increasing inflationary expectations. The Phillips curve was stable.

D. EXPLAINING THE REAL WORLD

1. Labor market discrimination is one of the factors that determines the natural rate of unemployment. Any policy that lowers the NRU will lower the inflation rate. So to the extent that the NRU is increased by labor market discrimination, decreasing discrimination can lower the inflation rate.

2. Successful academies ease the transition from education to employment. As more and more students are enrolled in academies, the NRU should therefore decline. A decline in the NRU leads ultimately to a decline in the inflation rate as well.

3. The answer depends on many factors. Are expectations formed rationally or adaptively? Are they static? If expectations are static or adaptive, then the economic events after September 11 do not affect expectations, and the expected inflation rate would remain in the 1.5 to 2.0 percent range. But if expectations are formed rationally, then people are trying to figure out what will happen in the future. If the only factor to consider was the change in the government's budget deficit, then it would be reasonable to assume that people's expectations of inflation increased. But the economic shocks following September 11 included drops in consumption and investment spending. A great deal of uncertainty clouded expectations.

4. Rational expectations. If there is much economic uncertainty, then individuals are trying to form informed expectations as to the future. The best way to inform those expectations is to have some ideas, however vague, of how the economy functions.

5. Taxpayers apparently did not view that tax cut as a permanent reduction in taxes. To the extent taxpayers could form expectations of future tax policy, they apparently expected that the government would need to increase taxes in the future. When a tax cut is temporary, resulting in a temporary increase in disposable income, the marginal propensity to consume is very low. (See the textbook appendix to Chapter 6.)

6. It is conceivable that a skilled rhetorician could convince people and businesses to lower their inflationary expectations, particularly if there is poor public understanding of how the economy functions. In this case, the Phillips curve would shift down, lowering the inflation rate and the unemployment rate.

7. The unemployment rate is depicted graphically on the inside back cover of your textbook. If expectations are "rational," then all of the fluctuations in the unemployment rate correspond to fluctuations in the natural rate. Economists disagree. But the authors of your textbook and your study guide do not think that all of those actual fluctuations are fluctuations in the natural rate. Therefore it is difficult to conclude that expectations are always formed "rationally."

E. POSSIBILITIES TO PONDER

No solutions are given to these questions. The questions are designed to be somewhat open ended. Each question draws on your understanding of the concepts covered in this chapter.

Are you trying to figure out which economics courses to take next? Ask the undergraduate advisors in your department for their guidance. And consider these possibilities:

- Money and Banking, where you explore monetary policy and the banking sector
- International Finance, where you explore the determination of exchange rates and the worldwide flow of financial capital
- Economic History, where you explore how economic analysis can help us understand history, including such events as the Great Depression

Chapter 13

Stabilization Policy

- In the United States, monetary policy is conducted by the Federal Reserve. Fiscal policy is conducted by Congress with the approval of the President.

- The real-world conduct of stabilization policy is complicated by long and variable lags, uncertainty, and the possibility the structure of the economy may change in response to the policies themselves.

LEARNING GUIDE

Chapter 13 is the first of five applications chapters. We developed all of the macroeconomic theory in the previous twelve chapters. Now we can apply it to real-world situations. The focus in Chapter 13 is stabilization policy – the policies of the federal government and the Federal Reserve that can be used to stabilize the unemployment and inflation rates in the short run.

At this point in the course, time is usually limited and instructors have to make choices as to which material to cover. So which parts of Chapter 13 will be emphasized will vary from instructor to instructor. Because there is no point in memorizing lots of details that you might not need – especially if doing so means you miss the big picture – many of the minor details of Chapter 13 are not covered in the study guide.

Short on time?

Before you study this chapter, find out what you are expected to learn from it. Some professors will want you to be able to write thoughtful essay answers on the topics raised in this chapter; others may limit their testing to a few multiple choice questions.

You will want to be clear on who conducts monetary policy, who conducts fiscal policy, the advantages and disadvantages to using each type of policy to solve macroeconomic problems, and the power and limitations of policy.

A. BASIC DEFINITIONS

Before you apply knowledge, you need a basic grasp of the fundamentals. In other words, there are some things you just have to know. Knowing the material in this section won't guarantee a good grade in the course, but not knowing it will guarantee a poor or failing grade.

USE THE WORDS OR PHRASES FROM THE LIST BELOW TO COMPLETE THE SENTENCES. SOME ARE USED MORE THAN ONCE; SOME ARE NOT USED AT ALL.

Congress	*liquidity trap*
deposit insurance	*Lucas critique*
Employment Act of 1946	*money stock*
Federal Open Market Committee	*policy formulation*
Federal Reserve	*President*
fiscal automatic stabilizers	*recognition*
Alan Greenspan	*Adam Smith*
John Maynard Keynes	*Robert Solow*
lender of last resort	*stagflation*

1. The time it takes for policy makers to recognize that a problem has occurred in the economy is called the _____ lag.

2. In the United States, the _____ conducts fiscal policy.

3. A central bank is called the _____ because it can rapidly expand the money supply and directly lend to financial institutions when there is a financial crisis.

4. The economist whose work was seminal in establishing roles for monetary and fiscal policy to alter unemployment and inflation was _____.

5. The four measures of the _____ are called M1, M2, M3, and L.

6. In the United States, the _____ conducts monetary policy.

7. After a problem is recognized, the time it takes for policy makers to devise and implement policy is called the _____ lag.

8. The _____ is the primary policy-making body of the Federal Reserve system.

9. The _____ says that the structure of the economy depends in part on policy.

10. The possibility that monetary policy might be incapable of fighting recession because expected price deflation keeps the real interest rate high is called a(n)

    _____.

11. Financial panics are less severe in the United States than they were one hundred years ago because Congress instituted _____ during the New Deal.

12. A combination of relatively high unemployment and relatively high inflation is called

    _____.

13. When the economy enters a recession, the government's budget surplus automatically declines because of _____.

14. In the United States, the federal government formally accepted responsibility for stabilizing the economy with its passage of the _____.

CIRCLE THE CORRECT WORD OR PHRASE IN EACH OF THE FOLLOWING SENTENCES.

15. [REVIEW] In the short / long run, when government spending increases, output does not change.

16. [REVIEW] In the short / long run, when government spending increases, income increases.

17. [REVIEW] In the short run, prices are flexible / sticky.

18. [REVIEW] In the short run, when government spending increases, the unemployment rate rises / stays the same / falls, and the inflation rate rises / stays the same / falls.

19. [REVIEW] In the long run, prices are flexible / sticky.

20. [REVIEW] In the long run, when government spending increases, the unemployment rate rises / stays the same / falls, and the inflation rate rises / stays the same / falls.

21. When M1 is increasing, M3 is always / usually / sometimes / never increasing as well.

22. Monetary / Fiscal policy is the most powerful tool for stabilizing the economy.

23. In the United States, the Fed is / is not independent of the federal government.

24. Estimates of the slope of the IS curve are precise / imprecise.

B. MANIPULATION OF CONCEPTS AND MODELS

Most instructors expect you to be able to do basic manipulation of the concepts. Being able to do so often means you can earn a C in a course. But if you want a better grade, you'll need to be able to complete this next section easily and move on to Sections C and D.

HINT: Before you begin, be sure you know what determines the slope and location of the Phillips curve, and what determines the slope and location of the monetary policy reaction function. If you are not sure, review Chapter 12 before going further.

1. [REVIEW] In the short run, we can depict the determinants of the inflation and unemployment rates using the monetary policy reaction function (MPRF) and the Phillips curve (PC).

    A. Using the graph at the right, describe what happens in the short run to unemployment and inflation when government purchases increase. Assume the increase in government purchases is not fully anticipated.

    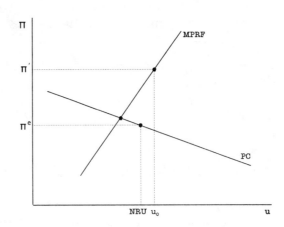

    B. Using the graph at the right, describe what happens in the short run to unemployment and inflation when the central bank decreases the real interest rate. Assume the decrease in the real interest rate is not fully anticipated.

    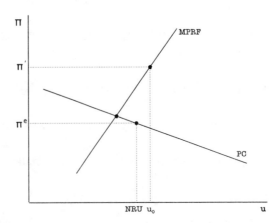

TO THE CHALKBOARD:
Explaining Figure 13.7

Figure 13.7 depicts the Phillips curves for 1955 - 1967 and 1975 - 1980. Here we focus on the curves and why they shift. The detail is left to the textbook graph.

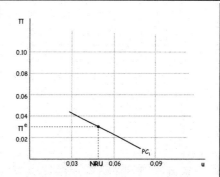

In the graph at the right, suppose that Phillips curve PC_1 describes the supply-side tradeoffs between the unemployment and inflation rates for 1955 - 1967. Now look at the textbook Figure 13.7. Most of the annual combinations of the unemployment and inflation rates for 1955 to 1967 are on or near the same curve, "Phillips Curve, 1955 - 1967." Between 1955 and 1967, the natural rate of unemployment was about 4.7 percent and the expected inflation rate was about 2.8 percent.

The United States involvement in the Vietnam conflict accelerated in the mid-1960s. In 1965, when the unemployment rate was 4.5 percent, the U.S. economy was already operating at or near the natural rate of unemployment. Nevertheless federal government spending increased, pushing the economy to produce beyond its potential. Employed workers put in many overtime hours; additional workers were relatively hard to find. Wages and prices began rising. As the Vietnam War wore on, people and businesses raised their expectations of the inflation rate. The OPEC oil crisis began in 1973, further increasing inflationary expectations.

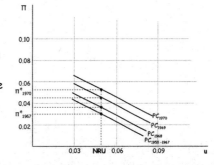

The increases in the expected inflation rate that began in about 1967 raised the Phillips curve. Expectations were adaptive in this period, so the expected inflation rate rose gradually. If we were to draw the Phillips curve for each year between 1967 and 1975, it would shift up a little bit each year. The messy graph shown at the right would result.

In the early 1970s, labor productivity growth slowed. Slower labor productivity growth raised the natural rate of unemployment. Increases in the natural rate of unemployment are shown as shifts to the right in the Phillips curve.

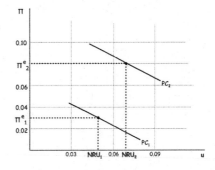

By 1975, the Phillips curve had shifted up and to the right. The expected inflation rate had risen to about 8 percent and the natural rate of unemployment had risen to about 6.7 percent. No further changes in either rate occurred through the end of the 1970s. As a result, the Phillips curve was again stable for those six years. In the graph at the right, the 1975 - 1980 Phillips curve is PC_2. This second Phillips curve takes into account both sets of changes: higher expected inflation rates and a higher natural rate of unemployment. Now look again at the textbook Figure 13.7. All of the annual combinations of the unemployment and inflation rates for 1975 to 1980 are on the same curve, "Phillips Curve, 1975 - 1980."

2. Suppose the Fed wants to lower real interest rates. What does the Fed do? How does their action lower the interest rate that Citibank charges to a local small business that wants to borrow $10,000 in order to purchase a new computer system?

3. Describe the source of the "inside" time lags that occur between the occurrence of an economic problem and its solution. How long is the inside lag for fiscal policy? How long is the inside lag for monetary policy?

 NOTE: The sections of Chapter 13 that describe the economic history of the United States are excellent. Don't miss them!

4. Look at the inflation rate data that are on pages 524 - 525 of your textbook.

   A. Form a guess for the expected inflation rate in each of the years 1965 - 1980. Write your guesses into the table at the right. Explain how you formed your guesses.

year	π^e		year	π^e
1965			1973	
1966			1974	
1967			1975	
1968			1976	
1969			1977	
1970			1978	
1971			1979	
1972			1980	

   B. Based on your answers to Part A, describe what happened to the Phillips curve between 1964 and 1980.

5. The quantity theory of money tells us $M \cdot V = P \cdot Y$, and therefore that $\%\Delta M + \%\Delta V = \%\Delta P + \%\Delta Y$.

    A. If the rate of growth of velocity, $\%\Delta V$, is predictable and the Fed's goal is to have an inflation rate of 2 percent and real GDP growth of 3 percent, do we need to have "activist" monetary policy? Explain.

    B. Look at Figure 13.8 in your textbook. During what years was the rate of growth of velocity predictable? When was it not predictable? During what years might it have been sensible to have an "automatic" central bank in the United States? During what years might it have been sensible to have an "activist" central bank in the United States?

6. Why is the money stock not a good leading indicator of the economy?

7. The money multiplier, μ, describes the relationship between the monetary base and the amount of money in the economy: $M = \mu \cdot B$. The expression for the money multiplier is

    $\mu = \dfrac{\dfrac{C}{D} + 1}{\dfrac{C}{D} + \dfrac{RR}{D} + \dfrac{XR}{D}}$. The size of the money multiplier depends upon the ratio of cash

    holdings to checking deposits, C/D; the required reserve ratio, RR/D, and the excess reserve ratio, XR/D. (**NOTE**: The symbols used in this question – C/D, RR/D, and XR/D – are different than what is used in textbook Box 13.4.)

    A. Suppose the cash to deposits ratio is 10 percent, the required reserve ratio is 12 percent, and the excess reserves to deposit ratio is 3 percent. What is the value of the money multiplier? If the Fed increases the monetary base by $100 billion, by how much will the money stock increase?

    B. Suppose cash holdings increase to 15 percent of deposits. What is the new value of the money multiplier?

8. The money multiplier is $\mu = \dfrac{\dfrac{C}{D} + 1}{\dfrac{C}{D} + \dfrac{RR}{D} + \dfrac{XR}{D}}$.

A. Explain why the money multiplier is lower when the cash to deposits ratio is higher.

B. Explain why the money multiplier is lower when the required reserve ratio is higher.

C. Explain why the money multiplier is lower when the excess reserve ratio is higher.

9. If the central bank lowers real interest rates on June 1, should they expect to observe a change in aggregate demand by June 30? Explain.

10. What are the three limits of stabilization policy?

TO THE CHALKBOARD:
Explaining – and Correcting – Box 13.5

Box 13.5 explains why policy makers will be cautious as they implement policy. Let's go through the example.

We are given the following information:
- Actual real GDP = $9,500 billion
- Target level of real GDP = $10,000 billion
- There is some uncertainty as to how much real GDP will respond to a change in real interest rates.
- The central bank's goal is to choose Δr so as to minimize $(Y - 10,000)^2$, the squared deviation of actual real GDP from the bank's target level.

A staff analyst – an interesting job, and there are Fed internships available to undergraduate economics majors – has estimated the possible responses of real GDP to a change in interest rates.

- 25 percent chance that $\Delta r = -1$ yields $\Delta Y = +0$ billion and thus $Y = \$9,500$ billion
- 50 percent chance that $\Delta r = -1$ yields $\Delta Y = +\$200$ billion and thus $Y = \$9,500$ billion $- 200 \cdot \Delta r$
- 25 percent chance that $\Delta r = -1$ yields $\Delta Y = +\$400$ billion and thus $Y = \$9,500$ billion $- 400 \cdot \Delta r$

The bank's goal is to minimize the squared deviation of actual real GDP from $\$10,000$ billion. The possible values of the squared deviation are:

- 25 percent chance that squared deviation $= (9,500 - 10,000)^2$
- 50 percent chance that squared deviation $= (9,500 - 200 \cdot \Delta r - 10,000)^2$
- 25 percent chance that squared deviation $= (9,500 - 400 \cdot \Delta r - 10,000)^2$

The **expected value (EV)** of the squared deviation is the sum of the products of the chance of each value and the value: $EV = \sum_{i=1}^{i=3} \left[probability_i \cdot (squared\ deviation)_i \right]$.

$$EV = 0.25 \cdot (9,500 - 10,000)^2 + 0.50 \cdot (9,500 - 200 \cdot \Delta r - 10,000)^2 + 0.25 \cdot (9,500 - 400 \cdot \Delta r - 10,000)^2$$
$$= 0.25 \cdot (-500)^2 + 0.50 \cdot (-500 - 200 \cdot \Delta r)^2 + 0.25 \cdot (-500 - 400 \cdot \Delta r)^2$$
$$= 0.25 \cdot (250,000) + 0.50 \cdot \left[250,000 + 200,000 \cdot \Delta r + 40,000 \cdot (\Delta r)^2 \right]$$
$$+ 0.25 \cdot \left[250,000 + 400,000 \cdot \Delta r + 160,000 \cdot (\Delta r)^2 \right]$$
$$= 250,000 + 200,000 \cdot \Delta r + 60,000 (\Delta r)^2$$

We thus have:

- When $\Delta r = 0$, $EV = 250,000 + 200,000 \cdot (0) + 60,000 \cdot (0)^2 = 250,000$
- When $\Delta r = -0.5$, $EV = 250,000 + 200,000 \cdot (-0.5) + 60,000 \cdot (-0.5)^2 = 165,000$
- When $\Delta r = -1$, $EV = 250,000 + 200,000 \cdot (-1) + 60,000 \cdot (-1)^2 = 110,000$
- When $\Delta r = -1.5$, $EV = 250,000 + 200,000 \cdot (-1.5) + 60,000 \cdot (-1.5)^2 = 85,000$

To find the value of Δr that minimizes the expected value of the squared deviation from $\$10,000$ billion requires a bit of calculus. The minimum value occurs at the value of Δr that makes the first derivative of the expected value of the squared deviation equal zero. (Think back to your calculus: when the first derivative is negative, the expected value of the squared deviation is falling; when the first derivative is positive, the expected value of the squared deviation is rising. So it must be that when the first derivative is zero, the expected value of the squared deviation has stopped falling and is just about to start rising – that is, the expected value of the squared deviation is at its minimum.)

So we want

$$\frac{min}{\Delta r}(EV) = \frac{min}{\Delta r} \left[250,000 + 200,000 \cdot \Delta r + 60,000 (\Delta r)^2 \right]$$

which means we must solve the following equation for Δr.

$$\frac{d}{d(\Delta r)} \left[250,000 + 200,000 \cdot \Delta r + 60,000 (\Delta r)^2 \right] = 0$$
$$0 + 200,000 + 2 \cdot 60,000 \cdot (\Delta r) = 0$$
$$200,000 = -120,000 (\Delta r)$$
$$\Delta r = \frac{-200,000}{120,000} = -1.67$$

When the real interest rate is decreased by 1.67 percentage points – for instance, from 4.0 percent to 2.33 percent – then the expected value of the squared deviation of actual real GDP from the target level will be minimized.

Notice that decreasing the real interest rate by 1.67 percentage points does **not** bring the expected value of actual real GDP up to the target level of $10,000 billion. When the real interest rate is decreased by 1.67 percentage points, there is a

- 25 percent chance that Y = $9,500 billion
- 50 percent chance that Y = $9,500 billion - 200·(-1.67) = $9,834 billion
- 25 percent chance that Y = $9,500 billion - 400·(-1.67) = $10,167 billion

So when the real interest rate is decreased by 1.67 percentage points, the expected value of real GDP is $9,834 billion, less than the target value of $10,000 billion.

Why would the central bank deliberately shoot low? Because there is still a 25 percent chance that lowering the real interest rate by 1.67 percentage points could push real GDP all the way to $10,167 billion, beyond the target level of $10,000 billion.

11. During World War Two, government purchases increased dramatically in the United States. If the Fed had been neutralizing fiscal policy, what action would they have taken? How is the combination of policies depicted in the IS-LM graph? How is the combination of policies depicted in the AS-AD graph that uses the MPRF and the Phillips curve?

12. Suppose the government increases tax rates and increases unemployment compensation payments. Do these changes increase or decrease the size of automatic stabilizers? Do they dampen or exaggerate changes in real GDP? Do they dampen or exaggerate changes in the government's budget deficit during a recession?

13. Give three reasons that are sometimes offered as to why policy should be driven by rules rather than left to the discretion of policy makers.

NOTE: In Chapter 11, the Taylor Rule said the central bank sets real interest rates in reaction to the inflation rate only. If you do not remember the Taylor Rule from Chapter 11, you might want to review study guide Chapter 11, Section B, Questions 27 to 32. Now we introduce a more realistic rule, allowing real interest rates to be set in reaction to both the inflation rate **and** the unemployment rate.

14. Suppose the Taylor Rule is $r = r^* + \phi' \cdot (\pi - \pi') - \gamma \cdot (u - u^*)$, where r* is 2 percent, π' is 2 percent, and u* is 4 percent.

   A. If the central bank places greater emphasis on achieving its inflation rate goal than it does on achieving its unemployment rate goal, which parameter will be larger: ϕ' or γ?

   B. Suppose $\phi' = 1$ and $\gamma = 0.25$. Complete the table at right.

u	π	r
4 %	2 %	
4 %	4 %	
6 %	2 %	
6 %	4 %	

NOTE: If you are interested in the realities of the Fed's monetary policy and the role of the Fed chairman, let me recommend the book *Maestro: Greenspan's Fed and the American Boom* by Bob Woodward (Simon and Schuster, 2000). It is a compelling account of the role and power of Alan Greenspan.

C. APPLYING CONCEPTS AND MODELS

Now we're getting to the good stuff. Being able to apply a specific concept or model to a real world situation — where you are told which model to apply but you have to figure out how to apply it — is often what you need to earn a B in a course. This is where macroeconomics starts to become interesting and the world starts to make more sense.

1. During Summer 2001, American taxpayers received tax "rebates" of $300 to $600. But consumption spending did not increase to the extent policy makers had expected. Use the Lucas critique to explain why actual consumption spending fell short of expected consumption spending.

2. When changes in real GDP are due to shifts in aggregate demand, will a money target or an interest rate target cause smaller fluctuations in real GDP? When changes in real GDP are due to fluctuations in velocity, will a money target or an interest rate target cause smaller fluctuations in real GDP? Use the IS-LM model to explain your answers.

D. EXPLAINING THE REAL WORLD

Most instructors are delighted when you are able to figure out which concept or model to apply to a real world situation. Being able to do so means you thoroughly understand the material and is often what you need to do to earn an A in a course. This is where you experience the power of macroeconomic theory.

1. In Fall 2001, the Federal Funds rate – the rate that banks charge on overnight loans to other banks – had been lowered by the Fed to 2.5 percent. Inflationary expectations were about 1 to 2 percent and falling. Some pundits were openly anticipating price deflation in the months and years to come. But the unemployment rate was rising and everyone was worried about recession. How effective can the Fed be in fighting unemployment by lowering the real interest rate?

2. During the credit crunch of 1991, potential borrowers could not obtain loans because banks refused to lend. Excess reserves increased. The Fed had difficulty making the money stock increase. Explain the connection between these statements.

3. During World War Two, government spending increased. The Federal Reserve and the U.S. Treasury had entered into an agreement under which the Fed promised not to increase nominal interest rates. In the absence of any other policies, what would have been the effect on the inflation rate? At the same time, rationing was imposed on consumers, limiting spending by households. Explain the economics effect of the combination of policies.

4. The unemployment rate began to rise in early 2001 as the rate of growth of real GDP slowed. All else constant, should the federal government's budget surplus in 2001 be more or less than the budget surplus in 2000? Explain.

E. POSSIBILITIES TO PONDER

The more you learn, the more you realize you have more to learn. These questions go beyond the textbook material. They are the sort of questions that distinguish A+ or A work from A- work. Some of them may even serve as starting points for junior or senior year research papers.

1. The monetary policy reaction function (MPRF) of Chapter 12 stated that the central bank sets the real interest rate in reaction to the inflation rate. In Chapter 13, the MPRF was expanded to allow the central bank to set the real interest rate in reaction to both the inflation rate and the unemployment rate. Do you think the emphasis the central bank places on unemployment and inflation – the sizes of the coefficients γ and ϕ' respectively – depends upon the actual levels of the unemployment rate and the inflation rate? How would the MPRF need to be changed if the central bank's reaction to the unemployment and inflation rates *did* depend upon the actual rates?

2. In the textbook, Professor DeLong asserts that "the prestige of the Federal Reserve is high." Do you agree? What are the economic effects of the Fed having – or lacking – prestige?

3. Can the U.S. economy fall into a liquidity trap similar to the trap Japan is in? Will it?

4. Economists generally believe that monetary policy is more effective than fiscal policy in changing the economy in the short run. What economic conditions could tip the balance so that fiscal policy is perceived as more effective than monetary policy? What political conditions could tip that balance?\

5. According to the textbook (p. 383), "Alberto Alesina and Lawrence Summers concluded that the more independent a central bank, the better its inflation performance." What factors might affect the extent to which central bank independence results in better inflation control? Should policy makers encourage all nations to establish a fully-independent central bank?

SOLUTIONS   SOLUTIONS   SOLUTIONS   SOLUTIONS

A. BASIC DEFINITIONS

1. recognition
2. Congress
3. lender of last resort
4. John Maynard Keynes
5. money stock
6. Federal Reserve
7. policy formulation
8. Federal Open Market Committee
9. Lucas critique
10. liquidity trap
11. deposit insurance
12. stagflation
13. fiscal automatic stabilizers
14. Employment Act of 1946

15. long
16. short
17. sticky
18. falls; rises
19. flexible
20. stays the same; rises
21. usually
22. monetary
23. is
24. imprecise

B. MANIPULATION OF CONCEPTS AND MODELS

1. A. See Chapter 12, Section B, Questions 16 and 22. When government purchases increase, income increases through the multiplier process and therefore unemployment falls. If the Fed does not change its estimate of the "normal" level of the real interest rate, r^*, then the unemployment rate that is associated with that "normal" interest rate falls. The MPRF shifts to the left. As unemployment falls, workers' bargaining power rises and they are able to obtain larger wage increases. Firms raise their prices. These effects are shown as a movement along the existing Phillips curve. The end result is an increase in the inflation rate and a decrease in the unemployment rate.

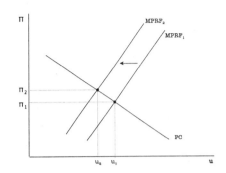

   B. The answer depends upon why the central bank has lowered the real interest rate. If the central bank has lowered the real interest rate because of a decrease in the inflation rate, then this sort of change in the real interest rate is depicted as a movement along the MPRF. We must then ask why the inflation rate decreased to cause the central bank to change the interest rate. Perhaps there was a supply "shock" that lowered prices; perhaps inflationary expectations fell; perhaps the NRU declined. Any of these factors would have shifted the PC to the left. The central bank's decrease in the real interest rate is then a reaction to the resulting drop in the inflation rate. The end result is a decrease in both the unemployment and inflation rates.

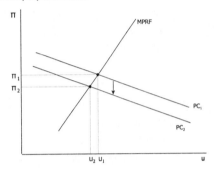

   On the other hand, if the central bank has lowered the real interest rate because of a decrease in its perception of the "normal" real interest rate or an increase in its target inflation rate, the decrease in the real interest rate is depicted as a shift up of the MPRF. At a lower real interest rate, real income will be higher. Unemployment will therefore be lower but the inflation rate will rise. See the graph at the right.

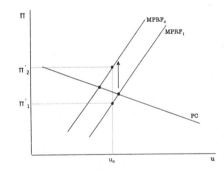

2. If the Fed wants to lower real interest rates, they will direct their bond traders to buy U.S. government bonds. These are bonds that were previously issued by the federal government when they needed to borrow to finance a budget deficit, and which are currently being held by the public: banks, businesses, mutual funds, businesses, and individuals in the United States and abroad.

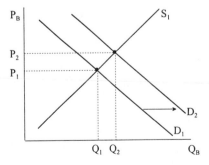

This increase in the demand for bonds is shown in a graph of the bond market as a shift to the right in the bond demand curve, as shown at the right. (**NOTE:** In the textbook, Prof. DeLong refers to the Fed's purchase of bonds as a "reduction in supply." Whether you model the Fed's purchase as an increase in the total demand for bonds or as a decrease in the supply, the price effect is the same. But the quantity effect differs. When you model the Fed's purchase as an increase in demand, you get the right quantity effect: more bonds are sold in the market for bonds.) The increase in the price of bonds corresponds to a decrease in the rate of return on bonds; that is, a decrease in the nominal interest rate. So long as the expected inflation rate does not decline to the same degree, there is also a decrease in the real interest rate on U.S. government bonds.

When the Fed buys bonds from the public, the Fed pays for the bonds by increasing the balance in the reserve account of the bank of the seller. For instance, suppose the Vanguard Group, a mutual fund company, sells $10 million in bonds to the Federal Reserve. If the Vanguard Group has its checking account at Citibank in New York City, then the Fed pays the Vanguard Group $10 million by making an "electronic transfer" to Citibank, where the Vanguard Group's has its corporate checking account. Citibank receives the $10 million electronic transfer as a deposit into its reserve account held at the Federal Reserve Bank of New York.

Citibank credits the Vanguard Group's checking account with the full $10 million transferred to it by the Fed. But of that $10 million that has been transferred to Citibank's reserve account, Citibank needs to keep only some fraction of the $10 million in its reserve account. That fraction is the **required reserve ratio** that is set by the Federal Reserve Board of Governors. Citibank can lend out the rest of those additional reserves.

Citibank is not the only bank to receive additional reserves. The Fed has repeated this process at hundreds of banks across the country. The banks are able to make additional loans. As banks try to make more loans, the supply of loanable funds increases, which decreases the price of loanable funds – the interest rate on loans. And finally we are to the small business that needs a small loan. Interest rates on loans made by Citibank have declined. After the Fed's purchase of bonds, the small business owner is quoted a lower interest rate when she calls Citibank to find out current loan rates than she would have been quoted before the Fed's action.

3. There are two general types of lags: the "outside lag" and the "inside lag." The "outside lag" is the amount of time that elapses between when an economic problem occurs and when policy makers know of the problem. It depends upon how many days, weeks, or months it takes for the various data-collecting agencies of the federal government to collect and release economic data. The "inside lag" is the time between when a policy proposal is made and when it becomes effective. It depends upon how many days, weeks, months, or years it takes between the time someone proposes a policy solution and when the economy fully responds to the policy. For fiscal policy, the inside lags are as long as one to two years. For monetary policy, the inside lags are no more than a few months.

4. A. Answers will vary. My guesses are shown at the right. Your guesses should be formed on the basis of static, adaptive, or rational expectations. In light of economic history, it makes sense to use static expectations through 1966 or so, to use some form of adaptive expectations through the mid-1970s, and then to use either adaptive or rational expectations for the end of the 1970s.

year	π^e		year	π^e
1965	1.5		1973	4.5
1966	1.5		1974	5.0
1967	2.0		1975	8.0
1968	3.0		1976	9.0
1969	3.5		1977	8.0
1970	4.5		1978	7.0
1971	5.0		1979	7.0
1972	5.0		1980	7.5

   B. Whenever the expected inflation rate rises, the Phillips curve shifts up. Whenever it falls, the Phillips curve shifts down. The tradeoffs between unemployment and inflation were changing in the 1970s. If the numbers above are close to accurate, it appears the Phillips curve shifted up about 1970, then shifted up again about 1975.

5. A. If the rate of growth of velocity is predictable, then there is no need for activist monetary policy. The central bank can simply program a computer to determine the desired rate of growth of the money stock: $\%\Delta M = \%\Delta P + \%\Delta Y - \%\Delta V$.

   B. Velocity was predictable from 1960 until about 1980. So from 1960 to 1980 it might have been sensible to have an automatic central bank. From 1980 to at least 1993, velocity was not predictable, so during that period we needed an activist central bank.

6. The money stock is not a good leading indicator of the economy because M1, M2, and M3 may behave differently. To use the money stock as a leading indicator, we would need to decide which measure of the money stock is the best. But there is no "best" measure of the money stock.

7. A. $\mu = \dfrac{0.10 + 1}{0.10 + 0.12 + 0.03} = \dfrac{1.10}{0.25} = 4.4$. If B increases by \$100 billion, M increases by \$440 billion.

   B. An increase in the cash to deposit ratio to 0.15 decreases μ to 3.8.

8. A. If individuals hold their money in the form of cash rather than as checking deposits, then banks have fewer reserves. With fewer reserves, banks can not make as many loans. Therefore for any change in the monetary base, the change in the amount of reserves will be smaller, so lending will be smaller, so the increase in the money stock will be smaller.

   B. If the required reserve ratio is higher, then banks must hold more reserves in their reserve account. Therefore for any change in the monetary base, the change in the amount of required reserves will be larger and the change in the amount of excess reserves will be smaller, so lending will be smaller, so the increase in the money stock will be smaller.

   C. If the excess reserve ratio is higher, then banks are holding more reserves in their reserve accounts. Therefore for any change in the monetary base, the change in the amount of lending will be smaller, so the increase in the money stock will be smaller.

9. It is probably unrealistic to expect to observe a change in aggregate demand in just a month. The change in real interest rates affects aggregate demand because it leads to a change in investment spending. But it takes time for businesses to plan investment projects. The bigger the project, the longer the planning process. Within a month, some small businesses might decide to go ahead and buy some new computer equipment, but even ordering specialized software would take more than a month. It would take a lot longer than one month for a residential construction company to begin a new housing development project.

10. The textbook lists these three limits of stabilization policy.

    - If the public loses faith in the central bank's ability to fight inflation, then stagflation can result.
    - Policy should respond slowly to changes in unemployment because forecasts are inaccurate and lags are long and variable.
    - We are uncertain as to how the economy responds to policy. If policy makers try to aggressively fight recessions, they may expand the economy too far and inflation may result. The policies may therefore prove to be counterproductive.

11. If the Fed wants to neutralize the increase in government purchases, it should raise real interest rates. In the IS-LM graph, the increase in government purchases would shift the IS curve to the right, and the increase in real interest rates would shift the LM curve up. If the expansionary fiscal policy was completely neutralized, the result would be a higher real interest rate but no change in real output. In the AS-AD graph, there would be no change. The increase in government spending shifts the MPRF to the left, but the increase in the real interest rate shifts it back to the right. The existing combination of equilibrium inflation and unemployment rates, where MPRF intersects PC, is unchanged, but occurs at a higher real interest rate.

12. Increased tax rates and unemployment compensation will increase the size of automatic stabilizers, dampen changes in real GDP, and exaggerate changes in the government's budget deficit during a recession.

13. The textbook offers these three reasons to favor rules.

    - The people appointed to conduct policy may be incompetent.
    - The authorities may not have the right objectives.
    - The central bank may get into a cycle where it wants to change its policy in an inflationary direction.

14. A. If the central bank places greater emphasis on achieving its inflation goal, then $\phi' > \gamma$.

    B.

u	π	r
4 %	2 %	2 %
4 %	4 %	4 %
6 %	2 %	2.5 %
6 %	4 %	4.5 %

C. APPLYING CONCEPTS AND MODELS

1. The Lucas critique states that the parameters of equations such as the consumption function may themselves depend upon policy. When Congress lowered tax rates, households formed expectations of future disposable income. In particular, they formed expectations of what would happen to tax policy and what might happen to their own income in the future. To the extent American taxpayers expected that the tax cuts implemented by Congress in Summer 2001 were likely to be reversed in the future, the marginal propensity to consume would have declined with the passage of the policy. The change in consumption would therefore have been smaller than policy makers would have predicted.

2. When fluctuations in real GDP are due to shifts in aggregate demand – to shifts of the IS curve – then real GDP will fluctuate less if the monetary authorities have a money target. In the graph at the right, LM_r is the LM curve when the authorities have an interest rate target and LM_m is the LM curve when they have a money target. With a money target, the increase in output which leads to an increase in the demand for money leads to an increase in the real interest rate, which decreases investment and gross export spending, partially offsetting

    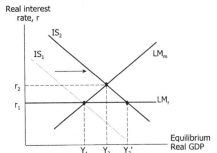

    the initial increase in aggregate demand. Real GDP increases from Y_1 to Y_2. On the other hand, with an interest rate target, when the increase in transactions demand for money puts upward pressure on real interest rates, the central bank supplies additional liquidity to the financial markets such that the real interest rates are unchanged. There are no changes in investment and gross export spending to offset the initial increase in aggregate demand. Real GDP increases from Y_1 to Y_2'.

    When fluctuations in real GDP are due to shifts in velocity – to shifts of the LM curve – then real GDP will fluctuate less if the monetary authorities have an interest rate target. In the graph at the right, LM_r is the LM curve when the authorities have an interest rate target and LM_m is the LM curve when they have a money target. When velocity increases, the nominal interest rate that clears the money market falls. With a money target, the increase in velocity decreases the real interest rate, and shifts the LM curve from LM_m to LM_m'. The decrease in

    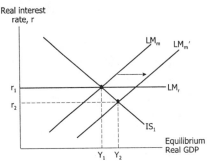

    the real interest rate increases investment and gross export spending, increasing real GDP from Y_1 to Y_2. On the other hand, with an interest rate target, when the increase in velocity puts downward pressure on real interest rates, the central bank responds by decreasing the money supply so that the real interest rate is unchanged. There are no changes in investment and gross export spending. Real GDP remains at Y_1.

D. Explaining the Real World

1. The Fed's power to fight unemployment by lowering the real interest rate is limited in this case. The Fed has already lowered the nominal interest rate to 2.5 percent. In theory, the Fed can lower nominal interest rates no lower than 0 percent. But political reality probably puts the lower limit of nominal interest rates at 1 percent. So starting with a nominal Federal Funds rate of 2.5 percent, the Fed can lower the nominal interest rate by no more than 2.5 percentage points and probably no more than 1.5 percentage points.

    With expected inflation rates falling, the Fed needs to lower nominal interest rates to prevent the economy from contracting. For every 1 percentage point decline in the expected inflation rate, the real interest rate rises by 1 percentage point. So the Fed would want to lower nominal interest rates by 1 point simply to keep the real interest rate from rising. But with the anticipated inflation rate falling from 1 or 2 percent to 0 or even –1 or –2 percent, the Fed has lost all of its wiggle room. Once nominal interest rates reach their lowest possible level, the Fed will be unable to lower real interest rates. Monetary policy will become completely ineffective in fighting the recession.

2. The credit crunch of 1991 was a time when banks decided to increase their excess reserve holdings. The ratio of excess reserves to deposits increased. As a result, the money multiplier declined. The Fed could buy bonds to increase the monetary base, but if banks refused to loan, then the money stock would not increase.

3. The increase in government purchases, absent other policies, would increase aggregate demand, increasing output, and lowering the unemployment rate at every interest rate. In the AS-AD diagram, the increase in government purchases would be shown as a shift to the left of the MPRF, increasing the inflation rate and lowering the unemployment rate. If the Fed promised not to increase nominal interest rates, then the increase in the inflation rate corresponds to a decrease in the real interest rate. In the language of the MPRF, the Fed is lowering its target real interest rate. In an IS-LM diagram, the policy is depicted as a shift down of the LM curve; in an AS-AD diagram, it is depicted as a further shift to the left of the MPRF. Inflation rises further and unemployment fall further. The addition of consumer rationing aids the economy. The increase in government spending is offset by the decrease of consumption spending. The decrease in consumption spending is shown as a shift of the IS curve back to the left. The inflation rate will not rise as high as it would have without consumer rationing, the real interest rate therefore will not fall as far as it would have without rationing, and in the graph the LM curve will not shift down as far as it would have without rationing. If the increase in government spending is fully offset by the decrease in consumption spending, inflation and unemployment will be unchanged. If the rationing only partly offsets the rise in government spending, the unemployment rate will fall and the inflation rate will rise.

    In the United States, government spending during World War Two was only partially offset by consumer rationing. The unemployment rate fell from over 10 percent in 1940 to about 2 percent by 1945. The inflation rate increased, but price controls prevented it from increasing as much as the AS-AD model might have predicted.

4. The budget surplus should decline in 2001 as unemployment rises, due to the automatic stabilizers in the government's budget. When unemployment rises, transfer payments automatically increase and tax revenues automatically decline. These changes alone will cause the budget surplus to fall.

E. POSSIBILITIES TO PONDER

No solutions are given to these questions. The questions are designed to be somewhat open ended. Each question draws on your understanding of the concepts covered in this chapter.

Chapter 14

The Budget Balance, the National Debt, and Investment

- Because automatic stabilizers change the government's budget balance whenever national income changes, we need to use the full-employment (or, cyclically-adjusted) budget balance to properly evaluate the short-run contractionary or expansionary effect of fiscal policy.

- An increase in the government's budget deficit benefits the economy in the short run by increasing output and decreasing unemployment. But it hurts the economy in the long run by decreasing national saving and thus decreasing capital-to-output ratios.

LEARNING GUIDE

This chapter contains some new concepts and a couple of minor models. It pulls together the short run and the long run as we consider the effects of government fiscal policy.

Chapter 14, more than any other chapter in the textbook, illustrates the challenges of writing a timely textbook. The textbook was finished before September 11; the study guide was not. After September 11, U.S. government purchases and transfer payments both increased sharply and tax revenues decreased. A year earlier, it seemed reasonable to talk about the future of government budget surpluses in the United States. But not anymore.

Short on time?

Before you study this chapter, find out what you are expected to learn from it. Some professors will want you to be able to write thoughtful essay answers on the topics raised in this chapter; others may limit their testing to a few multiple choice questions.

If you are not short on time, take the chance to think about the issues raised here. How will the events of Fall 2001 affect the economy? Every journalist and pundit would like to know.

BASIC DEFINITIONS

Before you apply knowledge, you need a basic grasp of the fundamentals. In other words, there are some things you just have to know. Knowing the material in this section won't guarantee a good grade in the course, but not knowing it will guarantee a poor or failing grade.

USE THE WORDS OR PHRASES FROM THE LIST BELOW TO COMPLETE THE SENTENCES. SOME MAY BE USED MORE THAN ONCE; SOME ARE NOT USED AT ALL.

bonds	generational accounting
capital budgeting	national debt
debt	stocks
deficit	surplus

1. A government borrows by selling _____ to individuals, businesses, and banks.

2. The lifetime impact of taxes and spending programs on individuals born in, say, 1980, is called _____ .

3. When government spending is less than tax revenues, the government is running a _____ .

4. The _____ is the amount of money that the government owes to people, businesses, and banks from whom the government has borrowed.

5. When government accounting reports government expenditures on long-lived assets separately from expenditures on other items, the government is doing _____ .

6. When government spending is greater than tax collections, the difference is a government _____ .

CIRCLE THE CORRECT WORD OR PHRASE IN EACH OF THE FOLLOWING SENTENCES.

7. The <u>full-employment / actual</u> budget balance changes as we move along a stable IS curve.

8. Fiscal policy is "sustainable" if the debt-to-GDP ratio is <u>increasing / constant / decreasing</u>.

9. According to the textbook, the "right" measure of fiscal policy is the <u>full-employment /</u> <u>actual</u> government deficit.

10. Changes in the full-employment budget deficit <u>shift / move us along</u> the IS curve.

$\mathcal{B}$. MANIPULATION OF CONCEPTS AND MODELS

Most instructors expect you to be able to do basic manipulation of the concepts. Being able to do so often means you can earn a C in a course. But if you want a better grade, you'll need to be able to complete this next section easily and move on to Sections C and D.

1. The government's debt builds up when there is a government deficit. Debt is reduced when there is a government surplus. That is

$$\Delta D = d$$

A. Suppose the government's debt was $4 trillion on 31 December 1990. Suppose the government ran a deficit of $280 billion during 1991 and a deficit of $200 billion in 1992. What was the value of the government's debt on 31 December 1991? What was it on 31 December 1992?

B. Suppose D = $5 trillion on 31 December 1999 and d = –$200 billion during 2000. That is, there is a government surplus during 2000. What was the value of the government's debt on 31 December 2000?

> The United States federal government debt currently exceeds $5 trillion. That debt was not accumulated gradually over the 200-plus-year history of the nation.
>
> Outstanding U.S. debt first exceeded $1 trillion in 1982
>
> Outstanding U.S. debt first exceeded $2 trillion in 1986
>
> Outstanding U.S. debt first exceeded $3 trillion in 1990
>
> Outstanding U.S. debt first exceeded $4 trillion in 1992
>
> Outstanding U.S. debt first exceeded $5 trillion in 1996
>
> It took the nation almost 200 years to accumulate $1 trillion dollars of debt. The next $4 trillion dollars – $4,000,000,000,000 – were accumulated in just 14 years. It doesn't matter how you look at those numbers, the government's late twentieth-century **peacetime** debt accumulation proceeded at an astounding pace.

2. What are two reasons – one short-run and one long-run reason – for economists to be interested in government debt?

3. In previous chapters, we combined transfer payments, TR, and tax payments, TA, into one term: net taxes, T. But it is sometimes easier to think about the political decision-making process and economic stabilization effects of government policy if we consider transfer and tax payments separately. Transfer payments programs include unemployment compensation, so when income rises, transfer payments decrease. But transfer payments programs also include Social Security, whose payments are independent of current income. Suppose

$$G = \$800 \text{ billion}$$
$$TR = \$700 \text{ billion} - 0.03Y$$
$$TA = 0.15Y$$

Suppose the actual level of income is $9,000 billion and potential output is $10,000 billion. What is the value of the actual deficit (or surplus)? What is the value of the full-employment deficit (or surplus)? Why are the two values of the deficit not equal?

4. Suppose the actual budget surplus is initially $200 billion. Suppose

$$\Delta G = +\$81 \text{ billion}$$
$$T = TA - TR = 0.20Y$$
$$C_y = 0.70$$
$$IM_y = 0.10$$

A. When government spending increases by $81 billion, by how much does income increase?

B. By how much does T increase?

C. What is the change in the budget surplus?

D. Explain why the change in the budget surplus is less than the change in government spending.

TO THE CHALKBOARD:
Explaining Box 14.1

In Box 14.1 Professor DeLong derives an expression we can use to assess the effect of fiscal policy. Here we go through the derivation step-by-step.

Step One: The Response to a Change in Government Purchases

What is the short-run impact of a change in government purchases, G, on national income? We answered that question in Chapter 9. National income changes by the change in government purchases times the multiplier.

$$\Delta Y = \frac{1}{1 - MPE} \cdot \Delta G = \frac{1}{1 - C_y(1 - t) + IM_y} \cdot \Delta G$$

Step Two: The Response to a Change in the Tax Rate

What is the short-run impact of a change in the tax rate, t, on national income? Calculus is needed to derive the expression that is given in Box 14.1. (If you haven't had calculus, don't fret. Just skip the derivation.) Assume A* is the amount of autonomous spending required to ensure that equilibrium income equals potential output, Y*.

$$dY = \frac{\partial}{\partial t}\left(\frac{A^*}{1 - C_y(1 - t) + IM_y}\right) dt \qquad \text{applying calculus rule}$$

$$dY = \frac{\partial\left(\frac{A^*}{1 - C_y(1 - t) + IM_y}\right)}{\partial(1 - C_y(1 - t) + IM_y)} \cdot \frac{\partial\left(1 - C_y(1 - t) + IM_y\right)}{\partial t} dt \qquad \text{applying more calculus rules}$$

$$dy = A^* \cdot \left[\frac{-1}{[1 - C_y(1 - t) + IM_y]^2}\right] \cdot (0 - C_y \cdot (-1) + 0) dt \qquad \text{taking derivatives}$$

$$dy = \frac{-A^*}{1 - C_y(1 - t) + IM_y} \cdot \frac{C_y}{1 - C_y(1 - t) + IM_y} dt \qquad \text{simplifying}$$

$$dy = -Y^* \cdot \frac{C_y}{1 - C_y(1 - t) + IM_y} dt \qquad \text{substituting } Y^* = \frac{A^*}{1 - MPE}$$

$$dy = \frac{-1}{1 - C_y(1 - t) + IM_y} \cdot C_y \cdot Y^* dt \qquad \text{rearranging terms to match text}$$

Mathematicians would shudder, as we noted in a previous chapter, but economists are content to assume the expression above holds for reasonably-sized changes in t, Δt. In that case,

$$\Delta Y = \frac{-1}{1 - C_y \cdot (1 - t) + IM_y} \cdot C_y \cdot Y^* \cdot \Delta t$$

Step Three: The Response to Simultaneous Changes in Government Purchases and Tax Rates

Now we have two expressions. One expression tells us by how much income changes when there is a change in government purchases. The second expression tells us by how much income changes when there is a change in the tax rate. We can combine the expressions into a third expression that tells us by how much income changes when **both** government purchases and the tax rate change.

$$\Delta Y = \frac{1}{1 - C_y(1 - t) + IM_y} \cdot \Delta G + \frac{-1}{1 - C_y \cdot (1 - t) + IM_y} \cdot C_y \cdot Y^* \cdot \Delta t$$

$$= \frac{1}{1 - C_y \cdot (1 - t) + IM_y}\left(\Delta G - C_y \cdot Y^* \cdot \Delta t\right)$$

Now we can play with this expression a bit to derive something that tells us how income changes when the government adjusts the **full-employment** budget deficit.

$$\Delta Y = \frac{1}{1 - C_y \cdot (1 - t) + IM_y}\left(\Delta G - C_y \cdot Y^* \cdot \Delta t\right) \qquad \text{expression for } \Delta Y \text{ when } G \text{ and } t \text{ both change}$$

$$\Delta Y = \frac{1}{1 - C_y \cdot (1 - t) + IM_y}\left(\Delta G - C_y \cdot \Delta T^*\right) \qquad \text{defining } \Delta T^* = Y^* \cdot \Delta t$$

$$\Delta Y = \frac{1}{1 - C_y \cdot (1 - t) + IM_y}\left(\Delta G - \Delta T^* + \Delta T^* - C_y \cdot \Delta T^*\right) \qquad \text{adding and subtracting } \Delta T^*$$

$$\Delta Y = \frac{1}{1 - C_y \cdot (1 - t) + IM_y}\left(\Delta G - \Delta T^* + (1 - C_y) \cdot \Delta T^*\right) \qquad \text{factoring out } \Delta T^*$$

$$\Delta Y = \frac{1}{1 - C_y \cdot (1 - t) + IM_y}\left(\Delta d^* + (1 - C_y) \cdot \Delta T^*\right) \qquad \text{defining } \Delta d^* = \Delta G - \Delta T^*$$

When Congress implements fiscal policy, the full-employment budget deficit, d* changes. If Congress has altered tax rates, the full-employment level of tax payments, T*, will also change. Both changes impact national income, Y.

5. Suppose the economy begins at full employment, and

$$G = \$1{,}300 \text{ billion}$$
$$TR = \$700 \text{ billion} - 0.03Y$$
$$TA = 0.15Y$$
$$C_y = 0.80$$
$$IM_y = 0.10$$
$$Y^* = \$10{,}000 \text{ billion}$$

A. What is the expression for net taxes, T? If the economy is at full employment, how large are tax revenues, T*? How large is the budget deficit, d*?

B. Suppose Congress increases government purchases by $105 billion. By how much does income, Y, change as a result of just the increase in government purchases?

C. Suppose Congress increases the tax rate by 1.05 percentage points. By how much does income change as a result of just the increase in the tax rate?

D. Suppose Congress institutes both the government purchases and tax rate increases simultaneously. What is the net effect on income of the simultaneous increases in G and t?

E. Congress increased the government spending by $105 billion and increased the full-employment tax revenues by $105 billion. Why did actual income rise?

NOTE: You may have read about the "Social Security lockbox." There never was any real "lockbox." Currently, Social Security tax revenues exceed Social Security payments, creating a "Social Security surplus." The Social Security lockbox was simply an idea embraced by many members of Congress who said that in assessing their spending and revenue plans, they would focus on the parts of spending and revenue that were not part of the Social Security program. This was never an economic idea. It was always a political one.

TO THE CHALKBOARD:
The Real Deficit

In Section 14.3, the expression for the real deficit is presented. The real deficit, d^r, equals the cash deficit, d^c, less the inflation rate, Π, times the debt.

$$d^r = d^c - \Pi \cdot D$$

The cash deficit includes the actual expenditures less actual revenues of the government. One of those expenditures is the interest payments on the debt. The interest payments on the debt depend upon the size of the nominal interest rate, i.

$$\text{cash interest payments} = i \cdot D$$

But since the nominal interest rate is the sum of the real interest rate, r, and the inflation rate, Π,

$$\text{cash interest payments} = (r + \Pi) \cdot D = r \cdot D + \Pi \cdot D$$

So

$$\text{cash deficit} = \text{cash interest payments} + \text{rest of cash deficit}$$
$$\text{cash deficit} = r \cdot D + \Pi \cdot D + \text{rest of cash deficit}$$

The real interest payments, $r \cdot D$, are part of the real deficit. Define the rest of the cash deficit – the spending for government purchases, transfer payments and the government's tax receipts – as also part of the real deficit. Then we have

$$\text{real deficit} = r \cdot D + \text{rest of cash deficit}$$
$$\text{real deficit} = r \cdot D + \text{rest of cash deficit} + \Pi \cdot D - \Pi \cdot D$$
$$\text{real deficit} = \text{cash deficit} - \Pi \cdot D$$

---

6. What are the four adjustments that Professor DeLong suggests we make to the actual budget balance?

7. Why doesn't the U.S. government do capital budgeting?

TO THE CHALKBOARD:
Deriving the Expression for the Steady-State Level of Debt-to-GDP

In the textbook, page 399, the steady-state level of the real value of the national debt to real GDP ratio is derived. Here we go through the derivation step-by-step.

Step One: The rate of growth of government debt. The real value of the debt increases from year to year by the amount of the budget deficit, d. But even if the government's budget was balanced year after year making d = 0 every year, the real value of the debt would change from year to year. Any time there is inflation, the real value of an outstanding debt declines. Therefore, the real value of the outstanding debt at the end of 2001 equals the inflation-eroded value of the debt that existed at the end of 2000 plus any additional borrowing undertaken during 2001. That is,

$$D_{12/31/2001} = (1 - \pi) \cdot D_{12/31/2000} + d_{2001}$$

The rate of growth of debt is then

$$D_{t+1} = (1 - \pi) \cdot D_t + d \qquad \textit{definition of debt growth}$$

$$D_{t+1} = D_t - \pi \cdot D_t + d \qquad \textit{distributing } (1 - \pi)$$

$$D_{t+1} - D_t = -\pi \cdot D_t + d \qquad \textit{subtracting } D_t \textit{ from both sides}$$

$$\frac{D_{t+1} - D_t}{D_t} = -\pi + \frac{d}{D_t} \qquad \textit{dividing both sides by } D_t$$

$$\frac{D_{t+1} - D_t}{D_t} = -\pi + \frac{d}{D_t} \cdot \frac{Y_t}{Y_t} \qquad \textit{multiplying by 1}$$

$$\frac{D_{t+1} - D_t}{D_t} = -\pi + \frac{d}{Y_t} \cdot \frac{Y_t}{D_t} \qquad \textit{rearranging terms}$$

$$\frac{D_{t+1} - D_t}{D_t} = \%\Delta D = -\pi + \delta \cdot \frac{Y_t}{D_t} \qquad \textit{defining } \delta = \frac{d}{Y_t}$$

Step Two: The rate of growth of real GDP. As established previously, the rate of growth of real GDP is

$$\%\Delta Y = n + g$$

Step Three: The rate of growth of the debt-to-GDP ratio. The proportional growth rules tell us that the rate of growth of a ratio, such as D/Y, is equal to the difference between the rate of growth of D and the rate of growth of Y.

$$\%\Delta(D/Y) = \%\Delta D - \%\Delta Y$$

If the debt-to-GDP ratio is stable, then its growth rate is 0. Therefore

$$\%\Delta\left(\frac{D}{Y}\right) = 0 \qquad \textit{definition of steady state}$$

$$\%\Delta D - \%\Delta Y = 0 \qquad \textit{applying proportional growth rule}$$

$$\%\Delta D = \%\Delta Y \qquad \textit{adding } \%\Delta Y \textit{ to both sides}$$

$$-\pi + \delta \cdot \left(\frac{Y_t}{D_t}\right) = n + g \qquad \textit{substituting}$$

$$\delta \cdot \left(\frac{Y_t}{D_t}\right) = n + g + \pi \qquad \textit{adding } \pi \textit{ to both sides}$$

$$\frac{\delta}{n + g + \pi} = \left(\frac{D_t}{Y_t}\right) \qquad \textit{multiplying both sides by } \left(\frac{D_t}{Y_t}\right) \textit{ and } \frac{1}{n + g + \pi}$$

If the debt-to-GDP ratio equals the deficit-to-GDP ratio divided by the growth rate of **nominal** GDP, then the debt-to-GDP ratio will not increase over time.

8. Suppose

$$\delta = d/Y = 0.025$$
$$n = 2 \text{ percent}$$
$$g = 1.5 \text{ percent}$$
$$\pi = 3 \text{ percent}$$

What is the steady-state level of debt-to-GDP?

9. Give two reasons why an increase in the government debt-to-GDP ratio increases the risk of lending to the government.

10. What are the three significant effects a deficit can have on the economy?

 NOTE: In the discussion of the three factors that brought an end to the 1980s and 1990s rise of U.S. government debt, the President Bush whose economic advisors persuaded him to go back on his campaign pledge of "read my lips; no new taxes" was President George H. W. Bush, the senior George Bush, who served as President of the United States from 1988 to 1992.

11. What were the three economic effects of the doubling of the government debt-to-GDP ratio in the 1980s and early 1990s?

> **NOTE:** Don't miss one of the most important lessons of macroeconomics. Policies that benefit the economy in the short run may hurt the economy in the long run. In particular, expansionary fiscal policy increases real GDP and decreases unemployment in the short run – a benefit. But unless the central bank maintains low real interest rates by allowing the money supply to increase rapidly, expansionary fiscal policy reduces government saving, reducing national saving, and thus raising real interest rates and slowing investment spending in the long run – a cost. If the central bank fully accommodates expansionary fiscal policy by maintaining low real interest rates, the money supply increases at a more rapid rate and the economy risks higher inflation rates in the long run – a cost. So whether the central bank allows real interest rates to rise or maintains them at existing levels, there are long-run costs to the short-run benefit of lowering unemployment.

12. One of the key lessons of macroeconomics is that government policies that benefit the economy in the short run may hurt the economy in the long run.

   A. Why is an increase in the government's budget deficit good for the economy in the short run but potentially bad for the economy in the long run?

   B. Suppose the increase in the government's budget deficit is due to increased spending for education. Would your answer to Part A change?

   C. Suppose the increase in the government's budget deficit is due to increased spending for public infrastructure such as the transportation or communications network. Would your answer to Part A change?

> **NOTE:** As you near the end of the term, you need to be able to use both the long-run analysis introduced in Chapter 4 and the short-run analysis of Chapters 9 through 12. If you are unsure of why the long-run effects of an increased budget deficit may be bad for the economy, review Chapter 4.

C. APPLYING CONCEPTS AND MODELS

Now we're getting to the good stuff. Being able to apply a specific concept or model to a real world situation — where you are told which model to apply but you have to figure out how to apply it — is often what you need to earn a B in a course. This is where macroeconomics starts to become interesting and the world starts to make more sense.

1. Congress proposes increasing unemployment compensation, increasing the size of checks received each week by unemployed workers. What effect would the increase in unemployment compensation have on the actual budget surplus? What effect would it have on the full-employment budget surplus? If the public judges fiscal policy based on changes in the actual budget surplus, and if the public believes any decrease in the budget surplus is "bad," what will be their evaluation of Congress's proposal?

2. During the War on Terrorism that the United States began in Fall 2001, what do you expect will happen to the government's budget surplus? What do you expect will happen to the ratio of U.S. government debt to GDP?

D. EXPLAINING THE REAL WORLD

Most instructors are delighted when you are able to figure out which concept or model to apply to a real world situation. Being able to do so means you thoroughly understand the material and is often what you need to do to earn an A in a course. This is where you experience the power of macroeconomic theory.

1. In the context of U.S. economic history, what was unique about the 1980s increase in the debt-to-GDP ratio?

2. Between 1 April 2001 and 1 September 2001, the estimates of the U.S. government's budget surplus for the fiscal year ending 30 September 2001 decreased by almost half. The U.S. Congress said (more or less), "Don't blame us!" Explain why we might not want to blame Congress for the 2001 decrease in the budget surplus.

3. In the wake of the September 11 attack, the Federal Aviation Administration (FAA) grounded all airplanes for four days. The airlines successfully lobbied for a federal government "bailout" to replace at least part of the revenues foregone during the four-day shutdown. Was the airline bailout an increase in government purchases or in transfer payments? How should the bailout affect the economy in the short run? All else constant, how should it affect the economy in the long run?

4. In the wake of the anthrax scare in October 2001 and associated fears of bio-terrorism, public health expenditures rose markedly. Every time someone feared anthrax and called 911, a local Public Health Department and the nation's Center for Disease Control (CDC) responded. Government purchases of antibiotics and vaccines increased. What is the short run economic effect of the increase in public health expenditures? What is the long run economic effect of the increase?

E. POSSIBILITIES TO PONDER

The more you learn, the more you realize you have more to learn. These questions go beyond the textbook material. They are the sort of questions that distinguish A+ or A work from A- work. Some of them may even serve as starting points for junior or senior year research papers.

1. Is the "era of [federal budget] deficits" in the United States over?

2. Suppose that legislators establish fiscal policy not with an eye to improving the economy, but instead with the goal of getting themselves reelected. Suppose the legislators believe that the likelihood of their getting reelected depends upon the public's perception of the benefits of any particular fiscal policy. If you could teach one economic concept to the public in such a way that everyone understood it fully, what would that concept be?

3. Suppose that government spending in any year depends upon tax revenues received in the previous year. If revenues increase in one year, then government spending will increase the next year. If revenues decrease in one year, government spending will decrease the next year. How would such a fiscal policy affect the economy in the short run?

4. Do you think "generational accounting" can be explained clearly to the general public? If so, should the government describe its spending and taxation policies using generational accounting?

5. Do policy makers focus on the long run? Why or why not? Should they?

SOLUTIONS SOLUTIONS SOLUTIONS SOLUTIONS

A. BASIC DEFINITIONS

1. bonds
2. generational accounting
3. surplus
4. national debt
5. capital budgeting
6. deficit

7. actual
8. constant
9. full-employment
10. shift

B. MANIPULATION OF CONCEPTS AND MODELS

1. A. $D_{12/31/1991} = 4,000 + 280 = \$4,280$ billion $= \$4.28$ trillion
   $D_{12/31/1992} = 4,280 + 200 = \$4,480$ billion $= \$4.48$ trillion
   B. $D_{12/31/2000} = 5,000 - 200 = \$4,800$ billion $= \$4.8$ trillion
2. Economists are interested in government debt and deficits because
   - Government deficits are a measure of fiscal policy's role in short-run stabilization policy.
   - Government deficits decrease national savings and thus reduce capital formation and long-run economic growth.

3. In general, budget surplus (BS) = TA - G - TR = 0.15Y - 800 - (700 - 0.03Y)

   Actual BS = 0.15(9,000) - 800 - [700 - 0.03(9,000)] = 1,350 - 800 - 430 = $120 b.

   Full-employment BS = 0.15(10,000) - 800 - [700 - 0.03(10,000)] = 1,500 - 800 - 400 = $300 b.

   The full-employment budget surplus is larger than the actual budget surplus because when income is lower than its potential, tax revenues are lower and transfer payments are higher than they would be if income was at its potential.

4. A. ΔY = $150 billion. $\Delta Y = \dfrac{1}{1 - C_y \cdot (1 - t) + IM_y} \cdot \Delta G = \dfrac{1}{1 - 0.7 \cdot (1 - 0.2) + 0.1} \cdot 81 = \dfrac{1}{0.54} \cdot 81 = 150$

   B. $\Delta T = 0.20 \cdot (150) = \$30$ billion

   C. $\Delta BS = \Delta T - \Delta G = 30 - 81 = -\$51$ billion. The budget surplus falls by $51 billion when government spending rises by $81 billion.

   D. The change in the budget surplus is smaller than the increase in government purchases because the increase in government purchases leads to higher income, which increases tax payments, offsetting part of the effect of government purchases on the budget surplus.

5. A. T = TA - TR = 0.15Y - (700 - 0.03Y) = -700 + 0.18Y

   T* = -700 + 0.18(10,000) = $1,100 billion

   d* = G - T* = 1,300 - 1,100 = $200 billion

   B. $\Delta Y = \dfrac{1}{1 - C_y \cdot (1 - t) + IM_y} \cdot \Delta G = \dfrac{1}{1 - 0.8 \cdot (1 - 0.15) + 0.1} \cdot 105 = \dfrac{1}{0.42} \cdot 105 = 250$

   C. $\Delta Y = \dfrac{-1}{1 - C_y \cdot (1 - t) + IM_y} \cdot C_y Y^* \Delta t = \dfrac{-1}{1 - 0.80 \cdot (1 - 0.15) + 0.10} \cdot 0.8 \cdot 10,000 \cdot 0.0105$

   $= \dfrac{-1}{0.42} \cdot 0.8 \cdot 10,000 \cdot 0.0105 = -\$200$ *billion*

   D. The net increase in income is $50 billion.

   E. Actual income increases because the tax rate increase does not have the same initial impact on the economy as does the increase in government purchases. The immediate effect of the increase in government purchases on aggregate demand is the full $105 billion. The immediate effect of the increase in tax rates on aggregate demand is less than $105 billion; increased taxes decrease disposable income which decreases consumption spending by some amount that is **less than** the change in disposable income. The mpc, C_y tells us by how much consumption spending changes when disposable income changes. In this case, with an mpc of 0.8, the increase in tax rates will decrease disposable income by $105 billion at full employment and thus decrease consumption spending by $84 billion. So the initial effects of the fiscal policy actions on aggregate demand is an increase in G of $105 billion offset in part by a decrease in C of $84 billion, for a net increase in aggregate demand of $21 billion. With multiplier effects, income increases by $50 billion.

6. The four adjustments that Professor DeLong suggests we make to the actual budget balance are adjustments for

   • the deviation of actual output from potential output.

   • the effects of inflation.

   • government purchases of long-lived assets.

   • the government's promises to make payments in the future.

7. The primary reason the U.S. government does not do capital budgeting is political. Who decides which items are capital expenditures? There is no objective, politically-free answer to such questions as "Are expenditures for Head Start a capital improvement?" Marian Wright Edelman would answer "Absolutely yes!" But not everyone would agree with her.

8. The steady-state level of debt-to-GDP is $\dfrac{D}{Y} = \dfrac{\delta}{n + g + \pi} = \dfrac{0.025}{0.02 + 0.015 + 0.03} = \dfrac{0.025}{0.065} = 0.38$

9. According to the textbook, when the government debt-to-GDP ratio increases, it is riskier to lend to the government because
   - if the debt-to-GDP ratio is high, then changes of government, peaceful or otherwise, are more likely to lead to a repudiation of debt incurred by the previous government than when the debt-to-GDP ratio is low.
   - if the debt-to-GDP ratio is high, the government has a greater incentive to reduce the real value of the debt via inflation than when the debt-to-GDP ratio is low.

10. According to the textbook, the three significant effects a deficit can have on the economy are
    - it may affect the political equilibrium that determines the government's taxing and spending levels,
    - it may affect the short-run level of real GDP, and
    - it may affect the long-run level of real GDP and standards of living.

11. According to the textbook, the three economic effects of the doubling of the government debt-to-GDP ratio in the United States in the 1980s and early 1990s were
    - probably negative effects on the formulation of government spending and taxation plans in subsequent years,
    - increased real GDP in the short run, and
    - decreased long-run potential for growth of real GDP.

12. A. An increase in the government's budget deficit increases real GDP and decreases unemployment in the short run. Unless the economy is already operating at potential output, most people agree a decrease in unemployment is good for the economy. But if the central bank does not maintain the real interest rate, an increased budget deficit reduces government saving, reducing national saving, raising real interest rates, and thus slowing investment spending in the long run. But lower investment spending in the long run reduces the rate of growth of the capital-to-output ratio, reducing the standard of living in the long run, which most people would agree is bad for the economy. If the central bank maintains the real interest rate when the government's budget deficit rises, then the money supply increases at a more rapid rate and the economy risks higher inflation rates in the long run, a cost that again most people would agree is bad for the economy. So whether the central bank allows real interest rates to rise or maintains them at existing levels, the long-run effects of an increase in the government's budget deficit are bad for the economy even though the increased budget deficit is good for the economy in the short run.

    B. If the increase in the government's budget deficit is due to an increase in spending for education, then the increased deficit may be increasing human capital, which might contribute to a higher level of labor efficiency (symbolized by E in Chapter 4). In this case, the answer to Part A might change. If the central bank allows real interest rates to rise, crowding out some investment spending, the decrease in private investment spending for machinery and buildings will be at least partially offset by the increases in human capital made possible by the increased government expenditure for human capital. If increased human capital increases efficiency, then standards of living will rise. The two effects – increased efficiency boosting the standard of living and decreased private investment spending lowering the standard of living – will result in less of a "bad" effect on the economy than was predicted in Part A.

    C. If the increase in the government's budget deficit is due to an increase in spending for public infrastructure, then the spending may contribute to a higher level of labor efficiency. In this case, again, the answer to Part A might change. If the central bank allows real interest rates to rise, crowding out some investment spending, the decrease in private investment spending for machinery and buildings will be at least partially offset by the increase in public investment spending for the economy's infrastructure. If improved infrastructure increases efficiency, then standards of living will rise. The two effects – increased efficiency boosting the standard of living and decreased private investment spending lowering the standard of living – will result in less of a "bad" effect on the economy than was predicted in Part A.

C. APPLYING CONCEPTS AND MODELS

1. If Congress passes legislation that increases unemployment compensation, then the actual budget surplus in a recession will be smaller than it would have been in the absence of the legislation. Because there are no unemployment compensation payments when the economy is operating at full-employment, the full-employment budget surplus would be unchanged. If the public judges fiscal policy based on changes in the actual budget surplus – the numbers they read in the newspapers – and if the public believes any decrease in the budget surplus is "bad," then they will oppose an increase in unemployment compensation.

2. Answers may vary, but it is very reasonable to expect that the War on Terrorism will increase government expenditures, decreasing the budget surplus (and probably to the extent that the federal government again runs budget deficits). The ratio of the budget deficit to GDP determines whether or not the debt-to-GDP ratio will increase. If the budget deficit-to-GDP ratio exceeds the rate of growth of nominal GDP, $n + g + \pi$, then the government debt-to-GDP ratio will rise. If the budget deficit-to-GDP ratio is less than the rate of growth of nominal GDP, then the debt-to-GDP ratio will fall.

D. EXPLAINING THE REAL WORLD

1. During the 1980s, the debt-to-GDP ratio increased markedly in the United States. But there was no war and there was no economic depression in the 1980s. Every other time the debt-to-GDP ratio increased in U.S. economic history, it was either during a period of war or a period of economic depression.

2. The actual budget surplus reflects not only policies implemented by Congress, but also the cyclical movements of the economy. In 2001, tax revenues fell and transfer payments rose as the growth of income slowed. Whether or not we should blame Congress for the drop in the budget surplus depends upon what happened to the *full-employment budget surplus* between 1 April 2001 and 1 September 2001, not upon the *actual budget surplus*. Congress was not entirely innocent; the tax cut signed into legislation during Summer 2001 contributed to the decline in the actual – and full-employment – budget surplus as well.

3. The government received no good or service in exchange for the money given to the airlines, and therefore the airline bailout was a transfer payment from the government to the airline corporations. In the short run, regardless of how the airline corporations spent the money, the bailout should boost real GDP and lower unemployment. (The specific sectors and workers who would benefit from the bailout depend upon precisely how the airline corporations spend the money.) In the long run, the airline bailout decreases the government's budget surplus, lowering government saving. If the Fed does not inject money into the economy in order to keep real interest rates from rising, then the real interest rate will increase, lowering private investment spending in all business sectors, lowering the rate of growth of private physical capital, and thus lowering the capital-to-output ratio in the long run. On the other hand, if the Fed chooses to maintain the real interest rate, it will need to increase the nominal money supply to meet its interest rate target. In the long run, unless the rate of growth of velocity slows or the rate of growth of potential output rises, a faster rate of growth of the nominal money supply will trigger higher inflation rates.

4. In the short run, the increase in government expenditures for public health increases real GDP and lowers unemployment. More workers are needed in public health departments. More workers are

needed to produce antibiotics and vaccines in pharmaceutical companies. Multiplier effects spread the gains to income and employment well beyond just these two sectors.

In the long run, the increase in government spending for public health may or may not be good for the economy. The answer depends upon whether or not we believe public health is part of the public infrastructure that contributes to the efficiency of labor. An increase in spending for public infrastructure, regardless of its effect on labor efficiency, lowers the government's budget surplus (equivalently, increases the government's budget deficit), lowering government saving. If the central bank allows real interest rates to rise, crowding out some private investment spending, the decrease in private investment spending for machinery and buildings will be at least partially offset by effect of the increase in public health spending on the public infrastructure. If improved infrastructure increases efficiency, then standards of living will rise. The two effects – increased efficiency boosting the standard of living and decreased private investment spending lowering the standard of living – may offset each other.

E. POSSIBILITIES TO PONDER

No solutions are given to these questions. The questions are designed to be somewhat open ended. Each question draws on your understanding of the concepts covered in this chapter.

Solutions Solutions Solutions Solutions Solutions

Have you enjoyed your Intermediate Macroeconomics class? Do you think your instructor did a good job? Tell him or her so. You might be surprised by how much we faculty members appreciate a note or email of gratitude. And if you think you've had a simply awesome professor this term – in this or any other class – consider nominating her or him for your school's teaching award.

Chapter 15

International Economic Policy

- Under a fixed exchange rate regime, economic disturbances in one country are transmitted to other countries. The gold standard is blamed by many scholars for the spread of the Great Depression from the United States to the world's economy.

- If there is very high capital mobility, a fixed exchange rate system renders monetary policy ineffective. For monetary policy to be effective in altering aggregate demand, a floating exchange rate system must be instituted when capital mobility is high.

LEARNING GUIDE

This chapter explores exchange rate systems. It focuses on the role of a fixed exchange rate system. Even though most of the world's economies now have floating exchange rates, we cannot understand economic history – and especially the worldwide nature of the Great Depression – if we do not understand the functioning of a fixed exchange rate system such as the gold standard.

The chapter draws on the material presented in Chapter 2 regarding real exchange rates. It introduces two new concepts: the balance of payments, and the role of foreign exchange reserves in determining real exchange rates in an environment of low international capital mobility.

Short on time?

Before you study this chapter, find out what you are expected to learn from it. Some professors will want you to be able to write thoughtful essay answers on the topics raised in this chapter; others may limit their testing to a few multiple choice questions.

If you find the material in this chapter interesting, consider taking an upper-division course in international finance where the determination of exchange rates and the role of exchange rate systems are considered in depth.

A. BASIC DEFINITIONS

Before you apply knowledge, you need a basic grasp of the fundamentals. In other words, there are some things you just have to know. Knowing the material in this section won't guarantee a good grade in the course, but not knowing it will guarantee a poor or failing grade.

USE THE WORDS OR PHRASES FROM THE LIST BELOW TO COMPLETE THE SENTENCES. SOME ARE USED MORE THAN ONCE; SOME ARE NOT USED AT ALL.

Bretton Woods
capital controls
gold standard

international currency speculators
International Monetary Fund
monetary policy authorities

1. When a country imposes limits on capital imports and capital exports, these limits are called _____.

2. The fixed exchange rate system that most of the world economy was on before World War I was the _____.

3. The international monetary system that was set up after World War II was called the _____ system.

4. Under a fixed exchange rate system with high capital mobility, _____ determine the exchange rate.

CIRCLE THE CORRECT WORD OR PHRASE IN EACH OF THE FOLLOWING SENTENCES.

5. Fixed / flexible exchange rate systems encourage international trade by reducing exchange rate risk.

6. A floating / fixed exchange rate system forces monetary authorities to focus its policy tools on achieving "external balance."

7. During most of the twentieth century, fixed / floating exchange rate regimes dominated.

8. A floating / fixed exchange rate system allows monetary authorities to focus its policy tools on achieving "internal balance."

9. When international capital mobility is low, changes in exchange rates <u>depend upon /</u> <u>are independent of</u> changes in the government's foreign exchange reserves.

10. Within the "Euro zone," exchange rates are <u>fixed / floating</u>, but between countries in the Euro zone and the United States, exchange rates are <u>fixed / floating</u>.

11. The gold standard system tended to be <u>inflationary / deflationary</u>.

$\boldsymbol{B}$. MANIPULATION OF CONCEPTS AND MODELS

Most instructors expect you to be able to do basic manipulation of the concepts. Being able to do so often means you can earn a C in a course. But if you want a better grade, you'll need to be able to complete this next section easily and move on to Sections C and D.

1. [REVIEW] Suppose real interest rates increase in England but not in the United States. What is the effect on the nominal exchange rate which is the dollar price of one British pound? Has the dollar appreciated or depreciated relative to the pound?

2. Suppose 1 ounce of gold sells for $35 in the United States and for 140 peso in Mexico. What is the dollar price of 1 peso? What is the peso price of 1 dollar?

3. Suppose that at the Treasury, you can exchange 1 ounce of gold for $35 or for 70 French francs. Suppose the market exchange rate is $0.40 per franc. Can these rates of exchange be maintained forever? Explain.

TO THE CHALKBOARD:
Explaining the Equation NX + NIA - FG = 0

The equations on page 414 of the textbook are balance of payments equations. They tell us what the relationship between net exports and net investment from abroad will be when the international financial payments system is in equilibrium. The explanation is clearer if we give the domestic economy a name; let's assume the domestic economy is the United States.

Currency – domestic and foreign – will flow between the United States and another country for three reasons.

- When goods and services are traded across national borders, currency flows between the two countries.
- When ownership of financial or real assets is traded across national borders, currency flows between the two countries.
- When the government acquires more foreign currency than it wishes to hold, or when it wishes to acquire additional foreign currency to meet the demands of its nation's households and businesses, currency flows between the two countries.

NX, or net exports, refers to the first of these three reasons. When someone imports goods or services into the United States, currency flows out of the United States to pay for those items. When someone in another country purchases goods or services produced in the United States, currency flows into the United States to pay for those items. When U.S. exports are greater than U.S. imports, more currency is flowing into the country than is flowing out. Therefore

when NX > 0, currency is flowing into the United States
when NX < 0, currency is flowing out of the United States

NIA, or net investment from abroad, refers to the second of the three reasons above. When someone in another country purchases U.S. assets, currency flows into the United States. This is called a **capital import**. When someone in the United States purchases foreign assets, currency flows out of the United States. This is called a **capital export**. When foreign purchases of U.S. assets (capital imports) exceeds U.S. purchases of foreign assets (capital exports), net investment from abroad is positive and more currency is flowing into the country than is flowing out. Therefore

when NIA > 0, currency is flowing into the United States
when NIA < 0, currency is flowing out of the United States

FG, or net inflows of gold, refers to the third reason above. When the U.S. government acquires more foreign currency than it wishes to hold, it trades the foreign currency for gold from the issuing government; gold flows into the United States. When the U.S. government wishes to acquire additional foreign currency, it trades U.S. gold for foreign currency; gold flows out of the United States.

when FG > 0, gold is flowing into the United States
when FG < 0, gold is flowing out of the United States

Case One: A Floating Exchange Rate System

When exchange rates can float freely, any imbalance in the balance of payments is eliminated by movements in the nominal exchange rate. Gold never flows between nations. For instance, if NX + NIA > 0, then more foreign currency is flowing into the United States than is flowing out. There is an imbalance in the balance of payments. As a result the exchange rate between the U.S. dollar and the foreign currency will fall, lowering net exports and bringing about balance of payments equilibrium with NX + NIA = 0. An imbalance in the balance of payments is quickly eliminated. Therefore it is typically the case that NX = -NIA; a trade surplus is offset by a capital deficit and a trade deficit is offset by a capital surplus.

Case Two: A Gold Standard System

When exchange rates are fixed by a gold standard, any imbalance in the balance of payments is offset by flows of gold. For instance, if NX + NIA > 0, then more foreign currency is flowing into the United States than is flowing out. Foreign currency will accumulate at the U.S. Treasury. The U.S. government will eventually sell that foreign currency back to the issuing government in exchange for gold; gold will flow into the United States. The size of the gold inflows will equal NX + NIA. Therefore we will have NX + NIA = FG, or NX + NIA - FG = 0.

4. Under a gold standard, can a country run a deficit in its balance of payments forever? (That is, can NX + NIA be less than 0 forever?) Can it do so in a floating exchange rate system?

5. What four factors are cited as the reasons the post-World War I gold standard was less stable than the pre-World War I gold standard?

NOTE: If you are interested in learning more about the gold standard and its contribution to the worldwide depression of the 1930s, I recommend *Golden Fetters: The Gold Standard and the Great Depression, 1919-1939,* by Barry Eichengreen (Oxford University Press, 1992).

6. Suppose the world is on a gold standard. Suppose income declines in the United States, lowering U.S. imports from abroad.

   A. What effect does the decline in U.S. imports have on NX + NIA in the United States? What effect does it have on gold flows into the United States?

   B. What effect does the decline in U.S. imports have on NX + NIA in the countries that are U.S. trading partners? What effect does it have on gold flows into those countries?

7. What are the three principles that guided the development of the Bretton Woods system?

8. Suppose the international economy operates with fixed exchange rates. Suppose there is inflation in the United States but not in other countries.

A. What is the effect on the real exchange rate, ε?

B. What is the effect on net exports, NX? On the flow of gold?

C. To stem the gold flows, the United States could change nominal exchange rates. Would the United States want to increase or decrease e, the price of foreign exchange? What effect would the change in fixed exchange rates have on net exports? On the flow of gold? On aggregate demand?

D. Alternatively, the United States could change real interest rates. Would the United States want to increase or decrease r, the real interest rate? What effect would this policy have on aggregate demand? On the flow of gold?

E. Why would domestic policy makers prefer to change exchange rates? Why would the world prefer that they instead change their domestic real interest rate?

TO THE CHALKBOARD:
Explaining Figure 15.4

Figure 15.4 depicts the relationship between the real exchange rate and the difference between the domestic and foreign interest rates. Changing the labels on the axes and shifting the vertical axis might make the graph clearer.

The graph is illustrating the equation
$$\varepsilon = \varepsilon_0 - \varepsilon_r(r - r^f).$$
Looking at the equation, it should be clear that if ε is on the vertical axis and $(r - r^f)$ is on the horizontal axis, then the intercept of the real exchange rate curve will be ε_0 and the slope will be $-\varepsilon_r$.

The long-run expected exchange rate is ε_0. When there is "no differential" between home and foreign interest rates, then $\varepsilon = \varepsilon_0 - \varepsilon_r(0) = \varepsilon_0$. The intercept of the real exchange rate curve on the vertical axis, where the real exchange rate is measured, is therefore ε_0. The real exchange rate curve slopes down, with a slope of $-\varepsilon_r$.

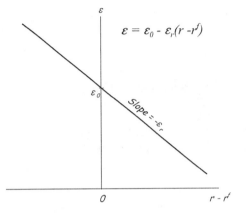

$$\varepsilon = \varepsilon_0 - \varepsilon_r(r - r^f)$$

Slope $= -\varepsilon_r$

9. In an economy with very high capital mobility, the real exchange rate depends upon the behavior of international currency speculators as captured in the equation $\varepsilon = \varepsilon_0 - \varepsilon_r \cdot (r - r^f)$. Suppose $\varepsilon = 4.2 - 10(r - r^f)$. Suppose the central bank's goal is $\varepsilon = 4.5$. If the foreign real interest rate is 3 percent, what will be the central bank's target for the real interest rate?

10. Suppose international financial capital mobility is very high and the international economic system has fixed exchange rates. Suppose there is an increase in real interest rates in European countries. If nominal exchange rates cannot be changed, what will be the impact on real interest rates and real GDP in the United States?

11. In the equation $\varepsilon = \varepsilon_0 - \varepsilon_r \cdot (r - r^f) + \varepsilon_R \cdot \Delta R$, which parameters change and in which direction when international capital mobility increases?

12. When capital mobility is low, real exchange rates are determined by the equation $\varepsilon = \varepsilon_0 - \varepsilon_r \cdot (r - r^f) + \varepsilon_R \cdot \Delta R$. Suppose $\varepsilon = 4.2 - 10(r - r^f) + 0.002(\Delta R)$.

   A. Suppose $r = 0.05$, $r^f = 0.04$, and $\Delta R = 200$. What is ε?

   B. Suppose $r = 0.05$, $r^f = 0.08$, and $\Delta R = 200$. What is ε?

13. Suppose $\varepsilon = 4.2 - 10(r - r^f) + 0.002(\Delta R)$.

   A. Suppose the government uses its foreign exchange reserves to stabilize real exchange rates. Suppose $r^f = 5\%$, $r = 2\%$, and the goal is to have $\varepsilon = 4.5$. By how much will the government allow its foreign exchange reserves to change in order to achieve its goal for the real exchange rate?

   B. Suppose now foreign real interest rates increase to 7 percent. Suppose the government's goal remains a real exchange rate of 4.5. If the government changes its foreign exchange reserves to achieve its goal, what will be the necessary change in foreign exchange reserves? If the government instead increases the real interest rate in order to achieve its goal, what will be the new value of the real interest rate? If the government's second goal is to stabilize the unemployment rate, which policy will it pursue: changing real interest rates or changing foreign exchange reserves.

C. APPLYING CONCEPTS AND MODELS

Now we're getting to the good stuff. Being able to apply a specific concept or model to a real world situation — where you are told which model to apply but you have to figure out how to apply it — is often what you need to earn a B in a course. This is where macroeconomics starts to become interesting and the world starts to make more sense.

1. Suppose a country is on a gold standard. Suppose that initially the country's international payments are balanced: NX + NIA - FG = 0. Suppose there is then an international crisis of confidence in the political stability of the country, lowering capital imports into the country. What effect will the international crisis of confidence have on the balance of payments? If the monetary authorities want to maintain the country's gold reserves, will they increase or decrease real interest rates? Why? What short-run effect will the monetary authorities' actions have on the economy?

2.   Suppose investors in a country lose confidence in the political stability of another country where they previously had invested substantial sums of money. Capital exports therefore decline. What happens to the gold reserves in the investors' home country? What, if anything, will the monetary authorities do in response to the gold flows?

3.   Compare your answers to the previous two questions. Explain why a gold standard creates occasional pressure to increase real interest rates and contract the economy, but never creates pressure to decrease real interest rates.

D. EXPLAINING THE REAL WORLD

Most instructors are delighted when you are able to figure out which concept or model to apply to a real world situation. Being able to do so means you thoroughly understand the material and is often what you need to do to earn an A in a course. This is where you experience the power of macroeconomic theory.

1.   Many economic historians argue that the gold standard worsened the Great Depression and, in particular, caused several European economies to suffer along with the United States. Explain.

2.   A recession began in the United States during summer 2001 and worsened markedly following the September 11 attack. The economies of the world are worried that the U.S. recession will spread throughout the world. Explain. (*Note*: Most economies have floating exchange rates.)

3.   Over the last two decades, the internet and the associated advent of online global trading has increased international capital mobility. When the real interest rate is increased in other countries, is the impact in the United States greater or less today than it would have been twenty years ago? Explain.

E. POSSIBILITIES TO PONDER

The more you learn, the more you realize you have more to learn. These questions go beyond the textbook material. They are the sort of questions that distinguish A+ or A work from A- work. Some of them may even serve as starting points for junior or senior year research papers.

1. Some pundits advocate that the world's economies return to a gold standard. They argue that if the money stock was tied to gold, domestic economies would be more stable. Should the United States and the world's industrialized economies go back on a gold standard? Explain.

2. Should we encourage all countries in the world to have the highest possible rate of capital mobility? Explain.

3. Can the United States avoid international financial crises in the future?

SOLUTIONS   SOLUTIONS   SOLUTIONS   SOLUTIONS

A. BASIC DEFINITIONS

1. capital controls
2. gold standard
3. Bretton Woods
4. international currency speculators

---

5. fixed
6. fixed
7. fixed
8. floating
9. depend upon
10. fixed; floating
11. deflationary

B. MANIPULATION OF CONCEPTS AND MODELS

1. [REVIEW] If real interest rates increase in England but not in the United States, the foreign exchange speculators will increase their demand for assets denominated in British pounds and decrease their demand for dollar-denominated assets. In the market where pounds are traded for dollars, the demand for pounds rises as the supply of pounds offered in exchange for dollars falls. The nominal exchange rate rises. The dollar falls or depreciates relative to the pound.

2. If 1 oz of gold = $35 and 1 oz of gold = 140 peso, then $35 = 140 peso. Therefore $0.25 exchanges for 1 peso, and 4 pesos exchange for $1.

3. No, these rates cannot be maintained forever. The Treasury rate is $0.50 per franc and the market exchange rate is $0.40 per franc. Arbitragers could take 700 French francs to the Treasury, exchange them for 10 ounces of gold, exchange the gold for $350, then take the $350 to the market where they could exchange the $350 for 875 French francs. Their small investment of time resulted in a gain of 175 French francs, or 25 percent. But as arbitragers continue trading francs for gold, gold for dollars, and dollars for francs, their actions will eventually lead to a change in the market rate of exchange. The market rate of exchange will rise as a result of the increased demand for French francs.

4. No, a country cannot run a deficit in its balance of payments forever when it is on a gold standard. The country will eventually run out of gold, forcing a devaluation. With a floating exchange rate system, a country also will not run a deficit in its balance of payments forever; the balance of payments deficit will lead to a change in exchange rates that brings the balance of payments back to 0.

5. The four factors that are cited as the reasons the post-World War I gold standard was less stable than the pre-World War I gold standard are

   • After World War I, people believed governments would abandon their gold standards in an emergency as they had done during World War I. But before World War I, the gold standards were perceived as more inviolable.

   • After World War I, everyone knew the governments would adjust real interest rates not just to maintain gold flows but also to produce full employment.

   • After World War I, many countries held their reserves in foreign currencies, not in gold. Those countries that still held gold therefore faced potentially enormous gold outflows during rough economic times.

   • After World War I, economies with balance of payments surpluses (France and the United States, in particular) did not lower real interest rates to limit gold inflows.

6. A. When U.S. imports from abroad decline, U.S. net exports (NX) rise, increasing NX + NIA for the United States. A decline in U.S. imports from abroad means that foreign currency is accumulating in the United States. Individuals in the United States who are holding foreign currency will exchange the foreign currency for gold at the Treasury. The Treasury in turn will exchange its accumulating pile of foreign currency for gold from the issuing countries. Gold inflows into the United States (FG) will increase. The increase in gold inflows, FG, will offset the increase in net exports, NX, such that NX + NIA - FG = 0.

   B. From the perspective of the United States' trading partners, the decline in U.S. imports from abroad is a decline in their gross exports, lowering their net exports. The trading partners will have fewer dollars coming into their economy. Those who wish to obtain dollars will exchange the foreign currency for dollars at their central bank. The central bank in turn will need to buy dollars from the United States, and so will exchange some of its gold reserves for dollars. Gold outflows from the U.S. trading partners will increase.

7. The three principles that guided the development of the Bretton Woods system are

   • In ordinary times, exchange rates should be fixed because fixed exchange rates make foreign prices relatively predictable, encouraging international trade.

   • In extraordinary times such as a Great Depression, exchange rates should be changed through a devaluation or revaluation of a currency.

   • An institution is needed to provide a financial safety net to countries in need. The institution that was created was the International Monetary Fund (IMF).

8. A. When there is inflation in the United States, all else constant, the real exchange rate falls. That is, the relative price of foreign goods and services declines.

B. When the real exchange rate declines, U.S. exports fall. Although our model did not say so, U.S. imports also rise. (To see this, consider the gross exports equation from the Canadian perspective. If gross exports from Canada to the United States decline by X_ε when the real exchange rate ε rises by 1, then clearly an equivalent statement is that imports into the United States from Canada are declining by X_ε when the real exchange rate ε rises by 1.) The decline in exports and rise in imports both contribute to a decrease in net exports, NX, into the United States. If net exports decline, then dollars are accumulating in other countries, leading ultimately to an increase in gold outflows.

C. If the United States wanted to slow gold outflows, they could increase the nominal exchange rates, reversing the decline in the real exchange rate. The increase in nominal exchange rates — a devaluation of the dollar — would increase real exchange rates, decreasing U.S. imports and increasing U.S. exports. The increase in net exports would offset the previous decrease in net exports and stem the flow of gold. Aggregate demand would rise.

D. If instead the United States slowed gold outflows by changing real interest rates, they would need to increase real interest rates. An increase in real interest rates would decrease aggregate demand due to declines in both investment and gross export spending, followed by multiplier effects that lowered consumption spending. Higher real interest rates in the United States would also increase capital imports into the United States, increasing net investment from abroad, NIA. The increase in NIA would offset the decrease in NX brought about by the change in the real exchange rate, stemming the outflow of gold.

E. Domestic policy makers would prefer a currency devaluation. A currency devaluation solves the gold problem and benefits the domestic economy by increasing aggregate demand. But the rest of the world suffers as their exports fall. The rest of the world would prefer that the domestic policy makers raise their own real interest rates, so that the negative aggregate demand effects would be chiefly limited to the domestic economy.

9. The target rate for the domestic real interest rate will be 6 percent.

10. An increase in foreign real interest rates will lead to gold outflows from the United States as capital exports from the United States rise, lowering U.S. net investment from abroad (NIA). Gold will flow out of the United States. To stem the outflow of gold from the United States, real interest rates in the United States will need to rise. Real GDP in the United States will therefore decline.

11. When international capital mobility increases, ε_r increases and ε_R decreases.

12. A. $\varepsilon = 4.2 - 10(0.05 - 0.04) + 0.002(200) = 4.5$

    B. $\varepsilon = 4.2 - 10(0.05 - 0.08) + 0.002(200) = 4.9$

13. A. $4.5 = 4.2 - 10(0.02 - 0.05) + 0.002(\Delta R)$, so $\Delta R = 0$. The government does not need to change its foreign exchange reserves at all in order to reach the goal of $\varepsilon = 4.5$.

    B. $4.5 = 4.2 - 10(0.02 - 0.07) + 0.002(\Delta R)$, so $\Delta R = -0.2/0.002 = -100$ if the government uses foreign exchange reserves to achieve its goal.

    $4.5 = 4.2 - 10(r - 0.07) + 0.002(0)$, so $r = 0.04 = 4\%$ if the government uses the real interest rate to achieve its goal.

    If the government uses the interest rate policy to achieve its exchange rate goal, the necessary increase in the domestic real interest rate will cause unemployment to rise. Therefore if the government wants to stabilize unemployment as well, it should pursue the policy of changing foreign exchange reserves.

C. APPLYING CONCEPTS AND MODELS

1. The decrease in capital imports lowers "NIA," net investment from abroad. Less foreign exchange is being traded for the domestic currency, so foreigners who are holding the country's currency instead exchange the currency for gold. The decrease in foreign demand for the country's currency thus leads to an outflow of gold; FG decreases. The balance of payments will again be balanced.

   But there is a limit to how far the country's gold reserves can fall. If the monetary authorities decide to stem the outflows of gold, they will increase domestic real interest rates. An increase in domestic real interest rates will make domestic assets more attractive to foreign investors, increasing foreign demand for the country's currency and thus offsetting the negative effects of the international crisis of confidence.

   The increase in domestic real interest rates, while stemming the outflow of gold, leads to decreases in aggregate demand and thus in real GDP, contracting the domestic economy. Under a gold standard, an international crisis of confidence thus ultimately creates a domestic recession.

2. The decrease in capital exports leads to an inflow of gold and increased gold reserves in the investors' home country. The monetary authorities will probably do nothing in response to the increase in gold reserves. More gold is always a good thing to have.

3. When there are gold outflows, there is a limit – zero – to how low a country's gold reserves can fall. Monetary authorities therefore have an incentive to increase real interest rates. But when there are gold inflows, there is no limit to how high a country's gold reserves can rise. Monetary authorities have no incentive to limit gold inflows, and thus no incentive to lower real interest rates in response to gold flows.

D. EXPLAINING THE REAL WORLD

1. Countries that maintained the gold standard found themselves forced to raise interest rates and contract their money supplies in order to avoid large gold losses. But higher interest rates led to contractions of aggregate demand and income, and rising unemployment. Countries that abandoned the gold standard and allowed their currencies to float were able to avoid raising interest rates and thus avoided the worst of the economic downturn. (See textbook Figure 15.3.)

2. The drop in income in the United States will lead to a drop in U.S. imports from the rest of the world. From the perspective of the rest of the world, a drop in imports into the United States is a drop in exports by the rest of the world, lowering their income.

3. Increased international capital mobility means international financial shocks are more quickly transmitted to the domestic economy. Therefore an increase in foreign interest rates today will have a greater and more immediate effect on the U.S. economy today than it would have had before the advent of online global trading.

E. POSSIBILITIES TO PONDER

No solutions are given to these questions. The questions are designed to be somewhat open ended. Each question draws on your understanding of the concepts covered in this chapter.

If you are considering graduate work in economics, now is the time to start planning your undergraduate course schedule accordingly. The most important courses for you to take if you want to earn a Ph.D. in economics are **not** economics courses. The most important ones are math courses. Your ability to get into a good graduate program depends largely upon your score on the quantitative portion of the GRE exam. This portion of the GRE exam is very similar to what you saw when you took the SAT exam. Your ability to survive the first year of graduate school depends upon your knowledge of the material covered in several math classes. Be sure you take "real" calculus, not some watered-down version that is labeled "for social scientists" or the equivalent. Take the year-long calculus sequence that the math majors take. Also be sure to take one semester of real analysis and one semester of linear algebra. Finally, my personal advice – which I did not heed – is to take a year or two off between undergraduate and graduate studies. You will then come to graduate school with a much clearer idea of what you want to study and why. And with good planning, you'll come with some savings, too.

Chapter 16

Changes in the Macroeconomy and Changes in Macroeconomic Policy

- The structure of the economy – who purchases output, what sectors produce it – has changed markedly over the last hundred or so years. In the United States, proportionately less output is produced by the agriculture and manufacturing sectors and proportionately more output is produced by the service sector.

- Ignoring the Great Depression, economic downturns in the United States today last about as long as did downturns that occurred before 1920, but economic booms last longer than they used to. Successful conduct of stabilization policy – especially monetary policy – seems to be responsible for prolonging the good times.

LEARNING GUIDE

This chapter is a terrific presentation of recent macroeconomic history. I recommend it highly.

The chapter was written before the September 11, 2001 attack and subsequent economic downturn. As you read the chapter, think about the most recent economic events and how they are – or are not – part of the trends in the macroeconomy and in macroeconomic policy described by Professor DeLong.

There are no Section B or Section C questions for this chapter.

Short on time?

 Before you study this chapter, find out what you are expected to learn from it. Some professors will want you to be able to write thoughtful essay answers on the topics raised in this chapter; others may limit their testing to a few multiple choice questions.

Macroeconomic history and changes in the structure of the economy are discussed in much more depth in courses in economic history. If you enjoy thinking about the issues raised in Chapter 16, check your college's course catalog to see if they offer an economic history course.

A. BASIC DEFINITIONS

Before you apply knowledge, you need a basic grasp of the fundamentals. In other words, there are some things you just have to know. Knowing the material in this section won't guarantee a good grade in the course, but not knowing it will guarantee a poor or failing grade.

CIRCLE THE CORRECT WORD OR PHRASE IN EACH OF THE FOLLOWING SENTENCES.

1. Better information technology that improves businesses' ability to control inventory holdings will worsen / dampen economic fluctuations.

2. In the United States and other industrial economies, labor productivity growth in the late nineteenth century was due primarily to capital deepening / increased labor efficiency and labor productivity growth in the twentieth century was due primarily to capital deepening / increased labor efficiency.

3. In western Europe, it is / is not possible to understand unemployment and inflation after 1970 using the standard Phillips curve.

4. As economic globalization continues, increased international trade will further increase / decrease the spending multiplier.

5. Research by Professor Christina Romer reveals that the average pre-World War I recession was shorter / about the same length / longer than the average post-World War II recession, and that the average pre-World War I recovery was shorter / about the same length / longer than the average post-World War II recovery.

6. As liquidity constraints are removed, the marginal propensity to consume should increase / stay the same / decrease.

7. The Federal Reserve has / has not created recessions in order to fight inflation.

8. In the United States and other industrialized economies, the decline in relative employment in the agricultural and manufacturing / service sectors since 1900 has been offset by a rise in relative employment in the manufacturing / service sector.

9. In the United States, it is / is not possible to understand unemployment and inflation after 1960 using the standard Phillips curve.

10. Increased financial flexibility makes it more / less difficult to conduct monetary policy.

11. By 1933, unemployment in the United States had reached 5 / 15 / 25 / 35 percent of the labor force.

12. The structure of the macroeconomy is constant / changing over time.

TO THE CHALKBOARD:
But What About September 11 . . .

Textbook Section 16.3 begins (p. 453), "For almost all of your lives – 'you' being the typical reader of this textbook – the business cycle has been relatively quiescent." How quickly the world can change. The textbook was completed before September 11, 2001.

So what will happen to the economy following the September 11 attack? As I write this section, it is late in October 2001. Some data are available; some trends are apparent; much is still unknown. Aggregate demand fell after September 11 as airline travel and tourism declined, and as a combination of fear and reconsidered life priorities lowered consumption spending more generally. The decline in airline travel was expected to lower demand for airplanes, an investment good. The stock market lost a great deal of value on September 17, but recovered much of that value within a month. The increased stock market volatility – especially downside volatility – worried some financial investors.

The multiplier effects will kick in next. Newly unemployed workers will no doubt reduce their spending, leading to layoffs of workers who produce consumer goods and services.

But are the autonomous declines in spending over? Can we depict the changes as just a one-time shift to the right in the Monetary Policy Reaction Function? Or will there be additional autonomous declines in spending? Have Americans been led to reconsider their priorities and values? Will they decide that latest gadget or those expensive shoes or the fastest computer can be foregone? Will they increase their saving, set aside some funds for a "rainy day"? Will families spend more time – and less money – together? Only time will tell.

And how will the policy makers respond? The public health system is woefully underfunded; will government spending for public health be increased? Will the federal government run budget deficits, stimulating the economy? Or will they increase taxes to cover the new areas of spending? Will the Fed be able to stimulate the economy by lowering interest rates? Or will nominal interest rates reach their minimum? Will the United States economy fall into a liquidity trap? Again, only time will tell.

Professor DeLong no doubt considers these issues in an essay (or two, or three) on his website: http://econ161.berkeley.edu. But you now have learned enough macroeconomic theory that you can formulate your own reasonable guesses as to what might happen or, if things are back to "normal," what did happen. What do you think?

D. EXPLAINING THE REAL WORLD

Most instructors are delighted when you are able to figure out which concept or model to apply to a real world situation. Being able to do so means you thoroughly understand the material and is often what you need to do to earn an A in a course. This is where you experience the power of macroeconomic theory.

1. It was much easier to obtain a credit card in 1998 than it had been in 1978. Practically every college bulletin board had a credit card offer on it. Credit card offers arrived in the mail at an almost obscene rate. What effect *should* the increased availability of consumer credit have had on consumption spending? What effect *did* the increased availability of consumer credit seem to have on consumption spending?

2. President George Bush, when calling for Congress to pass the landmark tax cut that was subsequently implemented in Summer 2001, suggested that American families needed the tax cut in order to pay down their credit card bills. If he was correct, then what effect would the tax cut have had on consumption spending? If he was correct, what was President Bush implying about the relative size (small or large) of the marginal propensity to consume? Do you think it was reasonable to expect that families would use the tax "rebate" checks distributed during Summer 2001 to reduce their credit card debt?

3. What should policy makers do when an economy falls into an extended period of economic decline?

E. POSSIBILITIES TO PONDER

The more you learn, the more you realize you have more to learn. These questions go beyond the textbook material. They are the sort of questions that distinguish A+ or A work from A- work. Some of them may even serve as starting points for junior or senior year research papers.

1. In a world in which both goods and financial capital flows across borders, political stability of foreign governments may be a prerequisite to that nation's participation in the global economy. What is the proper role of the government of countries such as the United States in assuring such stability?

2. Professor DeLong writes (p. 444), "Economists are good at analyzing how asset markets work if [the markets] are populated by far-sighted investors with accurate models of the world and long [time] horizons." Presumably, the more economics those investors know, the more accurate their models. Should economics be a required course of study for everyone?

3. Professor DeLong writes (p. 453), "Somehow the American economy at the end of the 1920s was very vulnerable in the sense that a small shock could cause a big depression." Was the American economy similarly vulnerable at the end of the 1990s? Will the economic effects of the September 11 attack be a "small shock" that could cause a big depression?

SOLUTIONS   SOLUTIONS   SOLUTIONS   SOLUTIONS

A. BASIC DEFINITIONS

1. dampen
2. capital deepening; increased labor efficiency
3. is not
4. decrease
5. about the same length; longer
6. decrease
7. has
8. manufacturing; service
9. is
10. more
11. 25
12. changing

D. EXPLAINING THE REAL WORLD

1. Increased availability of credit cards – a form of consumer credit – should smooth consumption spending as liquidity constraints are eased. When consumers can borrow against future income, consumption spending is less directly tied to disposable income than it is when consumers are liquidity constrained. Increased availability of credit cards *should* have lowered the marginal propensity to consume.

   But in fact, it appeared that increased availability of credit increased consumer spending. Saving rates fell to zero as consumer indebtedness soared. Unless consumers were borrowing against far-future income, such a drastic decline in the saving rate is hard to reckon with the expected consumption-smoothing effect of increased availability of credit.

2. If President Bush was right in suggesting that American families needed the tax cut in order to pay down their credit card bills, then the tax cut would have had very little, if any, effect on consumption spending. Families had "spent" the tax cut in previous months or years, when they incurred the credit card debt they would be paying down with the tax "rebate" check. In this case, President Bush was implying the marginal propensity to consume was quite small.

   It probably was reasonable to expect that families would use the tax rebate check to reduce credit card debt. Liquidity constraints on consumption spending had eased noticeably in the 1990s as access to credit card accounts increased. With lower liquidity constraints, consumers will borrow against future income to smooth consumption. The rebate check would not affect consumption spending in that case, because consumption was not constrained much by an inability to borrow against future income.

3. According to Professor DeLong (p. 459), "Everything."
   - Run a substantial government budget deficit.
   - Push the nominal interest rate close to zero.
   - If necessary, deliberately create inflation so that real interest rates decline.

E. POSSIBILITIES TO PONDER

No solutions are given to these questions. The questions are designed to be somewhat open ended. Each question draws on your understanding of the concepts covered in this chapter.

Chapter 17

The Future of Macroeconomics

- Macroeconomics as it is taught today is based on the work of John Maynard Keynes in *The General Theory*, as modified in response to challenges by monetarists and rational expectations economists.

- The future of macroeconomics may lie in confronting questions about the determinants of aggregate supply, the determinants of consumption spending, or the power of monetary policy.

LEARNING GUIDE

Chapter 17 contains a summary of the history of macroeconomic thought and Professor DeLong's musings regarding where macroeconomic thought might go in the future. The questions of Sections 17.2 and 17.3 might be good springboards for undergraduate research projects.

There are no Section C, D, or E questions for this chapter.

Short on time?

Before you study this chapter, find out what you are expected to learn from it. Some professors will want you to be able to write thoughtful essay answers on the topics raised in this chapter; others may limit their testing to a few multiple choice questions.

If you have time during the term to ponder the issues raised in this chapter, I congratulate you on your ability to organize your time well during final exams! Most instructors will skip this chapter because of time pressures. But if you are interested in macroeconomics, be sure to take time to read the chapter some day.

A. BASIC DEFINITIONS

Before you apply knowledge, you need a basic grasp of the fundamentals. In other words, there are some things you just have to know. Knowing the material in this section won't guarantee a good grade in the course, but not knowing it will guarantee a poor or failing grade.

USE THE WORDS OR PHRASES FROM THE LIST BELOW TO COMPLETE THE SENTENCES. SOME ARE USED MORE THAN ONCE; SOME ARE NOT USED AT ALL.

coordination failures
Brad DeLong
Milton Friedman
John Maynard Keynes
Keynesian
Robert Lucas

menu costs
monetary
New Keynesian
rational expectation
real business cycle

1. The microfoundations of price stickiness are considered by _____ theories.

2. According to _____ theories, production fluctuates because the nominal value of output and labor productivity fluctuate.

3. The General Theory of Employment, Interest, and Money was written by _____.

4. The costs of changing prices are called _____.

B. MANIPULATION OF CONCEPTS AND MODELS

Most instructors expect you to be able to do basic manipulation of the concepts. Being able to do so often means you can earn a C in a course. But if you want a better grade, you'll need to be able to complete this next section easily and move on to Sections C and D.

1. What four principles did Keynes emphasize in *The General Theory*?

2. What were the four major parts of Milton Friedman's 1960s critique of macroeconomics?

3. What were the two key features of the critique offered by rational expectations economists?

4. Use the Ricardian view associated with Robert Barro to explain why consumption spending did not increase very much when American taxpayers received their tax "rebate" checks during Summer 2001.

5. What is the "puzzle" about consumption today?

```
SOLUTIONS    SOLUTIONS    SOLUTIONS    SOLUTIONS
```

A. BASIC DEFINITIONS

1. New Keynesian
2. Real business cycle
3. John Maynard Keynes
4. Menu costs

B. MANIPULATION OF CONCEPTS AND MODELS

1. In *The General Theory*, Keynes emphasized these four principles.
   - the role of expectations
   - the volatility of expectations
   - the power of fiscal and monetary policy
   - the multiplier process

2. The four major parts of Milton Friedman's 1960s critique of macroeconomics were
   - Models used in the 1960s overestimated the government's ability to manage and control the economy.
   - Models used in the 1960s overestimated the power of fiscal policy and underestimated the power of monetary policy.
   - The quantity of money is all you need to know.
   - High past inflation will increase future expected inflation and change the tradeoffs between unemployment and inflation.

3. The two key features of the critique offered by rational expectations economists were
   - Expectations should be modeled based on the assumption that when they form expectations, people do the best they can to figure out the structure of the economy.
   - Systematic changes in economic policy change the parameters of the consumption and investment functions and the location of the Phillips curve.

4. According to the Ricardian view associated with Robert Barro, people form expectations of future tax policy. A tax cut today is likely, they expect, to be followed by a tax increase in the near future. Therefore, consumption spending today will not change in response to the tax "rebate" because it is expected to be temporary.

5. The puzzle about consumption today is that the marginal propensity to consume is not lower than it actually is. Liquidity constraints today are very minor, according to Professor DeLong. But if liquidity constraints are minor, then consumption spending should depend upon our expected *lifetime* income, not upon our income in any particular year. And in that case, consumption spending in any particular year should not respond much to changes in disposable income in that year. But in fact, consumption spending *does* respond to changes in disposable income. Why?

Appendix

Notation Used in the Textbook

Notation	Introduced on page(s)	Definition
α (alpha)	71 (introduced)	parameter of Cobb-Douglas production function, $$\frac{Y}{L} = \left(\frac{K}{L}\right)^{\alpha} \cdot (E)^{1-\alpha}$$
α (alpha)	77 (introduced) 90 (explained)	parameter measuring diminishing returns to investment
β (beta)	333	$2.5 / \theta$, where θ is the slope of the short-run aggregate supply curve; the smaller β is, the flatter the Phillips curve
γ (gamma)	178	parameter of the utility function that indicates how much the consumer values consumption today as opposed to consumption in the future
γ (gamma)	386	how aggressively the central bank reacts to unemployment
δ (delta)	76	depreciation rate; rate at which physical capital (K) wears out
δ (delta)	399	deficit-to-income ratio; d/Y
ε (epsilon)	31 171	real exchange rate; relative price of foreign goods and services; $\varepsilon = e \cdot \dfrac{P^*}{P}$
ε* (epsilon)	420	the government's target real exchange rate
ε_0 (epsilon)	174	baseline level of the real exchange rate; the average foreign exchange trader's opinion of what the exchange rate should be if there were no interest rate differentials
ε_r (epsilon)	174	responsiveness of the real exchange rate to changes in the real interest rate
ε_R (epsilon)	422	responsiveness of the real exchange rate to changes in foreign exchange reserves
ε^s (epsilon)	333	supply shocks that can directly affect the inflation rate

Notation	Introduced on page(s)	Definition
θ (theta)	177	ratio of the length of the future period to the length of the current period
θ (theta)	324	slope of the short-run aggregate supply function
κ (kappa)	99	capital-output ratio
κ^* (kappa)	76	capital-output ratio in balanced-growth equilibrium
λ (lambda)	106	growth multiplier; $\lambda = \dfrac{\alpha}{1-\alpha}$
μ (mu)	375	money multiplier
π (pi)	226	price inflation rate; rate of change of price level; $\pi = \dfrac{P_{t+1} - P_t}{P_t}$
π^e (pi)	229	expected future inflation rate
π' (pi)	322	the central bank's target inflation rate
σ^S (sigma)	35	risk premium
ϕ (phi)	336	shorthand for a combination of several symbols; $\phi = \dfrac{1}{2.5} \times \phi' \times \dfrac{1}{Y^*}$.
ϕ' (phi)	322	part of the Taylor rule; shorthand for $\dfrac{\phi'' \times (I_r + X_\varepsilon \varepsilon_r)}{1 - MPE}$
ϕ'' (phi)	322	how aggressively the central bank reacts to inflation
A	252	autonomous spending; $A = C_0 + I + G + GX$
A_0	322	level of autonomous spending that generates income $= Y_0$
B	375	monetary base
C	53, 162	consumption spending by households; $C = C_0 + C_y Y^D$
C_0	162	baseline level of consumption
C_y	162	marginal propensity to consume, mpc; $C_y = \dfrac{\Delta C}{\Delta Y^D}$
d	392	government deficit; if d < 0, there is a government surplus
d*	394	full-employment budget deficit
d^c	396	cash deficit

Notation	Introduced on page(s)	Definition
d^r	396	real deficit
D	392	government debt
e	30, Figure 2.1	nominal exchange rate; domestic (U.S. dollar) price of 1 unit of foreign currency
E E_t	71 (introduced) 74 (defined)	level of technology, or (equivalently) efficiency of labor force
E	249	aggregate demand; planned expenditure
E^a	275	accounting earnings that corporations report
E^s	35	earnings per share of stock; $\dfrac{E^s}{P^s} = r + o^s$
E^s	275	long-run "permanent" earnings that investors expect to receive per share of stock
$F(\bullet)$	71 (introduced) 74 (defined)	aggregate production function
FG	414	flow of gold into the domestic economy
g	76 (introduced) 96 (explained)	growth rate of labor efficiency, $\%\Delta E$
$\bar{G}$	191	government purchases
G	53, 169	government purchases of goods and services
$g(\kappa_t)$	101	rate of growth of capital-output ratio; $\%\Delta(K/Y)$
$g(k_t)$	98	rate of growth of the capital-labor ratio; $\%\Delta(K/L)$
$g(y_t)$	101	rate of growth of output per worker; $\%\Delta(Y/L)$
GX	171	gross exports of goods and services to foreigners
i	229	nominal interest rate; $i = r + \pi$ or $i = r + \pi^e$
I	53, 166	investment spending by businesses
I_0	166	baseline level of investment spending
I_r	166	responsiveness of investment spending to changes in the real interest rate
IM	173	gross imports of goods and services purchased from foreigners
IM_y	173	responsiveness of import spending to a change in real GDP; marginal propensity to import
K	71 (introduced) 74 (defined)	real physical capital; real value of machines, buildings, and inventory holdings
K/L	71 (introduced) 74 (defined)	capital per worker

Notation	Introduced on page(s)	Definition
K/Y	76	capital-output ratio
L	71 (introduced) 74 (defined)	size of labor force
$L(r + \pi^e)$	229	relative demand for money
L^d	158	economy wide employment
L_{firm}	156	labor force of one firm
m	227	rate of growth of money stock; $\%\Delta M$
M	222	money stock
M	229	money demand
M	375	liquid money assets
M^d	301	nominal money demand
MPC	163	marginal propensity to consume
MPE	252	marginal propensity to spend; $MPE = C_y(1 - t) - IM_y$
MPL	156	marginal product of labor
M^S	301	nominal money supply
MUC	178	marginal utility of consumption
n	76 (introduced) 96 (explained)	labor force growth rate, $\%\Delta L$
n	183	number of years in the future
NIA	414	net investment from abroad
NX	53	real net exports
–NX	188	negative net exports; international savings
P	31	price level in domestic country (United States)
P	156	price level
P*	31	price level in foreign country
P^e	324	anticipated price level
P^s	35	price of one share of stock; $P^s = \dfrac{E^s}{r + \sigma^s}$
\$PV	183	present value
r	35	real interest rate
r*	322	the central bank's estimate of the normal real interest rate

Notation	Introduced on page(s)	Definition
r^f	174	foreign real interest rate
R	422	foreign exchange reserves
s	76 (introduced) 96 (explained)	savings rate, S/Y
S	177	saving
S^H	162	household saving; $S^H = Y^D - C$
$STREAM	184	stream of annual payments
$SUM	183	inflation-adjusted purchasing power to be received in the future
t	162	average tax rate; $T = tY$
T	161	net taxes; government tax revenues less government transfer payments
T*	394	full-employment tax collections
u	330	unemployment rate
u*	330	natural rate of unemployment
v	227	rate of growth of velocity; $\%\Delta V$
V	222 229	velocity of money; number of times a typical dollar changes hands in one year
V_0	229	baseline velocity
V_i	229	responsiveness of velocity to changes in the nominal interest rate
V^L	229	time-trend of velocity; financial technology-driven velocity trend
W	156	nominal wage
W/P	159	real wage
$\times$	throughout book	multiplication ("times") symbol
X_f	171	responsiveness of gross exports to changes in foreign income
X_ε	171	responsiveness of gross exports to changes in the real exchange rate
y	227	rate of growth of real GDP; $\%\Delta Y$
Y	53	real GDP; real national income
Y/L	71 (introduced) 74 (defined)	real GDP per worker

Notation	Introduced on page(s)	Definition
Y/L	90	$Y/L = F(K/L, E)$; output per worker is a function of the capital-labor ratio and the efficiency of labor
Y^*	160	potential output; potential real GDP
Y_0	322	level of real GDP when $r = r^*$
Y^D	162	disposable income; $Y^D = Y - T$
Y^f	171	foreign GDP
Y_{firm}	156	output of one firm